DON'T EAT YOUR HEART OUT COOKBOOK

OTHER BOOKS BY JOSEPH C. PISCATELLA

CHOICES FOR A HEALTHY HEART

CONTROLLING YOUR FAT TOOTH

THE FAT TOOTH FAT-GRAM COUNTER

THE FAT TOOTH RESTAURANT &
FAST-FOOD FAT-GRAM COUNTER

DON'T EAT YOUR HEART OUT COOKBOOK

SECOND EDITION

by Joseph C. Piscatella
Recipes by Bernie Piscatella

WORKMAN PUBLISHING, NEW YORK

Library of Congress Cataloging-in-Publication Data

Piscatella, Joseph C.
Don't eat your heart out cookbook / by Joseph C. Piscatella: recipes by Bernie Piscatella. — Rev. Ed.
p. cm.
Includes bibliographical references and index.
ISBN 1-56305-558-9
1. Heart—Diseases—Diet therapy—Recipes. I. Piscatella, Bernie II. Title.
RC684.D5P57 1994 94-32730
641.5'6311—dc20 CIP

Workman books are available at special discounts when purchased in bulk for premiums and sales promotions as well as for fundraising or educational use. Special editions or book excerpts can also be created to specification. For details, please contact the Special Sales Director at the address below.

Workman Publishing
708 Broadway
New York, NY 10003

Manufactured in the United States of America
First printing October 1994
10 9 8 7 6 5 4 3 2

The material in this book is provided for information only and should not be construed as medical advice or instruction. Always consult with your physician or other appropriate health professionals before making any changes in diet and/or physical activity.

ACKNOWLEDGMENTS

It takes many people to put a book together, and this one is no exception. *Don't Eat Your Heart Out* would not exist were it not for the support and help of many people. In particular, we are grateful to the medical professionals who gave of their time and expertise, providing information and insight and offering valuable suggestions concerning the manuscript. These include Beverly Utt, R.D., Anne Dattilo, R.D., Ph.D., Lynn Almon, R.D., Adam Drewnowski, Ph.D., John Nagle, M.D., Michael Davidson, M.D., Barry Franklin, Ph.D., L. Kent Smith, M.D., Philip Ades, M.D., and Kathy Berra, R.N.

And finally, our thanks to Peter Workman for his faith in our work and to Sally Kovalchick and Lynn Strong for their editorial prowess.

FOREWORD

The first edition of *Don't Eat Your Heart Out*, born out of Joseph Piscatella's own experience with coronary bypass, successfully bridged the gap between science and practical application for cardiac patients facing changes in their dietary and life-style patterns. I have found it at many hospitals in their cardiac education programs. Although the book has been updated periodically, the present revision is a major one. It applies the most current information on diet and cardiovascular health, and it provides a method of dietary change that is both realistic and effective.

I have found all of Mr. Piscatella's books to be easily readible and enormously helpful. I keep his *Fat Tooth Fat-Gram Counter* in my briefcase and periodically carry the *Restaurant & Fast-Food Fat-Gram Counter* into restaurants with me.

Joseph Piscatella knows what he's writing about. I strongly recommend the new revision of *Don't Eat Your Heart Out Cookbook*. If we all abided by what Mr. Piscatella says, the health of our nation would skyrocket.

William C. Roberts, M.D.
Director, Baylor Cardiovascular
Institute, Dallas, Texas
Editor-in-Chief, *The American*
Journal of Cardiology

PREFACE

For the millions of American patients and their families involved in the fight against heart disease, winning is what counts. This book and its author are winners. Imagine being told in the beginning of the prime of your life that you have heart disease. This was the message given to Joe Piscatella at age 32. As he so movingly and beautifully tells us in the Introduction, he was first shocked into a sense of disbelief. However, with the help of a sensitive and caring physician and a supportive and loving family, he accepted this harsh reality. He set about developing a winning strategy in his fight against the nation's number one killer. The first edition of *Don't Eat Your Heart Out Cookbook* was a sharing of this strategy with other patients and their families facing the reality of heart disease.

The widely acclaimed success of the first edition speaks well of the thought and dedication that the author puts into his strategy for success. The second edition builds upon this success and provides a timely and thorough update of advances in the personal approaches used to reduce the consequences of heart disease in individuals' lives.

As a cardiologist involved on a daily basis with the diagnosis and treatment of cardiovascular disease, I am very grateful for the appearance of the revision of *Don't Eat You Heart Out.* The information contained herein is first and foremost very clear and accurate. I would strongly advise the reading of this work from the Introduction through the first five chapters before proceeding to the "heart" of the matter: the dietary and cookbook information. Not only readers who have heart disease themselves but also their families will relate to the author as a true colleague in their own struggles. The first five chapters, included in the section "Understanding Heart Disease," contain some of the best information I have ever read regarding the heart and conditions that affect the health of this important organ. The clarity with which this information is presented is unprecedented. These five chapters lay the important groundwork for the "action" information that follows. I truly believe that the reader will find this information not only enlightening but also very encouraging. I would specifically call attention to Chapter Four, which discusses the very promising information regarding the reversal of coronary artery disease.

The subsequent five chapters lay the groundwork for an understanding of diet, both as friend and foe. Americans are blessed with an abundance of dietary choices. However, without a clear understanding of the positive vs. negative choices that can be made, diet can be as much an enemy as a friend. Therefore, the five chapters included in the section "Diet Is a Cardiac Risk Factor" should be required reading for any American who wishes to "eat to live" and not just "live to eat." Since the appearance of the first edition of this book, the food industry in America has also gotten the message. Therefore, as patients and their families prepare to do battle with heart disease in the 1990s, dietary strategies are much easier to put into place than they were a decade or two ago. This is due to the responsiveness on the part of the federal government, state and local authorities, as well as the producers and distributors of foods. The information contained in this section provides patients and their families with a superb understanding of what approaches they need to take and the choices they need to make if diet is to be part of their winning strategy.

The section entitled "Preparing for Dietary Change" draws the subject even more sharply into focus. The three chapters in this section can serve as a very specific guide to the key elements of the dietary and nutritional factors that form the major thrust of this book.

The final section, outlining seven steps to achieve permanent dietary change, addresses every problem or dilemma that heart patients and their families are likely to encounter. Very specific facts are provided here, along with some very helpful hints and suggestions as to how to put these specific details into daily use. Finally, the information contained in Chapter Twenty-Three supplements the nutrition or dietary information itself. This chapter discusses the advantages of exercise, an additional approach to fighting heart disease. The two-pronged approach, diet plus exercise, serves to reinforce each of the separate efforts. As Joe Piscatella points out in the Introduction, the heart patient can get "more practical information from a cardiac rehabilitation program." The reality is, nevertheless, that not all our patients have cardiac rehabilitation programs available to them or the financial means to participate in these programs. Therefore, with the exceptionally fine help and guidance of this book and the concurrence and supportive understanding of their physicians, patients and their families can look forward to winning the battle against heart disease.

L. Kent Smith, M.D., M.P.H.
Director, Cardiac Rehabilitation
Arizona Heart Institute

CONTENTS

PART III: PREPARING FOR DIETARY CHANGE

PART IV: SEVEN STEPS TO CHANGE YOUR DIETARY HABITS ONCE AND FOR ALL

CHAPTER TWENTY-ONE: STEP 4–HOW TO HANDLE EATING IN A RESTAURANT 239

CHAPTER TWENTY-TWO: STEP 5–HOW TO MODIFY YOUR OWN RECIPES 257

CHAPTER TWENTY-THREE: STEP 6–EXERCISE TO CHANGE YOUR DIET 267

CHAPTER TWENTY-FOUR: STEP 7–DEVELOP A SENSE OF PERSPECTIVE 282

COOKBOOK

RECIPES

INTRODUCTION

1994

It was 8:00 A.M. on a beautiful January morning, and I was in the waiting room of my cardiologist prepared to take my annual physical exam and treadmill. Five other patients were also waiting. "There are problems at the hospital," the receptionist told us, "so the doctor is running late. Just make yourself comfortable."

I wasn't happy, but I knew how hospitals could be and resigned myself to an hour wait. Looking around for reading materials, I noticed some copies of *Don't Eat Your Heart Out Cookbook*, my first book, which dealt with diet, cholesterol and health. Written soon after my coronary bypass surgery, the book had become highly recommended to patients by physicians, so I wasn't too surprised to see it in the waiting room.

Had it been almost 17 years since that surgery? It seemed just like yesterday—and at the same time a hundred years ago. I could picture myself, nervous and concerned, in this same waiting room. I picked up another copy of *Don't Eat Your Heart Out* and was drawn immediately to the Introduction.

1977

It was a hot July afternoon, and for the second time in a week I was seated in the office of Dr. John Nagle, a prominent cardiologist in Tacoma, Washington. I was bewildered as to why I was there.

Five days earlier I had been in to see my family physician, Dr. James Early, about what I thought was a lung problem. For about a month I had been experiencing some pain in my chest while I warmed up to play tennis. By the end of the warm-up, the pain would usually disappear. But the day before I saw Dr. Early the pain had remained with me through six hours of tennis. It was then that I decided to call him. He asked me to come in the following morning.

Dr. Early was concerned about the pain, more concerned than I was at the time, and he advised that an electrocardiogram, or EKG, be taken. An EKG measures the electrical impulses of the heart and is used as a standard indicator of cardiac health. A previous EKG had been taken just four months earlier, during my annual physical exam, and the results then had been normal. The results now, however, were drastically different.

"Joe, the EKG indicates a heart abnormality, perhaps indicative of a very serious heart problem," said Dr. Early. "I want you to see a cardiologist immediately."

So, three hours after my "routine" exam with Dr. Early, instead of meeting a business associate for lunch as planned, I found myself in Dr. Nagle's office undergoing a thorough cardiac examination. Jim Early is a respected and competent physician. I did not take his sending me to a cardiologist lightly. But I did not believe there was anything seriously wrong, either; I was certain it was a mistake.

The result of Dr. Nagle's examination was the same: a heart problem existed. But he could not tell how serious the problem was. There was only one way to determine its extent, and that was to undergo a surgical procedure in which the heart and the coronary arteries are x-rayed. Two days later I underwent this procedure.

Now Dr. Nagle was ready to review the results with me. "Joe," he said, "you have a severely blocked coronary artery, about a 95% obstruction from what we can tell, which is causing the chest pain, called angina. This condition is identified as *coronary heart disease.* The blockage is a buildup of fat and cholesterol on the artery walls. It's badly located, being in the coronary artery that supplies the main pumping chamber of the heart. The smallest blood clot could stop the flow of blood completely and trigger a heart attack. The result could be fatal.

"We could put you on drugs to try to keep the artery open, but I don't think it would be very effective in the long run. I would recommend that open-heart surgery be done immediately . . . I mean within the next few days. At this moment you are a heart attack statistic just waiting to happen."

I was 32 years old.

The shock of his words hit me like a slap in the face. This couldn't happen to me. I was not prepared to hear what he had to say; I had difficulty understanding his words. He was speaking about a heart problem—*my heart problem!*—that psychologically I could not accept. Thoughts of escape filled my mind. "Just get up and leave," I told myself. "It's all a mistake. You're not supposed to be here." Once safely back in my world, I reasoned, I would surely awaken from this horrible nightmare.

As I continued to listen numbly to Dr. Nagle, I was confused. Like most people, I knew something about the workings of the heart, but the information was principally of the Biology 101 variety. It had been a number of years since I'd had cause to study the human body, so the details concerning the heart were nebulous at best. About the coronary arteries, those tiny channels that supply blood to the heart; about the blockage, the result of high blood cholesterol; and about the potential result, a heart attack, I knew nothing.

It wasn't that information about the heart and heart disease was not available. The American Heart

Association, among others, had produced and disseminated a tremendous amount of it. But, quite frankly, it had been of remote interest to me. Such information, indeed the entire subject itself, was simply not relevant to my life. What did blocked arteries or heart attacks have to do with me? There was plenty of time, I thought, to read all those Heart Association pamphlets while I was rocking in retirement. There were many other things in my life that were of more immediate importance to me.

Unknowingly, I had succumbed to the "what I don't know won't hurt me" syndrome. But in reality what I didn't know could not only hurt me but kill me.

What I didn't know was that coronary heart disease develops silently, insidiously, over a long period of time—generally 20 to 40 years. Once it surfaces, however, the primary result, a heart attack, is often immediately devastating.

What I didn't know was that over 6 million Americans have coronary heart disease and that every year some 1.5 million people are struck by heart attacks, causing over 500,000 fatalities. In graphic terms, American heart attack deaths in one year equal the casualties from 10 Vietnam wars. Or, put a different way, American heart attack deaths are the equivalent of four fully loaded 747s crashing *every day* with no survivors.

What I didn't know was that over 70 million Americans have some form of cardiovascular disease and that every minute two people die from it.

What I didn't know was that heart disease causes almost 45% of all deaths in the United States each year—more than cancer, AIDS, auto accidents, floods and airplane disasters combined.

What I didn't know was that for about one-third of all heart attack victims, the first heart attack was the only one, resulting in sudden death.

What I didn't know was that while family history is important, the vast majority of Americans with heart disease have it because of poor life-style habits involving diet, exercise, stress and smoking.

And what I didn't know was that our life-style habits—the way we choose to live—could alter the course of coronary heart disease and that my dietary habits had resulted in a culturally induced heart problem.

Such information was simply outside the realm of my everyday life. But it all changed for me on that hot July day. Listening to Dr. Nagle, I became intensely interested. I had reached what many health professionals call a "teachable moment," a time when a person is ready to listen, to learn and to take action. I recalled the words of El Cordobés, the famous Spanish matador, who once said that his interest in the bullfight increased in direct ratio to the closeness of the bull's horns. Confused, but "close to the horns," I struggled to understand the nature of the problem and the solutions.

My second reaction was one of frustration and anger, the typical "why me?" response. I was young and in the midst of building a career, raising a family and contributing to my community. I was physically active and had no health problems. Moreover, I didn't beat my wife, steal from the poor or kick the family dog. What could have caused such a thing as coronary heart disease to strike me and imperil my life? It wasn't fair. There was no logic in the selection process. It was like being seated with 100,000 others in the Rose Bowl and having your ticket number announced as the winner in a lottery . . . for a firing squad. Why me?

Then I remembered a comment made by John F. Kennedy reflecting the fact that life was unfair, that unfairness was part of its nature. There were no guarantees. The randomness of death existed for everyone. All at once I understood. Why not me?

I was gripped by pure stomach-churning fear. Dr. Nagle said the surgery should be performed "immediately . . . in the next few days." Any delay was inadvisable because of the great potential for a fatal heart attack. I was, in his words, a heart attack waiting to happen. The prospect of death, of leaving my wife Bernie, and our children, Anne, then six, and Joe, age four, was crushing.

I had never carried that weight before. At 32, I had felt a kind of immortality that only the young experience. The concept of death had been a remote one for me. I pictured it at the end of a long life, after years of accomplishment, fulfillment and joy. Old age was something that I looked forward to sharing with Bernie. For death to take me in my prime had never been contemplated.

On that July day the alarm clock of reality rang. I realized that not only *could* death happen now, but it probably *would* happen now, the result of a time bomb located inside my chest.

As we talked that afternoon, Dr. Nagle calmly and deliberately explained the many facets of the problem. We talked about the physiology of the heart and the coronary arteries, and of the impact of the disease ("It's like rust accumulating in an old water pipe"). We talked about some of the reasons that could cause the disease to develop, the so-called risk factors ("Your cholesterol level is a major problem, Joe"). We talked about why bypass surgery was necessary ("We can't clean out the existing artery, so we'll create a new one for you"); about how it was performed; about the potential problems ("The operation is a serious one—anytime you're on the heart-lung machine, there's a risk of stroke and cardiac arrest, which could be fatal"); and about the long-term risks ("About 10% of all bypasses close up during the first year; we don't know the long-term results because the surgery itself is so new").

Soon the late afternoon shadows began to grow, and I knew that the day was almost done. Like the day itself, I was out of time. A decision was needed. Treat the problem with drugs and be satisfied with the half-life of a cardiac cripple? Or undergo coronary bypass surgery, a risky procedure that at the time was less than 10 years old and could promise no long-term success?

I chose the surgery.

Less than a week after my meeting with Dr. Nagle, Dr. Kari Vitikainen, a gifted surgeon practicing in Tacoma, performed a five-hour operation during which he took a piece of saphenous vein from my left leg and used it to create a new arterial channel to my heart. The new channel would allow blood in the coronary artery to flow freely around the blockage. It literally "bypassed" the blocked area, hence the name of the operation. The procedure was not without problems and I had to return to surgery two days later because of complications. Ultimately, however, it was a success. Life-sustaining blood was once again flowing freely to my heart.

Ten days after surgery, I was recovering at home. Initially, I felt terrible and was in considerable pain. I was weak and had neither strength nor stamina; I felt as though I had been hit by a train. In this physical condition, my mental faculties were taxed to the limit with simple decisions. It was a time of physical and mental challenge, but I was elated simply to be alive.

As I began to mend, I gradually came to understand what had taken place and began to think about what was ahead for me. Despite the sheer joy of survival, I was very concerned about the unknowns in my future. Surgery had circumvented the disease, but it had not stopped it. Bypass did not "cure" me. I asked a number of questions: How did I get coronary disease? What had caused its development? Would new blockages develop in the future? What could be done to stabilize or reverse the disease?

There were many things about coronary heart disease that I did not know. But there were some things that I did know. I knew that I did not want the disease to progress in me. I knew that I did not want to die a premature death from a heart attack. I knew that I did not want to live the half-life of a coronary cripple. And I knew that I did not want to get three or four years down the road only to find out that I needed another coronary surgery. I was seriously concerned about how I was going to live the rest of my life to prevent future heart problems. I understood how lucky I had been. Coronary heart disease could have killed me, but it didn't. Instead, I was alive and recuperating. The surgery was in the past; my interest now was in the future.

It was a turning point in my life. I could slip back into my comfortable old life-style, which had contributed to my coronary problem. Or I could develop a different, more healthful life-style, one that would reduce coronary risk.

There was really no choice. Opting for healthier life-style habits was the only reasonable thing to do to enhance my cardiac health and, with it, the quality and longevity of my life. But I was immobilized by a lack of clear direction. What should I do? How should I do it? It became obvious that no serious life-style change could be accomplished based on fragments of information. I needed to better understand the causes of coronary heart disease before I could determine how to alleviate those causes. Again I turned to Dr. Nagle.

"I'm glad you're interested in cardiac risk factors," he said. "In my opinion the identification and control of risk factors will be the key to the future health of your heart. During the past three decades, a number of major developments have taken place in cardiac medicine. You've already benefited from some of them, Joe, such as the arteriogram, the heart-lung machine, and the bypass surgery technique itself. As important as these developments are, they may prove to be less significant in the long run than the realization that life-style habits can increase—or decrease—the risk of coronary heart disease.

"This is especially important for you to understand, Joe, as you have demonstrated coronary heart disease. Bypass surgery may take away the pain, but it offers no guarantee against future angina and heart attack. You need to reduce your future risk, and surgery cannot do that for you—only life-style changes can.

"The way a person lives to a great extent dictates how healthy his or her heart will be. Because many life-style habits can be modified, there is a definite ability to influence our own cardiovascular health. We often live as if our life-style habits don't matter. They do. Half of the 10 leading causes of death in the United States are primarily related to life-style, and coronary disease leads the way. At least 90% of premature heart attacks and strokes are preventable. They are caused not by genetics or age but by the ill effects of a fatty diet, a sedentary life-style, too much stress and cigarette smoking—making heart attacks in the United States a culturally induced epidemic. Unlike the developments like angioplasty that deal in correction, the management of cardiac risk factors provides us with a means to *prevent, stabilize* and in some circumstances even *reverse* the disease."

Dr. Nagle went on to explain that the most common cardiac risk factors are family history, elevated cholesterol, cigarette smoking, physical inactivity, overweight, high blood pressure and stress.

"Obviously," he said, "family history is beyond our control. Of course, someone with a strong family history could protect himself greatly by minimizing his coronary risk factors. But studies show that less than 15% of those with heart disease have it because of bad genes. The overwhelming majority have it because of controllable risk factors such as high cholesterol, high blood pressure, obesity and smoking. In your case, Joe, diet pattern is a primary risk factor. You've eaten the contemporary American diet, rich in total fat, saturated fat, cholesterol and calories, and the result is an elevated level of blood cholesterol—a condition that dramatically raises the risk of coronary heart disease. And you're not alone. Millions of Americans have high cholesterol, yet people in other countries do not. Why? Because of what we eat. The high-fat American diet pattern may be the single largest contributing factor to the enormous incidence of coronary heart disease and heart attack in this country."

"Does anyone else know about this?" I interjected. "Why isn't it better publicized?"

Dr. Nagle smiled. "Many people are aware of it," he said. "The American Heart Association has been working for a change in our diet pattern since 1961. The National Institutes of Health, the Surgeon General, the National Cancer Institute and many other organizations are concerned with the makeup of the American diet and have called for changes. And in general the population understands. Americans are a nutritionally literate people. We know about diet and health, but we simply have not put that knowledge into action. While it may look as if we're making some progress, the reality is that we are a nation that discusses its cholesterol level over Danish pastry!

"The consequence is that coronary heart disease has become a modern epidemic. Pathologists report that less than 50 years ago arterial blockages were infrequent and not a cause for concern. Today these blockages are present in virtually all adult Americans and in many children as well. They are responsible for almost 45% of American deaths each year. I think that one of the most important things you can do for yourself, Joe, is to institute a more healthful way of eating."

As he was speaking, I realized the extent of my ignorance. I knew very little about my diet or my nutritional needs and absolutely nothing about diet as a cardiac risk factor. While I suspected that not all foods on my diet were healthful, I had little inkling that this diet could produce such a negative impact on my health. I was encouraged by Dr. Nagle's words, however, for I believed that we had identified a risk factor about which I could take some action.

All that was needed, I thought, was for Dr. Nagle to fill in the blanks—to explain clearly the relationship of my diet to my health, to design a new diet for me, and to tell me how to institute and maintain it. He would tell me what to do and how to do it, and it would all easily be accomplished.

Unfortunately, we were dealing with realism. "Much as I would like to do the whole thing for you," Dr. Nagle said, "the fact is that few physicians can offer much more than general advice and direction in the reorientation of diet. Frankly, you'll get more practical information from a registered dietitian or a cardiac rehabilitation program. The starting point is, of course, understanding the role of diet in coronary health and identifying the problem areas. I can certainly help you in that regard. I can tell you about tested principles, and I can direct you to research and clinical studies that can provide more in-depth information.

"Once you understand the problems with your

diet, you'll have solved one-third of the equation. The remaining two-thirds are the really difficult tasks: to design a new diet pattern that meets your physical and emotional needs and also fits your lifestyle, and to sustain it for the long term. Many patients become highly motivated and immediately institute a diet extremely low in fat—say, about 10% of calories from fat. Then they get bored with it, or find that it takes too much time or that the food is unpalatable, so they go back to their old, high-fat diet—probably with about 40% of calories from fat. According to the National Institutes of Health, over *one-half* of all bypass patients are off a low-fat diet within six months of surgery. Understanding what constitutes a heart-healthy diet is one thing. Making it work in the real world is quite another. Only you can do that."

I wasn't happy about what Dr. Nagle had to say. I was looking for an easy answer—a pill or a prescription. Instead he'd given me straightforward information: the task would not be easy, and the responsibility was mine. It was my heart, my life, my diet. It had to be my effort.

I spent the next six months studying the many facets of diet and cardiac health. I struggled with medical texts and papers about the heart and the coronary arteries, about cholesterol and about coronary heart disease. I attended lectures and clinics from coast to coast and interviewed a number of physicians, registered dietitians and other health professionals. I digested every cookbook, pamphlet and article published by the American Heart Association. And I continued to visit with Dr. Nagle. Finally, after much work, I was able to complete the initial one-third of the equation: I understood the mechanics of my coronary problem, how my diet had contributed to that problem, and what had to be done to change my diet, reduce my cholesterol and lessen the risk of future coronary problems.

The process of collecting and evaluating information was not an easy one. As a layman, my background and experience were not suited for medical research, and often my limitations were reached. At the same time, however, I knew there had to be a way for ordinary people to more clearly understand the nature of coronary heart disease and the role of diet in the disease process.

It was not my role, as I saw it, to discover something new; I merely wished to synthesize and evaluate current information and to arrive at a rational conclusion as to what was the best, most healthful diet pattern for me. My research led me to the following conclusions.

Dietary pattern is a cardiac risk factor. The evidence linking diet to coronary heart disease comes from various epidemiological studies that have surveyed the incidence and potential causes of disease in different populations. Studies of populations since World War II have illustrated a strong correlation between dietary fat, blood cholesterol and coronary heart disease. While diet is not the only factor in the development of the disease, clearly it is a major factor.

The American diet significantly increases the potential for coronary heart disease. Americans eat well by world standards, but our national diet is a major factor in the great number of coronary fatalities in the United States. While much of the world suffers from nutrient deficiency diseases, Americans suffer from chronic diseases caused by excesses. Too much total fat, saturated fat, dietary cholesterol, salt, sugar and calories have contributed to elevated levels of blood cholesterol, overweight, high blood pressure, stroke and heart attack. With a diet consisting of over 37% fat, 24% sugar and 5% alcohol, many nutritionists consider Americans to be the most overfed and undernourished people in the world. The American diet is a significant coronary risk factor.

Dietary pattern can be managed and cardiac risk can be diminished. Numerous trials and studies have shown that instituting a low-fat diet pattern can produce a reduction in blood cholesterol, which in turn can stabilize disease development and, in some cases, produce coronary regression, a reduction of blockages in the coronary arteries. During World War II, for example, Scandinavians were denied their typically high-fat diet, and consequently the incidence of heart attack diminished; after the war, their high-fat diet was resumed and the incidence of heart attack also increased. More recently, a number of studies have shown that it is possible to stabilize or reverse the buildup of coronary artery blockages through a low-fat diet.

Responsibility for dietary change rests with the individual. Help is available from family, friends, medical professionals and organizations. But they cannot make the change happen. Only the individual can do that. One physician stated it succinctly: "We doctors are trained in disease. That is why coronary problems can be diagnosed and corrected. But diet management in order to reduce coronary risk is not disease. It is health. And health, strangely enough, is not our field. Health is the responsibility of each person."

So, armed with basic knowledge about diet and coronary health, and motivated by an intense desire to reduce my cardiac risk, I began to translate what I had learned into a specific, practicable and workable program of dietary change. The science behind the need for healthy eating was good to know. But now I had to bridge the gap between knowledge per se and the application of that knowledge in real-life situations. In other words, I had to make the principles of healthy eating work in the real world.

This was neither an easy nor a quick effort. Progress was slow and was measured in small increments. Trial and error ruled. Some meals were disasters; others were great. Some new cooking techniques worked well; others did not and had to be abandoned. Sometimes I ordered well in a restaurant (salmon instead of prime rib); at other times high-fat still ruled (the salmon came swimming in a butter sauce!). Some days I could easily stay on a healthy diet; other days I succumbed to strong cravings for chocolate candy, cookies and milk shakes.

I wished for a plan that I could simply follow, but none existed. Most of the pop-nutrition diet books, concerned chiefly with quick weight loss, were useless. Some of the medically sound books counseled diets so low in fat as to be unrealistic for most people. And most of the so-called "healthy-heart" cookbooks told me how to prepare a recipe but not how to maintain a permanent change in dietary habits.

I was on my own to produce a new, practical diet plan, and the experience was frustrating. I was building the proverbial bicycle as I was riding it. Many times I came close to giving up the struggle, but I knew that the alternative—returning to my old diet—was not the answer. Finally, progress started to take root and a new way of eating began to take shape. The new dietary program that evolved was realistic, practical and workable, and it had a positive impact on my coronary health. For that reason, I called it the Positive Diet.

After a year on the Positive Diet, I returned to see Dr. Nagle for a checkup. He was well pleased with my condition. My cholesterol had gone from a high of almost 300 mg/dl to a low of 165 mg/dl. My weight was down from 185 pounds to 162 pounds. Blood pressure and triglycerides had fallen.

Dr. Nagle remarked that all his cardiac patients and their families should follow such a diet.

"Why don't they?" I asked.

"For a variety of reasons," he replied. "Many patients are not as young as you are, and most would not be able to put in the effort to design and implement such a diet. Nevertheless, they need it as much as you do."

It was then that I first thought of writing *Don't Eat Your Heart Out*, a personal statement of how one person and his family altered their dietary life-style in order to enhance cardiac health. It was developed not as an academic exercise, but as a program of survival to better control cardiac destiny. Although it includes information about healthful eating, menus, recipes and cooking tips, the book is not simply a compilation of dietary facts. It is a "how-to" book, a step-by-step outline showing how to achieve a lasting change in dietary habits. It is dedicated to the premise that no one—least of all a cardiac patient—should suffer a heart attack as the result of inadequate or insufficient information.

1994

As I put the book down, I was amazed at the emotion I still felt. The surgery itself, the struggle with dietary change and the effort to write the book came alive for me again.

I looked around the waiting room and noticed a middle-aged couple reading and talking about dietary changes they had to make. The husband, I learned, had had a heart attack six weeks earlier at age 55, and their life together had changed on a dime. They were scared and confused as they began their personal struggle to institute a healthy diet, and I felt a kinship and a connection with them. I wanted to tell them, "It isn't that hard to do. The world isn't the same as 17 years ago. The general public—not just heart patients—is more disposed toward low-fat eating. We know more about how to make it work. Low-fat food selections in grocery stores are so much better. It's easier to get what you want in a restaurant. It's easier to read and understand food labels. It's a different ball game from when I went through surgery."

It was then that I decided to write a new edition of *Don't Eat Your Heart Out.* There were a number of reasons, I felt, for doing so.

First, I had 17 years of research and personal experience to share. Since the publication of *Don't Eat Your Heart Out,* I had continued to do research and to make dietary changes in my own life. And I had written three other books: *Choices for a Healthy Heart, Controlling Your Fat Tooth* and *The Fat Tooth Fat-Gram Counter & Restaurant Guide.* In that period of time my diet had moved in stages from 40% fat to about 20% fat. I had much to share about the evolutionary process of sustained—yet moderate—dietary change.

Also, there was a world of new information and food products. When I went through surgery, for example, the American Heart Association did not recommend shellfish because it was "too high in cholesterol." That position has now changed due to new evidence that saturated fat has a greater impact on the elevation of blood cholesterol and that shellfish is low in saturated fat. Similar changes in thinking have occurred with regard to olive oil and other foods. It was important, I felt, for people to get straight, scientifically sound, current information on what constitutes a healthy diet.

The products available today offer a much wider range of choices, so selecting lower-fat items is not as difficult. When I went through surgery, tuna salad was made with either regular mayonnaise or, if you wanted to cut the fat, a blend of mayonnaise and low-fat yogurt. But today you can buy commercial mayonnaise in "regular," "light" and "fat-free" versions. There are low-fat and fat-free salad dressings, cookies and cheese, to name but a few items. While there are still problems with several such products (many fat-free cookies, for instance, are high in sugar and calories, which can be problems for weight and triglycerides), the fact remains that the world of food products has changed for the better.

In addition, I had developed a perspective based on research and experience about what works in the real world. And what works is a 20% fat diet. It is moderate and realistic, and it results in positive cardiac outcomes.

Virtually everyone agrees that the high-fat American diet penalizes health, yet that information by itself is not enough to produce lasting dietary change. If it were, we would be eating far less fat and far more fruits, grains and vegetables. Dr. Nagle had cited the fact that over half of bypass patients, who certainly have a reason to be motivated, are off a low-fat diet within six months of surgery. Cardiac rehabilitation programs cite "dietary noncompliance in patients" as their single greatest problem. And fewer than 30% of the 10 million Americans enrolled in weight loss programs will be eating a low-fat diet a year from now.

At the other end are very restrictive diets, usually about 10% fat. "These have come about," says dietitian Faye Berger Mitchell, "because people have taken the *low-fat* message to mean *no fat*, or very little fat. But in actuality, people do need some fat in their diets." In addition, such extremely low-fat diets, often considered boring and restrictive, can set people up for frustration and failure. The fact is that dietary fat does not have to be totally eliminated. By moderating its intake, cardiac benefits result—without the hassle of restrictive diets and with much more palatable food.

People on restrictive diets often have lists of

"good foods" and "bad foods" and live their lives trying to eat one and avoid the other. Until one day, in a moment of weakness, an Oreo cookie is eaten and the healthy diet is over! Today we know from research that a "fat tooth"—a craving for fatty foods—exists in most people and that we could better manage our diets by realizing that all food is "good food." How foods go together in the course of a day is what's important. An Oreo cookie by and of itself is not harmful. If it comes at the end of a day that saw a croissant for breakfast, a cheeseburger for lunch and prime rib for dinner, then it compounds the fat problem. However, if it follows a daily diet of oatmeal for breakfast, a grilled chicken sandwich for lunch and pasta marinara for dinner, then an Oreo is not much of a problem. The way foods go together can be managed by "fat budgeting," the most practical and realistic way to control dietary fat.

I have learned that moderation and balance are the keys to success. Although some heart patients may need a diet lower in fat, for most of us a diet with about 20% of calories from fat provides the best of both worlds: a balance of good food and good health. (The American Heart Association has historically suggested a goal of no more than 30% of calories from fat; however, many health professionals today think this is too generous, particularly for people with coronary disease.)

And finally, my own situation needs to be shared. At age 47, I went through a second bypass surgery. The situation, like most in life, contained bad and good elements. The bad news was that one of my original bypass grafts had worn out. Saphenous veins, taken from the leg, were used for most grafts at the time of my first surgery. Unfortunately, these veins are not designed by nature to go forever. As Dr. Nagle told me, "The average usable life span of a saphenous bypass graft is about five to seven years.

That's the average. Some people get more; some get less. But you got 15 years out of your graft because you took care of it by leading a healthy life-style. That's two or three times the average. But now it's a problem. We need to replace it with an internal mammary artery, which can last 25 to 30 years with good care."

The good news was that the rest of my cardiovascular system was found to be in excellent shape. I have developed collateral circulation, which is the growth of new coronary arteries; my main coronary arteries have gotten larger; and, most important, *I have less disease now than at the time of my first surgery.* "You've experienced coronary regression, Joe," said Dr. Nagle. "You have less cholesterol buildup than 17 years ago. The diet you've practiced has worked."

The updated *Don't Eat Your Heart Out* is designed to give the reader the latest information about how to institute and maintain a heart-healthy diet in the real world. The book describes coronary heart disease and explains why diet is a cardiac risk factor. It provides the perspective, plan and strategy necessary for successful dietary change. And it outlines the seven steps needed to change your dietary habits once and for all. The Cookbook section provides more than 300 delicious, heart-healthy recipes put together by my wife Bernie.

As a bridge between medical science and real-life application, the book is practical and usable. And it works.

Joseph C. Piscatella

PART I

UNDERSTANDING HEART DISEASE

CHAPTER ONE

THE HEART AND THE CORONARY ARTERIES

Understanding the nature of coronary disease is important as the basis for making heart-healthy life-style changes. The starting point is the heart and the coronary arteries. Until the time of my bypass surgery in 1977, I had felt no need to understand how the heart works. Its health, much like freedom, was something I took for granted. With the shock of surgery, however, came the desire to learn about the heart. Suddenly I was hungry for information about its functions, about the role of the coronary arteries and about the complex arrangement of blood vessels in the circulatory system. I knew that the heart had to be understood before an appreciation of the role of coronary heart disease could be gained.

The Heart

Throughout the ages, the word "heart" has covered such a wide range of meanings that one would expect its primary definition to be somewhat spectacular. In fact, it is not. Webster defines the heart itself simply as a "hollow muscular organ which by rhythmic contractions and relaxations keeps the blood in circulation." When all its complexities are removed, the essential nature of the heart remains . . . it is a pump.

But to describe the heart merely as "a pump" is like referring to Mt. Everest simply as "a mountain" or the Amazon as "a river." The heart is not just a pump—it is THE PUMP! Every day this unbelievable organ pumps 2,100 gallons of blood continuously at the rate of over one gallon a minute through some 60,000 miles of blood vessels to reach over 300 trillion body cells. It takes an average of just 24 seconds for a drop of blood to circulate through the entire body and return to the heart. In order to accomplish this monumental task, the heart must beat over 100,000 times a day. At this rate, in an average lifetime the heart will beat over 2.5 billion times and pump more than 135 million gallons of blood—or enough to fill more than 13 supertankers. And this is just when it's resting. It can pump six times its resting volume during exercise!

This pumping is such an amazing feat that its magnitude is often difficult to comprehend. Two and a half billion heartbeats . . . it's like talking about the national debt. The figures are just too large to be realistic. Perhaps that's why the heart is taken for granted by most people and often is not appreciated until a problem occurs.

Many misconceptions abound about the heart. For instance, upon learning the awesome amount of work it does, I assumed that the heart must be rather large. It is, in fact, quite small, about the size of a clenched fist, and usually weighs between 7 and 12 ounces depending on the size of the person. By comparison, the heart of a bull elephant can weigh over 50 pounds.

A second misconception concerns the location of

the heart. Most people believe, as I did, that the heart is located in the left breast. In actuality, it sits in the center of the chest directly behind the protective breastbone. Smug in my hard-won anatomical knowledge, I smile inwardly each time I stand in Seattle's Kingdome and see 60,000 people sing the national anthem with a hand over their left lung.

A third misconception concerns the shape of the heart. Quite simply, the heart is not "heart-shaped." It does not remotely resemble the classic valentine heart. While it may come as a shock to romantics and candy manufacturers alike, the heart is really shaped like . . . an eggplant! Suspended in a protective sac called the pericardium, the heart looks exactly like a grocery store eggplant in a plastic bag. Can you imagine Valentine's Day with chocolate eggplants and eggplant-shaped boxes of candy? For some people, myself included, this might take "truth in advertising" one step too far.

HOW THE HEART WORKS

The human body is made up of over 300 trillion individual cells. Each of these cells is a life unto itself, and each has a metabolic need for oxygen and nutrients in order to produce energy and new cellular material. Each cell also has a need to expel waste products and carbon dioxide. In this respect, the life of each cell parallels the life of the body as a whole.

The process defined as "in with the good, out with the bad" must occur continuously if the cells are to remain healthy. Any disruption in the process—not enough oxygen and nutrients going in, too little waste and carbon dioxide coming out—will negatively impact their health. Of critical importance to each cell is an uninterrupted oxygen supply, for no cell can live for more than 30 minutes without oxygen. Some cells, notably those in the brain and the heart, live for a considerably shorter time when deprived of oxygen.

For this reason, blood is constantly being circulated throughout the thousands of miles of arteries, arterioles, capillaries, veins and venules that make up the blood vessel system. The blood vessels are the conduits through which the blood carries oxygen and nutrients to the cells and removes waste and carbon dioxide. Picture the enormous network of roadways that serve a major city by accommodating the incoming flow of food and the outgoing flow of refuse; any slowing or stopping of this traffic could result in famine or disease. It's the same for the body. Blood must circulate constantly throughout the blood vessel system. But it can do so only as a result of the pumping action of the heart.

While the heart is considered a single organ, physiologically it is two distinct pumps that work together: the right heart and the left heart. The two pumps are completely separated from each other by a wall of muscle. Each half has two chambers: the atrium, or holding chamber, and the ventricle, or pumping chamber. The right heart receives venous blood containing waste products and carbon dioxide in the right atrium. Venous blood, called "poor blood," is low in oxygen. (Contrary to social myths concerning the blue-blooded rich, "poor blood" is characteristically blue; arterial blood, called "rich blood," is high in oxygen and is characteristically red.)

After the right atrium is filled, the venous blood is sent to the right ventricle, which in turn pumps it to the lungs. This is a fairly easy activity for the heart due to the low pressure maintained in the lungs. Only an easy pumping action is required, and this fact is reflected by the relatively thin walls of the right ventricle.

A Cross Section of the Human Heart

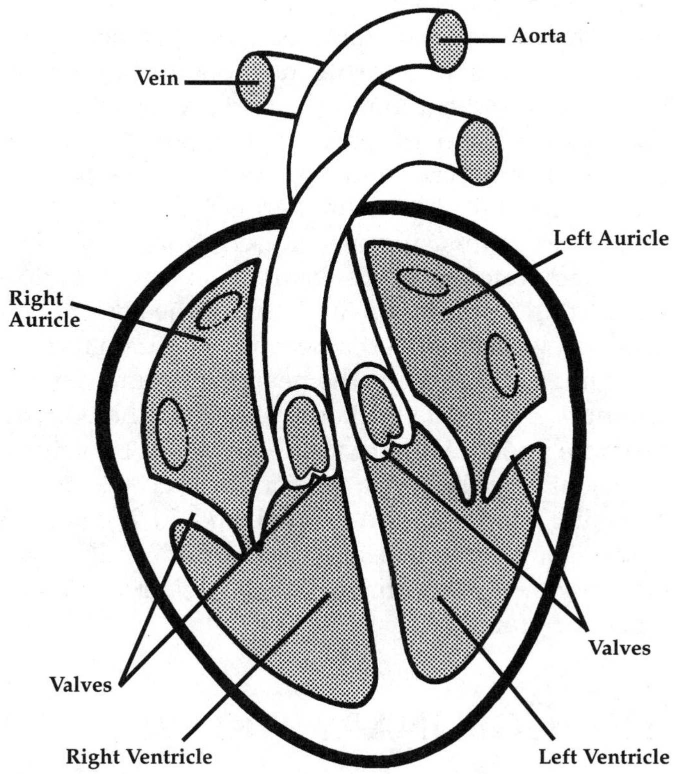

Once in the lungs, venous blood is cleansed of carbon dioxide, takes on oxygen and is transformed into arterial blood. It then moves from the lungs into the left heart, where it is received and stored in the left atrium and is subsequently passed to the left ventricle. The left ventricle is the powerhouse—the chamber that pumps blood to distant parts of the body, under high pressure and against much resistance, through arteries and into capillaries that may be only 1/2,500th of an inch in diameter.

This pumping takes tremendous power. As such, the left ventricle is a heavily muscular chamber with walls measuring one-half inch in thickness. The pressure necessary to drive the blood out of the left ventricle is so great that if the aorta were opened in the neck, a column of blood would spurt to a height of five or six feet. Intense pressure is essential in order to keep the blood circulating.

Even from this simplistic description of the purpose and function of the heart, it's easy to understand the importance of cardiac health. When supplied with the blood it needs to maintain its constant muscular activity, the heart can pump oxygen and nutrients to the farthermost cells of the body to promote good health. But when it doesn't receive a sufficient supply of blood for its own needs, its pumping ability is diminished and ill health can result. The heart—this small and wonderfully powerful organ—is essential to life. Its health cannot be taken for granted.

THE CORONARY ARTERIES

While the heart is often viewed as the key element in the body's delivery system, its own dependence on oxygen and nutrients is often overlooked. The heart is a super-organ in terms of energy and efficiency. However, like all other organs and body tissue, it cannot operate without fuel. The cardiac muscle has a need to be served—and this need is met by blood that flows through the coronary arteries.

I had assumed that the heart was somehow nourished by the thousands of gallons of blood that pass through its chambers. This is not the case. The heart, like the rest of the body, must be served by arteries. Only the blood that reaches the heart through the coronary arteries can provide nourishment.

The right and left coronary arteries, originating from the aorta, lie on the surface of the heart and divide into smaller branches so that every portion of the heart has a blood supply. The right main coronary artery nourishes the right side of the heart and has branches that extend to the back of the cardiac muscle. The left main coronary artery begins as a single artery and quickly branches into two main arteries: the left anterior descending artery, which supplies the front of the heart, and the left circumflex artery, which carries blood to the back of the heart. The coronary arteries surround the heart and actually curl around its surface like a crown.

The Coronary Arteries

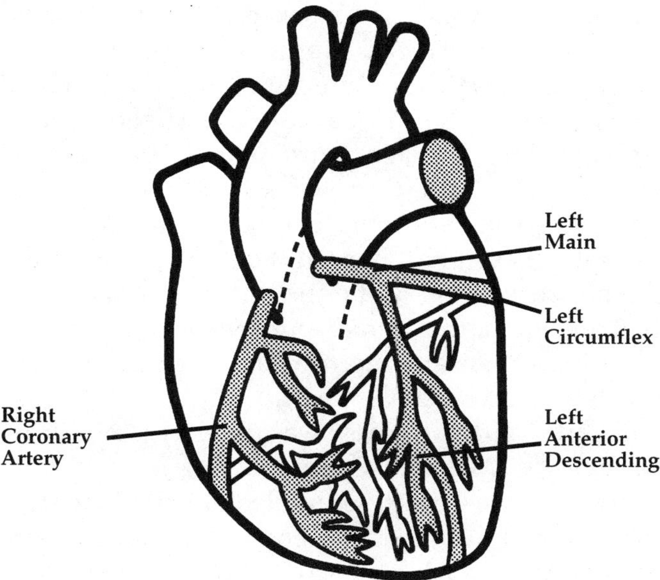

In establishing the coronary arteries as supply lines for the heart, nature has developed an efficient delivery system. Each time the heart pumps rich blood through the aorta to the body, a portion of that blood is siphoned through the coronary arteries back to the heart itself. It's like a commission that the heart pays itself for the work performed. Of the rich blood pumped into the aorta, 95% is supplied to the body and 5% finds its way back to the heart. So, every time it pumps, the heart works to nourish itself. The fact that only 5% of the rich blood is sufficient to meet the needs of the heart is due to the heart's ability to extract more oxygen per milliliter of blood than any other organ in the body.

Although the location of the coronary arteries and the 5% commission system are designed in combination to provide all areas of the heart with an adequate blood supply, that design is fraught with potential problems. The arteries themselves are extremely small—approximately an eighth of an inch in diameter, or about as wide as a piece of cooked spaghetti. Thus a blockage and/or clot could easily impede the blood supply to the heart.

And it doesn't take much for these arteries to become clogged. The earliest obstruction, often present by the teenage years, is a "fatty streak"—a layer of fatty, fibrous cholesterol-laden deposits on the interior walls of the coronary arteries. These deposits thicken and harden the artery walls, making the arteries less elastic and hampering their ability to expand and contract in response to the heart's pumping. They also narrow the channel through which blood reaches the heart.

Coronary artery disease was described in 1705 by physiologist William Cowper, who observed an artery that "very much resembled the bit of the stem of a tobacco pipe, its sides were so thick, and its bore consequently much lessened." Though not the only ingredient in the fatty streak, cholesterol is the most important. The rate at which a fatty streak develops depends primarily on how much cholesterol is in the blood. The more there is, the more is available for deposit.

Unlike other arteries that are protected by muscle tissue, the coronary arteries are afforded no protection by the heart itself. Located on the heart's surface, they are forced to move, stretch and kink as the heart muscle contracts and relaxes. This constant movement can cause much wear and tear, especially at the points where the arteries bend, and promotes the development of small fissures on the inner walls. In addition, certain aspects of life-style—such as cigarette smoking and excessive stress—tend to cause more arterial wounds. Such wounds often become important in the development of arterial blockages because it is at these injury sites that cholesterol can begin to collect, form a blockage and harden the artery.

The fact that the coronary arteries are unprotected and can easily be injured is a major reason for the development of blockages. (Ironically, because of their location on the surface of the heart, bypass surgery is possible.) And the fact that coronary arteries are very small is a significant reason such blockages can impede blood flow and cause a heart attack. These are things over which we have no control. But the amount of cholesterol in the blood, which is most often a product of diet, is controllable.

The coronary arteries, the weak link in the circulatory chain, are the real Achilles heel of mankind. But they don't have to be.

CHAPTER TWO

WHAT IS CORONARY HEART DISEASE?

Cardiovascular disease, which includes coronary heart disease, high blood pressure, stroke and rheumatic heart disease, is found in epidemic proportions in the United States today. An estimated 70 million Americans, or about one in four people, are afflicted. While cancer and AIDS may get the headlines, cardiovascular disease has the deadly distinction of being the number one killer, taking the lives of almost one million Americans every year.

One American dies from cardiovascular disease every 34 seconds. This means that by 7 o'clock in the morning, on any given day of the week, 741 Americans have already died from cardiovascular disease. By noon the figure has risen to 1,270 deaths, and by midafternoon some 1,558 people have died. By 7 o'clock in the evening, heart disease has claimed 2,012 American lives. And by the time the 11 o'clock news has ended, the total deaths nationally from cardiovascular disease stand at 2,488. Based on an average life span of 75 years, cardiovascular disease costs us 5.4 million years of potential life and more than $117 billion every year in medical costs and lost productivity resulting from disability.

Leading Causes of Death in the U.S.:

Cardiovascular disease	45%
Cancer	25%
Chronic lung diseases	6%
Accidents	5%
Pneumonia and influenza	4%
AIDS-related causes	1%
All other causes	14%

Source: American Heart Association.

The type of cardiovascular disease most responsible for heart attacks is called coronary heart disease. This is the disease I have, along with some six million other Americans. Coronary heart disease causes over 1.5 million heart attacks and a staggering half-million deaths each year.

Most people are aware of the great number of heart attacks in the United States. You'd have to be from another planet not to recognize the tremendous impact of heart disease on American society. Virtually everyone knows someone or some family touched by heart disease. And yet the details of the disease are not clear to many people.

Coronary heart disease is a condition in which layers of cholesterol and fat, called plaque, are formed on the inner walls of blood vessels. These layers can severely obstruct the flow of blood. The coronary arteries are like thin-walled rubber tubes that expand and contract as the heart pumps. But as the disease progresses, cholesterol deposits thicken arterial walls. One result is a narrowing of the channels through which blood flows to the heart. Another is that the arteries themselves lose their ability to expand. The consequence is that a steady supply of blood to the heart is threatened, a state that can seriously impair cardiac performance and put the heart—and life itself—at great risk.

A prime characteristic of the disease is its slow and silent progression over 20 to 40 years, usually with no outward signs or symptoms of its debilitating effects. This is why so many people are surprised by the "sudden" manifestation of the disease. In reality, these "sudden" signs usually signal advanced heart disease. The disease progresses in three stages. The first stage, called *hypercholesterolemia,* is characterized by elevated blood cholesterol and is often accompanied by high blood pressure. While genetics may play a role in a person's cholesterol level, the interaction of diet with genetics is most important. "Only 1% of high cholesterol is caused by bad genes," says Dr. William Connor of the Oregon Health Sciences University. "Ninety-nine percent has to do with diet. We can prevent hypercholesterolemia in most people by better dietary management."

Elevated cholesterol leads to the second stage, called *atherosclerosis,* literally translated from the Greek as "hard mush." This is an apt description of an arterial blockage that begins as a soft, mushy accumulation of fat and cholesterol and ends up as a deposit of hard, encrusted material. Its product is a narrowed, thickened and inelastic blood vessel.

Atherosclerosis, which is enhanced by cigarette smoking, lack of physical activity, and stress, leads directly to stage three—coronary heart disease.

How Coronary Heart Disease Develops

The exact sequence of events leading to the development of coronary heart disease is unknown. However, it is thought that the disease process is linked to injury on the inner wall of the blood vessel and to elevated levels of cholesterol in the blood.

Coronary wall injury is the result of both physiology and life-style. Coronary arteries are lined with a smooth tissue, the *intima,* which by its nature helps the blood to move freely. Early in life, minute fissures begin to develop in the intima as the coronary arteries twist and flex each time the heart contracts and relaxes. And with the heart beating 100,000 times in a single day, it is not surprising that the natural wear and tear on these arteries would produce such an injury. As time goes on, certain aspects of life-style—particularly cigarette smoking and chronic stress—can significantly increase arterial wounds. Nicotine and carbon monoxide from cigarette smoke can irritate the lining of the artery, as can powerful hormones that race through the blood vessel system when an individual is under stress. Although it makes sense not to increase injuries as the result of life-style choices, the fact is that coronary artery wounds are very common and each of us carries many of them.

Normally, when an injury occurs, blood cells and clotting material are rushed to the wound in order to repair it. In the case of an external cut or scrape, a "patch" of new cells covers the wound and soon a protective scar is formed. This mechanism works well unless the blood contains too much cholesterol. Then the bloodstream deposits not only blood cells and clotting materials but also cholesterol, which is quickly absorbed by the cells that surround the wound. As more and more cholesterol is deposited and absorbed, the surrounding cells are forced to multiply rapidly in order to maintain the absorption rate. The result can be a wild, cancer-like growth of new "foamy" cells that soon become swollen to the bursting point. The waxy, fatty deposit formed by the accumulation of these cholesterol-filled cells is called a "fatty streak." Sometimes the fatty streak becomes stable and ceases to grow. In such cases it may not significantly disrupt blood flow. But should the "foamy" cells continue to absorb cholesterol, they will eventually burst. A lot of scarring and inflammation follows, resulting in an uneven and hardened plaque or bulge called an *atheroma,* which gradually narrows the arterial channel and seriously impedes blood flow to the heart. It is estimated that well over half of adult Americans harbor one or more of such coronary artery blockages.

The Development of Artherosclerosis

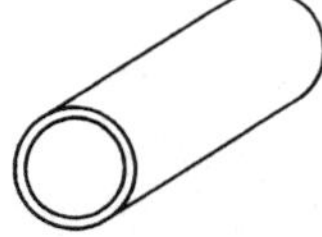

No atherosclerosis

Moderate atherosclerosis

Severe atherosclerosis

THE CONSEQUENCES OF CORONARY HEART DISEASE

Coronary heart disease commonly causes three cardiac conditions. The first is called *angina,* or *angina pectoris* (Latin for "pain in the chest"), which can result when the heart muscle receives insufficient oxygen to maintain its workload. It is estimated that over three million Americans have angina. For many people, it is a sharp pain in the chest, neck, jaw, arm or shoulder. For many others, it is a discomforting sensation of tightening in the chest or heavy pressure behind the breastbone. One cardiac patient told me it felt "like having an elephant sit on my chest." Frequently angina is misinterpreted as gas pain or indigestion that will not go away. For me, it was a burning sensation in the area of my lungs brought on by physical activity. Health professionals suggest seeing a doctor if angina symptoms occur with the four common triggers—exertion, eating, exposure to cold, severe emotional stress—and are relieved by rest. If the onset of angina is not relieved by rest, you should seek *immediate* medical care. New technology can potentially save heart muscle from certain damage if you can get to the hospital within four hours of the onset of severe angina.

Whatever its manifestation, angina is generally sufficient to force a person to curtail physical activity until the sensation passes. For many, angina dictates a life-style modification that precludes physical activities. Jogging, tennis or, in some cases, just walking up a hill requires the heart to pump blood at an increased rate to those working muscles that need oxygen. A jogger's legs, for instance, may demand six times the amount of blood when running as when at rest. This increased demand in workload usually poses no problem for the heart. But when coronary artery blockages prevent the heart from receiving sufficient oxygen to maintain its high workload, angina becomes the warning sign that the heart is in trouble.

When physical activity ceases, the heart is allowed to return to its slower beating pattern. With the workload reduced, the oxygen requirement is diminished and angina generally dissipates. Sometimes drugs are needed to produce relief. Angina is a significant indicator that coronary artery blockages exist and are of sufficient size to warrant concern about a heart attack.

The second consequence of coronary heart disease

is a heart attack, also referred to as a *myocardial infarction*, or *MI*. A heart attack takes place when the blood supply to the heart is restricted or denied to the point where the cardiac muscle can no longer function normally. Without oxygen for too long a period of time, cardiac muscle tissue will suffocate and die. Scar tissue replaces muscle tissue. The affected area can be large or small; however, once dead, the muscle *remains* dead. There is no healing or rejuvenating process that will restore the original muscle. Unfortunately, scar tissue does not have the ability to contract and is useless in the pumping activity of the heart. The scarred area consequently causes the heart to lose some of its effectiveness as a pump.

The clogging of the arteries by plaque was once thought by itself to cause a heart attack by depriving the heart muscle of oxygen-bearing blood. Today, however, doctors know that plaque rarely grows so large that it completely cuts off the flow of blood to the heart. While narrowing of the arteries most certainly sets up the attack, the immediate cause is usually a blood clot, or thrombosis, that forms when encrusted plaque ruptures. Says Dr. Scott Goodnight, a cardiovascular disease expert at the Oregon Health Sciences Center, "The actual heart attack is caused by a blood clot more than 95% of the time." This is particularly common if the blood is thick with cholesterol and fat, which promotes the final clot. Such a clot can act as an extension of the blockage, so that the combination of clot and blockage might be of sufficient size to obstruct the arterial channel completely and stop all blood to the heart. When this happens, a heart attack results. (The same mechanism occurs in other parts of the body. A blockage in the blood vessel that leads to the brain can cause a stroke. Other blocked vessels can result in gangrene of the legs or loss of kidney function.) The clotting mechanism is necessary for good health. It's fine for sealing a cut finger or a skinned knee. But when it blocks a coronary artery, heart muscle is destroyed.

The Heart Attack

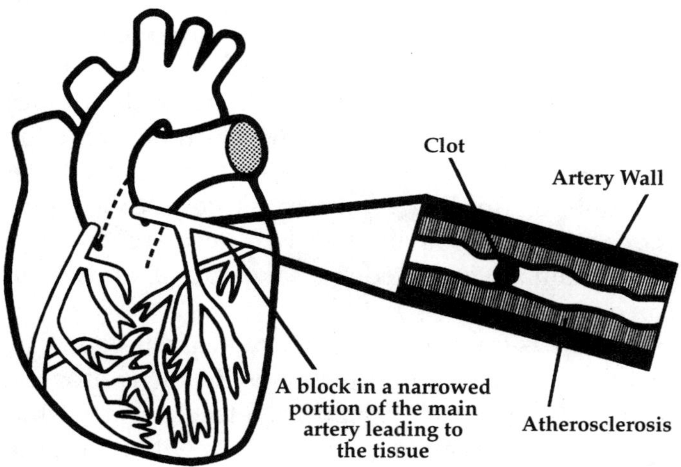

The good news is that deaths by heart attack have dropped by about 100,000 per year in the last decade. The bad news is that well over a half-million people per year still die from heart attack. Indeed, in about one-third of persons experiencing a first heart attack, the result is immediate death. About 300,000 people a year die of heart attack before they reach a hospital. Of those who survive a first heart attack, some 15% to 20% experience a second heart attack within four years. Many of those who survive, however, lose normal functioning of their heart muscle, which can result in an impaired life-style.

A third condition caused by coronary heart disease is *congestive heart failure.* This can occur when a heart attack has reduced the pumping power of the heart so that blood backs up in the veins leading to the heart. A heart attack often causes significant scar tissue to form in the area of the left ventricle, the principal pumping chamber. When this happens, the left ventricle may no longer have the ability to pump vigorously. But if the right ventricle is without damage, it will continue to pump blood into the lungs at a rapid rate. The difference in pumping ability of the two chambers may cause blood to back up in the lungs and the veins, disrupting the normal circulatory flow and causing distention of the tissues and a leaking of fluid into the abdomen and the extremities. The swelling due to abnormally large amounts of fluid in the body tissue is called pulmonary edema. The liver and kidneys are susceptible to damage when edema takes place, and death can occur.

No one is immune to coronary heart disease. The insidious aspect of the disease is its silent progression, its capacity to remain undetected until it has reached an advanced stage. Only when arterial blockages seriously restrict blood flow to the heart does the disease become noticeable. Often it is too late. While a heart attack may be described as "sudden," the blockages that produce the attack do not "suddenly" grow but instead develop silently over a period of years.

Nonetheless, coronary heart disease can be prevented. The evidence is strong that by applying low-fat dietary principles to reduce blood cholesterol (along with weight reduction, physical activity and quitting cigarettes), the problem can be nipped in stage one. But what about heart patients, those with known coronary heart disease? Evidence shows that heart disease can *progress, stabilize* or *be reversed.* The way that life-style, particularly dietary life-style, is managed goes a long way in influencing cardiac destiny.

CHAPTER THREE

CARDIAC RISK FACTORS

The onset of the epidemic of coronary heart disease began after World War I. Indeed, Dr. William Osler, one of America's foremost physicians, remarked in 1908 that only two or three cases of angina pectoris were seen each year in the large metropolitan hospitals of this country. That is because Americans, in Osler's time, had fewer cardiac risk factors. They did not smoke as many cigarettes. They were more physically active. They ate a diet lower in fat and higher in fiber. And they were less obese.

It would be wonderful if coronary heart disease could be traced to a specific cause, such as a virus. Then the chances of finding a "cure" would be greatly improved. Unfortunately, the disease does not have a readily identifiable single cause. It is a multifactorial disease in which more than 250 risk factors of varying degrees have been identified. Some of these factors are relatively minor. For example, research shows that men who are severely bald at the top may be three times more likely to suffer heart attacks than those with full heads of hair. Despite the "risk" from baldness, I doubt that too many bald men are losing sleep over it.

Other risk factors are more significant, such as elevated blood cholesterol. Some of the major risk factors, according to the American Heart Association, are listed on the following page.

Major Risk Factors

- Personal history of cardiovascular events
- Family history of heart disease
- Age
- Gender
- Low HDL ("good") cholesterol
- Elevated LDL ("bad") cholesterol
- Elevated levels of other blood lipids such as triglycerides
- High-fat diet (particularly saturated fats and trans fatty acids)
- Tobacco use
- Diabetes
- High blood pressure
- Excess iron in the body
- Obesity (particularly abdominal)
- Sedentary life-style
- High levels of clotting factors in the blood
- Chronic stress (particularly where anger and hostility are involved)
- Social isolation
- Syndrome X (high trigliceriden and low HDLs)

Research has shown the development of atherosclerosis and coronary heart disease to be a complex interaction of genetic and life-style factors. Although all of the above factors may be applicable to a large population, their impact will vary from individual to individual. A key point is that multiple risk factors are not additive; instead, they multiply coronary risk by many fold. The more risk factors present, the greater the likelihood of a heart attack. The illustration that follows shows how risk increases for three 45-year-old men: one who smokes cigarettes, one who smokes and has elevated cholesterol, and one who smokes and has elevated cholesterol and high blood pressure.

Cumulative Impact of Heart Attack Risk Factors

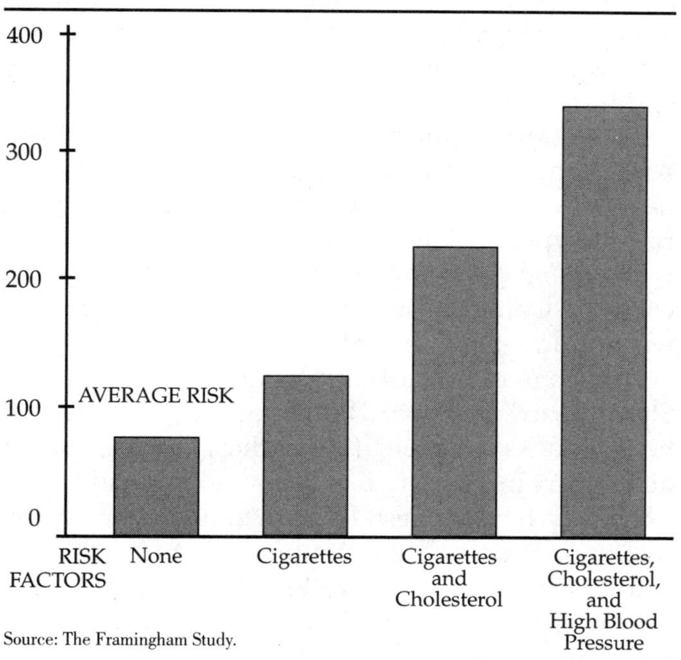

Source: The Framingham Study.

NONCONTROLLABLE RISK FACTORS

It is important to distinguish noncontrollable risk factors from controllable risk factors. Noncontrollable risk factors are those that are out of your hands. A *family history* of heart disease, for instance, is a noncontrollable risk factor. You can't change your parents, even though you might not like their legacy.

People with a genetic history of heart disease are simply more prone to developing it than those with a family history free of the disease. The fact is that if you have a parent or sibling who had a premature heart attack (before age 55 in a man or age 65 in a woman), you are at increased risk of coronary heart disease. (But even in these situations the impact of controllable risk factors must be considered. Did the family have heart disease because of bad genes? Or did they simply eat the same high-fat diet, smoke, and watch TV together?)

Race is also a noncontrollable risk factor. African-Americans, for example, have an elevated risk of heart disease, primarily because they have a higher risk of hypertension and diabetes than whites do.

Increasing age is another risk factor that cannot be changed. Coronary heart disease is mostly identified with middle-aged and elderly people. Indeed, the average age of a heart attack patient in the United States is now over 65. The young people in whom heart attacks do occur (the earliest reported heart attack was in a child 18 months old!) usually have extremely high cholesterol due to a genetic abnormality. For most of the population, it is rare for a heart attack to occur before 40 years of age. After 40, however, the number of coronary events in men rises sharply, peaking in the late 50s. For men, being over age 45 is a coronary risk factor. It works the same with women, but there is a 10-to-12-year delay. For women, being postmenopausal is a coronary risk factor.

The unfortunate fact about coronary heart disease is that by the time symptoms appear, the blockages in the coronary arteries are usually severe. Having no symptoms does not mean that there is no disease. This is why prevention must begin early in life, long before symptoms appear.

So, while middle age and beyond is when the

disease is most often made manifest, many young people carry arterial blockages, and traces of the disease are common in American children by age 10. Dr. Charles J. Guleck of the University of Cincinnati has found elevated cholesterol levels—a prime indicator of the disease—in children as young as eight years old. In addition, autopsies performed on children killed in auto accidents have confirmed that coronary artery blockages exist even in young children.

Other studies have confirmed that youth offers no immunity to coronary heart disease. Autopsies of young soldiers killed in combat during the Korean and Vietnam wars revealed that, despite an average age of 22, many of them suffered from severe coronary heart disease. It was concluded that some 35% of these young men were well on their way to heart attacks.

The salient point is that coronary heart disease is not the inevitable outcome of aging. It is clear that the disease develops slowly over a period of 20 to 40 years, so that its effects appear later in life. But these effects have less to do with the aging process itself than with early life-style habits. In populations where blood cholesterol levels are low throughout life, for example, so is the incidence of the disease at all ages.

And finally, *gender* is a noncontrollable cardiac risk factor. Just as youth provides no immunity, neither does gender. In the past, heart disease was thought to be exclusively a male problem. Perhaps this thinking grew out of the fact that males between the ages of 30 and 49 are 6.5 times more likely to have a heart attack than females of the same age. The lower rate for females is probably due to the production of estrogen, a sex hormone that seems to protect against coronary heart disease in women of childbearing age. But as females age, the risk of developing heart disease increases. Shortly after menopause, the odds become equal to those of males. What doctors now know is that female hormones do not allow women to *avoid* the disease; they merely *postpone* it. Between the ages of 45 and 64, one out of nine women has coronary heart disease. Over age 65, the ratio is one out of three. Indeed, women suffer almost the same amount of heart attacks and heart attack deaths as men. The difference is in the timing.

While women tend to fear cancer, twice as many females die of heart and blood vessel disease than of all forms of cancer combined. In addition, women who develop heart disease do not do as well as men with heart disease. Women tend to have more complications after bypass surgery and heart attack. Women also seem to have more complications during and immediately after angioplasty. Whether this is related to their older age when they develop coronary heart disease or to smaller coronary arteries compared to men is unclear.

The fact remains, however, that women, particularly postmenopausal women, need to be as aggressive as men in controlling their coronary risk factors. (Postmenopausal women should also discuss the pros and cons of hormone replacement therapy with their physicians.) For all Americans, men as well as women, heart disease is the single greatest cause of death.

Controllable Risk Factors

The real focus should be on cardiac risk factors that can be controlled, e.g., smoking, elevated cholesterol, overweight and high blood pressure. "Life-style habits are responsible for most heart disease in Americans," says Dr. William Roberts, editor of the *American Journal of Cardiology.* "For every one person who has atherosclerosis because of family genes, there are 499 people who have it because of life-style decisions."

Scientists now know more about the major controllable risk factors for heart disease than for most other diseases. Most controllable risk factors can be countered by simple preventive measures. In 1992 Dr. JoAnn Manson and her colleagues from Harvard University reviewed nearly 200 studies on coronary heart disease to evaluate the role of known preventive measures. The results, published in the *New England Journal of Medicine,* suggest the steps outlined on the following pages.

STOP SMOKING

Most people are unaware that smoking causes more deaths from cardiovascular disease than from cancer. Anywhere from 20% to 40% of all cardiac deaths (100,000 to 200,000 every year) are directly attributable to smoking. Tobacco use increases the risk of coronary heart disease by damaging the inner wall of the arteries, by increasing blood clotting, and by causing artery spasm and constriction. In addition, smoking reduces HDL cholesterol by 10% to 20% in regular smokers.

Studies show that smoking more than doubles the risk of developing coronary heart disease. In one study, the mortality from coronary heart disease in those smoking 25 or more cigarettes per day was nearly triple that of nonsmokers. It's the same for stroke. Results from the Harvard University-based Physician's Health Study of more than 22,000 doctors show that the risk of stroke among smokers is twice that of nonsmokers.

The good news is that within two to three years

after quitting smoking, the risk of heart attack and stroke in men and women declines to levels similar to those of men and women who had never smoked. And within five years after quitting, former smokers have a 50% to 70% lower risk of heart attack than current smokers.

Reduce Blood Cholesterol

Dr. Robert Levy, former director of the National Heart, Lung and Blood Institute, points to blood cholesterol as "the chief risk factor for heart attack." This is particularly true, he says, if LDL cholesterol (low-density lipoprotein), the so-called "bad" cholesterol, is elevated and/or HDL cholesterol (high-density lipoprotein), the so-called "good" cholesterol, is low.

There is much research to support elevated blood cholesterol as a prime risk factor. Data from the Framingham Study, an ongoing study of risk factors in 6,000 men and women begun in 1948, show that the risk of heart attack for a person with a total blood cholesterol level of 260 mg/dl is four times higher than for a person with a level of 200 mg/dl.

Just as increased blood cholesterol levels can cause the incidence of heart attack to rise, decreased levels can cause it to drop. One study involved over 4,000 middle-aged men *without* known coronary heart disease who were divided into two groups. One group took a cholesterol-lowering drug; the other group did not. The group that took the drug reduced their blood cholesterol levels by 25% and suffered half the heart attacks and sudden deaths of the group without the drug.

The consensus of medical experts today is: *Reduce your total blood cholesterol by 1% and you will reduce your risk of heart disease by 2% to 3%.* This holds true for the elderly as well as the young, and for all racial groups. Other studies in men and women *with* known coronary heart disease have shown that a dramatic reduction of total cholesterol through diet and/or drug therapy can stabilize and in some cases reverse coronary heart disease.

The results of major clinical trials clearly show that by lowering blood cholesterol:

- **Heart attack risk can be reduced in people without preexisting coronary heart disease; and**

- **Stabilization and reversal of coronary heart disease can result in people with existing coronary heart disease.**

Research also shows that elevated blood cholesterol levels are predictive of a greater incidence of coronary disease later in life. One study examined 1,337 male medical students in 1947. Forty years later, these students' 1947-era cholesterol levels were compared with their current risk of heart disease, heart attacks and death. The researchers found that those in the highest quarter of the group in 1947 had six times the risk of a heart attack as those in the lowest quarter. In addition, heart attacks in the top quarter were just as likely to occur before age 50 as afterward. Says Dr. Michael Klag, director of the study, "This was a young, healthy, lean population. It's remarkable how strong the relationship is between blood cholesterol at age 22 and cardiovascular disease 30 years later."

Cutting cholesterol seems to have become an American pastime, but the results are mixed. On one hand, the average adult's blood cholesterol level has dropped from 220 mg/dl in 1960 to 205 mg/dl today. Researchers attribute most of the drop to health education about cholesterol, which has resulted in dietary changes and exercise.

On the other hand, according to the National Cholesterol Education Program, more than half of us (approximately 100 million Americans) are at risk for coronary heart disease because of blood cholesterol levels over 200 mg/dl. Indeed, 25% of all adults have a cholesterol count of over 240 mg/dl and consequently are at considerable risk of coronary heart disease.

With the exception of a minority of people with elevated cholesterol due to genetics, the vast majority of Americans have high blood cholesterol levels because of the inordinate amount of fat, particularly saturated fat, in their diets.

For a more detailed explanation of cholesterol, LDLs and HDLs, please see Chapter Five: "Understanding Cholesterol."

Avoid or Control High Blood Pressure

The condition in which blood pressure exceeds an upper limit for an extended time is called *hypertension,* or *high blood pressure.* Blood pressure is measured when the heart beats (systolic pressure) and rests between beats (diastolic pressure) and is expressed as two numbers representing millimeters of mercury (mm Hg). The first number, systolic pressure, is optimally less than 130 mm Hg. The second number, diastolic pressure, is optimally between 70 and 80 mm Hg. A "normal" blood pressure might be expressed as 110/70, or "110 over 70." While there is no clear definition of when hypertension begins, most experts agree that in adults a systolic pressure of 140 or more and/or a diastolic pressure of 90 or more constitutes high blood pressure.

About 63 million Americans have high blood pressure. This condition significantly increases the risk of heart attack, stroke and death from other vascular problems. According to the Framingham Study, a man in his thirties with a diastolic pressure between 85 and 94 has five times the risk of a heart attack as a man with a diastolic pressure below 70.

Elevated blood pressure indicates that the heart is working harder than normal, putting greater stress both on itself and on the arteries. Over time, this added strain can lead to a bulging and rupture of the arteries (called an aneurysm), hardening of the arteries, stroke and/or heart attack. In addition, raising blood pressure can cause enough damage to the walls of the coronary arteries to create a potential site for fat and cholesterol deposition. The higher an individual's blood pressure, the greater the risk. But lowering blood pressure reduces risk. For every one-point drop in diastolic blood pressure, there is a 2% to 3% drop in the risk of heart attack.

Overweight, a sodium-rich diet and chronic stress contribute to the development of hypertension. The other side, however, is that losing weight, reducing the amount of sodium (salt) in the diet, exercising regularly and practicing stress dissipation techniques (exercise or meditation, for example) can help to lower blood pressure.

MAINTAIN A HEALTHY WEIGHT

Dr. Kenneth Cooper, father of the "aerobics boom," regards obesity as one of the top three or four cardiac risk factors. Indeed, obese individuals at least double their risk of heart attack. While not all medical professionals agree with Dr. Cooper, there is a consensus that carrying too much weight is a risk for elevated cholesterol, hypertension, gallbladder disease, diabetes and other diseases. It is estimated that one in every three American adults is obese, defined as weighing 20% or more than his or her "desirable" weight. In fact, the U.S. population currently ranks among the world's fattest, with the typical American adult male weighing 20 to 30 pounds too much and the typical female being overweight by 15 to 30 pounds.

Coronary disease risk seems to rise with extra weight. For example, an eight-year study of more than 115,000 American women aged 30 to 55 revealed that those women who were as little as 5% overweight were 30% more likely than their lean counterparts to develop heart disease. That risk increased to 80% in those who were moderately overweight, while those who were obese were over 300% more likely to develop coronary heart disease. But maintaining an ideal body weight, as compared with being obese, can reduce the risk of coronary disease by 35% to 55%.

The link between coronary disease and overweight is particularly strong if the excess weight is carried around the middle. Says Dr. William Castelli of the Framingham Study, "People with wide hips and flat bellies may be overweight, but the extra weight does not seem to increase their cardiac risk as much as that of people with narrow hips and potbellies. Abdominal obesity, which is really more of a male problem, is predictive of coronary heart disease."

Obesity is a well-established cause of blood lipid abnormalities, diabetes and high blood pressure—all coronary risk factors. Yet, despite knowledge of this link, the proportion of overweight adults in the United States has steadily increased during the past several decades, especially among women. A national survey by Louis Harris and Associates found that two out of three Americans were overweight in 1992, compared with one out of two in

1983. The state of our national overweight problem has less to do with genetics than with diet and exercise habits.

REDUCE TRIGLYCERIDES

Triglycerides, the form in which fat is carried in the bloodstream, can be measured in the same blood test that is used for cholesterol. Triglycerides are made from foods high in fat (such as butter) and sugar (such as alcohol). Normal triglyceride levels range from about 50 to 200 mg/dl, depending on the age and sex of the individual. A "desirable" level is less than 120 mg/dl. Triglyceride levels above 250 mg/dl are associated with a greater risk of heart disease, though not as great as the blood cholesterol connection.

In the past, triglyceride levels were not seen as an independent risk factor for coronary heart disease. That view is now changing. More and more studies have found elevated triglycerides to be an independent predictor of coronary heart disease, especially in women and diabetics, when accompanied by low HDL levels. A review of 26 studies reported in *Circulation* by Dr. Melissa Austin showed that those men and women with the highest triglyceride levels also had the highest rate of heart attack. "This is just what we found in Framingham," says Dr. William Castelli. "Elevated triglycerides are an *independent* risk factor."

The combination of high triglycerides (levels over 250 mg/dl) and low HDL cholesterol (levels under 40 mg/dl) is identified as a new cardiac risk factor called *Syndrome X.* Often people with Syndrome X have "normal" total cholesterol levels, even under 200 mg/dl, so the new risk factor may be overlooked. It is now recommended that if triglycerides are high and HDL cholesterol is low, treatment should be started regardless of total cholesterol level.

The same methods that boost HDL levels and lower LDL levels can help lower triglycerides: cut dietary fat, especially saturated fat; cut dietary sugar; increase fiber; exercise regularly; and lose weight.

Be Physically Active

Many people have the impression that we are in the midst of a fitness boom. Almost everyone seems to be walking, jogging or working out on a stair climber. Sales of shorts, sweatsuits and other exercise gear have soared. Indeed, a quarter of all shoes sold today are athletic shoes. But the belief that Americans exercise regularly is a myth. According to government data, about a quarter of American adults lead a completely sedentary life-style and half of us do not even exercise moderately. A Louis Harris survey shows that fewer people are exercising today than 10 years ago.

This is a tragic trend because people who are physically inactive have an increased risk of coronary heart disease. Conversely, people who are physically active have a reduced risk. A study of the life-styles of 16,936 Harvard University alumni conducted by Dr. Ralph Paffenbarger yielded the finding that active men had one-third fewer heart attacks than their sedentary counterparts. In addition to showing that people who exercise have a lower number of heart attacks, the study demonstrated that fit persons who suffer heart attacks are more likely to survive.

Some of the resistance to exercise may have come from the traditional guidelines that called for at least 20 minutes of vigorous, continuous exercise—jogging, swimming or an aerobics class, for example.

This recommendation was based on scientific literature that examined the effects of training on physical fitness.

Newer recommendations from the Centers for Disease Control and Prevention and from the American College of Sports Medicine call for 30 minutes a day of moderate, intermittent exercise, e.g., a brisk walk, stair climbing or gardening. The big difference is that the exercise does not have to be continuous and can be of moderate intensity. Five minutes here, 10 minutes there—as long as it adds up to at least 30 minutes and as long as it's brisk. The new recommendation is based on the relationship between physical activity and the risks of chronic disease and death. *Nonetheless, some form of aerobic exercise is still considered the best exercise for optimal cardiovascular health.*

Studies show that regular exercise can decrease the risk of having a heart attack from 35% to 55%. While the mechanism between physical activity and cardiac prevention is not clear, many experts believe that it centers on the ability of exercise to increase HDL cholesterol, decrease LDL cholesterol and triglyceride levels, reduce blood pressure, dissipate stress, strengthen the heart muscle, help prevent adult-onset diabetes and maintain weight control. A couch-potato life-style provides none of this protection.

Avoid or Control Diabetes

Non-insulin-dependent diabetes, also called adult-onset diabetes, is an important risk factor for both coronary heart disease and hypertension. Diabetes increases heart disease risk in men by 2% to 3%, but in women three to seven times. Even people who have a slightly elevated blood sugar level but no detectable diabetes are at increased risk. Weight control and exercise can improve the utilization of blood sugar and prevent or slow down the onset of diabetes.

Dissipate Stress

Americans live in a fast-paced, stressful society. Virtually everyone is subject to chronic stress. In addition, many people are so-called "Type A" personalities, characterized by intense time-consciousness and a sense of extreme competitiveness. Findings suggest that "Type A" people who hold in hostile or angry feelings may increase their risk of heart disease.

While few scientists believe that stress actually causes heart disease, it can still have a devastating effect on cardiovascular health. First, excessive stress can trigger the release of powerful stress hormones into the bloodstream. That these hormones can cause injury to artery walls was shown in a study involving two groups of monkeys fed the same low-fat, low-cholesterol diet. One group was subjected to social stress; the other was not. The study revealed that the stressed monkeys developed extensive coronary artery blockages, whereas the unstressed group did not—even though both groups ate the same diet.

Second, chronic stress can increase blood pressure. Studies by Dr. Robert S. Elliott have shown that about 20% of Americans are "hot reactors" whose response to even mild stress is skyrocketing blood pressure. Intermittent high blood pressure may eventually lead to chronically elevated blood pressure.

Third, stress can increase the stickiness of blood platelets and promote clotting, an increased risk for heart attack. A study at the University of Pittsburgh found that men under stress showed a higher secretion of the chemical ATP, which in turn fosters blood clotting, artery damage and narrowing of blood vessels. Says Dr. Susan Malkoff, "We're talking about the stress that happens when there's time pressure and some frustration or interference in getting something done."

And finally, stress has been shown to elevate cholesterol levels in many people. One study looked at the cholesterol levels of certified public accountants when facing tax deadlines in April and again when on vacation in August. Cholesterol levels were twice as high in April as they were in August, with no change in diet.

Stress seems to "come with the territory" in modern life. Few of us can escape it. However, stress can be dissipated through exercise, stress-reducing techniques such as meditation or deep-breathing exercises, and other outlets such as reading or playing cards with friends. Stress need not be a contributing factor to the development of coronary heart disease.

FOCUSING ON THE REAL PROBLEM

While the consequences of heart disease rightly demand our attention, it is imperative not to lose sight of the real problem—the root causes of the disease. The question must be asked: "Why do so many Americans suffer from heart disease?" For most of us, the answer lies in controllable risk factors. While some people are genetically predisposed to coronary heart disease, over 85% of Americans with the disease have it because of poor life-style habits. Says Dr. JoAnn Manson, "When it comes to heart attacks, most of us control our own destiny."

Behavior Changes	Estimated Reduction in Heart Attack Risk
Stop smoking	50% to 70% lower risk within 5 years of quitting
Reduce blood cholesterol level	1% reduction produces 2% to 3% decline in risk
Manage high blood pressure	1 mm Hg reduction in diastolic pressure produces a 2% to 3% decline in risk
Regular exercise	Active life-style reduces risk by 45%
Maintain ideal weight	35% to 55% lower risk, as compared with those who are obese

The beginnings of coronary heart disease lie in the small wounds in the artery lining that are a product of the human condition. About that we can do nothing. But the festering development of the disease is the product of an elevated blood cholesterol level, a situation greatly impacted by our eating and exercise habits. About that we can do much, and that should be our focus. As a cardiologist friend of mine, Dr. Steve Yarnall, says, "You need to use common sense in life-style decisions. You don't have to be a scientist to understand that the grease you sandblast from your oven and soak off your dishes isn't something you want inside your arteries. You don't have to be a physiologist to understand that regular, moderate exercise is preferable to no exercise. And you don't have to be a genius to figure out that setting fire to tobacco leaves and inhaling the smoke doesn't make a whole lot of sense."

CHAPTER FOUR

CAN CORONARY HEART DISEASE BE REVERSED?

This question has been posed since coronary heart disease was first diagnosed and linked to life-style habits. We know, for instance, that a high-fat diet can increase blood cholesterol and promote arterial blockages. But can changing to a low-fat eating pattern decrease blood cholesterol and lead to stabilization or reversal of heart disease? The answer appears to be "yes" in many people.

Early studies involved rhesus monkeys, which have a basic metabolism not unlike ours. When fed a diet with a fat content similar to that in the American diet, these monkeys showed a rise in blood cholesterol levels. After two and a half years, a number of them suffered heart attacks and died. (Note that rhesus monkeys in the wild never have heart attacks.) During autopsies it was discovered that the animals had multiple coronary artery blockages not unlike those of humans with severe atherosclerosis. Some of the remaining monkeys were then fed a low-fat diet, *which produced a lowering of blood cholesterol and a 35% to 75% reduction in coronary artery blockages.*

Recent studies involving humans have illustrated the same results. Hundreds of angiographic studies have indicated that reversibility of established coronary blockages may occur at the rate of 1% to 2% per year if blood cholesterol levels and particularly LDL levels are greatly lowered. At first glance, this rate of reversibility does not seem great. However, taking into account the fact that coronary heart disease progresses at the rate of 2% to 4% a year when cholesterol stays elevated, the net gain from lowering cholesterol may be as much as 6% a year. Furthermore, once the plaque has been stabilized and begins to reverse, the tendency for clotting seems to be much less, so that the heart attack rate is diminished even before much reversibility has been demonstrated.

At least 10 trials have examined reversibility. Two of the most important were conducted by Dr. David Blankenhorn at the University of Southern California and Dr. Greg Brown at the University of Washington. Each trial used a combination of dietary change and drug therapy to reduce blood cholesterol. Both trials showed a slowing of disease progression with the majority of patients and reversal of the disease process in 16% to 30% of patients who achieved significant reduction in blood cholesterol. Dr. Brown's study also showed fewer cardiac events, less cardiac death and less unstable angina. The key in both studies seemed to be the achievement of an LDL cholesterol level below 100 mg/dl. Those patients who lowered their LDL cholesterol levels to below 100 mg/dl improved the most.

Trials involving intensive dietary and life-style changes alone, without drug therapy, have produced similar results. A notable study was conducted by Dr. Dean Ornish at the Preventive

Medicine Research Institute in Sausalito, California. The 48 men and women in this study had arteries that were 40% to 100% clogged. The entire group was counseled to follow standard medical recommendations such as quitting smoking and exercising aerobically three times a week for 30 minutes. However, half the group followed the standard American Heart Association 30% fat diet. The other half (22 people) ate a strict vegetarian diet (only 8% fat), exercised moderately at least three hours a week, meditated regularly for stress management, and met twice weekly in group sessions to help reinforce the changes they were being asked to make. (It should be noted that the second group had to make a tremendous time commitment. This program required 12 hours a week plus cooking time.) When coronary arteries were remeasured after a year, the first group showed a cholesterol drop of only 13 points, with most people staying the same or getting worse. The second group, however, experienced a drop in cholesterol of 55 points, with the vast majority of subjects showing less disease. More important, 17 people in the vegetarian group experienced a slight regression.

But not all researchers believe that such a radical diet is required to begin to unclog arteries. In Heidelberg, Germany, Dr. Gerhard Schuler conducted a study of 56 men who were suffering from angina due to partially blocked arteries. These men were put on a fairly stringent low-fat diet (no more than 20% of calories from fat) and a program of regular exercise (at least three hours per week). After a year, 60% of the study group showed no disease progression and 32% had experienced coronary regression.

The work of Drs. Ornish and Schuler, which is representative of other research, is important for two reasons. First, it illustrates that coronary heart disease may continue to progress on a 30% fat diet, which has been the standard-of-care dietary recommendation. Indeed, for heart patients wanting to improve their condition, such a diet may not do the job. Second, both studies illustrate the effectiveness of aggressive dietary and life-style changes. While only slight increases in the arteries openings were achieved in each study, major health benefits resulted. "What appears to happen is that you stabilize the plaque," says Dr. John LaRosa of George Washington University. "So, even though the opening hasn't changed all that much, the plaque is no longer susceptible to clot, spasm and hemorrhaging, which are probably the things that cause the final closing off of the blood vessel."

While the outcomes of both studies were much the same, the dietary means of producing such outcomes differed greatly, so a sense of perspective is necessary. Dr. Schuler recommended a 20% fat diet. This, in my opinion, is the more practical choice because it is easily practiced at home and in restaurants, and offers a balance between taste and health that is critical to long-term compliance. My own coronary regression is to a great extent attributable to such a diet.

Dr. Ornish recommended a strict vegetarian diet of just 8% to 10% fat consisting mostly of vegetables, grains, beans and fruit. No meat, poultry, fish or whole-milk products were allowed. In fact, no animal foods at all were eaten except for a daily cup of nonfat milk or nonfat yogurt and the occasional egg white. Such a diet is so low in fat that many health professionals have expressed concern over the practicality and long-term compliance of a dietary program not easily practiced at home by most people. Even Dr. Ornish himself states, "The point of our study was to determine what is possible, not what is practicable." He concedes that adherence to the program would have to be "very good" for improvement to occur. While a very restrictive dietary recommendation may be a useful *goal* for some people with significant coronary disease, it should certainly not be recommended as a *standard*. And it should not be recommended as a lifetime plan for healthy people who simply want to manage cholesterol and lose weight. This would simply set them up for failure.

Another concern shared by many health professionals is the small number of people involved in trials using extremely low-fat diets. In contrast to the thousands of people in major studies involving cholesterol levels, exercise and smoking, the Ornish study put just 22 people on a very low-fat diet. Said Dr. Neil Stone at the 1993 American Heart Association's Scientific Symposium, "We simply do not have enough evidence from this small study to recommend such a diet to all patients." In addition, despite the publicity accorded to extremely low-fat diets, many health professionals caution not to view such diets as a "magic pill." Says Dr. Michael Mogadam of the Georgetown University Medical School, "What is responsible for improved cardiovascular health is a *package* of life-style changes—giving up cigarettes, stress management, exercise, weight loss, control of blood pressure, improving various lipid abnormalities, and altering other risk factors. To give all credit to a low-fat diet misses the point."

Working with an easy-to-use diet, such as a 20% fat diet, is especially important in light of studies showing that men who begin, then quit, a healthy regimen actually increase their risk of heart attack over those whose life-styles remain unchanged. A study of 1,222 men revealed that the heart condition of those who dieted and exercised improved while those treatments continued. After treatment stopped, however, those men were more at risk than men who never had been treated. "If there is a message here, it is 'Don't stop,' not 'Don't start,' " says Dr. Stuart Rich, chief of cardiology at the University of Illinois at Chicago. And "don't stop" often is dependent on a low-fat diet pattern that is interesting, tasty and easy to use.

The point to remember is that stabilizing and reversing coronary heart disease has been established in numerous studies using diet and drugs. While more testing is necessary, using larger groups and improved methods, at this point the data provide much hope for cardiac patients. Findings show that each person with coronary heart disease has an opportunity through realistic life-style changes and, if necessary, drug therapy to improve chances for regression and, more important, to avoid progression.

CHAPTER FIVE

UNDERSTANDING CHOLESTEROL

When it comes to notoriety, cholesterol ranks near the top of the list. After all, it's a prime contributor (along with high blood pressure, cigarette smoking and physical inactivity) to heart disease and stroke, the number one and number three killers of Americans. Interest in cholesterol runs high in the United States. We compare our numbers, talk about HDL ratios and read labels for the "cholesterol-free" guarantee. Although it seems as if everyone knows about cholesterol, a great many misconceptions exist.

One misconception is that cholesterol is a fat like lard, oil or butter. While it is indeed "fat-like" in its pearly, waxy appearance, it is not a fat.

Another misconception is that cholesterol is a dangerous, poisonous substance. This is the result of cholesterol's "bad press" as the principal culprit in the development of coronary heart disease. In truth, cholesterol, which is found in all tissues in humans and other animals, is necessary to the normal chemical processes of the body. It performs many important functions and is essential to life. Cholesterol is utilized in cell wall construction, for the transmission of nerve impulses and for the synthesis of important steroid and sex hormones. No cell could survive without cholesterol.

And finally, there is a misconception that *dietary cholesterol* (which we eat in food) is the only source of *blood cholesterol* (which circulates in the bloodstream). Actually, blood cholesterol comes primarily from the body itself. The liver, for example, can make about 1,500 milligrams of cholesterol per day. Under normal circumstances, this is all the cholesterol the body needs. A problem occurs when too much dietary cholesterol is added through foods eaten. For the average person, cholesterol produced in the body is supplemented by another 400 to 500 milligrams of dietary cholesterol consumed each day.

Dietary cholesterol is found in all foods from animal sources—meat, eggs, fish, poultry and dairy products. No plant-derived food contains cholesterol. What's more important is that animal foods also contain saturated fat, a type of fat that promotes cholesterol production in the body. *Experts agree that saturated fat has more to do with elevated blood cholesterol than does dietary cholesterol.* In other words, the butter used to scramble an egg may have more to do with your blood cholesterol level than the cholesterol in the egg itself. So, for most of us, it makes sense to moderate animal foods (and thus reduce the intake of total fat and saturated fat as well as dietary cholesterol) to better control blood cholesterol and cardiac risk.

THE LABORATORY TEST

Knowing your blood cholesterol level is a good first step toward cardiovascular health. It can tell you if you have a potential cardiac risk and can help you to formulate a strategy to reduce that risk.

The amount of cholesterol in the blood is determined by a blood test and is expressed as the number of milligrams (mg) of cholesterol in one deciliter (dl) of blood. For example, a person with 210 milligrams of cholesterol in a deciliter of blood has a cholesterol level of 210 mg/dl, popularly expressed as a total cholesterol "count" of 210.

When you have your cholesterol tested, it's important to use a laboratory that your physician trusts to give reliable measurements. Not all laboratories are standardized or well regulated, and test results can vary. In addition, certain factors can affect your blood cholesterol count:

- Smoking before a test may cause higher readings.

- Not fasting for 12 hours before a test may cause higher readings.

- Lying down for a test may cause lower readings; sitting up tends to cause higher readings.

- Time of day (morning levels are usually higher than those later in the day).

- Exercise, stress, dieting, body weight change, medications and the phases of a woman's menstrual cycle can affect readings.

Most experts agree that fingerstick tests at shopping malls, health fairs and health clubs are a practical way to screen large numbers of people, but they warn that results can vary from 30 to 50 points higher or lower than laboratory test results. In general, if you have a reading over 200 mg/dl, have your doctor recheck it.

Much as with blood pressure, it is recognized that a single cholesterol reading is not etched in stone. Many health professionals now recommend being tested for cholesterol at least twice. The second measurement should be obtained within one to eight weeks of the first; if this reading is within 30 mg/dl of the first reading, then the *average* of the two values is used. Otherwise, a third test should be performed and the *average* of the three tests used.

In general, all adults over age 20 should be tested for total cholesterol, including HDL and LDL cholesterol, at least once every five years. However, if you have coronary heart disease, or if you have two or more cardiac risk factors, your doctor should retest you at least annually.

What Do the Numbers Mean?

Okay, you've had your blood test and now you're going over the numbers. There are four important pieces of information you should know from your laboratory test.

What Is Your Total Blood Cholesterol?

Total blood cholesterol is a key predictor of future incidence of heart attack, particularly when other risk factors are present. The higher the total cholesterol level, the greater the potential for coronary heart disease and heart attack. For example, a person with a blood cholesterol of 260 mg/dl has four times the risk of heart attack as a person with a level of 200 mg/dl.

The Lipid Research Clinic Trial indicates that for every 1% rise in total cholesterol above 150 mg/dl, the risk of heart attack goes up by 2%. However, the opposite is also true: a 1% reduction in blood cholesterol can result in a 2% drop in heart attack risk.

A relative scale has been established by medical

authorities to define the relationship of blood cholesterol level to cardiac risk:

Total Cholesterol	Classification
Less than 200 mg/dl	Desirable
200 to 239 mg/dl	Borderline-high risk
Over 240 mg/dl	High risk

In general, the public health goal for the nation is a "desirable" blood cholesterol level below 200 mg/dl. Indeed, studies show that lower is even better, particularly for those who already have coronary heart disease. Part of the problem in understanding these guidelines is not realizing that *normal* or *average* values are not necessarily *desirable* values. In the past, many people with levels well over 200 mg/dl were told they were "normal." This happened to me just a few months before my first bypass surgery. My "normal" blood cholesterol was 250 mg/dl. What I had not understood was that the term "normal" referred to a statistical average and had little to do with optimal health.

If your blood cholesterol level is somewhere around 200 mg/dl, you are normal (average) by today's standards. But that is not the best level for good cardiac health. The optimal, or ideal, blood cholesterol level is actually around 150 mg/dl. It is in this context that the goal of "under 200 mg/dl" makes sense.

***The bottom line:* If you have a total blood cholesterol level in excess of 200 mg/dl, you may be at increased risk for coronary heart disease.**

The Higher Your Cholesterol, the Higher Your Risk

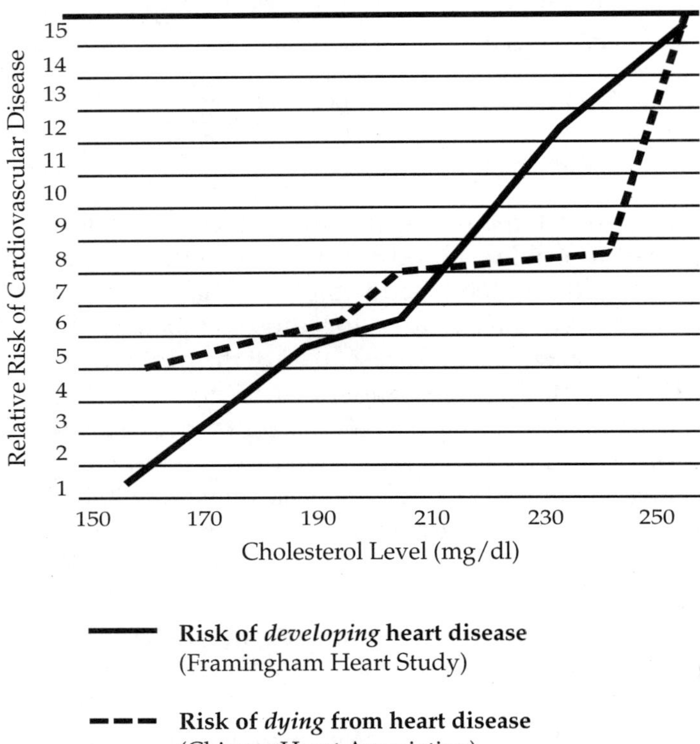

Risk of *developing* heart disease (Framingham Heart Study)

Risk of *dying* from heart disease (Chicago Heart Association)

WHAT IS YOUR LDL-CHOLESTEROL LEVEL?

Important though it is, total blood cholesterol level seems at best to be a crude indicator of risk. Knowing only the number for that level may leave you dangerously uninformed, since most heart attacks occur among people with only slightly elevated total cholesterol. The fact is that the whole, in this case the total cholesterol number, is less important than the sum of its major parts—so-called "bad" and "good" cholesterol.

Just as oil will not dissolve in water, waxy cholesterol by itself cannot dissolve in blood. It must first be combined with fat and protein molecules into a chemical package called a *lipoprotein*, nature's "vehicle" for transporting cholesterol throughout the body. Most lipoproteins contain cholesterol and triglycerides in their core, with protein and fat forming an outer coat. Various types of lipoproteins have different sizes, shapes and functions, contain different amounts of cholesterol, triglycerides and protein, and are usually classified on the basis of their density or compactness. Two of the most important are *low-density lipoproteins*, or LDLs, and *high-density lipoproteins*, or HDLs.

LDLs, which are predominantly fat and contain very little protein, are responsible for carrying cholesterol through the bloodstream. Circulating in the blood for several days after their creation, they drop off cholesterol wherever it's needed for useful work such as cell building. LDLs are not stable chemical packages and come apart quite easily. Should they penetrate an artery wall and "unravel," unused cholesterol could be released and deposited in susceptible blood vessels, thus beginning the clogging process. Since it takes cholesterol into the system, LDL is commonly called "bad" cholesterol. It can combine with oxygen (oxidize) in the bloodstream, and this may enhance its ability to produce the artery-blocking plaque that can lead to a heart attack.

LDL cholesterol level is a better predictor of cardiac risk than total cholesterol. The higher the level of LDL cholesterol circulating in the bloodstream, the greater the risk for arterial buildup. Because LDLs are the lipoproteins most directly related to cardiovascular risk, many physicians believe that the measurement of LDL cholesterol is an independent factor in predicting the potential for future heart attacks. Research shows that for every increase of one mg/dl of LDL cholesterol, the risk of cardiovascular events increases by 2%. So, the lower LDL cholesterol, the better.

A value below 130 mg/dl is "desirable." For a person with no other risk factors, many experts believe that up to 160 mg/dl is the upper limit, called "borderline-high risk." Individuals above 160 mg/dl are at "high risk." *For cardiac patients, LDL cholesterol should be below 100 mg/dl.*

LDL Cholesterol	Classification
Less than 130 mg/dl	Desirable
130 to 159 mg/dl	Borderline-high risk
160 mg/dl and above	High risk

The bottom line: **If you have an LDL cholesterol level in excess of 130 mg/dl, you may have an independent risk factor for coronary heart disease—no matter what your total blood cholesterol. If you are a heart patient, your LDL cholesterol should be under 100 mg/dl.**

Good ways to decrease LDL cholesterol are to lose weight, cut down on foods rich in saturated fat (such as red meat and whole-milk dairy products) and trans fatty acids (such as hydrogenated margarine) and increase foods rich in soluble fiber (such as oat bran, oatmeal and beans).

What Is Your HDL-Cholesterol Level?

High-density lipoproteins, primarily protein and very little fat, assist in undoing the damage wrought by LDL cholesterol. If LDL cholesterol is in excess of 90 mg/dl, body cells get more cholesterol than they can use. The excess is either stored as artery deposits or excreted from the liver. HDL cholesterol is key to the excretion process. As HDL circulates in the bloodstream, it pulls cholesterol from tissues—including artery walls—and brings it back to the liver for excretion. Because of this key role in reverse cholesterol transport, HDL cholesterol has been dubbed "good" cholesterol.

While HDL cholesterol averages only about 25% of total cholesterol, it is crucially important in determining heart attack risk. Low HDL cholesterol, defined as 35 mg/dl or below, is thus now considered an independent risk factor for coronary heart disease. *A high HDL level, defined as 60 mg/dl or more, is considered protective.* It is estimated that for every one mg/dl increase in HDL cholesterol, there is a 4% decrease in cardiac risk.

Average HDL levels are 45 mg/dl for men and 55 mg/dl for women. Female sex hormones tend to raise HDL levels, a difference that in part explains the lower rates of coronary heart disease in women of childbearing age. Risk classifications for HDL cholesterol are as follows:

HDL Cholesterol	Classification
More than 45 mg/dl*	Desirable
35 to 44 mg/dl	Borderline-high risk
Less than 35 mg/dl	High risk

*According to the National Cholesterol Education Program, the "most desirable" HDL cholesterol level is more than 60 mg/dl.

While experts today emphasize that HDL and LDL levels are separate and independent risk factors for heart disease, the ratio of total cholesterol to HDL cholesterol is often helpful in estimating cardiac risk.

Total Cholesterol/ HDL Ratio	Classification
Less than 5.0	Desirable
5.1 to 6.0	Borderline-high risk
More than 6.0	High risk

***The bottom line:* If your HDL cholesterol is under 35 mg/dl, you may be at increased risk for coronary heart disease no matter what your total cholesterol and LDL-cholesterol levels. If you are a heart patient, a minimum HDL level of 40 mg/dl is needed.**

Good ways to increase HDL cholesterol are to lose weight, increase physical activity, stop smoking and choose monounsaturated oils (such as olive oil) over polyunsaturated oils (such as corn oil) and saturated fats. Women on birth-control pills who have low HDL cholesterol may want to discuss alternatives with their physician as a means of elevating HDL levels. This would be especially true for women with additional coronary risk factors and/or a strong family history of heart disease. A drink or two a day of alcohol may also boost HDL levels, but this is controversial since the risks of heavy drinking outweigh the potential benefits for the heart.

What Is Your Triglyceride Level?

Triglycerides are getting more attention as the result of new studies linking high levels to an increased risk of heart disease. Normal triglyceride levels range from about 50 to 200 mg/dl, depending on age and sex. According to the National Cholesterol Education Program, the following are risk classifications for triglycerides:

Triglycerides	Classification
Less than 200 mg/dl	Desirable
200 to 400 mg/dl	Borderline-high risk
More than 400 mg/dl	High risk

As outlined in the chapter on cardiac risk factors, the view of triglycerides has changed. First, high levels are now seen as an independent risk factor for coronary disease. Over 26 studies have shown that people with the highest levels of triglycerides also have the highest rate of heart attack.

Second, triglycerides are a main component of the new cardiac risk factor called Syndrome X. People with this condition typically have a moderate level of total cholesterol (many times under 200 mg/dl) but have elevated triglycerides and low HDL cholesterol, often accompanied by abdominal obesity and elevations in blood pressure, blood sugar and uric acid. The profile of a 51-year-old male in the Framingham Study showed the following:

Total cholesterol	195 mg/dl
LDL cholesterol	108 mg/dl
HDL cholesterol	32 mg/dl
Triglycerides	264 mg/dl

Because his total cholesterol is not high (it's actually better than the national goal of 200 mg/dl) and his LDL level is "desirable," an assumption might be that this man has a low cardiac risk. But according to Dr. William Castelli, such an assumption is in error. In fact, this man has progressive coronary heart disease caused primarily by elevated triglycerides and low HDL cholesterol. Says Dr. Castelli,

"Syndrome X is a new cardiac risk factor, and the people who have it form a new group. In Framingham, we've found that when triglycerides are over 250 mg/dl and HDL is below 40 mg/dl, the risk of heart attack doubles . . . even when total cholesterol is in line. We've also found that when you fatten up in the abdomen, you start to move your triglycerides and HDL toward Syndrome X."

Methods to lower triglycerides and increase HDLs include reducing dietary fat (especially saturated fat) and sugar, increasing fiber, increasing physical activity, losing weight and drug therapy.

***The bottom line:* If your triglycerides are in excess of 250 mg/dl and your HDL cholesterol is below 40 mg/dl, you may have an increased cardiac risk.**

Other Things to Ask Your Doctor

Although total blood cholesterol, LDLs, HDLs and triglycerides are of the greatest importance in assessing your cardiac risk, there are related areas that you should discuss with your physician to better understand the whole picture. This is particularly true if you have confirmed coronary heart disease.

What About Alcohol?

There has always been a great deal of interest in the role—if any—of alcohol in a heart-healthy diet. Some of the early research was conducted in the 1970s by Dr. Arthur Klatsky, a cardiologist with Kaiser Permanente in Oakland, California. Using the computerized health records of the more than 100,000 people served by Kaiser Permanente,

Dr. Klatsky looked for factors that significantly affected the risk of heart disease. "Lo and behold," he said, "we found that moderate drinkers, those who consume from one to three drinks per day, have a lower risk of dying from heart disease than either those who abstain altogether or those who drink heavily."

More recently, a certain amount of controversy about alcohol has centered on the so-called "French Paradox": why it is that the French seem to be able to consume large amounts of alcohol and food high in saturated fat and cholesterol, and still have one of the industrial world's lowest rates for cardiovascular disease. Studies by the World Health Organization in 21 countries indicate that moderate consumption of alcohol, especially wine, appears to protect against heart disease. "We know that people who drink wine suffer less heart disease," says Dr. Curtis Ellison of Boston University. "Moderate" is defined as one to two drinks a day. A study at Brigham and Women's Hospital in Boston showed the same results. Among the reported benefits are an elevation of two forms of protective HDL cholesterol (HDL2 and HDL3) and a reduction in the risk of clot formation in the coronary arteries. "There is little doubt that alcohol is protective," writes Dr. Klatsky in the *New England Journal of Medicine.*

Not all experts agree. According to Dr. William Connors, author of a study at the Oregon Health Sciences University, fruits, vegetables and unsaturated oils (chiefly olive oil)—not wine—may be the reason the French suffer fewer heart attacks.

What both sides do agree on is that heavy drinking is damaging to health. "More than a drink or two a day, and the benefits are outweighed by the increased risks of other health problems," says Dr. Michael H. Criqui, an expert in this area. People who consume too much alcohol suffer more high blood pressure and stroke, and women who do so have an increased cancer risk. Regular and excessive drinking damages the heart muscle in nearly one-half of heavy drinkers and causes damage in the liver, brain and the entire nervous system. In addition, at 7 calories per gram, alcohol is an excellent way to develop a "beer belly." It contributes to overweight (and in turn to elevated triglycerides) by inhibiting the burning of body fat, by being metabolized itself much as dietary fat is, and by being rich in calories.

At this point, most health professionals find it inadvisable to recommend alcohol as part of a healthy diet to raise "good" HDL, reduce the tendency of blood to form clots or reduce the risk of heart attacks. However, for most adults (excluding pregnant women), there is no evidence that having one or two drinks per day, particularly with meals, is harmful to the heart. One drink is defined as 12 grams (one-half ounce) of pure alcohol, the amount consumed in 12 ounces of beer, 1.5 ounces of 80-proof liquor or 5 ounces of wine.

So, the bottom line is to be responsible. Know your own situation. If you need to lose weight, for example, the extra calories in alcohol simply will not help. If you can enjoy alcohol in a way that does not negatively impact your life, or the lives of others, enjoy it in appropriate amounts, at appropriate times and in appropriate places. Otherwise, avoid it altogether.

What About Aspirin?

According to the *New England Journal of Medicine*, aspirin appears to help prevent heart attacks by making blood platelets less sticky, thereby reducing the risk of clotting within the coronary arteries. A key study of this effect, begun in 1983, involved more than 22,000 doctors all of whom were in apparently good health. Half the group took a buffered aspirin every other day; the other half received a placebo. For those taking aspirin, the risk of a heart attack was cut by 47%, "a highly statistically significant reduction," according to Dr. Charles Hennekens of Harvard Medical School. The extremely beneficial effect of aspirin was so apparent that doctors monitoring the trial recommended that it be stopped and those volunteers getting the placebo be informed so they could take aspirin if they wished.

The decision to take aspirin should always be made with a physician. Aspirin is not for everybody. The drug can cause nausea and internal bleeding (aggravating gastric ulcers, for example) and may slightly increase the risk of stroke. In addition, it is not a magic cure-all and should not be a substitute for smoking cessation, lowering blood cholesterol, exercising regularly or reducing high blood pressure.

For those who can take aspirin, doctors usually recommend one buffered tablet (325 milligrams) every other day. Gobbling more tablets or higher doses will not help to further reduce risk and may increase side effects.

Remember, never self-medicate. Talk to your physician before making your decision about aspirin or any other drug.

WHAT ABOUT ANTIOXIDANTS?

During normal biological activities, the body produces small amounts of unstable substances called *free radicals,* which can potentially damage everything they come in contact with—including the cells that produce them. Fortunately, "balancing" antidotes in our cells neutralize most free radicals as soon as they are produced. Some free radicals have unstable oxygen atoms that can oxidize LDL cholesterol, resulting in LDLs being absorbed rapidly by the cells of the artery walls. This in turn starts the buildup of plaque, which leads to atherosclerosis.

Several recent studies suggest that vitamins A (beta carotene), C and E act as *antioxidants.* According to Dr. Ishwarlal Jialal of the University of Texas Southwestern Medical Center in Dallas, "Antioxidants scavenge free radicals and neutralize them, thereby blocking LDL oxidation and curbing the earliest stages of plaque formation."

In addition, studies have found that high blood levels of vitamin C correlate with elevated HDLs and with lower blood pressure. "The evidence is mounting that antioxidants really protect against cardiovascular events," says Dr. Joan Manson of Harvard Medical School. In the Harvard Nurses Study, Dr. Manson found that women who ate at least five servings a day of fruits and vegetables high in antioxidant vitamins lowered their risk of future heart attack by 33% and stroke by 71%. These reductions are among the largest gained by any means, including other life-style changes and prescription drugs. This research provides new support for the existing recommendation that people eat at least five servings of fruits and vegetables per day.

Although strong links have been found between high doses of these vitamins and disease prevention, researchers have not as yet determined optimal daily intake. Says Dr. Diane Tribble of the University of California at Berkeley, "We simply do not know enough at this point to recommend daily dosages. And we do not know if getting vitamin C, for instance, from a supplement works as well as getting it from an orange." Dr. Manson observes, "We can't yet say that antioxidant vitamins, as opposed to foods high in antioxidants, can reduce the risk of heart attack and stroke." It is clear, though, that the amounts needed to fight disease are considerably higher than the U.S. Recommended Daily Allowances (USRDA). Those nutritional levels are described as generous minimums needed to prevent deficiency diseases.

Research so far suggests that the optimal level of vitamin C may be 500 to 1,000 milligrams per day, compared with the USRDA of 60 milligrams. The optimal level of vitamin E may be 100 to 800 International Units (IU), or 133 to 533 milligrams, compared with the USRDA of 30 IU, or 20 milligrams. For beta carotene, which has no USRDA, the optimal level may be as low as 5 milligrams a day or, as some suggest, in the range of 25 to 30 milligrams.

As a general rule, it is always preferable to get vitamins and minerals in a nutritious diet rather than through supplements. One reason is that other factors in vitamin-rich foods may play a role; another is that taking vitamins can become an excuse to ease up on other healthy behavior. Later in the book I will address foods that are rich in vitamin C (such as oranges, grapefruits, strawberries, peppers and tomatoes), vitamin E (such as safflower and corn oils, and leafy green vegetables) and beta carotene (such as carrots, sweet potatoes, cantaloupe and broccoli). However, should you opt for using vitamin supplements, be sure to clear it first with your physician.

WHAT ABOUT DRUG THERAPY?

Drug therapy has been shown to be very effective in reducing LDL cholesterol and triglycerides and in increasing HDL cholesterol. If there has been a problem at all with such therapy, it is that physicians often prescribe drugs too quickly, claiming that their patients will not make the needed behavioral changes.

It is critical to understand that the primary recommendation for lowering LDL cholesterol is dietary change to reduce foods high in fat and saturated fat. However, if dietary change does not produce adequate LDL reduction, drug therapy should be considered with your physician. In general, the guideline is:

- LDL cholesterol greater than 190 mg/dl in people without definite coronary heart disease or two other risk factors

- LDL cholesterol greater than 160 mg/dl in people with definite coronary heart disease or two other risk factors

The interaction of diet and drugs must be understood for success. LDL-lowering drugs, usually bile acid sequestrants, work best when combined with a low-fat diet pattern. Indeed, high-fat foods can often offset the drugs.

Dr. William Connor described the example of a female patient in his lipid clinic who had a genetically induced cholesterol level of over 400 mg/dl. The patient was placed on a drug that rapidly cut her LDL and total cholesterol. In monitoring her progress, Dr. Connor noticed that her cholesterol level would jump periodically. There seemed to be no reason for the change until he matched her cholesterol levels with her calendar. Lo and behold, when the woman was at home in Portland, Oregon, her cholesterol level was in line. The drug was working. But when she visited her sister in Wisconsin and practiced "souvenir eating" with cheese, ice cream and bratwurst, her cholesterol level shot back up despite the drug.

The point is that if you're using a drug to reduce total and LDL cholesterol, be sure to practice low-fat eating habits to get the most out of the drug.

With regard to raising HDLs, niacin has been shown to be very effective in many people. But it takes megadoses of this over-the-counter B vitamin to achieve these results—doses so high that it's considered a drug, not a vitamin. In addition, niacin usually causes unpleasant flushing and may aggravate stomach ulcers, liver problems, diabetes or arthritis, particularly gout. *Large doses of niacin should be taken only under a doctor's supervision.* If you think you need therapeutic doses of niacin, talk to your doctor.

WHAT IS APO B?

Current research in medical science is focusing on other aspects of blood chemistry that may have a great impact on the development of coronary heart disease. Scientists now believe that cardiac risk may also be determined by levels of *Apolipoprotein B,* or *Apo B.* Apo B is the protein part of the lipoprotein that allows the transfer of cholesterol from the lipoprotein to the cells. If the balance is correct, i.e., if the amount of Apo B matches up to the amount needed by the cells, there is no problem. However, if there is more Apo B than is needed, the excess circulates at high levels in the bloodstream. Unfortunately, Apo B has an affinity for artery walls. Excessive amounts in the bloodstream contribute to the buildup of blockages.

WHAT IS LP(A)?

New research has also suggested that a particular form of low-density lipoprotein, *Lipoprotein (a),* or *Lp(a)* (usually called "Lp little a"), may be an underlying cause of a quarter of premature heart attacks. Studies by Stanford University and Jewish Hospital of Cincinnati show that Lp(a) cholesterol can permit the cells that make up the walls of the arteries to proliferate unchecked and lead to the clogging of the heart's coronary arteries. In addition, Lp(a) seems to increase the clotting ability of the blood, thus dealing the heart a double blow. Unlike the production of LDL cholesterol, which is responsive to diet, the production of Lp(a) is genetically determined and can vary in individuals by a factor of 1,000. At this point there is no dietetic treatment that can lower Lp(a), although some studies show that niacin and estrogen may be effective medical treatments. For persons with high levels of Lp(a), intensive treatment of *all* coronary risk factors is extremely important.

FOCUS ON KEY VALUES

Coronary heart disease is the product of a complex interaction of genetic and dietary factors. No factor is more important than elevated blood cholesterol. While cholesterol is a complicated subject, research clearly shows that you may be at increased cardiac risk if:

- Your total blood cholesterol is greater than 200 mg/dl.
- Your LDL cholesterol is above 130 mg/dl.
- Your HDL cholesterol is under 35 mg/dl.
- Your triglyceride level is over 250 mg/dl and your HDL cholesterol is below 40 mg/dl.

Fortunately, for the vast majority of Americans, cholesterol values can be improved with life-style changes, particularly those changes involving diet and exercise.

PART II

DIET IS A CARDIAC RISK FACTOR

CHAPTER SIX

THE AMERICAN DIET MAY BE HAZARDOUS TO YOUR HEALTH

More than two centuries ago the German poet Goethe wrote that "Man is what he eats." This statement made no sense to me until my coronary problem forced me into a better understanding of the relationship between diet and cardiac disease. Only then could I fully appreciate Goethe's insight.

Like most people, I lived on a diet that had little to do with what I needed to eat for good health. My dietary decisions were based on impulse, convenience, economics, status, taste and cravings—on a number of influences other than nutritional value. After heart surgery, the need to change the way I ate was evident. Still, making the change was a cultural shock. For 32 years I had eaten the typical American "meat and milk" diet, built on the recommended "four food groups." My eating habits were premised on the belief that the more I consumed of these foods, the healthier I would be. So first my mother, then my wife, dutifully prepared meals rich in red meat and whole-milk dairy products, and I dutifully consumed them. After all, we thought, fortified with quantities of protein and calcium, I would grow straight and strong, have sparkling teeth, live to a ripe old age and leap tall buildings in a single bound.

But nothing was ever said about the fact that this high-fat way of eating might be the single most important factor in the development of coronary heart disease. Somehow the information linking diet to atherosclerosis—*the fact that the American diet is hazardous to my health*—fell through the cracks.

The truth is that from the standpoint of cardiac health, diet is a double-edged sword. It can penalize your health. Or it can work for you. The evidence from population studies, animal experiments, molecular biology, and human metabolic and clinical trials is clear:

- If you want to increase blood cholesterol, LDLs, triglycerides and cardiac risk, eat a diet rich in total fat, saturated fat, trans fatty acids, dietary cholesterol and excessive calories associated with abdominal obesity.

- If you want to reduce blood cholesterol, LDLs, triglycerides and cardiac risk, eat a diet that emphasizes fruits, vegetables, grains, beans and seafood; is rich in foods that contain fiber, particularly soluble fiber, and antioxidants (vitamins C and E, and beta carotene); is moderate in animal protein; and contains reduced calories (coupled with increased physical activity) to avoid abdominal obesity.

Today, more people are beginning to understand this advice. The "Basic Food Group Wheel" studied in school has been discarded. Instead, the U.S. Department of Agriculture has developed "The Food Guide Pyramid" as an outline of what to eat each day. (See page 70.) It asks us to picture our daily eating program as a pyramid, with the wide base representing the foods we should eat more of and the narrow peak representing the foods we should restrict. The pyramid retains much of the "food groups" idea but illustrates how to proportion choices among the different groups. For example, by emphasizing fruits, vegetables, grains, pasta and breads in its broad base, the pyramid promotes foods with vitamins, minerals, complex carbohydrates and dietary fiber.

We now know and accept that what and how much we eat can have a direct impact on our health, appearance and longevity. We know that our national diet contributes not only to coronary heart disease but also to an imposing list of typically American diseases such as cancer, stroke, diabetes and high blood pressure, not to mention the less threatening but still serious problems of gout, osteoarthritis, gallbladder disease and obesity.

The relationship between diet and health has been clearly recognized by major health organizations. A recent Surgeon General's Report on Nutrition and Health, painting a picture of Americans gobbling their way to the grave, links a high-fat diet to 5 of the 10 leading causes of death. In 1990, 10 voluntary and governmental agencies agreed on Dietary Guidelines for Americans, issued in a special report entitled *The Healthy American Diet.* For people two years of age or older, the report provides seven guidelines for a healthful diet:

- Eat a variety of foods.

- Maintain healthy weight.

Food Guide Pyramid

A Guide to Food Choices

KEY ● Fat (naturally occurring and added)
▼ Sugars (added)
These symbols show fat and added sugars.

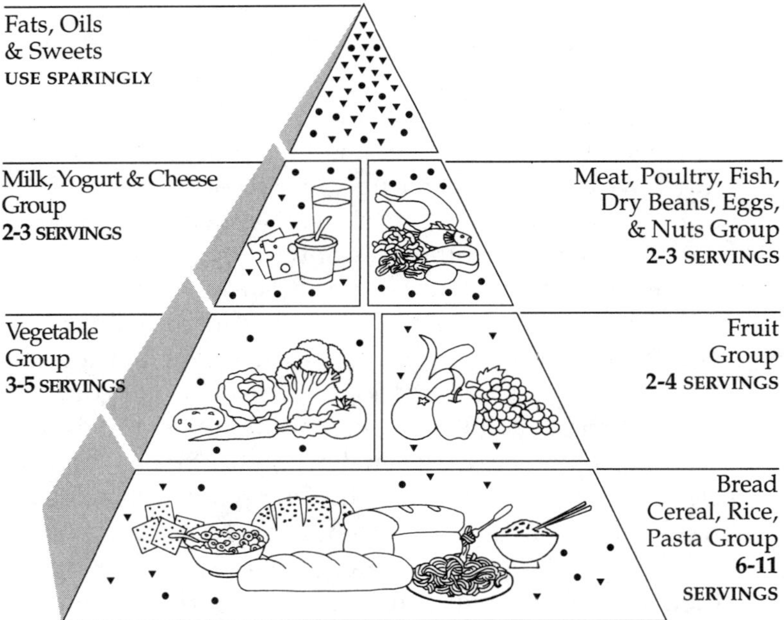

Looking at the Pieces of the Pyramid

The Food Guide Pyramid emphasizes foods from the five major food groups shown in the lower sections of the Pyramid. Each of these food groups provides some, but not all, of the nutrients you need. Foods in one group can't replace those in another. No one of these major food groups is more important than another. For good health, you need them all.

Source: U.S. Department of Agriculture, Human Nutrition Information Service, August 1992, Leaflet No. 572.

- Choose a diet low in fat, saturated fat and cholesterol.

- Choose a diet with plenty of vegetables, fruits and grain products.

- Use sugars only in moderation.

- Use salt and sodium only in moderation.

- If you drink alcoholic beverages, do so in moderation.

These guidelines tell us what we *should* eat for better health. However, when contrasted with what we *do* eat, fundamental problems become evident: too much dietary fat, salt and sugar, and not enough complex carbohydrates and fiber. The following chapters will look at these problem areas in depth and offer practical solutions.

CHAPTER SEVEN

TOO MUCH DIETARY FAT

While many aspects of our national diet are of concern to health professionals, there is a consensus when it comes to the greatest dietary hazard: *too much fat!* Reducing total fat intake (and with it saturated fat and dietary cholesterol) has become the nation's highest dietary priority.

The American diet today is much richer in fat than in the past. Figures from the U.S. Department of Agriculture show that in 1910 dietary fat made up just 27% of calories consumed, while today it accounts for about 37.5%. (Many experts dispute this figure, claiming that it underestimates fat consumption by 100 to 200 calories, or up to 20 grams of fat per day. This would mean that many of us are actually consuming over 40% of calories from fat, or over 100 grams of fat per day!)

Since much of this fat comes from animal foods, the intake of saturated fat and dietary cholesterol has also risen. At the same time, the consumption of refined sugar has doubled, while that of high-carbohydrate, high-fiber foods has fallen by about 25%. The result is a modern diet in which fat contributes far too many calories.

Is fat inherently harmful? The answer is no. Like cholesterol, fat itself is not bad and plays a legitimate and important role in maintaining good health. Along with protein and carbohydrate, fat is one of the main classes of foods essential to the body. Polyunsaturated fats (mostly from vegetable oils) supply the body with linoleic acid, an essential fatty acid. Dietary fat is also used in the transportation of important fat-soluble vitamins in the body; without fat in the diet, we would not be able to absorb vitamins A, D, E and K.

Dietary fat also provides the body with a concentrated source of energy (calories). At 9 calories per gram, fat packs twice the calories as the same amount of protein or carbohydrates. This is especially important for children under two years of age, who can use the higher energy from fat to meet increased growth needs. The body stores fat as an energy reserve and draws upon it when extra fuel is needed.

There is nothing wrong with dietary fat when it's consumed in the proper amounts. From a nutritional standpoint, the daily requirement for fat can fully be satisfied by consuming the equivalent of one tablespoon of vegetable oil. The average American, however, eats eight times that amount—between 800 and 1,000 calories, or about the equivalent of one full stick of butter a day, some 130 pounds of fat a year!

It is this overconsumption of fat that constitutes a health issue.

Fatty foods are central to the way America eats. According to the USDA, the top three sources of dietary fat are red meats, poultry and fish; visible fats such as cooking and salad oils; and whole-milk dairy products. Other significant sources include baked goods, fast foods, snack foods such as chocolate candy and potato chips, and convenience foods such as frozen dinners. In addition, frying and deep-fat frying are favorite methods of cooking, while fatty sauces and gravies are routinely used as flavor enhancers.

Why Do We Eat So Much Fat?

Despite fat reduction as a prominent nutritional goal, Americans continue to eat fatty foods in abundance. According to data from the National Institutes of Health, very few people are able to stick to a low-fat diet, including heart patients and people who have gone through expensive weight-loss programs. Experts have identified four factors that give insight into our love affair with dietary fat.

The Push for Protein

Much of the increase in high-fat foods since World War II came as a result of an overemphasis on protein. Protein is a needed nutritional building block, so the call to eat more protein-rich foods seemed reasonable. Unfortunately, it was not taken into account that many protein-rich foods actually contain far more fat than protein.

Red meat, for example, is a good protein food, but it also supplies three of the top five sources of fat in our diet. While a T-bone steak gets 30% of its calories from protein, 68% come from fat! It's even worse for bacon, which gets 17% of its calories from protein but 81% from fat. Even lean ground beef is 37% protein and 60% fat. Many cuts of red meat certainly should not be called "high-protein" foods without acknowledging their "high-fat" content.

A general misconception also exists about the amount of protein needed for good health. The fact is that protein, like fat, is not required in abundance. The table that follows shows the Recommended Daily Allowance (USRDA) for protein, along with the average protein consumption by age and gender.

Sex and Age	USRDA for Protein (grams)	Average Protein Consumption (grams)
Males		
11–14	45	92
15–18	59	122
19–24	58	105
25–29	63	105
30–59	63	93
60–69	63	79
70+	63	69
Females		
11–14	46	66
15–18	44	63
19–24	46	65
25–49	50	65
50–69	50	55
70+	50	49

For adults, the USRDA for protein is no more than 0.8 grams per kilogram (2.2 pounds) of body weight. (Athletes need about 1.2 grams per kilogram of weight.) To put this in perspective, a person could consume 42 grams of protein—more than half the requirement for a full day—in a lunch consisting of a turkey sandwich (four ounces of turkey breast, two slices of whole-wheat bread) and an eight-ounce glass of nonfat milk. Far too much protein is consumed by Americans, and far too much of what is consumed is in the form of high-fat animal foods.

The Push for Calcium

The same type of misinformation exists for calcium, with much the same result. No question about it, calcium is essential in building strong bones and teeth and is especially important for women in preventing osteoporosis. The recommended daily calcium intake for adults is about 800 milligrams (more for pregnant or nursing women).

When most people think of calcium, they think of dairy foods such as milk, cheese and ice cream. Many of these foods are *good* sources of calcium but *great* sources of fat! Most cheese, for instance, is over 60% fat, while whole milk and ice cream are over 50% fat. In actuality, the USRDA can be met by nonfat or low-fat calcium sources. This is illustrated by the following comparison of the fat and calcium content of various types of milk.

Type (1 cup)	Calories	% of Calories from Fat	Milligrams of Calcium
Whole milk	150	51%	288
2% milk	125	38	287
1% milk	105	22	300
Nonfat (skim) milk	80	2	302
Nonfat buttermilk	90	2	285

The daily requirement of calcium for most people can be met by two glasses of nonfat milk and a cup of nonfat yogurt. There is no need to consume high-fat dairy products to ensure sufficient calcium in the diet.

"Fat Tooth" Food Cravings

Another factor that has contributed to excessive dietary fat is a lack of understanding about the impact of food cravings on food selection. In the past, many people who tried to eat healthfully but succumbed to the craving for a chocolate-chip cookie saw themselves as "weak" or "undisciplined." Often they were so dejected that they ate the whole box of cookies, felt even worse, and then gave up on low-fat eating altogether. The Calvinistic approach that willpower determines eating habits has fallen into disrepute according to numerous nutritional experts. Nutritional scientists at the Massachusetts Institute of Technology, the University of Michigan and Rockefeller University, among others, have found a physiological connection between hormones and brain chemistry levels on one hand and food choices on the other.

Dr. Adam Drewnowski, head of the Human Nutrition Center at the University of Michigan, categorizes the phenomenon as a "fat tooth." "The fact is that most of us are born with a natural preference for fat," he says. "It may be that evolutionary pressures have provided us with inherited tendencies toward fatty foods, which are important to survival in primitive conditions. It may be that hormone and brain chemical levels direct us to certain fatty foods to offset an imbalance. Certainly we were not meant to eat as much fat as we do, but the easy access we have to high-fat foods, combined with the body's inborn preference, makes it difficult to just say no. The point is that our preference for fatty foods, and often an abnormal appetite for them, is in reality a biological, not a moral issue."

The innate craving for fatty foods is termed a "fat tooth" because many of the foods most commonly desired, such as pastry, chocolate and ice cream, are mistakenly thought to be high in sugar and are actually much richer in fat. A glazed chocolate doughnut, for example, derives just 20% of its calories from sugar but 80% from fat. Indeed, in most "sweet tooth" foods, sugar actually masks a higher fat content. One reason it's so hard to fight a "fat tooth" is that our appetite for fat is virtually bottomless. With sugar or salt your taste buds will eventually say "enough," but there seems to be no saturation point for fat. Rarely is anything too rich.

The salient point is that the craving for fatty foods is natural and normal, and to deny it can set up pendulum-like swings between abstention and bingeing. I go into much detail about such cravings in my book *Controlling Your Fat Tooth.* However, it suffices here to understand that the "fat tooth" predisposes many people to crave fat and thereby causes them to maximize fatty foods in their dietary choices. The good news is that biology doesn't have to control dietary destiny. It is possible to retrain your "fat tooth" to like specific low-fat foods, which may help you to change the high-fat nature of your diet. What this means for many of us is a more practical approach to fat reduction. It may be more effective to *reduce* fatty foods (but include some to satisfy "fat tooth" cravings) than to try to *eliminate* them completely. In doing so, our chances of instituting low-fat dietary habits are greatly increased.

A Pro-Fat Environment

Without question, the style of modern life has created a pro-fat environment. Extended work hours, longer commuting times, two-income families, single-parent households—the result is less time available for shopping, cooking and even eating. According to Dr. Nancy Wellman, former president of the American Dietetic Association, "Many of us try to reduce fat in our diets, but our life-style overrides our good intentions. Demographic changes, the number of meals eaten away from home, the convenience pull, nutritional naiveté and plain confusion confound our attempt." People are eating on the run and settling for "what is available" from restaurants, take-outs and food stores. "We've become a nation that has denigrated the role of preparing, serving and sharing food in society," says Joel Weiner of Kraft General Foods. "We've moved from eating to grazing to refueling." The shift from home-cooked meals to restaurant food, fast food, frozen meals, deli take-out, snack foods and junk foods demonstrates a willingness on the part of modern Americans to trade nutrition for high-fat convenience.

In addition, society seems to be reacting to a call to be perfect—to lead a fat-free, abstemious, healthful, aerobicized life-style—with an attitude adjustment that trend-watcher Faith Popcorn calls the "pleasure revenge." It is a backlash against the relentless beating of those obsessed with promoting extremely low-fat diets. It seems that Americans are starting to loosen up. A 1993 national telephone poll of 1,000 adults conducted by the American Dietetic Association found that only 39% of the responders said they were doing everything they could to eat a healthier diet, as opposed to 44% in 1992. This is also reflected in television and print advertising. According to Competitive Media Reporting, diet-product advertising was down $309 million in 1993, while non-diet advertising was up by $1.6 billion.

Whatever the reason, the American diet continues to be based on too much dietary fat. The result has been an epidemic of twin health problems—coronary heart disease and obesity.

Dietary Fat and Blood Cholesterol

One of the first studies on cholesterol in humans was initiated in the 1940s at the University of Minnesota by Dr. Ancel Keys, a pioneer in cardiac research. In this study 281 businessmen in their forties and fifties were observed over a 15-year period.

During that time, some of the men had heart attacks and some did not. It was found that those suffering heart attacks had a significantly greater amount of blood cholesterol than those who did not have heart attacks. Dr. Keys concluded that a direct relationship existed between a high level of blood cholesterol and a greater incidence of heart attack. People with elevated blood cholesterol, it seemed, were much more likely to have heart attacks than those with normal or low blood cholesterol. This was the first time that blood cholesterol level was linked to coronary heart disease in humans. However, the study did not concern itself with diet pattern.

Not until the early 1950s was the role of diet as a risk factor seriously examined. Dr. Keys instituted a study of three groups of Japanese subjects, each of which resided in a different environment. Differences in heredity and physiology, which were evident in prior studies, were set aside in this study, allowing Dr. Keys to concentrate on the diet patterns and blood cholesterol levels of the three groups. The first group lived in Japan and ate a traditional low-fat Asian diet. This group had low blood cholesterol levels and a low incidence of heart attack. The second group lived in Hawaii and ate a mixture of low-fat Asian and high-fat American meals. They had higher levels of blood cholesterol and a greater incidence of heart attack. The third group lived in Los Angeles and consumed the American diet exclusively. Their blood cholesterol levels and incidence of heart attack were much higher than the second group and significantly higher than the first group.

This study concluded that blood cholesterol level is influenced directly by diet pattern. Coupled with earlier findings that elevated blood cholesterol increases the incidence of heart attack, it opened the door to the modern medical approach to diet as a coronary risk factor.

Another notable trial was the Seven Country Study, in which diet, blood cholesterol and frequency of heart attack were measured in communities in Finland, Greece, Italy, Japan, the Netherlands, the United States and Yugoslavia. In all, some 12,000 men in the 40-to-49 age range were tested and observed. The study illustrated that cultures in which fat, particularly saturated fat, made up a significant percentage of total caloric intake demonstrated an elevated level of blood cholesterol and a high incidence of coronary heart disease. Thus the Finns, who ate 20% of their calories as saturated fat, had blood cholesterol levels that averaged 265 mg/dl. The Japanese ate only 5% of their calories as saturated fat and had correspondingly low levels of cholesterol, averaging just 165 mg/dl. A most important point was that the heart attack rate for middle-aged Finnish men was six times greater than for Japanese men of the same age.

A further study divided the continent of Europe into two distinct geographic areas based on dietary patterns. "High-fat Europe," with a diet similar to that of the United States, comprised the British Isles, Germany, Holland, Scandinavia, northern France, Belgium and northern Switzerland. This group was categorized as a "beer and butter" culture, and their diet pattern, while differing in national foods, was uniformly rich in fat. "Low-fat Europe," on the other hand, exhibited a diet pattern that was lower in fats; in addition, many of the fats used were unsaturated. This group, categorized as a "wine and oil" culture, consisted of Spain, Italy, southern France, southern Switzerland and Greece. The study illustrated that elevated blood cholesterol and a high incidence of heart attack existed in "high-fat Europe," while just the opposite occurred in "low-fat Europe." It concluded that blood cholesterol levels and incidence of coronary heart disease cut across geographic and ethnic boundaries where similarities in diet patterns did the same.

More recently, studies such as the Framingham Heart Study, the MRFIT trial and the NIH Cholesterol Study have shown that a reduction in dietary fat, particularly saturated fat, can cause blood cholesterol level to fall, thereby reducing the threat of heart attack. In other studies in which lower blood cholesterol was achieved with diet and/or drug therapy, coronary stabilization and regression resulted for some people. In sum, research now very clearly shows that the intake of dietary fat does indeed have an impact—good or bad—on blood cholesterol levels and the development of coronary heart disease.

What's the Problem?

One problem involves the *amount* of fat consumed. We eat a lot of fat because it is a basic component of so many foods. Fat provides flavor, texture and moisture (it "melts in the mouth") and is digested slowly, so it provides an enjoyable feeling of satisfaction after a meal. In addition, the natural craving for fat known as the "fat tooth" predisposes some of us to select foods rich in fat.

The result is that about 37.5% of all calories consumed are in the form of fat. The American Heart Association, the Surgeon General and the National Cancer Society recommend that fat constitute no more than 30% of calories consumed. While this may be an acceptable level for healthy people, a growing number of health professionals today believe that 30% is still too generous, particularly for heart patients who need to stabilize or reverse their disease and for people who need or want to lose weight. In light of our national problems of heart disease and obesity, and my personal experience, I agree. What makes sense to me is the following guideline:

If you are a cardiac patient, have two or more cardiac risks in your life-style, have a strong family history of heart disease, need to lower cholesterol or need to lose weight, choose a diet with about 20% of total calories from fat.
(*Note:* I recognize that some heart patients should be on a diet lower in fat. However, as a general rule, very few people can or will stay for long on a very restrictive diet, while a 20% fat diet is realistic and attainable. In addition, positive cardiac outcomes—stabilization and reversal—have been achieved with a 20% fat diet.)

If you are not a cardiac patient, do not have two or more cardiac risks in your life-style, do not have a strong family history of heart disease, do not need to lower cholesterol or do not need to lose weight, choose a diet with about 25% of total calories from fat.
(*Note:* I recognize that some people can eat junk all day and never gain weight or increase cholesterol. But for the rest of us, a diet with 25% of calories as fat is a good balance between healthy eating and living in the real world.)

In my opinion, based on research and over 18 years of personal experience, a 20% fat diet provides the best combination of foods for good cardiac health and good taste. Heart disease has been shown to progress with diets containing more than 30% fat. The other extreme, diets down around 10% fat, simply are not workable for most people because they do not suit the demands of modern life-style and the choices that exist in restaurants and supermarkets. For most of us, such diets invite failure.

A second problem concerns the *type* of fat consumed. All fats and oils are a mixture of three types of fatty acids: saturated, polyunsaturated and monounsaturated. No fat is made up exclusively of one type of fatty acid. Rather, fatty acids are found in differing amounts. For example, canola oil, which is 6% saturated, 62% monounsaturated and 32% polyunsaturated, is described as a "monounsaturated fat." On the other hand, coconut oil, which is 87% saturated, 6% monounsaturated and 2% polyunsaturated, is clearly a "saturated fat." These distinctions are important because, from a cardiovascular standpoint, not all fats are equal.

The fat most harmful to cardiac health is saturated fat, found in animal foods such as the visible fat on steak, bacon drippings, cheese, lard and butter. A rule of thumb is that saturated fat stays hard at room temperature. It is also found in three vegetable oils: palm oil, palm kernel oil and coconut oil. Saturated fat makes up about 16% to 18% of calories on the American diet. However, for many people in this country, saturated fat makes up as much as one-third of total calories. Since the major dietary influence on blood cholesterol is saturated fat, which tends to stimulate the internal production of LDL cholesterol, experts now recommend that it make up no more than 10% of calories. "Please remember," says Dr. Virgil Brown, past president of the American Heart Association, "that 10% is an upper limit, not a target. A better goal is in the 7%-to-10% range—and below that if you have heart disease."

Better for cardiac health are the unsaturated fats—polyunsaturated and monounsaturated. Unsaturated fats can, in fact, help to lower blood cholesterol level when they replace saturated fats. A good rule of thumb is that unsaturated fats remain liquid at room temperatures.

Polyunsaturated fat is found chiefly in vegetable

oils such as safflower, soybean, sunflower, corn, cottonseed and sesame oils. Many people mistakenly believe that polyunsaturated oils can do no harm and are actually good for you. This myth is perpetuated by the advertising of margarine and vegetable oil. There are two cautions regarding polyunsaturated fats from vegetable sources. First, they lower protective HDLs as well as harmful LDLs, thereby blunting some of the beneficial effect. Second, when liquid polyunsaturated oils are hardened or stiffened into solid fats, a process called hydrogenation, a chemical change takes place that produces trans fatty acids. Unfortunately, some trans fats can raise blood cholesterol in much the same way that saturated fat does. In the Harvard Nurses Health Study, women who ate lots of foods rich in trans fatty acids had a 66% higher risk of heart disease than those who did not. Hydrogenated or partially hydrogenated vegetable oils are used to make margarine, solid shortening, cookies, crackers, potato chips and other processed foods.

One source of polyunsaturated fat that does not carry these drawbacks is seafood, including shellfish. Omega-3, a fatty acid found in fish oil, has been shown to protect against coronary heart disease. It is thought that fish oil actually reduces the stickiness of the blood platelets that otherwise would cling to damaged blood vessel walls and form dangerous clots. In addition, fish oil markedly lowers high triglycerides. According to the *New England Journal of Medicine,* eating "as little as two fish dishes a week (about 7.5 ounces of fish) may cut the risk of dying from heart attack in half." Fish with high fat content include salmon, mackerel, herring, fresh tuna, whitefish and lake trout.

Monounsaturated oils include olive, canola, peanut, avocado and nut oils. Studies in Canada and the United States indicate that monounsaturated oils reduce the risk of clot formation within coronary arteries, lower "bad" LDL cholesterol and minimize the decrease of "good" HDL cholesterol when substituted for saturated fats. Olive oil and canola oil in particular may be instrumental in reducing the risk of coronary heart disease. This may explain the low incidence of heart problems among Mediterranean populations who use olive oil and Asian populations who use canola oil as replacements for saturated fats.

A Key Point: Reduce Total Fat

There is no doubt that polyunsaturated and monounsaturated fats are "more healthful" than saturated fats. However, there is no need to consume large amounts of any fat, whether it comes from a steer or from plants such as corn. Indeed, there is evidence that too much fat *of any kind* can help to develop artery blockages. The key is to eat less fat. Period.

As one physician said to me, "If a patient used to make a sandwich with butter on two pieces of bread, but now makes it with margarine on two pieces of bread, that's not much of a change. But if he makes the sandwich with a thin smear of margarine on one piece and mustard on the other, that's a change." So, the proper perspective is this: *When you eat fat, substitute unsaturated for saturated fats. But use all fats in moderation.*

What About Dietary Cholesterol?

Many people erroneously believe that the most important dietary step is to cut out cholesterol-rich foods such as eggs and organ meats. In truth, however, dietary cholesterol is less important than dietary fat. "Actually, dietary cholesterol has a minimal effect on blood cholesterol," says Dr. Margaret Denke of the American Heart Association. "Only about 15% of dietary cholesterol is absorbed into the bloodstream. The main problem with cholesterol-rich foods is that they also tend to be high in dietary fat, particularly saturated fat." The emphasis on total fat and saturated fat, rather than dietary cholesterol, is a change from times past when experts counseled to stay away from foods "too high in cholesterol." Today it is known that cholesterol-rich foods are less responsible for elevated blood cholesterol than are foods rich in saturated fat. Says Dr. Ernst J. Schaefer of Tufts University, "Reducing saturated fat consumption by 50% may lower blood cholesterol twice as much as a similar drop in dietary cholesterol." The American Heart Association recommends no more than 300 milligrams of cholesterol per day. When the consumption of animal foods is reduced to lower total fat and saturated fat intake, a natural consequence is a reduction in dietary cholesterol.

Dietary Fat and Overweight

The Duchess of Windsor once remarked that in the United States a person can be neither too rich nor too thin. Her statement, while perhaps not complimentary, is certainly a perceptive view of one of our most cherished national fantasies—to be thin.

American culture is, to put it mildly, preoccupied with weight. A recent survey by *Better Homes and Gardens* revealed that 90% of the population, including small children, think they weigh too much. A Gallup poll showed that a third of American women aged 19 to 39 diet at least once a month. Everyone seems to be concerned about weight, but the irrefutable fact is that Americans as a people are overweight by an estimated 1.5 billion pounds.

This should be no surprise to anyone familiar with the American diet pattern of fatty meat and dairy products, sugar and alcohol. After all, when you eat too much, when you eat too often, when what you eat is too high in calories, you get fat!

A number of scientific studies have illustrated the impact of high-fat dietary choices on obesity. One study conducted at St. Luke's–Roosevelt Hospital Center in New York City found that while many people blame their inability to lose weight on bad genes or sluggish metabolism, it actually has more to do with food choices. "Most people really cannot invoke some genetic cause as the only explanation for obesity," says Dr. Steven Heymsfield, medical director of the hospital's weight control unit. "The main reason they are overweight is that they are overeating."

Metabolism does contribute to obesity. So does genetic inheritance. But researchers say these factors are probably far less important for most people than the simple act of taking in too many calories. And when your diet is high in fat, it's hard not to take in too many calories.

Obesity Is a Cardiac Risk Factor

Most people are concerned with weight for reasons of appearance and self-esteem. While these are important considerations and should not be minimized, clearly the most important reason for weight control is good health.

Medical research has shown that being overweight can constitute a serious health risk. Actuarial studies by insurance companies have found that the death rate from all causes increases as weight rises, and that this risk becomes substantial for people who weigh more than 20% above their ideal weight. A National Institutes of Health report estimates that a quarter of cardiovascular disease can be attributed to obesity.

Carrying excessive body fat is also associated with an increased risk of certain cancers, high blood pressure, diabetes, respiratory problems, gallbladder disease, arthritis and gout. Says Dr. Charles H. Hennekens of Harvard University, "Obesity is right up there with cigarette smoking and heavy alcohol consumption as a major cause of excess morbidity and mortality in the United States. Overweight people tend to have higher total cholesterol and lower HDL levels than normal-weight people."

ARE YOU AN "APPLE" OR A "PEAR"?

New research shows that *where* you carry excess fat may be more important than *how much* you carry. Both men and women are known to be at greater risk for diabetes, high blood pressure and heart disease if their excess fat is deposited around the waist and in the abdomen rather than on the hips and thighs. According to the Framingham Study, abdominal fat also tends to increase triglycerides and reduce HDLs, which can produce the cardiac risk factor called Syndrome X.

According to one study, people can be categorized as "apples" or "pears." Men are typically "apple-shaped," while women are more typically "pears." The study showed that "apples" are three to five times more likely than "pears" to suffer heart attacks. This effect may result from the fact that abdominal fat is much more metabolically active than fat stored in thighs, hips and buttocks. It may also explain why men are initially more at risk for the disease.

Are you an "apple" or a "pear"? To determine your status, use a tape measure to find the circumference of your waist at its narrowest point when your stomach is relaxed. Next, measure the circumference of your hips at their widest (where your buttocks protrude the most). Finally, divide your waist measurement by your hip measurement. For men, if the ratio is greater than 1.0, the risk of heart attack is elevated. (Example: a man with a 40-inch waist and 36-inch hips would have a 1.1 ratio.) The same is true for women with a ratio exceeding 0.8. (Example: a 33-inch waist and 36-inch hips would yield a ratio of 0.9.)

How Dietary Fat Makes You Fat

Eating supplies the body with energy in the form of calories. As long as energy input (calories consumed) is in balance with energy expenditure (calories burned in exercise, physical activity and basic bodily functions), all is well. But when caloric input is greater than output, the extra calories are stored as body fat. It takes 3,500 extra calories to create one pound of body fat. For most of us, gaining weight as body fat is not a short-term affair. A bit more calories coming in, a bit fewer going out, over time is what causes body fat to accumulate. As few as 50 extra calories a day, a single chocolate-chip cookie, can add 350 calories a week, or a total of 18,200 in a year. That's equal to a gain of 5 pounds in a year, or 52 pounds in a decade. It is, of course, possible to gain weight by overeating any type of food. Eat enough fruit, pasta or carrots, and you could be overweight. But most of the problem comes from too much dietary fat. A gram of fat is not the same as a gram of carbohydrate or protein, either in the number of calories it contains or in the way it is metabolized by the body.

Dietary Fat Contains More Calories

At 9 calories per gram, dietary fat has more than twice as many calories as carbohydrates and protein at 4 calories per gram. High-fat foods are calorically dense, which means they pack a lot of calories into a small amount of food. A small package of M&M peanut candies, for example, contains 250 calories, 47% of them from fat. This isn't a lot of food (actually only 1.74 ounces), but it contains a king-size amount of calories because it's so rich in fat. Just the opposite is true of low-fat foods, which are calorically light. An entire pound of apples contains only 240 calories—less than the small bag of M&Ms.

Research shows that people who eat high-fat diets actually take in less food but a lot more calories and therefore gain weight. On the other hand, people who eat a diet low in fat but rich in complex carbohydrates and fiber eat more food but lose weight.

Dietary Fat Converts Easily to Body Fat

For many years, scientists held to the belief that "a calorie is a calorie." A growing body of evidence now suggests that once a calorie is eaten, this simple rule of dieting dogma doesn't always hold true. The fact is that there are marked differences in the body's metabolic response to dietary fat.

The process of converting calories into body fat takes energy, and some of the calories being converted are used to produce that energy. This represents the "handling costs" of turning calories into stored body fat.

Not all foods call for the same amount of energy

in the conversion process. One hundred calories of butter, a dietary fat, uses only 3 calories in processing, which means that 97 calories can be converted to body fat. One hundred calories of baked potato, a complex carbohydrate, uses 23 calories in processing, which means that just 77 calories are available to be converted to body fat. In reality, only about 1% of calories from carbohydrate and protein end up as body fat because the body would rather use them up right away than waste energy to store them.

So, by eating a low-fat diet, not only do you consume fewer total calories, but the calories you do eat are less likely to be converted into body fat.

A Last Word

Overconsumption of fat is our greatest nutritional hazard. The medical effects of a high-fat diet are devastating. Heart disease, stroke, cancer, high blood pressure, diabetes, osteoarthritis, gallbladder disease, gout and obesity—all are products of a diet too rich in fat. In addition, by overconsuming fatty foods, we often underconsume foods rich in dietary fiber, vitamins, minerals, antioxidants and other substances in complex carbohydrates that protect health. The more fat we consume, the less we eat of other foods that have protective benefits. The result is a double whammy against health.

CHAPTER EIGHT

NOT ENOUGH COMPLEX CARBOHYDRATES AND FIBER

The call to cut down on fat is also a call to eat more foods rich in complex carbohydrates and fiber, i.e., more fruits, vegetables, beans and grains. The fact is that dietary change based exclusively on negatives—foods you should avoid—has little chance for success. To create new and healthier dietary habits, you must center your diet pattern on foods you can have. Complex carbohydrates fill this need. They are the secret to a diet pattern that promotes good health with delicious food.

Complex carbohydrates should be the primary source of calories in the diet. Specifically, complex carbohydrates should make up at least 55% of total calories. The Committee on Diet and Health of the National Research Council advises: "Every day eat five or more servings of vegetables and fruits, especially green and yellow vegetables and citrus fruits. Also, increase intake of complex carbohydrates by eating six or more daily servings of a combination of breads, cereals, pasta, rice and legumes."

Historically, complex carbohydrates have been the chief source of calories for humans: corn for American Indians, bread for Europeans, rice for Asians, grains and beans for Africans and South

Americans. In many parts of the world starchy carbohydrates still make up the bulk of the diet, but in the United States and other industrialized civilizations the proper role of complex carbohydrates in the diet has been altered. First, the consumption of all carbohydrates has fallen off in favor of fat. Since the early 1900s, along with an increase in affluence, the American diet has systematically substituted animal foods and refined foods for whole fruits, grains, beans and vegetables. Second, the type of carbohydrate eaten has changed. In the past, Americans ate most of their carbohydrates in the form of whole foods. Today, most carbohydrates come from refined and processed foods such as commercially baked goods, processed grains and canned vegetables. The result is a diet that is too high in fat and too low in complex carbohydrates—a diet that should be changed for a variety of reasons.

Complex Carbohydrates Are Not Fattening

Of all the dietary misconceptions that exist, none is farther from the truth than the notion that starchy carbohydrates cause people to get fat. This myth is what causes many dieters to avoid starchy foods such as bread, potatoes, rice and pasta. Indeed, nutritionists counsel that if you want to lose weight, you should eat more starchy foods and less fatty ones.

This advice is premised on the fact that starchy carbohydrates are not rich in calories. Like protein, carbohydrate contains just 4 calories per gram. Fat, on the other hand, bulges with 9 calories per gram. So, while one ounce of lamb, a fat-rich food, is about 100 calories, the same amount of rice, a starchy carbohydrate, has only 30 calories. Fruits, grains and vegetables by their nature contain fewer calories than do high-fat foods.

It is the fat in food, *including the fat added to complex carbohydrates,* that makes you fat. A medium-size baked potato, for instance, contains just 110 calories. But add fatty toppings—butter, margarine, sour cream, bacon bits, cheese—and the calories jump to 400. It isn't the potato that packs the calories, it's the added fat. It isn't the rice that adds pounds, it's the butter sauce. It isn't the bread, it's the margarine. And it isn't the pasta, it's the cheese, meatballs and cream sauce.

Another important point is that fatty foods lack mass, so they can be eaten in greater amounts. Complex carbohydrates are just the opposite. They are low in calories, high in fiber and high in mass, so they fill you up before you eat too much. Foods that need a lot of chewing, like apples or carrots, take a long time to eat and therefore provide sufficient time (about 20 minutes) for satiety to be attained. These foods also absorb water in the digestive system, thereby helping to create a feeling of fullness and satisfaction that keeps you from overeating. The fact is that most overweight people cannot eat enough complex carbohydrates to maintain their weight. They lose weight automatically when they replace fatty foods with fruits, grains and vegetables.

COMPLEX CARBOHYDRATES CONTAIN FIBER

Fiber, often called roughage, bulk or bran, is the nondigestible part of plant food such as fruits, vegetables and grains. Examples of fiber sources include cellulose, hemicellulose, pectin, gums and lignins. Fiber aids weight control because it passes through the digestive system intact, which means that not all calories consumed stay with the body. In addition, high-fiber foods reduce the risk of colon cancer by pushing food through the digestive system faster, thereby reducing the time the colon wall is exposed to potential carcinogens.

The American diet is too low in fiber, a circumstance that contributes to a number of serious health problems such as cancer of the colon and rectum, diverticulosis, gallstones, varicose veins, hiatus hernia, appendicitis, hemorrhoids and heart disease. Americans consume on average 11 grams of dietary fiber each day. This is short of the American Dietetic Association recommendation of 20 to 35 grams of fiber per day. For an idea of how much this is, remember that 28 grams equals one ounce, so the total amount of fiber in your daily food intake does not have to be large.

You *can* overdo a good thing. Eating more than 50 or 60 grams of fiber a day may decrease the amount of vitamins and minerals your body absorbs.

Getting adequate fiber is the result of making better food choices. First, find out which foods are high in fiber. The tables on the following pages will be of help. Then make smarter choices:

- Choose whole fruits instead of juice.
- Eat a baked potato with the skin on.
- Choose high-fiber snacks: popcorn, fresh fruits, raw vegetables and, occasionally, nuts.
- Plan for a cooked vegetable *and* a salad at dinner.
- Remember that breakfast is a good place to add fiber-rich foods such as oatmeal, bran cereals, and low-fat oat bran or wheat bran muffins.

Food	Amount	Grams of Dietary Fiber	Calories
Fruits			
Apple (with skin)	1 medium	3.0	81
Banana	1 medium	1.8	105
Blueberries	½ cup	2.7	41
Cantaloupe	¼	1.1	47
Figs, dried	2	3.5	95
Orange	1 medium	3.1	62
Peach (with skin)	1	1.4	37
Pear (with skin)	1 medium	4.3	98
Prunes, dried	3	1.8	60
Raisins, seedless	¼ cup	1.9	108
Strawberries	1 cup	3.9	45
Vegetables, Cooked			
Broccoli	½ cup	2.0	23
Brussels sprouts	½ cup	3.4	30
Potato, baked (with skin)	1 medium	3.6	220
Spinach	½ cup	2.0	21
Summer squash (zucchini)	½ cup	1.3	18
Sweet potato	½ medium	1.7	59
Vegetables, Raw			
Carrots	1 medium	2.3	31
Celery	1 stalk	0.6	6
Cucumber, sliced	½ cup	0.5	7
Lettuce, romaine	1 cup	1.0	8
Mushrooms, sliced	½ cup	0.5	9
Spinach	1 cup	1.5	12
Tomato	1 medium	1.6	24
Legumes, Cooked			
Baked beans, plain or vegetarian, canned	½ cup	9.8	118
Kidney beans	½ cup	7.3	110
Lentils, cooked	½ cup	3.7	97
Breads, Grains and Pasta			
Bagel	1	1.2	163
French bread	1 slice	0.8	102
Pumpernickel bread	1 slice	1.9	79
Rice, brown, cooked	½ cup	1.7	109
Spaghetti, cooked	½ cup	1.1	99
Whole-wheat bread	1 slice	1.9	61

Food	Amount	Grams of Dietary Fiber	Calories
Snack Foods			
Peanuts, dry-roasted	¼ cup	2.9	214
Popcorn, air-popped	1 cup	0.9	23
Sunflower seeds, oil-roasted	¼ cup	2.3	208
Walnuts, English	¼ cup	1.4	193
Breakfast Cereals			
All-Bran	⅓ cup	8.5	71
Bran Chex	⅔ cup	4.6	91
Bran flakes	¾ cup	5.3	93
Cornflakes	1¼ cup	0.6	121
Granola	¼ cup	3.2	149
Oat bran, raw	⅓ cup	4.9	76
Oatmeal, regular, quick and instant, cooked	¾ cup	1.6	108
Raisin bran	¾ cup	4.8	115

Source: U.S. Department of Agriculture, Human Nutrition Information Service.

Complex Carbohydrates Benefit Cardiac Health

A diet rich in complex carbohydrates can benefit cardiac health in four ways. First, studies throughout the world show that people who habitually consume a diet rich in plant food have a low risk of coronary heart disease, probably because such a diet is usually low in cholesterol-raising animal fat and high in fiber and other important nutrients.

Second, complex carbohydrates aid in the reduction of excess body fat, which by itself is a cardiac risk factor. Such foods are lower in fat and, because of their mass, can help keep you from overeating.

Third, fruits and vegetables (particularly citrus fruits and green and yellow vegetables) provide important antioxidants—vitamin C, vitamin E and beta carotene (a relative of vitamin A)—that may reduce the risk of heart disease. A study at the University of Texas, for example, found a 30% reduction in the risk of heart disease in men whose daily intake of vitamin C equaled that found in one or two oranges and who consumed an amount of beta carotene equal to that found in one or two carrots. The Harvard Nurses Study showed that those who ate at least five servings a day of fruits and vegetables *lowered their risk of heart attack by 33% and of stroke by 71%*. Such research provides a strong argument for eating at least five servings of fruits and vegetables per day.

And finally, there is clear evidence that complex carbohydrates rich in soluble fiber can reduce blood cholesterol. As it moves through the digestive system, soluble fiber forms a gel that interferes with the absorption of cholesterol and helps to reduce it in the bloodstream. Soluble fiber is particularly effective in people with blood cholesterol levels above 200 mg/dl, as demonstrated in studies at the University of Kentucky conducted by Dr. James Anderson. These studies showed that such individuals could reduce their cholesterol by 13% to 19% by consuming one cup of oat bran, or about three bowls cooked, per day. (Eating three bowls of oat bran a day is not a dietary recommendation. It's important to get sufficient soluble fiber from a variety of foods.) Less compelling data are available on cholesterol reduction in people with blood cholesterol under 200 mg/dl; however, since a 1% reduction in blood cholesterol produces a 2% reduction in the risk of heart attack, even a small drop in blood cholesterol can be of significance.

Foods rich in soluble fiber include oat bran, oatmeal, dried beans and peas (black-eyed and split peas, lentils, kidney, navy and pinto beans), vegetables (carrots, peas, corn, sweet potato, zucchini, cauliflower, broccoli) and fruit (pears, prunes, apples, bananas, oranges). Psyllium, sold commercially as Metamucil, also contains soluble fiber. It's important to remember, however, that foods rich in soluble fiber help only when they become part of an eating plan that is healthful overall, low in fat (particularly saturated fat) and cholesterol, and accompanied by exercise.

A Last Word

The significance of a diet to lose weight, lower cholesterol and promote health lies not just in what is taken away (fat) but also in how it bears on what is put back (complex carbohydrates). By increasing fruits, vegetables and grains from a variety of sources as a means to reduce dietary fat, you can lower blood cholesterol and lose weight at the same time. So, in addition to cutting fat, concentrate on the following nutrition priorities:

- Plant foods come first: vegetables, fruits, whole grains and legumes.

- Include foods high in antioxidants, which appear to be good defenders against heart disease and cancer.

- Get fiber up to the recommended 20 to 35 grams a day—and stay there. Be sure to include foods rich in soluble fiber to help lower your cholesterol naturally.

CHAPTER NINE

TOO MUCH SALT

It's dinnertime, and throughout the United States people sit with family and friends to enjoy a meal together. Somewhere between grace and the first forkful of food comes the inevitable hallmark phrase of American table conversation: *Please pass the salt!*

For most Americans, salt constitutes a basic dietary component. It's used in cooking and as a condiment, and next to sugar it's the most widely used additive in processed foods. But recently many people have begun to question the amount of salt consumed on the typical American diet. The reason? Excessive salt (sodium) intake has been linked to high blood pressure, stroke, kidney and thyroid disease, and edema. Next to fat, sodium intake constitutes the greatest dietary concern. A number of health organizations now advise Americans to limit sodium consumption to no more than 2,400 milligrams a day. "The recommendations that today's high salt intake be reduced are based not on any one study," says Dr. Jeremiah Stamler of Northwestern University. "They're based on hundreds of studies, over many decades, using every method of medical research."

Salt Is Found Everywhere

Salt is the major source of sodium for most Americans. The National Research Council has stated that an "adequate and safe" level of sodium intake is between 1,100 and 3,300 milligrams daily. This is about one-half to one and a half teaspoons of salt. Many experts feel that 2,400 milligrams of sodium daily should be a maximum number. (Indeed, people with kidney problems, high blood pressure and certain heart conditions may want to keep their intake below 2,400 milligrams a day. If you have special problems, consult a physician for guidelines.) The average American consumes two to four teaspoons of salt daily, which translates into 4,000 to 8,000 milligrams of sodium. Our salt-rich diet produces a per capita consumption of 15 pounds of salt per person per year, which has caused sodium intake to go well beyond the "adequate and safe" levels.

Where does all this salt come from? About 15% comes from natural sources such as meat, fish, dairy products, vegetables and drinking water. Another 35% is table salt used as a condiment and as a cooking spice. But fully 50% is derived from processed foods. Salt and other sodium products are used by food manufacturers as a curative for fish and meats; as a brine agent for pickles, olives and sauerkraut; as a leavening agent in bread and crackers; and as a fermentation control in cheese. Using 2,400 milligrams a day as a guideline, it's easy to see how common foods can cumulatively produce an excess of sodium:

Food	Milligrams of Sodium
1-oz. bag of Lay's potato chips	95
1-oz. serving of Planters salted cashews	110
1-oz. bag of Doritos Cool Ranch tortilla chips	170

Food	Milligrams of Sodium
Hamburger bun	230
16 Wheat Thins	240
2 slices of white Wonder Bread	240
1-oz. serving of Smartfood white popcorn	260
10 saltines	360
4-oz. serving of Healthy Choice spaghetti sauce	380
½-cup serving of chicken-flavor Stove Top stuffing	580
1-oz. serving of Snyders Very Thin pretzels	730
4-oz. serving of Ragú Old-World Style spaghetti sauce	740
1 McDonald's Big Mac	890
2-oz. serving of salted popcorn	1,100
3-oz. slice of ham	1,115
10.75-oz. serving of Campbell's Chunky chicken noodle soup	1,120
1 cup sauerkraut	1,755
1 large dill pickle	1,940
1-oz. serving of Kikkomen soy sauce	2,075

It's no surprise that these foods contain salt. After all, they taste salty. What *is* a surprise is the number of low-sodium foods that turn into high-sodium products because of added salt. A 5.5-ounce potato, for instance, contains just 5 milligrams of sodium; processed as potato chips, it contains 1,560 milligrams. A tomato has 15 milligrams of sodium; processed into tomato sauce, one cup contains about 1,500 milligrams. One-half chicken breast has 70 milligrams of sodium; a fast-food chicken dinner can have 2,250 milligrams. According to *Consumer Reports:*

- One ounce of corn flakes has nearly twice the sodium as an ounce of salted peanuts.

- Two slices of white bread contain more sodium than 14 potato chips.
- One-half cup of prepared chocolate pudding has more sodium than three slices of bacon.

There is no natural affinity for the taste of salt. Unlike "fat tooth" cravings, the preference for salt is something we acquire. Many people learn to like the taste of salt as babies when their mothers salted their food or served salty commercial baby food. Says Dr. Lot Page, a Harvard hypertension specialist, "Salt appetite is determined by early dietary habits and has no relationship to salt need." This means that a taste for salt can be *un*learned.

WHAT'S THE PROBLEM?

The warnings issued about salt are very serious. In order to understand the health risks associated with excessive salt consumption, it is first necessary to distinguish *salt* from *sodium.* Salt, or sodium chloride, is a combination of two minerals: sodium, a metal, and chloride, a gas. Approximately 40% of salt is sodium. Thus a diet that is high in salt is also high in sodium, and the amount of sodium consumed is a health issue.

Sodium, which is essential to life, has both positive and negative characteristics. On the positive side, it is the chief regulator of the fluid balance of the body. The tissues in the human body must constantly be bathed in a saline solution. The correct sodium-to-fluid ratio in this solution is critical to proper metabolic functioning. Sodium regulates this balance by triggering a thirst sensation when body fluid is too low or sodium content too high. For example, when you lose fluid by sweating, the ratio of sodium is increased, causing you to become thirsty. By drinking liquids to satisfy your thirst, you also replace the fluid necessary to restore the proper balance. This relationship of excess sodium to thirst has long been understood by savvy bartenders who offer free salted peanuts or popcorn to their patrons.

When the concentration of sodium in the body is constantly high, as it often is as a result of a high-salt diet, the fluid-balance mechanism can be perverted to produce negative health results. A characteristic of sodium is that it holds liquid. When the body contains too much sodium and consequently too much liquid, the excess is eliminated through the kidneys. Should this happen occasionally, it generally poses no health problem. But when the kidneys are required constantly to eliminate excess sodium and fluid, they become overworked and are placed under great strain. They simply become unable to perform at the required level of elimination, and kidney damage or failure results.

Excessive amounts of sodium and fluid in the blood vessels also tax the heart by increasing the volume of blood to be circulated. When this happens, the heart is required to pump harder and create more pressure in order to move additional pounds of fluid in the bloodstream. At the same time, sodium causes the small blood vessels to constrict, thereby increasing resistance to blood flow. The heart is forced to respond by further increasing blood pressure, which is a significant strain on the cardiac muscle.

High blood pressure, or hypertension, is the most serious health consequence of excessive sodium intake. Over 63 million Americans are afflicted with the condition. Like atherosclerosis, it progresses silently. Blood pressure may increase year after year with no overt symptoms until quite suddenly, usually in middle age, the condition appears. By this time it's often too late to repair the damage done to the heart, kidneys and blood vessels. Chronic illness and death often occur. According to the National Heart, Lung and Blood Institute, over 45% of Americans with hypertension are unaware that they have the condition.

The causes of hypertension are not fully understood. Many factors, such as weight, age, stress, genetics and diet, are thought to contribute to it. Although a cause-and-effect relationship between high-salt intake and hypertension is difficult to prove, numerous studies have established a link. These studies have shown that in low-salt societies, such as New Guinea, the Kalahari Desert and parts of Brazil, hypertension is virtually nonexistent and blood pressure does not rise steadily with age. In high-salt societies, such as Japan and the United States, hypertension is rampant. In Japan, where salt consumption can be 20 times that of the West, areas can be found where over 40% of the adult population suffers from serious hypertension; in fact, the disease is that country's leading cause of death.

Not everyone with an excessive sodium intake is susceptible to the condition. In many people the excess is promptly excreted no matter how much is consumed. But in about 10% to 30% of the American population, there exists a genetic predisposition to hypertension. For these people, a diet rich in salt (and therefore rich in sodium) can increase the risk of high blood pressure and heart disease. Unfortunately, there are no tests that will let you know whether or not you're sodium-sensitive; consequently, individuals with sodium-rich diets are playing Russian roulette with their health.

CHAPTER TEN

TOO MUCH SUGAR

It seems that people have always enjoyed sweet foods. Even the Bible describes the Promised Land as "flowing with milk and honey." At least in early childhood there seems to be a biological basis for this preference. Even infants show a strong desire for sugary foods. Indeed, no other animal (with the possible exception of cats) demonstrates such a powerful inclination for foods that taste sweet. This craving, however, is sufficiently strong to affect our dietary decisions throughout life.

Until the Industrial Revolution, the craving for sweet foods was met by *naturally* sweet foods such as fruits and berries. Because they contain vitamins, minerals and fiber, these foods were important nutritionally as well. With the advent of sugar refining in the early 1800s, fruits and berries were replaced by pastry, cakes and candies. Industrialization produced a more "civilized" life-style for many people, including dietary changes that called for sweeter and richer foods as a symbol of affluence and status. Cream, butter and refined sugar became dietary staples.

Very little refined sugar was consumed in the early 1800s—only about two pounds per person annually—because refined sugar was expensive and not everyone could afford it. Moreover, taste preferences did not dictate large amounts of sugar. The preference or craving for sweet foods could be satisfied with only two pounds of sugar a year.

Advances in technology reduced the cost of producing refined sugar, and by the late 1800s it was available to the entire population. By 1875, the average American consumed 40 pounds of refined sugar. By 1910, it was 70 pounds. As people continued to increase sugar consumption, the amount of sugar needed to satisfy the craving also increased. The more sugar eaten, the more sugar desired. It took 35 times more sugar in 1910 than it did in 1800 to satisfy the national craving.

The development of the processed food and beverage industry in the 20th century has caused the consumption of refined sugar and other sugar concentrates to skyrocket. Sugar has replaced salt as the most popular food additive. The average American now consumes 143 pounds of refined sugar and sugar concentrates per year (or more than one-third of a pound, 600 calories, each day). The figure is even higher for children and adolescents: studies at Washington State University found that the average is over 12 ounces of sugar per day—or 274 pounds a year! It should be no surprise that sugar accounts for 24% of total calories on the American diet.

According to Dr. John Yudkin of London University and other experts, sugar is addictive for many people. The more sugar contained in the diet, the more is needed to satisfy the craving. The result is a modern diet that contains more sugar in a week than our forefathers consumed in an entire year.

Sources of Refined Sugar

Many people mistakenly believe that table sugar, or sucrose, is at the root of our high sugar intake. In actuality, it contributes about 30% of our total intake. Table sugar is used mostly in drinks such as coffee or lemonade, in cooking and baking, and as a condiment on fruit and cereal.

A much more substantial contributor is sugar added to processed foods such as soft drinks, jams and jellies, bakery goods such as cakes, cookies and pies, milk products such as ice cream, chocolate milk and flavored yogurt, cured meats, cereals, canned fruit, salad dressing, ketchup and candy. These foods provide 70% of the sugar we consume. This figure should not be astonishing in light of the fact that the average American eats 15 pounds of candy and drinks 40 gallons of soft drinks a year. For children, cold cereal supplies almost 10% of sugar consumption. Dr. John Yudkin, long a critic of sugar as a food additive, states that "if only a fraction of what is already known about the effects of sugar were to be revealed in relation to any other material used as a food additive, that material would promptly be banned."

WHAT'S THE PROBLEM?

Sweeteners such as table sugar and honey are called *simple carbohydrates*. Though less harmful than excess dietary fat, they pose a health hazard by contributing to tooth decay, obesity and diabetes when consumed in excessive amounts. And, according to experts such as Dr. John Farquhar of Stanford University, an overabundance of simple carbohydrates may constitute a risk for coronary heart disease as well.

One of the chief problems is that foods rich in refined sugar produce "empty" calories containing few or no nutrients. Such foods can take up space in the diet and often replace more nutritious foods that contain vitamins, minerals and fiber.

A second problem is the impact of sugar on

weight control. Actually, a teaspoon of sugar is just 16 calories, which makes it no more fattening than protein or carbohydrate and less than half as fattening as fats or oils. But we do not consume quantities of sugar by itself, teaspoon by teaspoon. The greatest amount is eaten in processed foods, small quantities of which can contain large amounts of sugar. The following are good examples:

Food	Calories	Teaspoons of Sugar	% of Calories from Sugar
Shasta Orange Soda (12 oz.)	172	11.8	100%
Coca-Cola (12 oz.)	144	9.3	100
Popsicle (1)	70	4.5	100
General Mills Boo Berry Cereal (1 oz.)	110	3.3	47
Snickers candy bar (2 oz.)	258	7.3	42
Milky Way candy bar (2.1 oz.)	270	9.0	21

In addition, many "sugary foods," such as candy bars, are actually far richer in fat (and thus high in calories), producing a double whammy on efforts to control weight. In light of the fact that abdominal obesity seems to increase cardiac risk, the excess calories from sugar and or sugar/fat are simply not prudent.

A third problem is that foods rich in sugar generally provide very little mass, which means there's no signal that you've had enough to eat. You can consume virtually an unlimited amount of candy bars (and a large number of calories) without feeling full. Foods containing refined sugar often result in the simultaneous extremes of being overfed yet still feeling hungry. Foods containing natural sugar—fruits, berries, vegetables and grains—are just the opposite.

These foods are low in calories but contain significant bulk. A great many strawberries at 55 calories per cup would have to be eaten before too many calories would be consumed. Because of the mass of the food, the person eating them would feel full before consuming too many calories.

And finally, studies in Japan, South Africa and the United States show that refined sugar can elevate triglycerides, which can work like cholesterol to clog coronary arteries. It is estimated that about 20 million Americans have a genetic predisposition to high triglycerides, which can be triggered by excessive sugar in the diet. Studies reveal that people with the highest triglyceride levels also have the highest rate of heart attack. In addition, the combination of high triglycerides and low HDLs produces Syndrome X, which significantly increases the risk of coronary heart disease.

PART III

PREPARING FOR DIETARY CHANGE

CHAPTER ELEVEN

THE BASIC PRINCIPLES

Changing dietary habits starts with a conscious decision. But simply making this decision does not guarantee success. Millions of people resolve to eat less fat and more fruits and vegetables, set out strongly to do so, yet fail in the end. Changes usually work well at first. Oatmeal replaces Danish pastry, apples take the place of candy, and carrots substitute for potato chips. But within a week or so, efforts typically become sporadic and begin to wane, and soon the old, comfortable eating pattern is reinstated. This is often a tough lesson to learn: it's one thing to alter food choices for a week, and quite another to change habits for a lifetime.

The word "diet" frequently has a singular connotation in our culture. It is a weight reduction program, a means of shedding excess pounds rapidly by controlling the intake of calories. Overweight people are concerned with a diet. Periodically they go "on" and "off" a diet, much like historian Arthur Toynbee's cyclical theory of history, until either the "on," or more likely the "off," eventually dominates. In this context, there often is no relationship between diet and health.

After researching diet as a cardiac risk factor, I came to understand that it was not a "diet" that was important. Rather, it was a "diet pattern" that was meaningful, long-term eating habits that could gen-erate positive or negative results. An analysis of my diet pattern showed it to be one that had produced a negative impact on my cardiac health. What was needed was a *positive diet*—a dietary life-style that would emphasize healthy eating. The question "How do I want to eat for the next week?" was no longer relevant. Instead, as the Positive Diet concept began to take shape, the question became: "How do I want to eat—and live—for the rest of my life?"

The Positive Diet is based on the following basic principles:

1. Reduce the intake of total dietary fat; when fat is used, substitute unsaturated fats for saturated fats.

2. Increase the intake of complex carbohydrates and fiber.

3. Reduce the intake of sodium.

4. Reduce the intake of refined sugar.

5. Exercise regularly.

Using my own experience as a guide, I determined that the Positive Diet must also meet the following four requirements.

It Must Be Grounded in Sound Nutritional Science. There are no magic foods or quick-fix solutions, as demonstrated by the oat bran and niacin hype of a few years ago. The principles for healthy eating proposed by the Positive Diet are based on the widely accepted Dietary Guidelines for a balanced diet promoted by 10 leading health agencies, including the American Heart Association, the National Cancer Institute and the Heart, Lung and Blood Institute.

It Must Be Achievable and Realistic.
Simply put, it must be in tune with the contemporary American life-style. This means a diet pattern that contains favorite foods, allows for meals away from home and does not entail undue sacrifice. I had too much experience to believe that a diet that doesn't taste good or feel good can be achieved.

What is needed is a diet pattern that is moderate yet effective. For example, while the 30% fat diet recommended by most health organizations is for the general population (many experts feel a diet lower in fat would be better), research shows it may not be sufficiently low in fat to stabilize or reverse coronary disease in most people. On the other hand, experience shows that many people (including some highly motivated heart patients) have an enormous problem staying with very rigid low-fat diets. Such diets, which usually derive about 10% of calories from fat, generally ignore quality-of-life issues and often make people slaves to an inflexible way of eating. Thinking it's an all-or-nothing affair, many people find themselves unable to stick with a 10% fat diet, feel like failures, and revert to their old high-fat diet. In such instances, the very low-fat regimen itself may set them up for failure.

What makes the most sense for heart health and weight control, based on my own research and personal experience, is a diet pattern with 20% of calories from fat.

Research shows that at this level stabilization and regression of coronary disease is possible. Yet such a diet pattern can provide a wide variety of foods, convenience and delicious taste. In addition, it is much more easily practiced in real-life situations such as a Christmas party or dining in a restaurant. A 20% fat diet is the best for effectively balancing good food and good health. For me, it simply means cutting my fat intake in half and doubling my intake of complex carbohydrates and fiber.

It Must Be Based on a Simple System.

There are three areas of concern for everyone who wants to change dietary habits: what you buy in a *supermarket*, what you order in a *restaurant* and what you prepare in your own *kitchen*. In addition, there are numerous dietary areas that impact cardiac health. For instance, saturated fat and trans fat can raise LDL cholesterol, while excessive salt can trigger high blood pressure in some people and excessive sugar can cause triglycerides to rise. But if you try to track every one of these areas, you'll turn eating into a chemistry project. Chances are then good that you'll become confused and frustrated, with the result that you'll return to your old eating habits.

The simplest and most effective way to manage fat intake (and promote more complex carbohydrates) is to maintain a fat-gram budget that tells you how much fat you can have in a day and still meet the prescription for a healthy diet. In managing total fat intake, by necessity you must moderate animal foods, reduce whole-milk dairy products and moderate processed foods. In doing so, you naturally reduce the intake of saturated fat, trans fat, sodium, sugar and total calories. By controlling total fat, you institute a management tool to provide control over other important dietary elements.

It Does Not Have to Be Implemented in One Fell Swoop.

The goal of the Positive Diet is a permanent change in dietary habits that involves an *evolutionary*—not *revolutionary*—process. Permanent change is not accomplished in a pressure-filled, "change everything at once" program. Instead, the Positive Diet uses a series of small steps, established over time, to achieve the long-term results: a 20% fat diet for heart patients, a 25% fat diet for others.

It was easy for me to understand and accept the "why" of the Positive Diet. Much information testifies to the fact that such a diet can be instrumental in good cardiac health. The difficulty was in the "how." When I left the hospital after surgery, I was issued a standard low-fat diet, really nothing more than a listing of so-called "good" and "bad" foods. It was based on the premise that some foods were healthful and should be eaten, while others were harmful and should be avoided.

The missing link was an explanation of how to apply the premise, how to use it to change the eating habits of a lifetime and how to make it work. It just said, "You better do it!" Granted, with the surgery fresh in my mind, my motivation to stay with a new diet was great. But how long, I asked myself, could I survive on carrot sticks—the Peter Rabbit approach to cardiac health—before reverting to my old, comfortable eating pattern? Without the "how," the new diet was meaningless.

"We can only make general dietary recommendations for you," said Dr. Nagle, my cardiologist. "We can't design a diet to specifically suit your needs and tastes, and we can't make it work for you. Many of my patients have started out with a strong motivation to modify their diet. Yet most have been unable to do so with any degree of success. A number have returned to their original diet—the same diet that contributed to their cardiac problem in the first place. Why? Because without a realistic, step-by-step program to follow, the patient never understands how a new diet can be accomplished. Information is not enough. I can give you a four-inch-thick study on cholesterol, but what does it mean to you when you go one-on-one with your refrigerator? For most people, nothing. After a few months of frustration, they give up trying to change."

Dr. Nagle's comments put the situation squarely into perspective. Changing to a healthy diet was critical for me, but how would I make it work? Could I come up with meals day in and day out that I liked and that would still be heart-healthy? Would too much time be spent in preparing them? Would the meals be more expensive? And what about eating in a restaurant or sitting down to Thanksgiving dinner?

Then I read a column by business guru Tom Peters, who said that instead of researching and researching we might be better off to focus on a goal, get off the mark and adapt as we get new information. This made sense not only for America's corporations but for me as well. My decision was to disregard the "woulds" and the "shoulds" and direct my attention to just getting started—but to do so in an orderly fashion with the clear goal of changing my eating habits. I did not believe that even with an understanding of diet and motivation to change, I could instantly reverse a 32-year-old behavior pattern.

As I experimented over the months and years to develop a healthier way of eating, Dr. Nagle's words became even more meaningful to me. It was obvious that if people were to succeed in changing their habits, a bridge needed to be built between science and practical application. My own bridge was built, plank by plank, with slow and often uneven progress. Some things worked; others did not. The author Graham Greene once said that there was no black or white, only shades of gray, and that was how the Positive Diet initially appeared to me—in an elusive, shadowy form. Gradually, however, it took on clarity in the light. After more than 18 years of work, it exists today not just in theory but in reality, as a practical way for good food and good health to come together.

Helping you to make permanent dietary change is the goal of this book. In order to allow yourself the greatest chance for success, you need to get ready for change. The following chapters will give you techniques and concepts to maximize your prospect for success.

CHAPTER TWELVE

MODERATION AND BALANCE

St. Thomas Aquinas, a very wise man, advised that for a happy and healthy life there should be "moderation in all things." Obviously he was unfamiliar with the American culture and its tendency to go to extremes, to test limits, to be excessive. This tendency has led to wonderful achievements in many areas, but in terms of diet it has led to downright swinishment and self-destruction. In any given day in the United States, we consume about 815 billion calories—about 200 billion too many. Simply put, we eat too much and drink too much. Just look at the daily consumption figures for the following items:

170 million eggs
60 million pounds of meat
50 million pounds of sugar
47 million hot dogs
47 million gallons of milk
16 million gallons of beer and ale
6 million pounds of chocolate
4 million pounds of bacon
3 million gallons of ice cream
1.5 million gallons of hard alcohol

The emphasis is evident from a comparison of advertising budgets from 1993. While the National Cancer Society spent just $400,000 promoting fruits and vegetables in its "Five a Day" campaign,

Kellogg alone spent over $13 million to promote Fruit Loops and over $34 million selling Frosted Flakes!

Fortunately, times are changing. People have become more nutritionally literate and better understand how diet impacts health. In less than one generation, the notion of healthful eating has gone from fad to fashion to fact of life. Knowing more about the health aspects of food, and about cooking and eating more sensibly, can help us all to live better, higher-quality lives.

But now we have to face another extreme. Instead of moderating fats in our diet, we try to cut them out altogether. Instead of reducing our intake of alcohol to a reasonable amount, we become rabid prohibitionists. Instead of increasing complex carbohydrates and fiber to a recommended level, we become oat bran junkies. Americans seem to prefer extreme dietary solutions: radical weight-loss regimens, megadoses of vitamins, diets built around one miracle nutrient. This simplistic view of nutrition repeatedly leads to a diet pattern that few people can live with, resulting in frustration and disappointment, and a pendulum-like swing back to the extreme of overeating and overdrinking.

The best way to develop dietary habits that produce lasting results is to steer a *moderate* course. A 40% fat diet is too rich in fat to be healthful. A 10% fat diet can be too bland, boring and complicated to hold our interest for very long. A diet with about 20% of calories from fat provides the best of both worlds, reconciling the pleasures of eating with the health advice of modern nutrition. Remember, developing low-fat habits is a process. If you can't get to 20% right away, do the best you can for now, but keep those figures before you as an achievable goal.

What does "moderation" mean? For one person,

it might mean topping off a low-fat restaurant meal with an occasional piece of chocolate cake shared with three other people. To another, it might mean cutting back from three pints a week to one pint of his beloved Ben & Jerry's. By healthy standards, this is still too much ice cream and too many calories from fat, but consider the substantial progress he has made in terms of calories and fat intake. Had he been given a list of "bad" foods that he was never to eat again, and had this list contained premium ice cream, a sense of deprivation would have set in and the regimen would have lasted one week, tops. As it is, he can build on his success to reduce fat further over time, changing his interpretation of moderation along the way.

Moderation is more easily achieved with some sense of serving size. After all, it's easy to overeat if you don't know what a cup, an ounce or a teaspoon looks like in practical terms. A good method is to use your own palm, fist and thumb:

1 Palm = 3 Ounces. The size of your palm is about the size of a 3-ounce serving of meat, fish or poultry.

1 Fist = 1 Cup. One cup of cereal, spaghetti, vegetables or cut fruit is about the size of your closed fist.

1 Thumb = 1 Ounce of Cheese. As a general rule, a chunk of cheese the size of your thumb is about 1 ounce.

1 Thumb = 1 Teaspoon. One teaspoon of butter, peanut butter, mayonnaise or sugar is about the size of the top joint of your thumb. Three such portions make up about 1 tablespoon.

1 or 2 Handfuls = 1 Ounce of Snack Food. For nuts or small candies, one handful equals about 1 ounce. For chips or pretzels, 2 handfuls is about 1 ounce.

Because it's not a rigid dietary prescription, moderation offers solid ground from which a person can begin to explore and practice dietary change. The methods recommended in the following chapters deal with how to construct a healthy dietary life-style. They are rooted firmly in the concept of moderation and balance, which is the way we want to live.

CHAPTER THIRTEEN

MEAL PLANNING AND CREATIVE SUBSTITUTION

If experience regarding food behavior has taught us anything, it is this: people will eat healthy, low-fat food only when it tastes good and is convenient. If the diet is bland and boring, or takes a spa chef to put it together, most people will not stick to it. That's the reason many patrons of weight loss programs, fresh off an expensive week of dieting, will undo everything with a slice of cheesecake.

Breaking the high-fat habit is too difficult to accomplish if it's approached in an "as-you-go" fashion. Habits change when you make a plan to change them. Two techniques that are critical to success are *meal planning* and *creative substitution.*

MEAL PLANNING

Meal planning is an important step to success and is critical to the establishment of low-fat habits. In a number of ways, the meal plan is like a game plan in football, providing advance direction for what to do to be successful. In football, it's the game plan that defines for the quarterback how he can best move his team against the opposition; it's the game plan that allows him to know in advance what plays he must run. Without such a plan, even an All-Pro quarterback could find himself approaching the line of scrimmage only to ask, "What do I do now?"

It's the same in establishing the Positive Diet. A meal plan defines in advance how to successfully stay on the diet. By preselecting foods/meals that appeal to you and that meet your fat budget, you minimize the selections left to chance. Moreover, meal planning does not have to be employed forever. Its use in the beginning is important to help you create new habits, but centering your diet on low-fat foods will become second nature over a period of time.

Meal planning does take some effort to be successful. Some people have simplified the process by mapping out a general plan for dinners. The following example maximizes foods such as pasta, rice, vegetables and seafood, while including poultry and meat in smaller amounts.

Day	Type of Food
Monday	Soups, stews, pasta
Tuesday	Poultry
Wednesday	Main meal salads
Thursday	Seafood
Friday	Stir-fry, casseroles, chili
Saturday	Restaurants, take-out
Sunday	Meat

This type of general plan provides much flexibility and variety. In the beginning you may find that your meal plan is repetitive. This is to be expected—

after all, you're attempting to change the dietary habits of a lifetime. After a while, however, you'll develop a larger selection of tested menus and recipes, which will give you more culinary choices. Then the meal plan will become more a guideline and less a rigid plan. You don't have to use *my* meal plans to begin and successfully maintain a program of low-fat eating. But it's necessary to use *a* meal plan.

A good way to begin the planning process is to take a two-week period and divide it into 21 meals each. Using the basic principles as a guide, plan a meal schedule that reduces high-fat foods, such as animal foods and whole-milk dairy products, while increasing healthier ones, such as fruits, grains, beans and vegetables. I suggest starting with dinner, since this meal is generally the highest in fat. Fatty red meat is an American dinner favorite, and often poultry and seafood are served fried or in fatty sauces. To ensure a change without totally "giving up" meat (unless, of course, you wish to), chart a meal plan that calls for lean meat at one dinner, poultry at one dinner, and seafood at two dinners a week. In addition, take portion size and cooking methods into consideration. The beginnings of a sample meal plan for dinner might look like this:

DINNERS

	Week 1	**Week 2**
Monday	Chicken Enchiladas	Roast Breast of Turkey
Tuesday		
Wednesday	Teriyaki Shrimp	Grilled Scallops Dijon
Thursday		
Friday		
Saturday	Grilled Swordfish Steaks	Grilled Salmon Fillets
Sunday	Roast Tenderloin of Pork	Marinated Flank Steak

(*Note:* Recipes are found in this book.)

By including some meat, most people avoid feeling deprived. But by eating it less frequently and selecting leaner cuts, low-fat cooking methods and smaller portion sizes, you get the best of both worlds: a low-fat diet that includes meat. Remember to be flexible. If meat for dinner once a week is not satisfactory for you and your family, plan it for two dinners. In addition, make certain that the meatless dinners are well prepared with variety and good taste. If you trade a juicy hamburger for an uninteresting poached whitefish, I can almost guarantee that you'll have a problem. But serve linguine in a spicy red clam sauce, and few people will miss the hamburger.

The meal plan also allows you to figure out how to eat fish and seafood twice a week. This is important because the oil in fish and seafood can dramatically reduce heart attack risk.

Next, consider how to increase complex carbohydrates—rice, beans, pasta, fruits and vegetables. These foods are filling, contain valuable fiber and antioxidants, and are low in fat. Your first effort might be to plan for more of them as side dishes. If in the past you ate a small salad, perhaps one vegetable, and a large serving of meat or poultry for dinner, consider a role reversal. Have a large salad, two vegetables and a smaller entrée—less than four ounces. A dinner of chicken stir-fry, for instance, includes vegetables such as green and yellow peppers, onions, broccoli, cauliflower and pea pods. Serve it with rice and a green salad, and have fresh fruit for dessert. You'll eat to your heart' s content, be full and satisfied, yet remain well within your fat budget. A good perspective when choosing your entrée is to ask, "What two vegetables look good today?" This thought helps ensure that your meals will be centered on complex carbohydrates.

The second way to increase complex carbohydrates is to serve them as entrées. Many meatless dishes that use pasta, rice, beans and vegetables are tasty and satisfying main meals. In addition, defatted chicken or turkey broth makes an excellent base for heart-healthy soups and stews. Examples of appetizing meals include Pasta with Marinara Sauce, Mostaccioli with Tomatoes and Basil, Stir-Fried Vegetables with Soba Noodles, Barley-Mushroom Soup, Red Beans and Rice, Three-Bean Soup, Rice, Smoked Turkey and Sun-Dried Tomato Salad, and Salade Niçoise, to name but a few recipes in this book. Soon dishes such as these will complete your meal plan:

DINNERS

	Week 1	**Week 2**
Monday	Chicken Enchiladas	Roast Breast of Turkey
Tuesday	Stir-Fried Vegetables with Soba Noodles	Italian Vegetable Soup
Wednesday	Teriyaki Shrimp	Grilled Scallops Dijon
Thursday	Penne with Sun-Dried Tomatoes	Salade Niçoise
Friday	Barley-Mushroom Soup	Mostaccioli with Tomatoes and Basil
Saturday	Grilled Swordfish Steaks	Grilled Salmon Fillets
Sunday	Roast Tenderloin of Pork	Marinated Flank Steak

Planning is instrumental in creating meals using savory, wholesome foods with enough palatability and variety to offset less meat. In addition, planned meals are economical. Monday's roast turkey breast, for instance, yields luncheon sandwiches later in the week.

Another advantage in using a meal plan is that it allows for certain favorite but not-so-healthy foods to be gradually phased out rather than eliminated abruptly. Abrupt elimination can cause a feeling of being unjustly deprived and result in resentment. For example, if for years you've regularly eaten a breakfast of ham and eggs, giving it up altogether could be discouraging. All the fat and cholesterol arguments in the world might not work. With planning, you could enjoy ham and eggs one day a week, perhaps Sunday morning, while the remainder of the weekly breakfasts center on cereals, breads, fruit, juice and low-fat dairy products. The result would be not only a reduction in fat, saturated fat and cholesterol, but also a more ready acceptance of the Positive Diet as a permanent way of eating.

Meal planning also involves *all* members of the family in the act of deciding what to eat. Eating is a family affair, and good health is the business of the entire family. When everyone in the family understands why healthy eating habits are advantageous and provides input as to what should be eaten, there is generally more cooperation. Total family participation reduces the number of surprises at meals and leads to a firmer commitment by each person to practice low-fat eating. It frequently results in a sharing of responsibility, pride and support, which helps everyone to establish healthful eating habits. And it's an important healthful model for family members who may be at risk for heart disease.

CREATIVE SUBSTITUTION

Creative substitution is the process of substituting healthful foods and ingredients for harmful ones while still preserving the taste and appeal of the food. In order for a healthy diet to become a habit, as much attention must be paid to good taste as to good health. It's one thing to strip a favorite, yet high-fat food from your diet. It's quite another to fill the void with an alternative that is low in fat, delicious, easily prepared and acceptable to your palate. Low-fat meals do no one any good if they taste so bad that they go uneaten.

The long-term challenge is to come up with delicious, satisfying low-fat meals so that high-fat foods will not be missed. Creative substitution is necessary for permanent dietary change to occur. Fortunately, it is not difficult to achieve. It is an art, and like any other art it can be perfected over time.

The successful employment of creative substitution is based on research showing most American families prepare 12 recipes 80% of the time. So, rather than trying to live with 400 new and unfamiliar recipes, take your family favorites and begin to change them by cutting fat . . . but only to the point where good taste remains. Mom's spaghetti sauce can still be Mom's spaghetti sauce, but with the excess fat removed.

Creative substitution takes three forms. The first is the simple *"one-for-one" exchange* of heart-healthy fare for less healthful food. This is relatively easy to do. Substitute barbecued salmon or broiled swordfish for a New York steak. Select nonfat milk instead of whole milk or "2%" milk. Choose linguine in red clam sauce over fettuccine Alfredo. Replace a salami sandwich with a sandwich of sliced chicken breast. One of the keys here is to substitute foods rich in complex carbohydrates and fiber for animal foods. Moving from chili with meat to chili with chicken is good, but substituting vegetarian chili brimming with beans, pasta and vegetables is better.

The second form involves *substituting low-fat ingredients* for high-fat items in a recipe. This is much more easily accomplished today because of the increased availability of low-fat and nonfat food products. For example, if you're making tuna salad for a sandwich, you now have a choice of regular mayonnaise at 11 grams of fat per tablespoon, light mayonnaise at 5 grams of fat per tablespoon or fat-free mayonnaise with virtually no fat. It's the same for yogurt, ice cream, cheese and hundreds of other food products. What this does is to allow a meal normally unacceptable on a heart-healthy diet to become acceptable by using creative substitution. For example, a chef's salad with cheese, ham and dressing might be too heavy in fat, but one made with low-fat cheese, lean turkey breast, and a low-fat or no-oil dressing would be acceptable . . . and great-tasting!

And finally, the third form of creative substitution is to *alter cooking methods*. French toast made from bread dredged in whole milk and whole eggs, then fried in bacon grease is an artery blocker. But heart-healthy French toast can be made using nonfat milk, egg whites and a nonstick griddle or pan. Traditional French fries are loaded with fat. But made in the oven or in a nonstick pan, "French fries" can be both low-fat and enjoyable.

Creative substitution takes planning, effort and practice, but with proficiency comes an increasing ability to turn negative diet dishes into Positive Diet meals. When this happens, you gain the best of both worlds.

PART IV

SEVEN STEPS TO CHANGE YOUR DIETARY HABITS ONCE AND FOR ALL

CHAPTER FOURTEEN

STEP 1-DETERMINE YOUR PERSONAL FAT BUDGET

A healthy, low-fat diet pattern should be premised on a clearly understood goal that answers the question: *What is the maximum amount of fat I should have in my diet?* While the American Heart Association and other organizations recommend a diet with no more than 30% of calories from fat, many experts counsel less.

As a general rule, my recommendations are as follows:

- If you're a heart patient, need to lose weight or lower cholesterol, or have more than two cardiac risk factors, a diet in which fat makes up no more than 20% of calories is appropriate.

- If you don't need to lose weight or lower your cholesterol, and don't have more than two cardiac risk factors, a diet in which fat makes up no more than 25% of calories is acceptable.

Obviously, you can go lower if you'd like, but in my opinion you should be prepared to sacrifice considerable taste and convenience. If you're interested in changing your dietary habits permanently (rather than eating a very low-fat diet for two weeks, then giving up and returning to your high-fat diet), the above recommendations will produce the best results.

Whatever level you select, a basic question remains: What does the percentage mean? Translating percentage of calories from fat into everyday-life food choices is not easy. For instance, how do you figure the fat percentage when there are four or five different foods on your dinner plate? Food labeling is even more of a problem. Luncheon meat labeled "95% fat-free" actually means that fat makes up only 5% of the product's *weight*. But fat may produce as much as 60% of the luncheon meat's *calories*. So-called "2% milk" is only 2% fat if you weigh it. If you drink it, 38% of the calories come from fat. The bottom line is that most people are simply too confused about percentages to make effective low-fat choices.

The Fat-Gram Method

Whether you decide to eat a diet with 20%, 25% or some other percentage of calories from fat, it's much easier to set a budget and monitor progress using grams of fat rather than worrying about percentages. Fat-gram budgeting is the most effective method of establishing low-fat eating habits. It works like this:

First, determine your *ideal weight*. One way to do this is to use the height/weight tables issued by the Metropolitan Life Insurance Company (see facing page).

Body Weight Guidelines

WOMEN

Height	Small Frame	Medium Frame	Large Frame
4'10"	92–98	96–107	104–119
4'11"	94–101	98–110	106–122
5'0"	96–104	101–113	109–125
5'1"	99–107	104–116	112–128
5'2"	102–110	107–119	115–131
5'3"	105–113	110–122	118–134
5'4"	108–116	113–126	121–138
5'5"	111–119	116–130	125–142
5'6"	114–123	120–135	129–146
5'7"	118–127	124–139	133–150
5'8"	122–131	128–143	137–154
5'9"	126–135	132–147	141–158
5'10"	130–140	136–151	145–163
5'11"	134–144	140–155	149–168
6'0"	138–148	144–159	153–173

MEN

Height	Small Frame	Medium Frame	Large Frame
5'2"	112–120	118–129	126–241
5'3"	115–123	121–133	129–144
5'4"	118–126	124–136	132–148
5'5"	121–129	127–139	135–152
5'6"	124–133	130–143	138–156
5'7"	128–137	134–147	142–161
5'8"	132–141	138–152	147–166
5'9"	136–145	142–156	151–170
5'10"	140–150	146–160	155–174
5'11"	144–154	150–165	159–179
6'0"	148–158	154–170	164–184
6'1"	152–162	158–175	168–189
6'2"	156–167	162–180	173–194
6'3"	160–171	167–185	178–199
6'4"	164–175	172–190	182–204

Source: Metropolitan Life Insurance Company (1959 tables).

Keep in mind that these tables are not very precise. If you do use a Met Life table, make certain it's the 1959 table and not the current table (issued in 1983), which allows for heavier weights. Also, be aware that frame size should not be an arbitrary judgment. A simple method to determine frame size is to measure your wrist just below the wrist bone (toward your hand) with a cloth measuring tape.

For women:
Under 6 inches indicates a *small frame size*
6 inches exactly indicates a *medium frame size*
Over 6 inches indicates a *large frame size*

For men:
Under 7 inches indicates a *small frame size*
7 inches exactly indicates a *medium frame size*
Over 7 inches indicates a *large frame size*

A better estimate of ideal weight, developed by Dr. Richard Freeman of the University of Wisconsin Medical School and based on healthy body-fat levels, is incorporated into the table on the facing page. But remember, ideal weight is a healthy weight guideline for people of average build. And guidelines are just that—guidelines! If your height and weight do not match this table, select your desired weight and follow the figures across that row. This formula has less to do with scale weight than with providing a statistical basis for determining your personal fat budget.

Once you know your ideal weight, you can estimate the amount of daily calories you need to maintain that weight. To a great extent, caloric intake depends on your level of activity. The more physically active you are, the more calories you can con-

Calories Needed Daily to Sustain Ideal Weight

WOMEN

Height	Ideal Weight	Extremely Inactive	Moderately Active	Active	Extremely Active
	1,425	1,710			
5'0"	100	1,100	1,300	1,500	1,800
5'1"	105	1,155	1,365	1,575	1,890
5'2"	110	1,210	1,430	1,650	1,980
5'3"	115	1,265	1,495	1,725	2,070
5'4"	120	1,320	1,560	1,800	2,160
5'5"	125	1,375	1,625	1,875	2,250
5'6"	130	1,430	1,690	1,950	2,340
5'7"	135	1,485	1,755	2,025	2,430
5'8"	140	1,540	1,820	2,100	2,520
5'9"	145	1,595	1,885	2,175	2,610
5'10"	150	1,650	1,950	2,250	2,700
5'11"	155	1,705	2,015	2,325	2,790
6'0"	160	1,760	2,080	2,400	2,880

MEN

Height	Ideal Weight	Extremely Inactive	Moderately Active	Active	Extremely Active
5'2"	118	1,298	1,534	1,770	2,124
5'3"	124	1,364	1,612	1,860	2,232
5'4"	130	1,430	1,690	1,950	2,340
5'5"	136	1,496	1,768	2,040	2,448
5'6"	142	1,562	1,846	2,130	2,556
5'7"	148	1,628	1,924	2,220	2,664
5'8"	154	1,694	2,002	2,310	2,772
5'9"	160	1,760	2,080	2,400	2,880
5'10"	166	1,826	2,158	2,490	2,988
5'11"	172	1,892	2,236	2,580	3,096
6'0"	178	1,958	2,314	2,670	3,204
6'1"	184	2,024	2,392	2,760	3,312
6'2"	190	2,090	2,470	2,850	3,420
6'3"	196	2,156	2,548	2,940	3,528
6'4"	202	2,222	2,626	3,030	3,636

Total calories you need every day: _______

sume. According to the American College of Sports Medicine and the American Dietetic Association, the following levels of activity will provide a guideline for estimating daily need:

Level of Activity	**Calories Needed per Pound per Day**
Extremely inactive, or sedentary	11
Moderately active, or light activity	13
Active, or moderate exercise and/or work	15
Extremely active, or heavy exercise and/or work	18

Multiplying your ideal weight by your level of activity gives an estimate of the number of calories needed daily. A 125-pound woman who is "active," for instance, needs about 1,875 calories each day to sustain her ideal weight.

Once you know your daily calories, you can then convert them into a budget of *grams of fat* per day. The following chart provides you with the maximum grams of fat per day on diets ranging from 15% to 30% of calories from fat.

Grams of Fat Allowed

Daily Caloric Intake	**Percentage of Calories from Fat**			
	15%	**20%**	**25%**	**30%**
1,200	20	27	33	40
1,300	22	29	36	43
1,400	23	31	39	47
1,500	25	33	42	50
1,600	26	36	44	53
1,700	28	38	47	57
1,800	30	40	50	60
1,900	31	42	53	63
2,000	33	44	56	67

Grams of Fat Allowed

Daily Caloric Intake	Percentage of Calories from Fat			
	15%	20%	25%	30%
2,100	35	47	58	70
2,200	36	49	61	73
2,300	38	51	64	77
2,400	40	53	67	80
2,500	41	56	69	83
2,600	43	58	72	87
2,700	45	60	75	90
2,800	46	62	77	93
2,900	48	64	80	96
3,000	50	67	83	100

(*Note:* Remember, these are *maximum* grams of fat in a day. Unless you're extremely active, e.g., you run 10 miles a day, or you work in very cold climates, there is no reason to budget more than 60 grams of fat per day. Anything above that figure on the chart is for reference only.)

WHAT ABOUT SATURATED FAT?

The recommendation is to keep saturated fat intake between 7% and 10% of total calories. A person who takes in 2,200 calories a day, for instance, could eat between 17 and 24 grams of saturated fat. Obviously, the lower, the better. By controlling your total fat with a fat-gram budget, and by replacing fatty foods with complex carbohydrates, you will naturally reduce saturated fat at the same time. Unless you wish to eat with a fork in one hand and a calculator in the other, it's much easier to control the one overriding problem—total fat. When your fat budget is in line, so will be your saturated fat intake.

THE CHECKBOOK APPROACH

Fat budgeting is the best method for balancing your diet. And it's easy. It works like a checking account. Let's suppose your fat budget is 40 grams. You start each day with that number of fat-grams in your "account." Then, as you make food choices throughout the day, you "spend" your budget. The key is to stay within the maximum number of fat-grams, which will automatically keep your percentage of calories from fat in line.

Let's use an example of a woman who eats 1,800 calories a day. On a 20% fat diet, she can have 40 grams of fat. She is home for breakfast and dinner but often eats lunch in a restaurant. Here's how a budget can help her to make smarter choices:

Food Choices	Fat-Grams*
Starting Balance	**40**
Breakfast	
Oatmeal, ½ cup	1
Banana, 1 medium	1
Nonfat milk, 1 cup	1
Whole-wheat toast, 1 slice	1
w/ strawberry jam	–
w/ 1 pat margarine	4
Coffee w/ whole milk, 2 Tbs.	1
Midmorning Snack	
Apple	1
Lunch	
McDonald's Grilled Chicken Breast Sandwich	4
Side salad	1
w/ lite vinaigrette dressing, 1 packet	2
Diet Coke	–
Dinner	
Grilled swordfish fillets, 6 oz.	10
Green Giant White & Wild Rice, ½ cup	2

Food Choices	Fat-Grams*
Stir-fried vegetables	–
Tossed salad	1
w/ no-oil dressing, 2 Tbs.	–
Sourdough roll	1
w/ 1 pat margarine	4
Raspberry nonfat frozen yogurt	–
Coffee w/ whole milk, 2 Tbs.	1
Evening Snack	
Pepperidge Farm Wholesome Choice Oatmeal Raisin Cookie, 2	2
Nonfat milk, 1 cup	1
w	
Total fat-grams spent	**39**

*Grams of fat are rounded off to the nearest whole number for ease of calculation. Remember, a fat budget is a guideline, not a rigid formula.

The above example illustrates a low-fat day (the woman stayed within her personal fat budget), yet one that contained delicious, satisfying food and even included lunch in a fast-food restaurant. (If the woman had opted for a vegetarian lunch or dinner, such as lentil soup for lunch or pasta with tomato and basil sauce, the figures for the day would be lower still.) No one would go hungry on such a day as above, yet total fat and saturated fat would be held to a minimum. The budgeting technique makes for the best of both worlds.

Once you've established your budget, it's easy to become more aware of the fat content of food. The budget becomes a criterion against which to measure your food choices in three important areas: grocery stores, restaurants and your own kitchen.

For example, when you buy food at a grocery store, pay attention to the nutrition facts on the label. Instead of guessing about two brands of so-called "low-fat" frozen chicken dinners, you can now determine from the nutritional label on each brand how many grams of fat are in one serving. Then make your decision based on a simple criterion: *Which dinner fits my fat budget?* Skip the hype about "low-fat" and "lean" and go right to the most meaningful figure: grams of fat per serving. The next chapter in this book will tell you what to do.

Restaurant meals present a challenge because they don't come with labels and you have little idea of what's in the food. Using general principles for low-fat eating such as no fried foods and skipping fatty sauces is a good beginning. However, if you want to have a better idea of how certain meals fit into your fat budget, a good reference is my book *The Fat Tooth Restaurant & Fast-Food Fat-Gram Counter*, which provides the average fat content for over 3,500 restaurant foods. This information lets you know that while a plate of pasta bolognese at your favorite Italian restaurant might be fine at 14 grams of fat, fettuccine Alfredo with 61 grams of fat may not fit your budget. The point is that if you know your budget, and you know the fat content of your food choices, fat budgeting can help you develop healthier food habits. In this book, the chapter on "How to Handle Eating in a Restaurant" is your guide.

And finally, when you cook at home, try to lighten up your favorite recipes. It makes much more sense to figure out how to strip away fat from these recipes—but only to the point where the food remains tasty—than it does to worry about introducing a hundred new foods to your family. The chapter on "How to Modify Your Own Recipes" will show you how it's done. Be sure to try the many delicious low-fat recipes in my books, other books and magazines that specialize in reducing fat. By understanding how others reduce fat from foods without sacrificing taste, you can develop your own technique for your favorite recipes.

Fat budgeting can also help you to overcome "fat

tooth" food cravings—the bane of a healthy diet. Let's suppose you're doing well with your low-fat efforts but suddenly have a craving for a cookie. Instead of denying it to the point of bingeing, you can budget for it. As in the example above, the two oatmeal raisin cookies have 2 grams of fat, certainly a reasonable amount to fit into most budgets. The beauty of fat budgeting is that it addresses a low-fat prescription yet allows for all types of foods, including those that satisfy "fat tooth" cravings.

And remember, you don't have to be perfect. There will be days when you splurge or simply "blow it." But such days will not upset a healthy diet pattern. If you go over your budget on one day, *compensate* on the next day or two by taking in less fat. The average for the week will still be within your budget.

Fat budgeting provides you with a simple, effective approach to managing dietary fat intake without deprivation or prohibition. It emphasizes freedom of choice, so no food is "good" or "bad." Instead, your fat budget provides a criterion against which to measure your food choices in grocery stores, restaurants and your own kitchen. By doing so, it puts the control in your hands. It's the first step toward creating healthy dietary habits. Do you have to "count" fat-grams for a lifetime? Certainly not! I'd never stick to a diet that required me to carry around a calculator to add up calories and fat. That isn't practical, and it doesn't work. But using a fat budget for a month or six weeks will let you develop habits for a lifetime. And habits, not diets, are what produce lasting changes and desired results.

CHAPTER FIFTEEN

STEP 2-LEARN TO READ FOOD LABELS

If you live in the real world, you eat packaged foods, so it's essential to know what's in them. You cannot purchase foods in a grocery store with an eye toward your personal fat budget if you have no idea of their fat content.

The proper intent of food labeling is to provide sound dietary advice to consumers. But putting that advice into practice has not always been easy. Finding out what's in the food has been a challenge for consumers and nutrition professionals alike. One reason for confusion in the past is that not all foods have been required to have a nutritional label. Obviously, without any data, consumers have virtually no nutritional information upon which to base their buying decisions.

Even where nutritional labels were required, few people really understood the information provided. What did the USRDA for riboflavin mean, anyway? Most consumers relied on advertising to help them make food decisions. Unfortunately, much food advertising has been more hype than information, often leading the consumer away from healthy choices. Advertising fat content by percentage of weight (as in "95% fat-free" cold cuts), for instance, has been a clever way to deceive customers about the true fat content of the product. Using weight as a standard can even allow hot dogs to be called "low-fat." Because half the weight of a hot dog is water, the fat content is about 30% by weight. But fat actually supplies over 80% of the calories! And what about foods termed "lite" or "light"? In the past, one "lite" cheesecake simply had a lighter texture, and "light" olive oil usually meant a lighter color.

Fortunately, the Food and Drug Administration (FDA) and the U.S. Department of Agriculture (USDA) have recognized the need to provide consumers with better information and are working together to reform nutritional labeling to make it more relevant to today's health concerns and today's marketplace. The new labeling law, effective in 1994, goes a long way in clearing up confusion about what is in the foods we eat. Is the law perfect? Of course not. But it does provide more consistency in describing food products and thus allows consumers to buy with more confidence.

PACKAGED FOODS

Packaged foods like potato chips and canned soup come under the FDA's jurisdiction. Its regulations require that most packaged foods in the grocery store must have a nutrition label and an ingredients list. (Small businesses that sell less than $50,000 worth of food a year are exempt from food labeling regulations, so don't expect to see the new food label on your favorite locally made jam.) In addition, claims like "low-cholesterol" and "fat-free" can be used only if the food meets new legal standards set by the government. Closing down this loophole alone—the ability of food manufacturers to use misleading claims—makes the new law worthwhile.

Each food label carries a section called Nutrition Facts, which summarizes the content of the food. See the facing page for explanatory comments.

Nutrition Facts

Serving Size ½ cup (114 g)
Servings Per Container 4

Amount Per Serving

Calories 90 Calories from Fat 30

	% Daily Value*
Total Fat 3 g	5%
Saturated Fat 0 g	0%
Cholesterol 0 mg	0%
Sodium 300 mg	13%
Total Carbohydrate 13 g	4%
Dietary Fiber 3 g	12%
Sugars 3 g	
Protein 3 g	

Vitamin A	80%	*	Vitamin C	60%
Calcium	4%	*	Iron	4%

* Percent Daily Values are based on a 2,000-calorie diet. Your daily values may be higher or lower depending on your calorie needs:

	Calories	2,000	2,500
Total Fat	Less than	65 g	80 g
Sat Fat	Less than	20 g	25 g
Cholesterol	Less than	300 mg	300 mg
Sodium	Less than	2,400 mg	2,400 mg
Total Carbohydrate		300 g	375 g
Fiber		25 g	30 g

Calories per gram:
Fat 9 Carbohydrate 4 Protein 4

More nutrients may be listed on some labels.

EXPLANATION

Calories tells how many total calories are contained in one serving (90 calories according to the sample label).

Total Carbohydrate. When you cut down on fat, you can eat more carbohydrates. Carbohydrates are found in foods such as bread, potatoes, fruits and vegetables. Information on simple sugars is important for people with blood sugar problems.

Dietary Fiber. Grandmother called it "roughage," but her advice to eat more is still up to date. That goes for both soluble and insoluble kinds of dietary fiber. Fruits, vegetables, whole-grain foods, beans and peas are all good sources and can help reduce the risk of heart disease and cancer.

Protein. Most Americans get more protein than they need. Where there is animal protein, there is also fat and cholesterol.

Vitamins & Minerals. Your goal here is 100% of each for the day. Don't count on one food to do it all. Let a combination of foods add up to a winning score.

Saturated Fat is listed separately because it's the key player in raising blood cholesterol. Since too much saturated fat is particularly likely to result in clogged arteries, it should supply no more than one-third of total fat intake. Note that one type of cholesterol-raising fat not covered is **trans fatty acids**. These are not broken out as a category but are included in the "Total Fat" figure.

Cholesterol. Too much cholesterol—a second cousin to fat—can lead to heart disease. Challenge yourself to eat less than 300 mg each day.

Sodium. You call it "salt," the label calls it "sodium." Either way, it may add up to high blood pressure in some people. So, keep your sodium intake low—2,400 to 3,000 mg or less each day.

Daily Values are listed for people who eat 2,000 to 2,500 calories each day. If you eat more, your personal daily value may be higher than what's listed on this label. If you eat less, your personal daily value may be lower.

For fat, saturated fat, cholesterol and sodium, choose foods with a low **% Daily Value.** For total carbohydrate, dietary fiber, vitamins and minerals, your daily value goal is to reach 100% of each.

g = grams (about 28 g = 1 ounce)

mg = milligrams (1,000 mg = 1 g)

Standardized serving size is now set by the FDA, rather than by food manufacturers, and is based on food consumption surveys to reflect the amount people actually eat. No longer will label readers have to compare a brand of spaghetti sauce that lists a serving as 4 ounces with one that lists a 6.5-ounce serving. This means that if you're trying to decide which brand of spaghetti sauce to buy, it will be easier because different brands will list the same serving sizes. *Servings per container* tells how many standard servings are in the container. For instance, suppose you buy a box of macaroni and cheese that contains 4 servings. If you're sharing this macaroni-and-cheese dinner with only one other person, you'll have to double the calories and fat (and other information) on the label.

Calories tells how many total calories are contained in one serving (90 calories according to the sample label).

Total fat is expressed in grams per serving. This figure is of great importance because it allows you to use your fat budget as a criterion against which to measure the packaged food. If your daily budget is 40 grams of fat, for instance, and a serving of the packaged food contains 13 grams of fat, you're in a position to make an intelligent decision by asking one question: "Does it fit my budget?" *Calories from fat* helps you to see how fat a food is. If you want to know the *percentage of calories from fat*, divide "calories from fat" by "calories." On the above label, for instance, you would divide 30 calories from fat by 90 calories and determine that the food is 33% fat.

Saturated fat is listed separately because it is a key player in raising blood cholesterol. Unfortunately, the new label overlooks trans fatty acids, which also raise blood cholesterol level. Trans fatty acids are included in the figure for "total fat." Many nutrition experts wish that they were listed separately.

The label also shows the amounts of particular nutrients—*dietary cholesterol, sodium, total carbohydrate, dietary fiber* and *simple sugars*—and *protein* in one serving. The above example shows that one serving contains no cholesterol, 300 milligrams of sodium and 3 grams of protein. The information on dietary fiber is particularly important since Americans usually fall short in this department. The information on simple sugars is important for people with blood sugar problems.

A Few Problems

The general consensus is that the new food labels clear up much of the confusion and help people to make healthy food choices. However, a few quirks and loopholes do exist.

While per-serving nutritional information in calories, grams and milligrams is straightforward and simple to understand, the *% Daily Value* may be confusing to some people. This new section replaces the old USRDA and is intended to show how a food fits into the overall daily diet. This is quite helpful when the nutrient considered has a recommended level that is consistent. The recommended level for dietary cholesterol, as an example, is less than 300 milligrams daily. Whether you're male or female, weigh 220 or 115 pounds, the recommended daily intake is the same: a maximum of 300 milligrams. So, if one serving of a food contains 30 milligrams of cholesterol, % Daily Value shows that it constitutes 10% of the recommended level. It's the same for sodium, with a recommended level of less than 2,400 milligrams daily, and for nutrients that carry no recommended level, such as sugars and protein.

But when dealing with fat, % Daily Value can be confusing in three ways. First, it is set for a *2,000-*

calorie-a-day diet. In the above example, the food contains 3 grams of fat, which represents just 5% of the fat you could consume if you happen to eat 2,000 calories a day. If you eat more or less than 2,000 calories, you have to make adjustments. And that's where the problem lies. While the FDA chose 2,000 calories because it falls in the midrange of the population's calorie needs, some health professionals are critical of its arbitrariness. Says Cecelia Henning, R.D., "How many average women five feet, four inches tall and weighing 125 pounds can eat 2,000 calories a day without gaining weight? How many teenage boys eat just 2,000 calories? The standard is unrealistic. And for those who do not eat exactly 2,000 calories a day, how many people will do the math to make adjustments? Not very many, I think."

A second problem with % Daily Value lies in the use of percentages itself. The foregoing example, which shows that one serving of the food contributes 5% of the % Daily Value for fat, may be very misleading for consumers. Some people will look at the label and assume that "5% fat" means that fat constitutes 5% of calories, making it a low-fat choice. But in actuality, the "5% fat" *has nothing to do with the percentage of calories that come from fat.* It simply means that if you happen to eat 2,000 calories a day, a serving of this food will constitute 5% of your recommended maximum fat intake for the day. The food is *not* 5% fat. The label shows that a serving contains 90 calories, 30 of which come from fat. This means that the food is 33% fat!

A better example is cream cheese, which derives 90% of its calories from fat. The small smear of cream cheese used on your morning bagel, however, makes up only 2% of the fat you could eat on a 2,000-calorie-a-day diet. So what does % Daily Value show? It states that the cream cheese is "2%"

fat. Some people will look at the label and think, "Wow! I've just found cream cheese that's only 2% fat. I can eat the whole tub!" Again, this is a good reason to concentrate on fat-grams as opposed to percentages.

And finally, it should be noted that % Daily Value is based on a diet in which 30% of calories come from fat—a standard that many experts consider too high for effective cholesterol reduction and weight control. I prefer a diet based on about 20% of calories from fat.

For me, the number of grams of total fat and the way it fits into my fat budget are far more meaningful than comparisons with an arbitrary daily value. This is why I pay attention to the left side of Nutrition Facts: grams of fat, milligrams of cholesterol, and such.

OLD TERMS, NEW MEANINGS

Food manufacturers and advertisers in the past were able to use terms like "light" and "low-fat" virtually as they wished. No longer. The FDA now requires such eye-catching nutrition terms to meet specific definitions so that consumers will know what they mean.

What the New Label Says	What the New Label Means
FREE	The product contains no or only negligible amounts of calories, cholesterol, fat, sodium or sugar.
Calorie-free	Less than 5 calories per serving.
Cholesterol-free	Less than 2 milligrams cholesterol and 2 grams or less saturated fat per serving.
Fat-free	Less than 0.5 grams fat per serving.
Sodium-free	Less than 5 milligrams sodium per serving.
Sugar-free	Less than 0.5 grams sugars per serving.

What the New Label Says	What the New Label Means
LOW	May be used on foods that can be eaten frequently without exceeding the dietary guidelines for fat, saturated fat, cholesterol, sodium, sugar and/or calories.
Low-calorie	40 calories or less per serving. *(When it comes to meals and main dish items like frozen dinners and entrées, this guideline translates into about 120 calories or less in 3.5 ounces of food.)*
Low cholesterol	20 milligrams or less cholesterol and 2 grams or less saturated fat per typical serving. *(If you're buying a main dish or meal, "low-cholesterol" means about 60 milligrams of cholesterol in a 10-ounce main dish.)*
Low fat	3 grams or less fat per 100 calories. *(Watch out for milk products, which have been exempted from the "low-fat" regulation. So, "2% milk" will be termed "low-fat," even though it contains 5 grams of fat per serving.)*
Low saturated fat	1 gram or less saturated fat per serving. *(A main dish can usually make this claim if less than 10% of its calories come from saturated fat.)*
Low sodium	140 milligrams or less sodium per serving. *(This translates into about 400 milligrams of sodium in a typical 10-ounce main dish meal, or 600 milligrams in a 16-ounce meal.)*
Very low sodium	35 milligrams or less sodium per serving.
HIGH	means the food must contain 20% or more of the Daily Value for a particular nutrient. "Rich in" or "excellent source" may be used instead of "high."
GOOD SOURCE	means that a serving of the food supplies 10% to 19% of the Daily Value for a particular nutrient.

What the New Label Says	What the New Label Means
LIGHT or *LITE*	can mean a number of different things: • If a food contains 50% or more of its calories from fat to begin with, such as sausage or cheese, "light" means that at least half its fat has been removed. • If a food is less than 50% fat to begin with, it can be called "light" if *either* the fat content has been cut in half *or* the calories have been reduced by a third. • For a main dish or meal, "light" means that the dish meets the definition of either "low-calorie" or "low-fat." • "Light" can also mean that the sodium content of a low-calorie, low-fat food has been reduced by at least 50%. However, if the sodium is reduced by 50% in a food that is not low in fat and calories, the label must state "light in sodium." • "Light" can also refer to color or texture, but the label must say so clearly. It can also be used without explanation when "light" has traditionally been part of the food's name, e.g., brown sugar or cream.
REDUCED	means that a product contains 25% less of a nutrient (such as fat) or of calories than the regular product.
MORE	tells you that a serving of food contains 10% more of the Daily Value for a nutrient than the regular food. The label on calcium-fortified orange juice, for example, could specify that the product supplies "more calcium" than regular juice.
LEAN and *EXTRA-LEAN*	describe the fat content of certain meats, poultry, seafood and game meats.

What the New Label Says	What the New Label Means
Lean	Less than 10 grams of fat, 4 grams of saturated fat and 95 milligrams of cholesterol per serving. *(With the exception of many main dishes and entrées, a "lean" food generally has more fat than a "low-fat" food and more saturated fat than a "low in saturated fat" food.)*
Extra-lean	Less than 5 grams of fat, 2 grams of saturated fat and 95 milligrams of cholesterol per serving. *(With the exception of many main dishes and entrées, an "extra-lean" food generally has more fat than a "low-fat" food and more saturated fat than a "low in saturated fat" food.*
PERCENT FAT-FREE	must now be used only on foods that meet the "low-fat" or "fat-free" definitions. However, it may still be misleading as it describes the percentage of fat by weight, not the percentage of calories from fat.

Fresh Meat and Poultry

Fresh meat and poultry are regulated by the USDA. In general, its new labeling regulations match up well with those of the FDA, making it easier for consumers to understand the information provided. However, there are a few exceptions.

The FDA requires nutritional labeling for meat and poultry products other than single-ingredient, raw meat and poultry products available for retail purchase. For instance, chicken franks, corned beef, meat burritos and frozen entrées with meat or poultry are products that must carry nutritional labeling. The label information is based on the product *"as packaged,"* which means that the label must list information about the nutrients in a serving of food at the time it is purchased, without considering further preparation. A label may, in addition, list information *"as consumed,"* provided that it clearly states preparation and cooking methods. "As consumed" information can be of help to the consumer when buying meat and poultry products whose nutritional content changes significantly during preparation. Bacon, which is quite different cooked from raw, is a good example. The nutritional labeling on meat and poultry items that require labels is virtually the same as that used on packaged foods governed by the FDA. So, whether it's a meat burrito or a bag of potato chips, consumers can easily spot grams of fat per serving.

Voluntary Labeling

Although raw, single-ingredient meat and poultry products are not required to carry nutritional labeling, *manufacturers may provide it voluntarily.* Ground beef, chicken breasts and whole unbasted turkeys are among the 45 meat and poultry products under the voluntary program. Major meat and poultry cuts affected include:

- *Beef*—chuck blade roast, top loin steak, rib roast large end, eye-round steak, top round steak, round tip roast, chuck arm pot roast, sirloin steak, bottom round steak, brisket, rib steak small end, tenderloin steak, regular ground beef and extra-lean ground beef.

- *Pork*—loin chop, loin country-style ribs, top loin chop boneless, loin rib chop, spare ribs, tenderloin, sirloin roast, shoulder blade steak, loin top roast boneless, ground pork.

- *Lamb*—shank, shoulder arm chop, shoulder blade chop, rib roast, loin chop, leg.

- *Veal*—shoulder arm steak, shoulder blade steak, rib roast, loin chop, cutlets.

- *Chicken and turkey*—whole (without neck and giblets), breast, wing, drumstick, thigh.

In addition, meat and poultry used for further processing and those in small, individually wrapped packages do not have to bear nutritional labeling.

This voluntary system raises a few concerns. First, although the USDA strongly encourages manufacturers to comply with the voluntary guidelines, there is no directive to do so. The result is that many frequently eaten foods, such as ground beef and chicken breasts, may carry no nutritional labeling. This situation certainly will not be of much help to the consumer. (It is thought that most stores will comply out of fear that noncompliance may turn "voluntary" into "mandated." However, the potential for no information still exists under the law.)

Second, nutritional information may not actually appear on the foods themselves but could be displayed on posters, brochures and other point-of-purchase materials. For example, the package of ground beef you pick up from the meat shelf in your grocery store may not have any nutritional information. Instead, the store may put up a poster or offer a brochure that describes calories, grams of fat and other nutrients in ground beef. This is fine, but it may have less of an impact on the consumer than would a nutritional label on the specific product being purchased.

Finally, serving size for meat and poultry (and seafood) has been set as 3 ounces, cooked. This may make the fat content look better, but many experts believe it to be less than what most people eat.

On the upside, voluntary nutritional information will cover the same food components as those on mandated labels, which include total fat in grams. This information is critical if you are to stay within your fat budget. In addition, the terms "lean" and "extra-lean" will match the definitions on packaged foods. "Lean" meat or poultry contains less than 10 grams of fat, 4 grams of saturated fat and 95 milligrams of cholesterol per serving. "Extra-lean" contains less than 5 grams of fat, 2 grams of saturated fat and 95 milligrams of cholesterol per serving. The standardizing of these terms, particularly for ground meat, is of great importance to consumers trying to reduce fat intake.

According to Dr. Anne Dattilo, a registered dietitian at the University of Georgia, one of the smartest things a person can do is to talk with the butcher to determine the fat content of the meat. "Start with 4 ounces of raw meat or poultry," she says. "This yields about 3.5 ounces cooked, or about 100 grams. If the butcher says the meat is 15% fat, then there will be 15 grams of fat in 100 grams of cooked meat."

KEEP YOUR FOCUS ON FAT

The Nutrition Facts section on labels is a definite improvement in educating the consumer about the makeup of packaged foods, and the new definitions will allow for greater truth in advertising that describes the food. But the sheer number of items to consider may make label reading a frustrating exercise for many people. Don't let it confuse you.

The most important point of information on the label is the number of grams of fat per serving.

Sure, there are a number of other things to be concerned about, but if you can only concentrate on one thing, make it fat. By being certain that packaged foods and fresh meat and poultry fit your fat budget, you manage not only fat intake but generally the consumption of dietary cholesterol, saturated fat, sodium and sugar automatically falls as well. Fat budgeting is the most effective management technique for reducing fat, and knowing how much fat comes in the food makes it work. So, while you might check the label for information on sodium, for instance, fat-gram content is the overriding piece of information upon which to base your food selection.

CHAPTER SIXTEEN

STEP 3-CHANGE THE FOCUS OF YOUR MEALS

The fundamental principles for establishing a diet pattern to reduce blood cholesterol and control weight are 1) moderate the intake of total fat and, when fat is used, substitute unsaturated for saturated fat; and 2) increase the intake of complex carbohydrates and fiber. These two basic principles go hand in hand.

Remember that Americans consume a diet that is 37.5% fat, and of this amount almost one-half is saturated. The average man eats a pound of fat every four days, over 6 pounds a month and 7,000 pounds of fat over a lifetime. The average woman eats a pound of fat every six days, 4 pounds a month and 5,000 pounds of fat over a lifetime. In addition, average daily cholesterol consumption is between 400 and 500 milligrams. And, to top it off, about 40% of American adults eat no fruit on any given day, 40% eat no vegetables and 80% eat no whole grains. The challenge is to reverse this pattern in a realistic way.

Many health professionals believe the proper guideline for fat to be between 20% and 25% of total calories. I agree with this recommendation but counsel a figure closer to 20%, particularly if you're a cardiac patient, have to lose weight or need to reduce blood cholesterol. If these are not problems for you, a diet of 25% fat is appropriate. Saturated fat should make up no more than 7% to 10% of calories. In addition, it is recommended that Americans increase fiber by eating more breads and cereals and by eating five servings of fruits and vegetables a day. A diet pattern based on about 20% of calories from fat is one that can offer delicious foods, and is practical and healthy.

One of the first things you should do is *identify the sources of fat* in your diet. Often simply keeping a three- or five-day record of what you eat will be enough to illustrate where fat is coming from. For most of us, meat supplies the majority of dietary fat, followed by dairy products, table fats and oils, convenience foods, snacks and desserts, and restaurant meals. Once your sources are identified, you can begin to move toward leaner eating habits by changing the focus of your main meals.

MODERATE MEAT

It should be understood that there is nothing wrong with meat. In fact, meat is a good supplier of protein, iron and B vitamins. Indeed, many other foods are higher in fat. A slice of apple pie, for instance, has more than double the amount of fat contained in 3.5 ounces of lean meat. The problem for most of us involves the type and amount of meat eaten. For many of us, meat meals are frequently over 50% fat, the portions are too large, and they are eaten too often. While reducing meat is an important goal, it's unrealistic to think that most people will give up meat altogether. A better way is to figure out how to moderate the amount of meat, not to eliminate it from your diet.

Begin by making a meal plan. As outlined in the previous chapter, plan to reduce meat dinners to one or two per week if you can. Such a plan is important because it strikes an achievable balance: meat is eaten less frequently at dinner but is still included in your diet. This helps to avert feelings of deprivation that can offset sincere efforts.

Next, select leaner cuts. Many favorite meat dinners, such as T-bone steak, prime rib, New York strip, rib eye, rib roast, brisket, pork spare ribs and lamb roast, can have 20 to 30 grams of fat per 3.5-ounce serving. (And few people limit themselves to such a small serving!) These cuts and types of meat could certainly break your fat budget, so they must be avoided. Fortunately, modern breeding and trimming methods have made many leaner cuts available that run between 6 and 9 grams of fat per 3.5-ounce serving. As a rule, beef cuts labeled "loin" or "round" are the leanest choices, particularly when cooked to "well done." According to the Beef Council, some of the best choices include tenderloin, London broil, flank steak, club steak, and eye of the round, round, and sirloin tip roasts.

Cut of Beef (3.5 oz.)	**Total Calories**	**Grams of Fat**	**% of Calories from Fat**
Top round, broiled	179	4.9	25%
Eye of round, roasted	166	4.9	27
Round tip, roasted	183	6.9	34
Top sirloin, broiled	192	7.1	33
Top loin, broiled	205	9.3	41
Tenderloin, broiled	208	9.9	43

Since most nutritional information on fresh meat will be limited (supermarkets will have posters or brochures), you can refer to my book *The Fat Tooth Fat-Gram Counter* for more information.

While it's relatively easy to choose leaner cuts of fresh meat, ground beef continues to be an issue because there is no such thing as a truly lean hamburger patty. However, you can certainly buy the leanest ground beef or ground round available. The new labeling law now defines ground beef in lean-to-fat ratios by weight. If a package is labeled ground beef, it must be at least 70% lean and no more than 30% fat. "Regular" ground beef, for instance, must be 73% lean / 27% fat. Get used to the percentages; descriptions such as "lean" or "extra-lean" will no longer be permitted. Look for ground beef with a higher percentage of lean and a lower percentage of fat.

Remember, the nutritional information on posters and in brochures is given in reference to three ounces of ground beef. Some nutritionists feel that a more realistic measurement is based on 4 ounces of raw ground beef, which when broiled yields a 3.5-ounce patty:

Common Measurements for Ground Beef

% Lean / % Fat by Weight	Calories	Grams of Fat
73% lean / 27% fat	291	21
80% lean / 20% fat	268	18
85% lean / 15% fat	240	14
90% lean / 10% fat	199	11
95% lean / 5% fat	155	6

Be sure to pay attention to the percentage of lean. There is a great difference in the fat content of beef that is "73% lean" and beef that is "95% lean." Read the food label and/or talk to your butcher to get the leanest ground beef available. Generally you'll have no problem finding up to "90% lean" ground beef; "95% lean" ground beef is not often available in most food stores.

Once you've selected the leanest meat, be certain to broil or grill (never fry) it to "medium" or "well done" so that the maximum amount of grease drips off. Patting it with a paper towel to soak up excess surface fat also helps. For pasta sauces and casseroles, cook ground beef in a nonstick pan, drain it well and blot with paper towels.

Keep in mind also that about 40% of beef fat is saturated. (You can multiply the fat-grams in beef by 0.40 to estimate saturated fat content.) So, a 3.5-ounce portion of top sirloin has just 7.1 grams of fat . . . but 2.8 grams are saturated.

For pork, lamb and veal, the leanest cuts are labeled "loin" or "leg." Like beef, many cuts of pork are leaner than in the past. Some lower-fat choices include tenderloin, Canadian bacon, pork center loin and fresh ham. Contrary to industry advertising, pork is not a "white meat" and is not comparable to poultry in fat content. Two of the leanest selections of lamb are loin chop and leg. For veal, the leanest cuts include leg and cutlet.

Keep in mind that pork fat is about 35% saturated. (You can multiply the grams of fat in pork by 0.35 to estimate saturated fat content.) So, a 3.5-ounce serving of roasted pork loin (lean only) contains 14 grams of fat . . . and 4.9 grams are saturated.

If you have access to wild game, a variety of such meats are low in fat. The following table shows that a 3.5-ounce portion, cooked, of certain wild game meat is lower in fat than either beef or chicken:

Type	**Calories**	**Grams of Fat**
Antelope	150	2.6
Buffalo	143	2.4
Deer	158	3.2
Elk	146	1.9
Moose	134	0.9
Pheasant breast (skinless)	133	3.6
Rabbit	173	3.5

Types of game that are not recommended include duck, pheasant with skin, quail with skin, goose and domesticated rabbit.

For lunches, the smartest choice is to avoid high-fat cold cuts and sausages and instead to select low-fat versions or alternatives. Some deli meats like pepperoni and hard salami have about 12 grams of fat per ounce, while bologna and summer sausage can have 8 or 9 grams. Many hot dogs contain 15 to 20 grams of fat. Look for truly lighter versions by reading Nutrition Facts. Hormel Light & Lean Franks and Healthy Choice Franks, for instance, have just a single gram of fat per serving, while Armour Premium Lean Hot Dogs contain 4 grams. An ounce of Oscar Mayer Corned Beef has less than one gram of fat, as does Hillshire Farm Pastrami. (Remember, the average sandwich contains three ounces of meat.) "Chopped" ham has between two and eight times more fat than "boiled," "cooked," "smoked" or "baked" ham. Oscar Mayer Baked Ham has just one gram of fat per ounce. Check food labels carefully for legitimately low-fat sandwich meats. Healthy Choice, for instance, has a line that averages about one gram of fat per ounce. Remember, if you're buying packaged meats, pay no attention to the "95% fat-free" type of labeling; just look for the number of grams of fat per serving. Other low-fat sandwich choices include roasted turkey breast, roasted chicken breast, lean roast beef, water-packed tuna (made with light or nonfat mayonnaise) and lean boiled or baked ham.

Don't offset a good choice by adding other high-fat foods to the sandwich. A tablespoon of regular mayonnaise, butter or margarine will add about 11 grams of fat to your sandwich. The same amount of mustard has just one gram or less. Add a slice of American or Swiss cheese, and you'll pick up another 8 or 9 grams of fat. Select potato salad or coleslaw as a side dish, and you'll easily overspend your fat budget.

Bacon, sausage patties, link sausage and breakfast

sandwiches (both fast-food and frozen) are too fat to be included on a heart-healthy diet. If you want to have meat in the morning, look to a moderate portion of Canadian bacon, but don't have it very often. Make certain the meat you choose is *trimmed of all visible fat* before cooking. You can't do much about marbling, the fat that runs through the muscle, except perhaps not to select a well-marbled cut in the first place. But visible fat must be trimmed or it will melt during cooking and make a high-fat meal out of a lean cut of meat. The difference can be significant even in low-fat cuts. Between trimmed and untrimmed round steak, for example, the difference is about 9 grams of fat per four-ounce portion.

Portion control is also essential to fat reduction. A three- or four-ounce serving of lean meat will not upset most people's fat budgets. Since this amount of cooked lean meat often contains fewer than 200 calories, it's easy to offset the fat in these calories by eating other foods during the day that are lower in fat, particularly fruits and vegetables. Unfortunately, many of us simply eat too much meat, even when we choose the right cut. (It's interesting to note that overconsumption of meat is more a problem for males than for females. When asked in government surveys to list their five "favorite and most frequently eaten meals," males listed meat three times: steak, hamburger and pizza with meat topping. Females did not include meat in their top five foods.) Large servings of meat are no longer appropriate in a population fighting obesity and heart disease. Instead, look to an average serving of about 3.5 ounces—about the same size as the palm of a woman's hand or a deck of cards.

A good way to curtail consumption of meat is to "stretch" it in soups, chili, casseroles and stir-fries by adding pasta, rice and beans. Borrow a concept from Asian cooking, in which meat is used as a condiment, garnish and flavor enhancer to make a little go a long way. It's the difference between serving a steak each to four people or using one steak, sliced thinly, stir-fried with a variety of vegetables and served with rice, to feed four people.

Cooking methods also make a difference. How you cook is as important as what you cook. Frying sears fat in, so it's the least desirable method. Cooking methods that allow fat to drip off include roasting, broiling, baking, grilling, stewing and barbecuing. In general, the longer meat cooks, the more fat is lost, so "medium" and "well done" are preferable to rare. It's also a good idea to braise lean beef or use it in stews so that it doesn't end up too dry. When using ground beef, sauté it in a nonstick pan and drain it on paper towels to defat the meat as much as possible. Be sure to pour off juices before adding other ingredients to browned meat. Less fatty cuts are usually less tender. To enhance flavor and tenderness, marinate these cuts for a few hours before cooking. Fortunately, there are many low-fat and nonfat marinades on the market. In addition, a number of no-oil salad dressings make for delicious marinades.

If you're relying on *frozen meat meals* and entrées for your meat dinner, be certain to make smart choices by reading the Nutrition Facts on the label. Many entrées come smothered in fatty sauces, contain too much sodium, are surrounded by high-fat foods or are sized as "he-man" portions. You need to know how many grams of fat each serving contains and whether or not that amount fits your fat budget. For instance, there's a big difference between Armour Dinner Classics Veal Parmigiana with 25 grams of fat per serving and Armour Dinner Classics Sirloin Roast with 8 grams of fat. The bottom line here is to read labels. If you do use a packaged entrée, be sure to add fresh vegetables, a salad and fresh fruit for dessert. Never trade nutrition for convenience.

MODERATE POULTRY

With the exception of duck and goose, poultry is generally lower in fat than meat. On your meal plan, have chicken or turkey make up one dinner per week. Remember, the recommendation is for a moderate amount of poultry in the diet, so *portion control* is as important here as it is with meat. "People have been heavily blitzed with the message to eat less fat," says Dr. Walter Willett, chief of nutrition at the Harvard University School of Public Health. "But instead of replacing fatty animal foods with grains, beans, vegetables and fruit, as they should, they're eating more low-fat animal foods. A huge chunk of chicken breast has replaced the 12-ounce steak in our culinary repertoire. This may seem sensible, but only if the steak is replaced by a moderate amount of chicken—say three or four ounces—surrounded by rice, pasta, vegetables and other foods rich in complex carbohydrates and fiber."

Poultry is an excellent one-for-one substitute for meat. Chicken breasts pan-fried in a nonstick pan are as easy to cook as minute steaks. Roast and broiled chicken take no more thought than a pork roast. Skewered turkey breast is a great alternative to beef or lamb on the barbecue. Chicken stew is an easy replacement for beef stew, as is teriyaki chicken for beef teriyaki. In addition, ground or shredded chicken and turkey breast can be used as a substitute for hamburger in many recipes, including tacos, taco salad, ravioli and lasagna. Chicken and turkey broths are a flavorful base for hearty soups and stews. Add rice, beans, pasta and vegetables, and you have a nutritious and delicious meal.

A simple rule will lead you to the *leanest cuts* of chicken and turkey: *choose a skinless, white breast*. Unlike meat, poultry is not marbled with fat. Instead, fat is concentrated just beneath the skin. By removing the skin before cooking, you'll save about 5 grams of fat per piece of chicken. If you do leave the skin on during cooking, be sure not to eat it with the meat.

The same relationship exists between light (white) and dark meat. Light meat contains about one-third less fat than dark meat, so a skinless breast is a much better choice than a drumstick or thigh. The following table shows that while a serving of skinless, light poultry would not break anyone's fat budget, dark meat with skin could put a real dent in it.

Poultry Meat (3.5 ounces)	**Total Calories**	**Grams of Fat**	**% of Calories from Fat**
Chicken, light meat, skinless, roasted	163	3.5	19%
Chicken, light meat, w/ skin, roasted	194	7.7	36
Chicken, dark meat, skinless, roasted	207	10.8	47
Chicken, dark meat, w/ skin, roasted	245	15.4	57
Turkey, light meat, skinless, roasted	155	3.1	18
Turkey, light meat, w/ skin, roasted	220	10.1	41
Turkey, dark meat, skinless, roasted	185	7.1	36
Turkey, dark meat, w/ skin, roasted	219	11.4	47

Poultry fat is about 30% saturated. (You can multiply the grams of fat in chicken or turkey by 0.30 to estimate saturated fat content.) So, a 3.5-ounce serving of roasted chicken breast contains 3.5 grams of fat . . . and about one gram is saturated.

If you're buying processed poultry, be sure to *read the label* for the number of grams per serving. This is particularly important when it comes to chicken hot dogs, turkey bacon and turkey bologna, since these and other such products often contain dark meat, skin and fat as well as light meat. These products generally are as fat as their beef and pork counterparts. *One of the worst offenders can be ground turkey.* Three and one-half ounces of some brands contain almost 13 grams of fat! Be sure the label says "ground turkey breast," or have the butcher grind a breast or cutlet for you. It's worthwhile to look for ground breast meat. Substituting ground chicken or turkey breast for regular ground beef can save 9 to 12 grams of fat per 3.5-ounce serving. Also, avoid whole turkeys that are self-basting since the basting solution contains added fat (usually coconut oil, soybean oil, corn oil or butter).

Hot dogs and luncheon meats made from chicken and turkey ride a crest of popularity for their perception of being lean, but many of them are fatty. Some poultry products may be lower in fat content than their beef and pork counterparts, but some are actually higher. In fact, most poultry franks supply as much as 76% of their calories from fat. One Perdue Chicken Frank, for instance, contains 10 grams of fat, while a Louis Rich Turkey Frank contains 11 grams—much more than many beef and pork franks. Chicken and turkey bologna at 8 grams of fat per ounce are by no means low-fat bargains.

Better choices for sandwiches are roasted or smoked turkey and chicken breasts. Use mustard, nonfat mayonnaise or light mayonnaise, and nonfat cream cheese instead of regular mayonnaise on sandwiches, and skip any full-fat cheese. And remember, most commercial chicken and turkey salads are not low-fat selections.

As with meat, *cooking methods* make a great difference. Frying a skinless chicken breast in oil or smothering it in fatty gravy will offset any low-fat benefit and play havoc with your fat budget. Use cooking methods that allow fat to drip off, such as roasting, broiling, barbecuing, baking, steaming and stewing. Don't add fat when cooking. Frying flour-coated or batter-dipped chicken in oil, lard, vegetable shortening or grease can add approximately 3 grams of fat per ounce of meat. Instead, use a nonstick pan with wetting agents such as cooking sprays, flavored vinegars, defatted broth or wine. If you do fry, cut the grease by pulling off the skin before cooking and by minimizing cooking time. Fat absorption is related to the time food spends in oil. After cooking, set the chicken on a paper towel to absorb surface fat.

Make soups, broth or stews a day ahead, refrigerate, then skim congealed fat before reheating. If you use a commercial broth, place it in the refrigerator about four hours ahead of time. When you open the can, remove congealed fat before heating.

Frozen meals can also be a challenge. As with meat, it's necessary to read the label for grams of fat per serving. While Healthy Choice Chicken Oriental with 2 grams of fat or Lean Cuisine Sliced Turkey Breast in Mushroom Sauce at 5 grams of fat would fit your budget, there is little chance that Swanson Hungry-Man Chicken Pot Pie with 41 grams of fat or Turkey Pot Pie with 42 grams of fat would work in anyone's budget.

INCREASE SEAFOOD

The fat in fish has been shown to speed up the clearance of dietary fat from the blood and to make the blood less prone to form clots. Because of the positive effect of fish oil on the prevention of heart attacks, health professionals recommend eating seafood at least twice a week. "Fish is very hard to beat as a food item," says Dr. William Castelli, director of the Framingham Heart Study. "There's something about fish and fish oil that is extremely beneficial and protects against degenerative cardiovascular diseases. In fact, I think people who have had a heart attack or know they have a cholesterol problem would be crazy not to eat fish at least twice per week."

Cardiac benefit seems to hold true for all types of fish, from oily salmon to leaner cod, from ocean fish to freshwater varieties. In the past people were advised to avoid shrimp and other shellfish because they were "too high in cholesterol," but recent evidence shows shellfish to be low in saturated fat and rich in protective oil, and these factors outweigh their cholesterol content. This is particularly true for oysters, clams, muscles and scallops.

Begin by including seafood twice a week in your meal plan for dinner. Since fish oil is so heart-healthy, making the *leanest selection* of seafood is less important than making the leanest selection of meat or poultry. However, the seafood you do select should still fit in your fat budget. (After all, you can gain weight with healthy oils!) Most types of fish contain no more than 5 grams of fat in a typical 3.5-ounce serving before cooking. Some types of fish are very low in fat, such as Dover sole with just one gram of fat. Others are oily and rich in fat, such as Chinook salmon with 10.5 grams of fat.

Fish with 3 grams or less of fat per 3.5-ounce serving include:

Abalone
Clams
Cod
Crab (Alaskan king and blue)
Crayfish
Flounder
Grouper
Haddock
Halibut
Lobster
Monkfish
Mussels
Ocean perch
Oysters
Pike
Scallops
Shrimp
Snapper
Sole (Dover)
Squid

Be sure to read the Nutrition Facts on canned fish labels. Many canned seafood products are preserved in vegetable oil, so there is no additional cardiac benefit from the extra oil. However, it does add a lot of calories. A four-ounce can of Bumble Bee oil-packed tuna, for instance, contain 20 grams of fat. The same size can of Bumble Bee water-packed tuna contains one gram of fat.

Cooking and preparation methods make an immense difference with fish. Frying or deep-frying fish in oil or butter, which adds more than a gram of fat per ounce, can make an unhealthy meal out of a healthy food. If you do fry, use a nonstick pan with a little cooking spray, but avoid butter, margarine, oil and lard.

Higher-fat fish, such as salmon, lends itself to grilling, baking, broiling and barbecuing. Leaner fish, such as halibut, does better with moist cooking methods such as poaching or microwaving. Avoid basting with butter or margarine. If added fat is need, brush the fish very lightly with olive, canola or safflower oil.

Perhaps the biggest problem with fish is the *fatty condiments*—butter, butter sauce, mayonnaise and tartar sauce. A single pat of butter will add 4 grams of fat to your meal; one tablespoon of mayonnaise or tartar sauce will add 11 grams of fat. It doesn't do much good to select a lean fish, cook it in an appropriate manner, and then cover it with tartar sauce. Better condiment choices include fresh lemon and lime, horseradish, tomato salsa, low-sodium soy sauce, flavored vinegars, vinaigrettes and oil-free dressings. Tuna salad is a particular problem, since mayonnaise used too liberally can turn a low-fat choice into a high-fat salad or sandwich. Better choices include light mayonnaise (about 5 grams of fat per tablespoon vs. 11 grams for regular mayonnaise), fat-free mayonnaise, a blend of nonfat yogurt and mayonnaise, and fat-free salad dressings.

Most seafood *frozen meals* today center on fish and shellfish that have been breaded, deep-fried and/or drowned in a fatty sauce, so it pays to read the label very carefully. There's a world of difference between Gorton's Salmon in Dill Sauce with 33 grams of fat and Mrs. Paul's Light Haddock Fillets with 5 grams of fat. The two questions to be asked about all frozen meals are: *How many grams of fat come in a serving?* and *Does it fit my budget?*

INCREASE COMPLEX CARBOHYDRATES

If you're going to change the focus of your meals by choosing leaner animal foods and eating smaller portions, then you must also increase the serving size of foods rich in *complex carbohydrates and fiber*—fruits, vegetables, legumes and whole grains. In addition, many of these foods contain disease-fighting antioxidants.

There are two practical ways to increase complex carbohydrates. First, you can surround a smaller entrée of meat, poultry or fish with larger servings of foods such as pasta, rice, potatoes, vegetables and fruits. These foods are bulky and will fill you up without added fat, keep you satisfied and make your new way of eating a success. This is very important because many people who try to cut down on animal foods without increasing complex carbohydrates find themselves continually hungry. *Complex carbohydrates are of critical importance for men and are a key to their success in changing eating styles.* Research shows that men who don't eat enough to be satisfied can think only about food, and many of them return to their old way of eating. If you're used to a small salad, a half-cup of rice and a large T-bone steak, for instance, changing to a small salad, a half-cup of rice and half a chicken breast may not be satisfying. In fact, you may be starving and look to supplement your meals with snacks or fast foods. Shift instead to a large salad, a full cup of rice or potato, two cooked vegetables (especially leafy green and yellow vegetables, and cruciferous vegetables such as broccoli, cauliflower, Brussels sprouts and Chinese cabbage), a moderate serving of London broil, chicken breast or salmon, and fresh fruit for dessert. By increasing grains, beans, fruits and vegetables, you'll feel full and satisfied and will be better able to cope with a change in eating habits.

A second way to increase complex carbohydrates is to make a meal plan that centers on plant foods. Among the recipes in this book, Spaghetti with Marinara Sauce, Stir-Fried Vegetables with Soba Noodles, Orzo with Steamed Vegetables, Linguine with Clam Sauce, Market Vegetable Salad and Rice, Smoked Turkey and Sun-Dried Tomato Salad are delicious, satisfying dinners and are very low in fat. For lunch, hearty soups such as Italian Vegetable Soup and Chicken Broth with Orzo can replace fast food and cold-cut sandwiches. And hot and cold whole-grain breakfast cereals like Shredded Wheat,

Fiber One and Kashi, whole-grain toast and English muffins, and fruit can replace breakfast meats and eggs. When you eat more complex carbohydrates, fat comes down, fiber and nutrients go up and, best of all, you get to eat more food without taking in more calories or fat.

PASTA

Pasta comes in a variety of shapes and sizes and lends itself to an assortment of dishes. Spaghetti, linguine, rigatoni, penne, fettuccine and vermicelli make delicious, low-fat main dishes when served with a low-fat sauce. Rotelle, fusilli, rotini and shells make tasty salads with fresh vegetables. And pastina and orzo make for hearty soups.

The type of pasta you choose is less important than how you serve it. Drenched in Alfredo sauce or served with a half-dozen meatballs, even the most healthful pasta will become a dish with 40 to 80 grams of fat. A better choice is a marinara sauce or a red seafood sauce with less than 10 grams of fat. Don't overlook Oriental noodles such as soba (buckwheat) and saifun (cellophane); they're particularly good in chicken broth with vegetables and make a tasty main course. Avoid canned, dehydrated and frozen foods and meals with noodles. Many come in fatty sauces or smothered with cheese.

RICE

Rice is a low-fat, nutrient-rich food that makes for excellent side and main dishes. White rice is polished, which makes it more attractive to the Western palate. A better choice is whole-grain brown rice. Like pasta, rice is a food that is often adulterated by fatty add-ons such as butter, butter sauce and gravy. It's better to serve it as a side dish with a few drops of sodium-reduced soy sauce or as a main dish covered with beans or stir-fried vegetables. Cook rice in defatted chicken broth, adding herbs and spices instead of butter. Wild rice is also excellent as a stuffing for poultry. Watch out for packaged rice dishes that contain added fat. Most rice can be prepared without the butter, margarine or oil suggested in the directions on the box. Don't be tricked into thinking that a rice dish is fat- free just because the Nutrition Facts list fat content as zero. Some manufacturers give nutritional information for their products "as packaged" so they don't have to include the fat called for in cooking directions.

Whole Grains

The changing image of whole grains has become a '90s nutrition theme. Once thought to be fattening, these much misunderstood foods are being hailed as nutritional bonanzas. They form the base of the Food Guide Pyramid, the foundation for a healthy diet. Grains have historically held an important place in the diets of all cultures and need to be rediscovered by modern Americans. Try barley (excellent in hearty soups and as a side dish), bulgur (as a breakfast cereal or to replace rice in recipes), triticale (a hybrid of wheat and rye that can also be cooked as a breakfast cereal or as a substitute for rice), couscous (made from wheat and the main ingredient in tabbouleh), cornmeal (eaten hot as corn bread or as polenta), millet, quinoa, amaranth, buckwheat (kasha) and whole-rye or wheat berries.

Potatoes

Potatoes are tasty and filling, high in carbohydrate but very low in fat. How you cook them and what you add to them, however, can turn them into a high-fat food. Frying potatoes changes the fat content dramatically. French fries, potato chips, potato sticks, fried potatoes and hash browns can get over 80% of their calories from fat. One ounce of commercial potato chips, for instance, has more grams of fat than an ounce of Brie!

A good alternative is to "fry" potatoes in a non-stick pan or "French-fry" them in the oven. Fatty condiments such as butter, margarine, sour cream, bacon bits and cheese can turn a low-fat baked potato into a high-fat food. Better toppings include nonfat sour cream, nonfat yogurt, salsa and fresh herbs such as chopped dill, parsley and chives. Defat gravy for mashed potatoes by placing ice cubes in it and then refrigerating it so that the congealed fat can be skimmed.

BEANS AND LEGUMES

Beans and legumes such as navy beans, pinto beans, black-eyed peas and green peas are great sources of fiber and nutrients, including protein, without fat. In addition, many contain soluble fiber, which can help to lower blood cholesterol. A good way to include beans, peas and lentils—the most common types of legumes—in the diet is to mix them with other foods. Examples are black beans and rice, white bean and tuna salad, pasta and beans, bean tacos and falafel. Or add lentils, split peas or black beans to hearty soups and stews. Use pinto beans for ground beef in tacos and burritos. And add navy, kidney and garbanzo beans to salads. A drawback in the past was that it took so long to prepare dried beans. Now, however, canned beans and legumes are available in supermarkets, as are many vegetarian items such as chili beans, bean soup and refried beans.

BREAD

The best choice for bread is whole-grain made from stone-ground flour. The next-best choice is 100% whole-wheat or other whole-grain bread such as rye or pumpernickel. These breads provide better fiber and nutrients than white bread. Read the label carefully when buying whole-grain breads. The words "wheat flour" instead of "whole-wheat flour" mean that the wheat bran and germ have been removed. You can't tell how much fiber is in a loaf of bread by its dark color, since raisin juice or other coloring may have been added.

Ethnic breads, such as French or Italian, contain minimal fat and are a good choice, but their crunchy crusts supply little more fiber than white bread. Most bread contains about one gram of fat per slice, making it less a fat problem in a sandwich than what is spread on the bread or what goes into the sandwich. The exception is a croissant sandwich, which can have 15 grams of fat—the equivalent of four pats of butter—in the croissant.

Bread is important in sandwiches because it can provide variety to keep lunches from becoming boring. Sliced turkey breast makes for a great sandwich, but how many times can you eat it in a week without becoming bored? By changing breads, however, you provide variety. A turkey sandwich made with dark rye on Monday seems different from one made with French bread on Thursday.

At breakfast, try bagels (skip the cream cheese or use a nonfat version) and whole-grain toast or English muffins instead of high-fat muffins, biscuits, Danish pastry or doughnuts. In Mexican recipes, use corn tortillas rather than flour tortillas, which have added fat.

Cereal Grains

Most cereal grains found on the American diet are made from wheat, corn, barley, rye and rice, and come in the form of breakfast cereals. Cereal grains have vitamins, minerals and fiber, and are low in fat. Some, however, have been processed to the point where fiber content is minimal, and many have refined sugar added, so it's important to read the Nutrition Facts. In general, whole-grain cereals such as oatmeal, oat bran, shredded wheat, whole-grain puffed wheat, rice and corn, whole-grain wheat, rice and oat flakes, and mixed-grain hot cereals are the best. A good rule of thumb is to make sure each serving contains 2 or more grams of fiber, no added fat and 5 grams or less of added sucrose or other sugars. Remember, 4 grams of "sucrose and other sugars" equals one teaspoon of sugar. Be aware that granola is usually high in fat and sugar. Brands that contain more than 10 grams of fiber per serving include Kellogg's All Bran with Extra Fiber and Bran-Buds, General Mills' Fiber One and Nabisco's 100% Bran.

Fruits and Vegetables

The consensus of health professionals is that five servings of fruits and vegetables should be eaten daily. (One serving is one-half cup, so we're not talking about a massive amount of fruits and vegetables.) These foods are instrumental to a healthy diet for a variety of reasons. First, they're low in calories and fat yet high in water content and bulk, so they make you feel more satisfied. One-half cup of watery vegetables such as asparagus, green beans, tomatoes, summer squash and broccoli contains less than 25 calories. Lettuce, radishes, celery and raw greens are so low in fat that they can be eaten freely. Compare the fruit you can eat for the equivalent of one tablespoon of oil, about 125 calories:

1 whole cantaloupe
1 whole grapefruit
5 Japanese plums
1.5 cups of raspberries
6 apricots
4 figs
1 cup of pitted sweet cherries
3 peaches
1 cup of prunes
2.5 cups of strawberries
1.5 cups of pineapple
4 tangerines

Second, many fruits contain natural sugars that can satisfy a craving for sweetness without loading up on calories. One medium apple, a banana, 30 fresh cherries and 2 cups of strawberries have about the same calories as 15 jelly beans. Summer fruits are particularly well-suited as substitutes for high-fat snacks. Eat a peach instead of potato chips, cantaloupe instead of a brownie, and you'll cut fat and calories. You can freeze banana slices and sweet, juicy grapes for candy-like snacks.

Third, fruits and vegetables contain fiber, a cancer fighter. Americans consume about 11 grams of fiber a day, but the recommendation is for 20 to 30 grams. Fruits and vegetables can help you reach the recommended level. One-half cup of blackberries, for example, contains 4 grams of fiber, and an apple has 3.5 grams, while ⅔ cup of corn has 6 grams.

And finally, many fruits and vegetables, particularly those that are dark green, orange and deep yellow, are rich in antioxidants that promote cardiac health. Study after study confirms the disease-fighting role of beta carotene (the parent of vitamin A), vitamin C and vitamin E. While the simplest solution might be to pop a vitamin pill or two (in fact, that may be the only way to get sufficient vitamin E to have a protective effect), it's better to get lots of beta carotene and vitamin C from foods. One reason is that foods contain substances that are believed to enhance or supplement the effect of vitamins. Says Jo Ann Carson, R.D., an associate professor of clinical nutrition at the University of Texas Medical Center, "It's much better to eat a diet rich in fruits and vegetables that give you lots of vitamin A and vitamin C, because you get not only those two specific antioxidant vitamins but also a wealth of wonderful other things . . . including fiber."

Beta carotene is concentrated in very dark green and deep yellow fruits and vegetables like broccoli, spinach, carrots, winter squash, pumpkin, cantaloupe, mustard greens, turnip greens, apricots and sweet potatoes. Experts recommend 5 to 30 milligrams of beta carotene a day for optimal antioxidant effect. This can be achieved with a little menu planning. A half-cup of cooked sweet potato and a couple of raw carrots will put you close to 25 milligrams a day.

Foods High in Beta Carotene

Food	Milligrams of Beta Carotene	Food	Milligrams of Beta Carotene
1 cup carrot juice	38	1 medium mango	5
½ cup cooked sweet potato	17	½ cup cooked spinach	4
½ cup cooked canned pumpkin	16	1 cup raw spinach	3
½ cup cooked carrots	11	½ cup dried apricots	3
½ medium cantaloupe	8	½ cup winter squash	3
½ cup raw carrots	5	1 cup cooked collard greens	2
		½ cup raw red pepper	2

For vitamin C, experts recommend 500 to 1,000 milligrams daily as an optimal level. A cup of orange juice, a cup of strawberries and a half-cup of broccoli will put you close to 200 milligrams.

Foods High in Vitamin C

Food	Milligrams of Beta Carotene	Food	Milligrams of Beta Carotene
½ medium cantaloupe	195	½ cup cooked Brussels sprouts	49
1 medium grapefruit	100	½ grapefruit (red/pink)	47
½ cup fresh black currants	100	½ cup grapefruit juice	47
½ cup raw red pepper	95	½ cup raw green pepper	45
1 cup honeydew melon	92	½ cup raw broccoli	41
1 cup papaya	87	½ grapefruit (white)	39
1 cup strawberries	84	½ cup raw cauliflower	36
1 kiwi fruit	75	1 cup raw tomato	34
1 medium orange	70	½ cup cooked sweet potato	32
½ cup orange juice	60	1 fresh lemon	31
½ cup cooked broccoli	58	1 cup raspberries	31
1 medium mango	57		

A few foods are excellent sources of both beta carotene and vitamin C. These include cantaloupe, sweet potato and raw red pepper. Some easy ways to boost beta carotene and vitamin C intake are listed below.

- Use spinach instead of iceberg lettuce for sandwiches and salads.
- Add chopped peppers to omelets, salads and casseroles.
- Add chopped or grated carrots to salads, muffins and casseroles.
- Substitute sweet potatoes for regular potatoes.

- Add tomatoes to salads and sandwiches.

- Carry dried apricots, peaches or prunes for a snack.

- Bake pumpkin bread and muffins (but watch out for fat and calories).

- Eat mangoes.

Vitamin E is the tough one to get through diet. The optimal level is 100 to 800 International Units (IU), or about 133 to 533 milligrams. Some foods are low-fat sources, such as Product 19 or Total breakfast cereals (20 mg per cup), wheat germ (5 mg per ¼ cup), cooked spinach (2 mg per ½ cup) and mangoes (2 mg per one medium mango). However, many sources are rich in fat, including sunflower seeds; sunflower, safflower, canola, corn, olive, peanut and soybean oils; mayonnaise; Brazil nuts and peanuts; and peanut butter. For those who want to supplement their foods with vitamin pills, it's important to first check with a physician or registered dietitian.

The most nutritious way to eat vegetables is raw. If you cook them, do it lightly by steaming in a vegetable steamer, cooking in a pan with a tight-fitting lid using a small amount of water, stir-frying in a nonstick pan or microwaving. Watch out for canned or frozen vegetables in butter, cream and cheese sauces.

And don't add to your fat problem by slathering vegetables with butter, margarine, cheese, cheese sauce, cream sauce or bacon fat. Better toppings include flavored vinegars, sodium-reduced soy sauce, lemon juice, hot sauce and butter-substitute sprinkles.

What About Snacks?

By this point, you should have a good idea of how to change your three daily meals to make them lower in fat. But what about snacks? Understanding how to make smarter choices is extremely important for two reasons.

First, everyone eats snacks. According to the National Eating Trends Report, snacking is a growth industry. Despite better nutritional awareness, the average person now consumes snack foods over 200 times in a year. To appreciate the impact of these foods, consider that the combined expenditure for potato chips, pretzels, corn chips and tortilla chips in 1993 topped $8 billion. Annual candy consumption recently jumped from 19 to 25 pounds per person. There is nothing inherently wrong with snacking. Indeed, some health professionals believe that it's probably healthier to eat many small meals throughout the day than to eat two or three large meals, particularly if they include a large meal at dinner. Eating more often, called grazing, is associated with lower weight and reduced cholesterol. Our problem rests more with what we choose to eat than with how often we eat.

And that is the second important reason: the most popular snacks are usually rich in fat (as well as sodium and sugar). Potato chips, the all-American favorite, are indicative of the problem. With some 50% to 60% of calories coming from fat, eating 8 ounces of chips is tantamount to adding 12 to 20 teaspoons of vegetable oil to a baked potato. A one-cup serving of the snacks listed on the facing page, a mere handful or two during a television program, would penalize your fat budget significantly.

Item	Calories	Grams of Fat
Corn chips	230	14
Cheese combos	510	21
Cheese puffs/twists	235	15
Corn nuts	375	12
Potato chips	150	10
Potato sticks	190	12
Tortilla chips	180	9

It's even worse for peanuts. The small bag served on airplanes has 9 grams of fat. And we usually eat two bags. Three good handfuls, or about a cup, of dry roasted peanuts contain 68 grams of fat. And a Hostess Apple Danish pastry has 20 grams of fat. The point is that just a few servings of high-fat snacks can add up to more than your daily fat budget. It doesn't do much good to refocus your main meals so you can cut down on fat if your snacking habits are working against those efforts. A better choice is to use low-fat alternatives, chiefly fruit and grains. You can snack on these foods practically all you want and still take in fewer than 10 grams of fat.

One of the first things to do is clean your cupboard of chips, candy and other high-fat snacks; it's much easier to avoid such snacks than to resist them. Replace them with a variety of low-fat snacks. Supermarket shelves today are bulging with low-fat choices. If you're looking for something crunchy and chewy, select pretzels, rice cakes, bagels, Armenian cracker bread, dry cereals, low-fat chips or popcorn. Popcorn is as American as apple pie—and can be a whole lot leaner. A four-cup serving (one ounce) of plain air-popped popcorn has only one gram of fat. For a richer taste, use one teaspoon of oil to pop one-half cup of kernels; this will add much more flavor for little fat. If you buy microwave popcorn, choose one of the "lite" versions and be certain to check the label. Good choices include Orville Redenbacher's Smart Pop, Pop-Secret, By Request and Weight Watchers. Each has about one gram of fat in a three-cup serving. Go easy on the salt (try garlic powder or curry powder instead) and never add butter or margarine.

Watch out for ready-to-eat popcorn, such as that found at movie theaters. It's generally high in fat, about 5 to 7 grams per cup. A study by the Center for Science in the Public Interest found that a medium-size bucket of movie popcorn may contain 43 grams of fat and 647 calories. Hit it with "butter" topping, and it climbs to 71 grams of fat and 910 calories. While total fat by itself is enough to condemn movie popcorn, a greater problem is that most of the fat is cholesterol-raising saturated fat. This is because many theaters pop their corn in coconut oil, which is 86% saturated, and use hydrogenated oils in their "butter topping." Compare the following:

Item	Grams of Saturated Fat
Movie popcorn, "buttered," medium size (11 cups)	41
Steak, baked potato with sour cream, salad with dressing, roll with butter	20
Big Mac and fries	14
Bacon, eggs, toast with butter	11

Pretzels are much lower in fat than chips because they're baked rather than fried. Few have more than a gram of fat in a one-ounce serving. Fat-free choices include Eagle Sourdough Hard Bavarian, Snyders of Hanover Old Fashioned, Mister Salty Twists and Michael Season's Organic Mini. Some brands that contain less than one gram of fat per ounce include Bachman Thin 'n Light, Petite and Hard; Mini Whole Wheat and Bavarian Whole Wheat; Uncle Henry's Whole Wheat and Health; Fat Free Gourmet Sourdough, Michael Season's Twist; Sunshine California; Keebler Traditional Knots; and Rold Gold Thin Twists. Some brands are quite high in sodium content, so be sure to check the label.

Many brands of tortillas and potato chips are now baked or microwaved rather than fried. A case in point is Guiltless Gourmet's Tortilla Chips, with just one gram of fat per ounce. Other brands that fall into this category include Smart Temptations Original and No Salt; Tostitos; Barbara's Amazing Bakes; and Fat Free Gourmet. At least two brands offer fat-free potato chips: Childer's 100% Fat Free Salted and Unsalted, and Friday Harbor. Childer's 97% Fat Free, Louise's Fat Free and Fitfoods Fat Free each contain just one gram of fat per ounce. And finally, American Grains Popsters and Tortilla Bites, and Health Valley Fat Free Cheese Puffs with Chili contain little fat.

While not necessarily fat-free, some major brands are offering fat-reduced products:

Product	**Calories**	**Grams of Fat**
1 ounce (about 15 chips)		
Doritos Light Nacho Cheese Flavored Tortilla Chips	110	4
Doritos Original	140	7
1 ounce (about 18 chips)		
Ruffles Light Potato Chips	120	6
Ruffles Original	150	9
1 ounce (about 34 pieces)		
Chee-Tos Light	120	6
Chee-Tos Original	150	9

Product	Calories	Grams of Fat
1 ounce (about 17 chips)		
Pringles Light Crisps	130	6
Pringles Original	160	11

Keep in mind that although the low-fat versions are lighter, if you "can't eat just one" (ounce, that is), the fat and calories still add up quickly—even for the lighter versions.

Rice cakes are crunchy and chewy, but I was never much of a fan until I tried Quaker's caramelized rice cakes. The added sugar is worth it to me, since these cakes taste great. Pretzels (at about one gram of fat per ounce) are a good alternative to potato chips (at 9 to 13 grams of fat per ounce). With the exception of most brands of granola, dry cereals generally have less than 3 grams of fat per serving, and many are fat-free.

Just because crackers and cookies are flat does not mean they're skinny. Some, like Ritz crackers, can contain several grams of fat in a handful. Fortunately, manufacturers now make a wide variety of low-fat versions. Nabisco's Snackwell line of crackers offers fat-free Cracked Pepper Crackers and Reduced Fat Cheese Crackers (at 2 grams of fat per ounce). Other good cracker snacks include Graham crackers, Armenian cracker bread, Ak-Mak, melba toast, Wasa, Kavli flatbreads, Pogens krisprolls, Finn crisp and RyKrisp.

If you like cookies and baked goods, there is a wide range of "fat-free" and reduced-fat versions. Snackwell's Devil Food Cookie Cakes and Chocolate Sandwich Cookies are both fat-free, for example, while the Chocolate Chip Cookies have just one gram of fat in six small cookies. Weight Watchers Chocolate Cake has 11 fewer grams of fat than Pepperidge Farm Chocolate Supreme Cake. Even many of the mixes for cookies and cakes now come in reduced-fat versions.

Type (1 oz. unless otherwise noted)	Calories	Grams of Fat
Standard Cookies		
Chocolate-chip (2)	130	6
Fig bar (2)	106	2
Cream-filled sandwich (3)	140	6
Ginger snap (4)	120	2
Oatmeal raisin (2)	120	4
Low-Fat and Fat-Free Cookies		
Archway Cinnamon Honey Gems (3)	100	0.5
Entenmann's Chocolate Brownies (2, or ¾ oz.)	80	0
Fat-Free Fig Newtons (1, or ¾ oz.)	70	0
Health Valley Fat-Free Raisin Oatmeal (3)	80	0
Pepperidge Farm Wholesome Choice		
Oatmeal Raisin (1, or ½ oz.)	60	1
Raspberry Tart (1, or ½ oz.)	60	1
Snackwell's Devil's Food (1, or ½ oz.)	50	0
Snackwell's Sandwich Cremes (1, or ½ oz.)	50	0
Weight Watchers Fruit-Filled Apple (1)	80	1

Be aware of a potential problem with "fat-free" baked goods. Although fat has been reduced, sugar content has been greatly increased. This poses two problems. First, less fat doesn't necessarily mean fewer calories. The sugar, corn syrup and other refined carbohydrates that often replace fat in "fat-free" products are quite caloric. This is why a small "fat-free" chocolate cookie can contain 50 or 60 calories. "You can get fat from eating too many of these products," says Chris Rosenbloom, an associate professor of nutrition and dietetics at Georgia State University. "In addition, research shows that if people are told a food is fat-free or lower in fat, they tend to eat more of it. The bottom line is that if you are looking to lose weight, loading up on fat-free foods may not be beneficial." A second problem is that a high intake of refined sugar can cause a rise in triglyceride level, which can be a risk factor for heart disease. Again, moderation is the key. It certainly doesn't make much sense to lower your fat budget by overeating "fat-free" baked goods rich in refined sugar.

If you're in the mood for sweet and smooth snacks, try fruit sorbet, frozen bananas or grapes, fruit-flavored gelatin, life savers or lemon drops, nonfat yogurt, nonfat frozen yogurt, ice milk, angel food cake, sherbet, sorbets, tapioca, juice and low-fat applesauce.

Dole's Fruit Juice Bars are sweet and satisfying, and the Frozen Yogurt Bars offered by Häagen-Dazs are practically indistinguishable from their rich and creamy ice cream.

And finally, don't overlook fresh and dried fruit (apples, oranges, grapes, grapefruit, pineapple, peaches, plums, melons and bananas) and vegetables (radishes, celery, carrots, zucchini and cucumbers). Watch out for party dips, especially those made with sour cream or cheese. Nothing adds zip or camouflages ho-hum flavor better than salsa; made from tomatoes, peppers, onions and spices, it's naturally light and goes with just about anything. Also, look in your supermarket for low-fat brands. Guiltless Gourmet, for instance, offers three delicious fat-free dips: Black Bean, Spicy Cheddar Queso and Spicy Pinto Bean.

Occasionally, it's reasonable to have a higher-fat dessert or snack. There will be times, particularly when your "fat tooth" kicks in, when nothing else will do. Then have the food and enjoy it without guilt. But budget for it and understand that it is an exception.

SUMMING UP

- Know your personal fat budget.
- Make use of meal planning to change the focus of your main meals. Think of vegetables, beans, grains and fruit first.
- Make use of creative substitution.
- When you eat meat, reduce the portion size. Choose the leanest cuts, trimmed of all visible fat. Broil, roast, bake, grill, stew, braise or barbecue, but never fry. Cook to medium or well done.
- Use meat as a condiment. "Stretch" it with vegetables, beans and rice to make it go further.
- Avoid high-fat luncheon meats, hot dogs, sausages and bacon. Better sandwich choices include roasted turkey or chicken breast, lean ham and lean roast beef. Check food labels for truly low-fat luncheon meats.
- Defat meat drippings and broths before using.
- Eat moderate portions of poultry. Always cook without the skin. Bake, broil, grill, roast, steam, poach, stew and barbecue, but never fry.
- Choose white breast meat over dark meat with chicken and turkey. Avoid processed products such as ground turkey, chicken hot dogs and turkey bologna.
- Eat fish more often. Preferred cooking methods are baking, poaching, grilling, steaming and broiling. Never fry or deep-fry. Watch out for fatty condiments such as mayonnaise, butter, butter sauce, cream sauce and tartar sauce.

- Base your diet on foods rich in complex carbohydrates and fiber. Plan a few meatless dinners each week. Avoid fatty sauces and condiments on pasta, rice, potatoes and vegetables. Make your daily bread whole-grain. Use more beans and legumes in soups, stir-fries and other dishes.
- Strive to include fruits and vegetables rich in antioxidants—beta carotene, vitamin C and vitamin E.
- Always read the Nutrition Facts on frozen meals to determine whether or not they fit your budget.
- Stock your home and office with a variety of low-fat snacks. Get rid of the high-fat versions. Remember, it's easier to avoid than to resist.
- Watch out for "fat-free" baked goods rich in sugar and calories.

CHAPTER SEVENTEEN

HOW TO REDUCE BUTTERFAT

Among the greatest sources of dietary fat for many Americans are dairy foods such as whole milk and "2%" milk, cheese, ice cream, and butter. Like meat, dairy foods have nothing inherently wrong with them. They're rich in vitamins, minerals and protein, and are a prime source of calcium. They should be included in a healthy diet. Unfortunately, many dairy products also come with unwanted baggage: too much fat. In addition, butterfat is saturated, so it has the same negative impact on cardiac health as does fat from meat. The challenge is to choose low-fat and nonfat dairy foods that provide taste and nutrition *without excess fat,* so it's critical to know the fat content of the food and how it fits into your budget.

The best low-fat choice is skim (or nonfat) milk, a product that gets only 2% of its calories from butterfat yet has all the benefits (calcium, protein) of whole milk. By drinking skim milk instead of whole milk, you'll save 8 grams of fat per cup. At 3 cups of milk a day, that's enough fat and calories saved in a year to equal 22 pounds! In addition, 3 cups of skim milk a day meets the USRDA for calcium and "costs" your budget just 1.2 grams of fat.

Switch to Skim Milk

Type of Milk (8 fl. oz.)	Total Calories	Grams of Fat	% of Calories from Fat
Whole milk	150	8.5	51%
Whole chocolate milk	208	8.5	37
2% milk	125	5.3	38
2% chocolate milk	179	5.0	25
1% milk	104	2.5	22
Buttermilk, skim	88	.4	2
Skim milk	81	.4	2

It takes about a month for most people to get used to the taste of skim milk. A principal problem is trying to change too abruptly. If you're used to whole or "2%" milk, switching to skim milk overnight usually doesn't work. A better method is to make the shift *gradually,* allowing your taste buds time to adjust. Change from whole milk to "2%" milk, then to "1%" milk, and finally to skim milk. (If you're unable to find "1%" milk, use a mixture of one part skim milk to three parts "2%" milk; then, over time, mix in more skim milk and less "2%" milk, until you finally arrive at 100% skim milk.) By making a gradual adjustment, you will greatly increase the chance for your taste buds to adjust.

For recipes that call for milk, cream or evaporated milk, good substitutions include low-fat and skim buttermilk, and skim evaporated milk. Low-fat buttermilk gives a rich, satisfying flavor to pancakes, waffles and baked foods, while skim evaporated milk can be used in puddings and soufflés.

AVOID BUTTER AND CREAM

A few dairy foods are so rich in fat that they fall outside the prescription for low-fat eating. Butter and cream fit this description.

Butter is a main source of fat for many people. It's used on toast, pancakes, waffles and French toast; on rolls, bread and in sandwiches; on potatoes, rice and vegetables; in snacks and desserts such as pies, cakes, cookies and popcorn; and in cooking (sautéing mushrooms, for instance). Not only is butter rich in fat—a single pat has 4 grams of fat, a tablespoon has 11 grams of fat—but over half its fat content is saturated. Ounce for ounce, butter has more fat than prime rib.

For a better understanding of fat impact, consider the following:

1 teaspoon of butter = 1 teaspoon of regular mayonnaise

= 2 teaspoons of French or Italian salad dressing

= 3 teaspoons of mayonnaise-type salad dressing

= 3 teaspoons of cream cheese

= 3 teaspoons of reduced-calorie mayonnaise

= 4 teaspoons of table cream

= 5 teaspoons of sour cream or whipped cream

Butter is an insidious product because you eat a pat here, spread a little there. It may not seem like much, but it adds up quickly. The best advice is to avoid it altogether. A more heart-healthy spread is soft, tub-type diet margarine (see pages 213–14 for more information) or olive oil used very judiciously. Use herbs, spices, flavored vinegars (such as balsamic or seasoned rice vinegar), lemon juice and imitation-butter sprinkles (such as Butter Buds) to flavor vegetables and baked potatoes without added fat. Dip shellfish such as crab and clams in fresh lemon juice instead of butter. Instead of frying or sautéing in butter, use a nonstick pan with lemon juice, flavored vinegar, defatted broth or cooking spray.

Cream is much the same. It's simply too rich to be regularly included on a healthy diet. Consider the following:

- A tablespoon of *half-and-half* has about 2 grams of fat.
- A tablespoon of *light table cream* has about 3 grams of fat.
- A tablespoon of *medium cream* has about 4 grams of fat.
- A tablespoon of *heavy whipping cream* has about 5.5 grams of fat.

If you drink three cups of coffee a day, using half-and-half or table cream can add from 5 to 9 grams of fat to your daily budget. Better choices are skim and "1%" milk. Watch out for nondairy creamers, since many of them contain the same amount of fat as table cream. In addition, some are made with coconut oil, palm oil or hydrogenated fat, which are heavily saturated. Some products, such as Mocha Mix, are made with unsaturated vegetable oils. While the oil used may be more heart-healthy, these products have the same fat and calories as half-and-half.

Whipped cream is so dense in fat that it will easily break your budget. Some imitation products are lower in fat, and some are not, so read labels. Frozen whipped topping such as Cool Whip and Reddi Wip come in "light" versions that contain about one gram of fat per tablespoon—much less than whipped cream.

BUDGET FOR CHEESE

According to the Stanford Center for Research in Disease Prevention, cheese is the hardest food for Americans to trim from their diet. Even in this age of low-fat awareness, we eat about 26 pounds of cheese per person each year. It is a particularly favorite food for women. While men list meat as a "favorite and frequently consumed food," women rank cheese much higher than meat. A good source of calcium and protein, cheese can also be a concentrated source of fat. Most regular cheese is between 65% and 75% fat. This means that a typical 1.5-ounce serving, about two slices of American cheese, contains as much fat as three and a half pats of butter—about 14 grams of fat—and most of the fat is saturated.

In general, hard cheese is usually fatter than soft cheese because it has less moisture and a higher concentration of fat solids. An ounce of cheddar, for instance, has over 9 grams of fat, while the same amount of Brie has about 7 grams. What many people don't realize is that most cheese is as fat—or fatter—than meat. Eat three cheese cubes at a cocktail party, for example, and you've just taken in more fat than 3.5 ounces of London broil! Some people will mistakenly reduce the meat in a recipe and increase the cheese, thinking that fat is being cut. In truth, the modified recipe may contain more fat than the original.

The fat content of most cheese is as follows:

- One ounce of *regular* or *full-fat cheese* has 9 to 11 grams of fat.
- One ounce of *reduced-fat* or *part-skim cheese* has 5 to 7 grams of fat.
- One ounce of *light cheese* has 2 to 4 grams of fat.
- One ounce of *fat-free cheese* has less than one-half gram of fat.

Most whole-milk cheese, such as cheddar, American, Monterey Jack and Swiss, contain more than 9 grams of fat per ounce. So, if you're going to include whole-milk cheese in your diet, budget for it very carefully. Know how much fat comes in an ounce and how many ounces you normally eat. You may have to restrict other foods severely to make whole-milk cheese fit your fat budget. Most of us should eat it only very occasionally.

A greater number of lower-fat and nonfat varieties are available today than in the past, but be sure to read the labels. Many products are now "lower in fat" than the original versions, which can save 6 to 10 grams of fat per ounce, but not "low in fat." Reduced-fat cheddar, for example, may contain 6 grams of fat per ounce. To be sure, it's less than regular cheddar at 9 grams per ounce, but it is not truly a low-fat food. Even the so-called "part-skim" cheeses may be richer in fat than you think. "Part-skim" mozzarella, for instance, has 5 to 6 grams of fat per ounce. Kraft and Healthy Choice offer nonfat American cheese slices that are excellent, and there are many brands of nonfat cottage cheese. Some brands of low-fat or nonfat cheese taste better than others, so keep trying different brands until you find one that you like. Watch out for "imitation" cheese—it's lower in saturated fat because it's made with vegetable oil, but in many cases it contains as much total fat as regular cheese.

Remember, cheese is an excellent food and can be part of a healthy diet. The key is to balance taste with fat content and your fat budget. If you find the low- and nonfat cheeses to be tasteless, budget for the higher-fat versions. Two ounces of Camembert, at about 15 grams of fat, may be the only cheese to ring your bell. If so, budget for it. But don't eat it often. And when you do, be certain to restrict fat in other foods that day.

Read labels for fat-gram information. And watch for serving size as well. Be aware that one ounce of cheese is a pitifully small amount for a real cheese lover. One way to stretch cheese is to grate it, then use teaspoons, not cups, to flavor vegetables, salads, soups and pasta. A sprinkle of sharp cheese (Parmesan, Romano, feta), added at the last moment, will season your meals with a minimum of added fat.

Look for Low-Fat Versions of Dairy Foods

Many dairy foods today have nonfat and low-fat versions. Yogurt, for instance, comes with a wide range of fat, so read the label.

- A cup of *regular yogurt* contains about 8 to 11 grams of fat.

- A cup of *low-fat yogurt* contains about 5 to 6 grams of fat.

- A cup of *nonfat yogurt* contains no fat.

Yogurt is an excellent source of calcium (one cup provides 20% to 25% of the USRDA). It can be eaten by itself or used as a substitute for regular sour cream, mayonnaise and commercial dressings in salads, dips and toppings. Make sure the one you choose fits your fat budget.

Many people enjoy sour cream as a topping on baked potatoes and Mexican dishes, or as an ingredient in recipes like beef Stroganoff. But full-fat sour cream can carry 10 grams of fat in 2 tablespoons. So, look for "light" and nonfat versions. As with cheese, some low-fat and nonfat brands taste better than others. Be sure to try more than one brand to find one that you really like.

Regular cream cheese has about 10 grams of fat per ounce. By comparison, an ounce of "light" cream cheese has 5 grams of fat. But the real find is nonfat cream cheese—one of the few nonfat products to taste almost as good as the full-fat version. Developed by Kraft and Alpine Lace, nonfat cream cheese is available nationwide. Made from skim milk, both brands contain zero grams of fat per ounce and work well as the base for creamy dips, baked in cheesecakes, beaten with powdered sugar for cream cheese icing and, of course, on bagels. Because of government regulations, these products cannot be labeled "cream cheese." Instead, look for "fat-free pasteurized process cream cheese product" on the tub. It doesn't sound good, but it tastes great.

Ice cream is a favorite American food. We eat about 18 pounds of it per person each year. *Premium ice cream* contains the most butterfat, generally about

30 grams of fat per cup. One cup of Häagen-Dazs Vanilla Swiss Almond, for instance, has a whopping 44 grams of fat! Other premium brands are Ben & Jerry's, Frusen Glädjé and Klondike. Many premium ice creams do not list fat content on the label, so you may want to refer to a fat-gram counter for more information. *Regular ice cream* generally contains about 12 to 20 grams of fat per cup. *Ice milk,* often called *light ice cream,* has about 6 to 8 grams of fat per cup. Many brands feature rich and creamy ice milk to rival the full-fat product. Light n' Lively Premium Coffee Ice Milk, at 3 grams of fat per one-half cup, is a viable option for Häagen-Dazs Coffee Ice Cream at 15 grams. *Fat-free ice cream* has no fat at all.

The point is that with ice cream you have many choices to balance taste preference with budgetary concerns. Ice milk or fat-free ice cream can save you 25 grams of fat or more over a cup of the premium stuff. Other good choices are fruit juice bars and sorbets, which are fat-free, and sherbets, which have about 1 to 2 grams of fat per serving. Don't be fooled into thinking nondairy frozen desserts are fat-free. They have no butterfat, but they're loaded with vegetable oil, usually soybean. A cup of Tofutti Vanilla, for example, contains 22 grams of fat.

Fat content in frozen yogurt can vary from 0 to 3 grams of fat per serving. One problem is that serving sizes are not standardized. One brand might list it as 3 ounces, which makes it look lower in fat than other brands of frozen yogurt, ice milk and ice cream that use 4 ounces as a serving. Another problem is that many people order low-fat or nonfat yogurt only to put back the fat with toppings. Two tablespoons of sprinkles, for instance, contain 6 grams of fat. On the positive side, some ice cream companies, such as Häagen-Dazs, are now offering low-fat frozen yogurt that is as creamy and satisfying as their premium ice creams.

What About Eggs?

This might be a good place to consider eggs, even though they're not dairy items. There was a time when an egg breakfast was considered a wholesome way to start each day. Then, with an increased awareness about cardiac risk factors, came an emphasis on eliminating foods rich in dietary cholesterol. As a result, organ meats, shellfish and eggs were severely restricted. More recently, experts have found that the saturated fat in foods has a far greater effect on blood cholesterol than does dietary cholesterol, so emphasis now is on the reduction of fat in general and of saturated fat in particular. On the other hand, it is well recognized that a diet too rich in dietary cholesterol can have an adverse effect on cardiac health, so it's prudent to restrict cholesterol-rich foods.

The American Heart Association recommends no more than 300 milligrams of dietary cholesterol a day. If you're a heart patient or have high blood cholesterol, the recommendation is for no more than 200 milligrams a day. Since most eggs contain from 200 to 250 milligrams of cholesterol, you could easily go over the limit with two eggs for breakfast. That isn't to say that whole eggs should never be eaten. For most people, two or three eggs a week is not a problem. Those who wish to reduce the intake of dietary cholesterol should avoid egg yolks, which contain 90% of an egg's cholesterol and 80% of its fat. Egg whites, on the other hand, contain most of the protein. The challenge is how to eat the whites but avoid the yolks.

Commercial egg substitutes, made primarily from egg whites, work well in scrambled eggs, French toast, omelets and pancakes. They can also be found on restaurant menus.

Comparison of Eggs and Egg Substitutes

Item (2-oz. serving)	Calories	Grams of Fat	Milligrams of Cholesterol
Egg white (1)	15	0	0
Egg Beaters	25	0	0
Healthy Choice	30	1	0
Better 'N Eggs	30	0	0
Second Nature	60	2	0
Scramblers	60	3	0
Simply Eggs	70	5	45
Whole egg	75	5	213

Instead of using egg substitutes, you can modify your recipes to include more egg whites. For example, in a recipe for French toast that calls for four beaten eggs, substitute one whole egg and three egg whites to cut cholesterol by 75% and fat by about 18 grams—with no change in taste. If your favorite potato salad includes hard-boiled eggs, use one cooked whole egg and three or four cooked egg whites.

A problem greater than the egg itself is how you cook it. It makes no sense to scramble egg whites in butter or margarine, for example, or to eat an omelet laced with cheddar or some other fatty cheese. You'd be better off to use a nonstick pan for the scrambled eggs and to emphasize vegetables, not cheese, in the omelet. As with other foods, the bottom line with eggs is moderation. And when you choose to have them, be sure to use low-fat cooking methods.

Summing Up

- Know your personal fat budget.

- Always read the Nutrition Facts on food labels for the number of fat-grams per serving.

- Drink milk for calcium, but make certain that skim milk is the beverage of choice. Learn to drink it over time by making gradual changes so that your taste buds will adapt.

- Avoid butter as a spread or sauce and in cooking. Nonfat cream cheese, jams and jellies are better alternatives as spreads. Use seasoned rice vinegar or balsamic vinegar for flavoring vegetables and other foods without adding fat. Sauté in broth, flavored vinegars or wine, or use a cooking spray, rather than fry in butter.

- Avoid whipped cream, half-and-half and table cream. Watch out for nondairy creamers made with saturated tropical oils.

- Budget for cheese. Most cheese contains more fat than a similar amount of meat, so select low-fat and nonfat cheeses for regular consumption. Save medium- and full-fat cheese for special occasions.

- Many dairy products are available in a wide range of fat content. Read food labels to determine low-fat and nonfat choices for cream cheese, sour cream, yogurt, frozen yogurt and ice cream.

- Limit egg yolks to no more than three per week. Use eggs whites as a substitute. Don't fry eggs in butter, margarine or oil. Avoid cheese, cheese sauce and other fatty sauces on egg dishes.

CHAPTER EIGHTEEN

HOW TO REDUCE TABLE FATS, OILS AND SALAD DRESSINGS

Most people are aware of the obvious sources of fat in their diet—meat, cheese, butter and ice cream. What many do not realize, however, is the enormous contribution made by table fats such as margarine and mayonnaise as well as by cooking oils and salad dressings. Because they're eaten in dribs and drabs, they are often not considered much of a fat problem. But those dribs and drabs add up. Even with more people watching their dietary fat intake today, the average American eats about 55 pounds of fat each year just from margarine, cooking oils and salad oils.

Part of the reason for this high intake is a misconception about table fats and oils. What is clearly understood is that *some fats and oils are more heart-healthful than others.* We know that saturated fats, which are primarily derived from animal sources, tend to raise blood cholesterol levels and are to be minimized. This is why a healthy diet contains moderate amounts of meat, cheese and poultry. We also know that monounsaturated and polyunsaturated fats, which come chiefly in the form of vegetable oils, are more heart-healthy. But while it's true that olive oil is more heart-healthy than butter, this does not amount to a license to eat an unlimited amount of olive oil. A better perspective is:

- **Reduce the intake of *all* fats. Strive for a diet in which fat makes up no more than 20% to 25% of calories. Remember, the overconsumption of fats—including "good" oils—can have "bad" health results.**

- **When you do eat fats and oils, be sure to choose the more healthful ones. The key is to replace saturated fats with monounsaturated and polyunsaturated oils.**

Choose the Best Oils

All vegetable oils contain 120 calories and about 14 grams of fat per tablespoon. (Butter and margarine have 110 calories and about 11 grams of fat per tablespoon; lard, 115 calories and 13 grams of fat.) Look for an oil that is low in saturated fatty acids and high in monounsaturated fatty acids:

Comparison of Various Common Oils

Type	Monounsaturated	Polyunsaturated	Saturated
	(grams of fat)		
Best			
Almond	10	2	1
Canola	8	4	1
Olive	10	1	2
Peanut	6	5	2

Type	Monounsaturated	Polyunsaturated	Saturated
	(grams of fat)		
Good			
Corn	3	8	2
Cottonseed	2	7	4
Safflower	2	10	1
Sesame	5	6	2
Soybean	3	8	2
Sunflower	3	9	1
Walnut	3	9	1
Worst			
Coconut	1	–	12
Palm	5	1	7
Palm kernel	2	–	11
Comparisons			
Butter	3	1	7
Margarine (stick)	5	4	2
Lard	6	2	5

Vegetable oils eaten in moderation do not generally increase cardiac risk, but there are exceptions. Tropical oils such as *palm oil, palm kernel oil* and *coconut oil* are sources of saturated fat and should be avoided. Tropical oils are found mainly in processed foods such as nondairy creamers, imitation whipped cream toppings, frozen meals, salad dressings, cake mixes, pie crusts, soups, cheese-flavored snacks, chips and crackers. Be sure to read the ingredients list on the food label. A telltale phrase is "made with one or more of the following oils." A number of oils may be listed, but you can't tell from the description which oil is actually used. It could be a tropical oil. If palm, palm kernel or coconut are listed, avoid the food.

Another thing to watch out for is the term "all-vegetable oil." This doesn't tell you which vegetable oil is used. Again, it could be a tropical oil. Canned shortenings often boast on the label of being "100% all-vegetable oil" but fail to tell you that palm oil is used. If the food label isn't specific about the term used, assume the worst.

From a cardiac viewpoint, monounsaturated and polyunsaturated oils are the best. But remember, a single tablespoon of *any* oil is rich in fat.

Choose the Best Margarine

Once seen as a healthful alternative, margarine in certain forms is now being categorized as no better than butter. The basic ingredient in margarine is vegetable oil, usually corn or safflower oil. The most healthful margarines have a liquid polyunsaturated oil as their main ingredient. Soft, tub-type margarine and liquid squeeze margarine are good examples. But a problem occurs when polyunsaturated oils are modified to make them solid or semisolid, a process known as hydrogenation. This causes a chemical change in the margarine that produces trans fatty acids, which works in the body like saturated fat to cause a rise in blood cholesterol. From a cardiac standpoint, stick margarine may be about the same as butter.

If you use margarine, look for one that lists "liquid" vegetable oils as the first ingredient. If the first ingredient is "partially hydrogenated" or "hardened," don't buy the product. Remember, all regular margarine has about the same fat content as butter (about 11 grams of fat per tablespoon), so be judicious in its use. You may want to try the many brands of "calorie-reduced," "fat-reduced" and "diet" margarines available today. Most have about 6 grams of fat per tablespoon, or about half that of regular margarine or butter, and only 1 gram of saturated fat. At least two brands—Nucoa Smart Beat and Promise Ultra Fat Free—offer margarine that has less than 2.5 grams of fat per serving and no saturated or trans fat. A good tip is to look for labels that claim the product in question is "saturated-fat-free." In order to qualify for this designation, the food must contain less than one-half gram of trans fat per serving. Other good alternatives are nonfat sour cream or nonfat yogurt on baked potatoes, nonfat cream cheese on bagels, and jam or jelly on toast.

Margarine is not the only food that uses hydrogenation. Watch out for cookies, crackers, potato chips and other processed foods. According to Dr. Helen Brown of the Cleveland Clinic, trans fatty acids make up 24% to 35% of the fat in fast-food French fries. Just one Dunkin' Donut has as much cholesterol-raising fat as a Big Mac, and over half the 61 grams of fat in a Taco Bell Taco Salad with Shell are cholesterol-raising.

Hold the Mayo!

Few foods are fatter than regular mayonnaise with 11 grams of fat per tablespoon. Ounce for ounce, it contains more fat than spareribs. This is why a tuna salad can have more fat than the same amount of meat. Fortunately, there are options. "Light" or "calorie-reduced" mayonnaise contains 4 to 5 grams of fat per tablespoon. And "fat-free" mayonnaise contains less than one-half gram of fat per tablespoon.

One of the keys is taste. Unlike the low-fat and nonfat versions of sour cream, which taste very close to regular sour cream, "light" and "fat-free" mayonnaise does not always have the taste and consistency of regular mayonnaise. Many people like "fat-free" mayonnaise on sandwiches, particularly when a spicy mustard is used. For others, only "light" mayonnaise will do, particularly when it comes to salads—tuna, potato, macaroni. Be sure to try different brands. If you're able to use a low- or nonfat mayonnaise, be sure to guard against using twice as much. The point is that there now exists a range of choices from nonfat to full-fat mayonnaise. Choose those with less fat and use them sparingly.

Item (1 Tbs.)	Grams of Fat
Kraft Free	0
Miracle Whip Free	0
Smart Beat Fat Free	0
Spinblend Fat Free	0
Weight Watchers Fat Free	0
Hellmann's/Best Foods Reduced Fat	3
Nasoya Nayonaise	3
Miracle Whip Light	4
Smart Beat Light	4
Hellmann's/Best Foods Sandwich Spread	5
Kraft Light	5
Weight Watchers Light	5
Miracle Whip	7
Hain Canola	11
Hellmann's/Best Foods	11
Hollywood Safflower	12
Kraft	12
Hain	12

CHOOSE LOW-FAT SALAD DRESSINGS

Most regular commercial salad dressings are about 90% fat, or about 9 grams of fat per tablespoon. This makes them richer in fat than an equal amount of hot fudge. To put it in perspective, a single packet of Thousand Island dressing at

McDonald's contains more fat than one cup of Ben & Jerry's premium chocolate ice cream!

If you use commercial dressings, be sure to try "nonfat" (also called "no oil") or "light (also called "calorie-reduced") versions. "Light" dressings will save, on average, about 7 grams of fat per tablespoon. However, fat-grams can add up rapidly even from "light" dressing if you have a heavy hand. The best choice for commercial dressings is "no fat" or "no oil." Try a variety to see which types and brands you prefer. Wishbone's Healthy Sensations Honey Dijon Salad Dressing, made from nonfat buttermilk, has just 25 calories per tablespoon. If you do eat "light" or "regular" dressing, serve it on the side. Dip your fork in the dressing, then eat the salad. You'll get all the flavor of the dressing but minimize fat intake.

While it's easy to pick up a bottle of salad dressing at the store, making your own at home requires little more effort. Often homemade versions have less fat and more flavor. One of the best ways to make an oil-and-vinegar dressing is to reduce the oil, increase the vinegar and smooth out the taste with broth, apple juice or tomato juice. The standard oil-and-vinegar dressing calls for three parts oil and one part vinegar. Our low-fat version calls for one part oil, one part vinegar and one part broth (or juice). It's delicious.

SUMMING UP

- Know your personal fat budget. Understand that small amounts of margarine, oil, mayonnaise and salad dressings could easily break it.

- When an oil is used, choose heart-healthy monounsaturated (olive, canola) and polyunsaturated (safflower, soybean, sunflower, corn, cottonseed and sesame), but use sparingly.

- Watch out for tropical oils—palm, palm kernel and coconut. Read food labels. Don't be fooled into thinking "all vegetable" oil is necessarily healthful.

- Avoid hydrogenated oils rich in trans fat. Choose soft tub-type and liquid squeeze margarine instead of stick margarine. "Light" and "diet" versions cut fat further but should be used judiciously.

- Never fry or sauté in margarine, cooking oil or other fats. Use a nonstick pan seasoned with flavored vinegars, lemon juice, defatted broth, wine or cooking spray. You'll save 14 grams of fat for every tablespoon of oil you don't use.

- Don't add fat to vegetables. Use seasoned rice vinegar or balsamic vinegar instead of margarine or butter for flavor without extra fat.

- Spread spicy mustard on sandwiches to reduce margarine and mayonnaise.

- Avoid regular mayonnaise in favor of "light" or "fat-free." Watch out for mayonnaise salads such as tuna, chicken and potato, and condiments such as regular tartar sauce.

- Choose "no-oil" or "light" over regular salad dressings. If you must use regular dressing, have it served on the side.

CHAPTER NINETEEN

HOW TO REDUCE SALT

It is widely recognized that reducing the intake of sodium is an important way to maintain good cardiac health. When you get too much sodium, your body may retain fluid as it tries to dilute the sodium. This puts an extra burden on the heart and blood vessels. It is especially important to reduce sodium intake if you have high blood pressure or congestive heart failure. If your doctor has you on a diuretic or "water pill," eating a diet high in sodium will work against the effectiveness of the medication.

The average American eats about 2,400 to 4,800 milligrams of sodium a day. The Food and Nutrition Board of the National Academy of Science suggests an "adequate and safe" daily level of 1,100 to 3,000 milligrams of sodium. Many experts recommend about 1,800 to 2,400 milligrams daily as a reasonable goal to strive for, but even this amount is well over the body's actual requirement for sodium. About 220 milligrams of sodium daily is all that is needed for the body to function properly.

Are sodium and salt the same thing? Not exactly. Sodium is a mineral that occurs naturally in almost all foods. Salt is actually sodium chloride, a compound that is about 40% sodium. Excess sodium is the health issue, and too much salt in the diet is a primary source of excess sodium. With a diet so rich in salt, it should be no surprise that over 60 million Americans have high blood pressure.

Humans are not born with a craving for salt. Rather, the taste for salt is learned. Says Dr. Lot Page of Harvard University, "Salt appetite is determined by early dietary habits and has no relationship to salt need." This means that the taste for salt can be *un*learned.

For many people, salt is a basic dietary component. It's used in cooking and at the table. It's found in foods such as pickles, bacon and potato chips. And it comes in processed foods such as soups, pork and beans, chili and frozen hash brown potatoes.

Identify the Sources of Salt

The *obvious sources* are those in which salt is expected to be found, such as the salt shaker, potato chips and pickles. *Hidden sources* are those in which salt and other forms of sodium are surprise ingredients, such as certain brands of peanut butter.

The obvious sources include:

- Table salt used as a condiment
- Table salt used as a seasoning in cooking
- Table salt used as a condiment in alcoholic drinks such as Bloody Marys
- Salty condiments such as seasoning salt, celery salt, garlic salt, onion salt, soy sauce and bouillon cubes
- Salty foods such as pickles, olives, anchovies, salted herring, sauerkraut, potato chips, pretzels, popcorn and salted nuts

No one is astonished to learn that the foregoing items contain salt. After all, they taste salty. While you might not know that a large dill pickle has 1,940 milligrams of sodium, or a cup of sauerkraut has 1,755 milligrams, one taste and you'd certainly know they contain salt. What surprises most of us are the hidden sources of salt and sodium, such as:

- Processed luncheon meats like bologna, salami and hot dogs
- Ham, bacon, sausage and cured pork
- Canned tuna and salmon packed in oil
- Cheese and cheese spreads
- Vegetable and tomato juices
- Commercial spaghetti sauce, tomato sauce, paste and purée
- Commercial salad dressings and marinades
- Condiments such as ketchup, barbecue sauce, relish, chili sauce, steak sauce and mustard
- Fast foods such as hamburgers, French fries, fried chicken and fish, and pizza
- Commercially baked bread, crackers, rolls, breadsticks, bread crumbs, pastry and desserts
- Candy bars, commercial cake icings and puddings
- Cereals, granola, frozen waffles and pancakes, and pancake mixes

- Salted butter and margarine
- Baking soda and powder
- Canned, frozen and dehydrated processed foods such as soups and chowders, chili, macaroni and cheese, noodle/potato/rice mixes, frozen entrées, baked beans and canned vegetables
- Chip dips
- Breakfast drinks
- Cooking wines
- Canned and dehydrated gravies
- Imitation bacon bits
- Seasoned meat tenderizers
- Antacids

If you eat kosher, be aware that meat is salted after slaughter to draw out excess blood and can contain twice as much sodium as nonkosher meat. You can reduce some of the sodium by peeling off chicken skin and by soaking beef in water for one hour before cooking.

Hide the Salt Shaker

The most obvious source of salt is the salt shaker, so this is the most logical place to start. Many people salt foods even before tasting them. In order to change this habit, the salt shaker should be removed from the table.

In the beginning this can be a problem. Saltless food by comparison may taste bland, particularly if fat has also been cut, and you may long to spice up your meals with a dash of salt. I resisted this temptation by reminding myself of the importance of salt reduction to my cardiac health and by handling reduction one day at a time. "Certainly you can last one day without your salt shaker," I told myself each morning. Soon a month had elapsed, and I noticed a subtle change taking place in my taste buds. I began to enjoy the natural flavor of unsalted foods. A tossed green salad with fresh vegetables, for instance, contained a myriad of pleasing tastes and textures. In the past it had existed merely as a vehicle for carrying salt. Now, with my taste buds no longer dulled, I could taste the many distinct flavors. I also began to appreciate other seasonings—black pepper, garlic and garlic powder, tarragon, chili powder, lemon juice and combinations of dried herbs and seasonings. Many commercial sodium-free seasonings (such as Mrs. Dash and Spike) are also available. Meals could be spiced up, I learned, without using the salt shaker.

After about two months of eating in this manner, I decided to test my taste buds. I made a large salad and salted it just as I had on my old diet. The taste was not as I had remembered it. The salad was too salty to be enjoyable; there was no taste to the food itself. I might as well have been eating cardboard. I knew then that my desire for salt could be diminished permanently and that I could live and eat well without my salt shaker.

If you're a person who has a problem eliminating table salt, consider using a one-hole shaker. Your wrist will give out before you get too much salt on your food. Or consider switching the salt and pepper shakers. Since pepper shakers have fewer holes, you'll get less salt. Salt substitutes, technically potassium chloride, are not always a good alternative. They often trick your taste buds into thinking you're still eating salt, so the craving for salt and salty foods doesn't go away. A better way is to restrict sodium to the extent that your taste buds are weaned away from salty foods. Only then will you be satisfied with less salt.

Reduce Salt in Cooking

The next step is to reduce the amount of salt you use in cooking. Begin by questioning whether salt is really needed at all. In many recipes, the answer is no. The traditional recipe for French toast, for instance, calls for one-fourth teaspoon of salt. What is salt doing in a recipe for French toast? If it isn't needed, do without it.

If salt *is* needed, reduce the amount called for by at least a quarter. If a recipe specifies one teaspoon of salt, use just three-quarters of a teaspoon. You'll find there is very little change in the taste of the recipe. After a few months, make a second reduction by another quarter. Again, you will not notice a change in taste. Then make a final cut of another quarter. The result will be a dramatic reduction in sodium intake with virtually no change in the taste of the food.

It's especially worthwhile to reduce the amount of salt when cooking with processed foods such as canned tomatoes, tomato sauce, tomato paste, and chicken and beef broth as these foods are already rich in sodium. To bring out natural flavors, rely on lemon juice, flavored vinegars, and herbs and spices that are low in sodium, and avoid salty condiments such as sea salt, garlic salt and soy sauce. (Reduced-sodium soy sauce, with about 160 milligrams per teaspoon, can be used in moderation.)

Sodium Content of Common Spices

Spice	Milligrams of Sodium per Teaspoon	Spice	Milligrams of Sodium per Teaspoon
Allspice	1.4	Nutmeg	0.2
Basil leaves	0.4	Onion powder	0.8
Bay leaves	0.3	Oregano	0.3
Caraway seed	0.4	Paprika	0.4
Cardamom seed	0.2	Parsley flakes	5.9
Celery seed	4.1	Pepper, black	0.2
Cinnamon	0.2	Pepper, chili	0.2
Cloves	4.2	Pepper, red	0.2
Coriander seed	0.3	Pepper, white	0.2
Cumin seed	2.6	Poppy seed	0.2
Curry powder	1.0	Rosemary leaves	0.5
Dill seed	0.2	Sage	0.1
Fennel seed	1.9	**Salt**	**2,300.0**
Garlic powder	0.1	Savory	0.3
Ginger	0.5	Sesame seed	0.6
Mace	1.3	Tarragon	1.0
Marjoram	1.3	Thyme	1.2
Mustard powder	0.1	Turmeric	0.2

Learn to Read Food Labels

Once your obvious sources of salt are under control, turn your attention to the more difficult dilemma of controlling the hidden sources. Most of the problem is with processed foods. The number of frozen, canned and dehydrated foods in which salt and other sodium products are a main ingredient is shocking. In light of a "reasonable" daily consumption of 1,800 to 2,400 milligrams of sodium, consider the following:

½ cup of Ragú Old World Style Spaghetti Sauce with Mushrooms has 740 milligrams of sodium

⅔ cup, prepared, of Rice-A-Roni Stroganoff has 1,245 milligrams of sodium

1 packet (2⅜ oz.) of Shake 'N Bake Chicken Coating has 2,557 milligrams of sodium

The amount of salt and sodium included in many processed foods is unbelievable, especially when contrasted with the sodium content of these same foods in their natural state. Fresh peas contain just .9 milligrams of sodium per one-fourth cup serving. The same amount of canned peas contains 230 milligrams. An ear of corn has about 1 milligram of sodium, while a cup of canned corn contains about 385 milligrams. A 3-ounce portion of steak has 55 milligrams, while a frozen meat loaf dinner has about 1,300 milligrams. Processed and convenience foods, mainstays of the "heat and serve" American diet pattern, guarantee a sodium intake high enough to be a health hazard.

One of the keys to restricting salt and sodium is to read the Nutrition Facts on food labels. This will tell you how many milligrams of sodium come in each serving and allow you to determine whether or not it fits your diet. In addition, advertising descriptions on food labels now have more meaningful definitions:

Low sodium means 140 milligrams or less per serving.

Very low sodium means 35 milligrams or less per serving.

Sodium free means less than 5 milligrams per serving.

Reduced sodium means at least a 25% reduction from the regular food.

Unsalted means no salt added (but not necessarily no sodium added).

Also, be sure to read the ingredients list on the food label for sources of sodium other than salt, such as sodium benzoate, sodium nitrate, monosodium glutamate (MSG), sodium bicarbonate and sodium phosphate. Remember, ingredients present in the greatest amount are listed first and those in the smallest amount last. So, if you find salt or sodium as one of the first three ingredients, it would be prudent to avoid the food.

You can make small changes in your food habits to further reduce sodium. Use fresh vegetables rather than frozen or canned. If you do use frozen or canned vegetables, choose those without salt or, if salted, drain off the liquid and rinse thoroughly. When buying deli food, select fresh-cooked turkey breast or lean roast beef over luncheon meats and sausages. Look for low-sodium cheese. While sodium in processed foods may not be as great a health problem as excessive fat, it still pays to read labels and watch for it.

Be Smart When Eating Out

Controlling sodium in a sit-down restaurant is relatively easy to do. Ask that your food be prepared without salt, garlic salt or MSG. Select meat, poultry or fish that is broiled or grilled, and avoid breading and sauces. When you're at the salad bar, skip the croutons, cheese, salted seeds and bacon bits (most of which you'd pass up for reasons of fat!) in favor of fresh, unprocessed fruits and vegetables.

Fast-food restaurants present more of a challenge because they generally prepare their foods one way only. While you're probably not going to eat a lot of fast food if you're concerned about fat intake, it pays to know that many items are loaded with sodium, making them a double whammy for health. The following table, prepared by the Center for Science in the Public Interest, shows the sodium content of some typical fast foods:

Food	Milligrams of Sodium
Hamburgers and Cheeseburgers	
Carl's Jr. Double Western Bacon Cheeseburger	1,810
Jack in the Box Ultimate Cheeseburger	1,176
Burger King Double Whopper with Cheese	1,245
Wendy's Double Big Classic with Cheese	1,555
Dairy Queen DQ Homestyle Ultimate Burger	1,110
Wendy's Big Classic	1,085
Hardee's Big Deluxe Burger	1,060
Hardee's Bacon Cheeseburger	1,030
McDonald's Big Mac	890
Chicken	
Arby's Chicken Cordon Bleu	1,824
Burger King Chicken Sandwich	1,417
KFC Colonel's Chicken Sandwich	1,060
McDonald's McChicken	770
KFC Original Recipe Side Breast	735
Wendy's Grilled Chicken Sandwich	715
Carl's Jr. Charbroiler BBQ Chicken Sandwich	680
Fish	
Subway Seafood & Crab Sandwich, 6"	1,306
Carl's Jr. Carl's Catch Fish Sandwich	1,220
Jack in the Box Fish Supreme	1,040
Hardee's Fisherman Fillet	1,030
McDonald's Fish-O-Filet	930
Subway Tuna Sandwich, 6"	905
Long John Silver's Clams, breaded	410

Food	Milligrams of Sodium
French Fries	
Hardee's Crispy Curls, 3 oz.	840
Wendy's, Biggie, 6 oz.	271
Burger King, medium, 4 oz.	238
McDonald's, large, 4.3 oz.	200
Carl's Jr., regular, 4.5 oz.	200
Dairy Queen, large, 4.5 oz.	200
Jack in the Box, regular, 4 oz.	194
Roast Beef	
Carl's Jr. Roast Beef Club Sandwich	1,950
Arby's Bac 'N Cheddar Deluxe	1,672
Carl's Jr. Roast Beef Deluxe Sandwich	1,340
Hardee's Roast Beef Sandwich with Cheese, large	1,062
Subway Roast Beef Sandwich, 6"	839
Arby's Regular Roast Beef	588
Salads	
Wendy's Taco Salad	1,110
Taco Bell Taco Salad with Shell	910
Jack in the Box Chef Salad	900
Hardee's Chicken Fiesta Salad	640
Subway Turkey Salad, small	479
Wendy's Garden Salad	60
Shakes and Malts	
Dairy Queen Heath Blizzard, regular	410
Wendy's Frosty Dairy Dessert, large	374
Dairy Queen Shake, regular	230
Arby's Chocolate Shake	341
Carl's Jr. Shake, regular	230
McDonald's, Low-Fat (average)	193
Pizza	
Pizza Hut Super Supreme, large, 2 slices	2,197
Pizza Hut Personal Pan Pizza, Pepperoni, whole	1,335
Pizza Hut Traditional Hand-Tossed, Cheese, medium, 2 slices	1,276

Food	Milligrams of Sodium
Domino's Cheese/Pepperoni, 16", 2 slices (thin-crust)	1,042
Domino's Veggie Pizza, 16", 2 slices (thin-crust)	1,035
Domino's Deluxe Pizza, 16", 2 slices (thin-crust)	954

SUMMING UP

The Positive Diet is not salt- or sodium-free. However, it is designed to moderate salt and sodium consumption with a few simple guidelines:

- Avoid using salt as a condiment; remove the salt shaker from the table.

- Reduce salt called for in recipes by 25% initially, by 75% ultimately. Never add salt to processed foods.

- Avoid using sodium-rich seasonings, seasoning salt and soy sauce. Instead, use lemon juice, flavored vinegars, fresh/dried herbs and spices.

- Moderate the intake of obviously salty foods such as pickles, salted nuts, sauerkraut and potato chips.

- Make smart choices in restaurants. Consider salt as well as fat.

- Moderate processed foods as much as possible. When using them, read Nutrition Facts carefully. Try to center your diet on fresh foods.

CHAPTER TWENTY

HOW TO REDUCE SUGAR

Americans love sugar. The average adult consumes more than a third of a pound of sugar each day—about 143 pounds per year. The figure is even higher for children and adolescents, almost 275 pounds per year. Thus sugar accounts for 24% of calories consumed on the American diet. (Alcohol, a refined sugar, accounts for an additional 5% of calories.) Contrary to popular belief, we do not get most of our sugar from the sugar bowl. Table sugar, or sucrose, is responsible for just 30% of total sugar intake. The preponderance of dietary sugar comes from processed foods and alcohol.

IDENTIFY THE SOURCES OF SUGAR

The first thing to do is to identify the sources of sugar in your diet. Some of the most common *obvious sources* include:

- Table sugar, powdered sugar and brown sugar used on cereal, fruit, berries and in coffee and tea

- Table sugar, powdered sugar and brown sugar used in cooking and baking

- Table sugar used in drinks such as iced tea and lemonade

The obvious sources revolve around table sugar added to foods and drinks, so they are somewhat expected. What generally is more of a surprise is the seemingly infinite number of foods that are *hidden sources* of sugar, including:

- Candy and sugary snacks such as gum drops, mints and chocolate bars

- Soft drinks such as soda pop and cocoa mixes

- Ice cream, shakes and flavored milk

- Commercially baked pastry and desserts such as pies, cakes (and frostings) and cookies

- Commercially baked bread, crackers, rolls, biscuits and breadsticks

- Canned fruits

- Sugared breakfast cereals

- Jams, jellies and marmalades

- Cured meats

- Salad dressings, ketchup and other condiments
- Peanut butter
- Processed foods such as baked beans, tomato sauce and soups
- Alcoholic beverages

HIDE THE SUGAR BOWL

Removing the sugar bowl from the table is important because many people routinely use table sugar liberally on fruit and cereals. To be honest, when I tried this, much of the food initially tasted bland. Again, I used the one-day-at-a-time method. By never looking forward more than 24 hours, the reduction of sugar became a short-term problem. Within six weeks, my taste buds became acclimated to the natural taste of foods. I began to relish new flavors and textures. A bowl of blueberries could now be appreciated for its natural sweetness; to add refined sugar was to gild the lily. The nutty flavor of breakfast cereal was discovered. The true flavor of fruit, cereal and other foods more than compensated for the loss of table sugar.

MODERATE SOFT DRINKS

Next, look at what you drink in the course of a day. You may be surprised to learn that much of it is rich in sugar. Soft drinks are the single greatest source of sugar in most people's diets. The amount of sugar that comes in a can or bottle can be almost incredible.

Soft Drink (12 oz.)	Calories	Teaspoons of Sugar	% of Calories from Sugar
Canada Dry Ginger Ale	130	8.0	94.8%
Canada Dry Tonic Water	140	8.4	97.7
Coca-Cola	144	9.3	100
Mountain Dew	178	11.0	100
On Tap Root Beer	162	10.3	100
Pepsi-Cola	158	10.0	100
Shasta Ginger Ale	118	8.0	100
Shasta Orange	172	11.8	100
Sprite	142	9.0	100

Some people have given up sugar-rich drinks in favor of "diet soda" made with aspartame, an artificial sweetener that is 180 times sweeter than real sugar. There were some concerns initially about the effects of aspartame. Certainly people born with the rare metabolic disorder called phenylketonuria, or PKU, have to avoid aspartame. That is why diet soda made with aspartame carries a warning label. Some people have complained of headaches, nausea and mood swings. And finally, there was the question of a potential link to cancer. After much study, however, the Food and Drug Administration gave aspartame a clean bill of health.

Nonetheless, while diet beverages may be safe, research shows that people often drink more of them and crave more sugary snacks. According to the Eating Disorder Clinic of Brigham Young University, sweet-tasting drinks (including those made with artificial sweeteners) often cause a craving for more and more sugar. Perhaps this is why, as the consumption of diet beverages has increased, so has the consumption of snack foods.

The solution is to avoid sugary beverages, drink diet beverages *only in moderation* and make water your first choice. Try to drink five or six glasses of water a day. Not only is it a better thirst-quencher, but it also helps to keep you feeling full and satisfied and to avoid overeating. Keep a pitcher of ice water and sliced lemons or limes in the refrigerator. Drink bottled mineral water on your "coffee breaks." Fruit juice diluted with club soda or mineral water is also refreshing and cuts calories in half.

Moderate Alcohol

Alcohol is a two-edged sword. On the one hand, moderate intake of alcohol has been shown to increase HDL cholesterol levels and reduce blood clotting, which may aid in the prevention of heart attacks. On the other hand, excessive alcohol is linked to high blood pressure, elevated triglycerides, breast cancer and overweight. While alcohol contains no fat, studies show that it slows the rate at which fat is burned in the body, making it more likely that fat will "stick" to the body as excess weight.

If you do drink alcohol, keep in mind that it is a source of concentrated sugar. You can get some idea of sugar's impact by understanding how rich in calories beer, wine and distilled liquor can be. Virtually all of the "empty" calories enumerated in the following table come from sugar. The smartest thing you can do is to plan ahead. If you're having a good wine with dinner, forgo the before-dinner cocktail. If you're at a cocktail party, plan to have one alco-

Beverage	Calories	Beverage	Calories
Scotch whiskey,		Brandy, cognac	
gin, vodka (1.5 oz.)		(1 oz.)	65
80-proof	95	Liqueurs (1 oz.)	75–100
86 proof	105	Dry wine (3.5 oz.)	85
90-proof	110	Sweet wine (3.5 oz.)	140
94-proof	116	Beer, ale (12 oz.)	140–165
100-proof	125	Light beer (12 oz.)	95–105

holic drink, then follow it with a glass of mineral water. If you choose to drink, the key is to do so in moderation.

Switch to Fresh Fruit

Sugar also poses a problem in home-baked and commercially baked goods, candy and snacks. These are favorite foods of Americans. Indeed, we eat almost 21 pounds of candy per person each year. But such foods are tremendously rich in sugar. A four-ounce piece of iced chocolate cake, for instance, contains about 10 teaspoons of sugar. One ounce of fudge has 4.5 teaspoons of sugar. There is no way to reconcile this amount of sugar (not to mention calories) with a healthy diet pattern. Fortunately, by the time many people begin to work on their sugar problem, a break has already been made from baked goods and candies due to their high fat content. When you have such foods, budget for them. But be realistic. What would a birthday be without cake, or Thanksgiving without pumpkin pie? Still, your fat budget could not afford many such luxuries, so sugar by necessity is also limited.

A better choice is fresh fruit: a ripe peach, a crispy apple or an ice-cold watermelon wedge. While not as appealing to the "fat tooth" as a piece of chocolate candy, such fruit can be satisfying. Frozen grapes and bananas are also recommended.

Learn to Read Food Labels

One of the most difficult areas to control is the hidden sugar used as an additive in processed foods. Sugar is often a surprise ingredient in such foods as frozen dinners, nondairy creamers and ketchup. It can even be found as an ingredient in pipe tobacco! Processed foods are the chief contributor to the 30-teaspoon-a-day habit of most Americans.

Many food processors routinely add concentrated sugar for sweetening, moisture control and spoilage control. For this reason, reading food labels is essential. Unfortunately, there is no dietary standard for sugar intake. Although the Nutrition Facts will give you the number of grams of sugar in a serving of the food, what does that number mean? What you want to remember is that *4 grams of sugars equals 1 teaspoon*. So, if the label tells you that a breakfast cereal has 12 grams of sugar per serving, you know that it contains 3 teaspoons of sugar. This is a more graphic and practical way to view sugar content.

Also, examine the ingredients list for sugar and its other names: sucrose, maltose, dextrose, lactose, fructose, malt, corn solids, corn syrup, honey, molasses, invert sugar, raw sugar, maple syrup, corn sweetener, malted barley, date sugar and turbinado, to name a few. A good rule of thumb is to avoid any product whose label lists sugar, under any name, among the first three ingredients.

Look for the number of times sugar appears on the ingredients list. In a study conducted by Washington State University and the Department of Agriculture, a cereal being test-marketed was shown to contain sucrose, brown sugar and corn syrup.

Also contained were four cereal grains—white flour, corn flour, cornmeal and rice flour. The food manufacturer circumvented the listing of sugar as the main ingredient by grouping the four flours into a single "cereal grain" category and by listing the three sugars separately, thus giving the impression that the cereal was primarily made up of grain. The label did not change the fact that sugar was the primary ingredient in the cereal. It only served to confuse the consumer about the real sugar content of the product.

Watch Out for "Fat-Free" Baked Goods

With so much emphasis on reducing dietary fat today, it's no wonder that consumers have flocked to reduced-fat and "fat-free" commercial products. While fat has indeed been cut in many of these foods, this has not always translated into lower calories. In many "fat-free" foods sugar has replaced fat in a big way. Now you can find a package of chocolate cookies that are free of fat but in which one small cookie contains 50 calories. The reason? The cookies are loaded with sugar and corn syrup. So, when you crave baked goods, be sure not only to budget for fat but also to check the calories and sugar listed on the label.

Summing Up

There is no shortcut to achieving a low-sugar diet pattern. Only through the reduction and moderation of sugar sources and the institution of fresh fruits and vegetables in their place can a permanent change in sugar level can take place.

The Positive Diet is not free of sugar. However, it is designed to moderate excessive sugar intake through the use of a few simple rules:

- Remove the sugar bowl from the table. Avoid using sugar as a sweetener.

- Reduce sugar in recipes by one-third. Look for substitutes like apple juice or applesauce in recipes for baked goods.

- Moderate commercially baked goods, including "fat-free" varieties. If you do eat foods such as cookies, candy and cake, budget for them.

- Moderate soft drinks.

- Drink more water.

- Eat more fresh fruit for dessert and snacks.

- Drink alcohol only in moderation.

- Read food labels carefully. Remember, 4 grams of sugar equals 1 teaspoon. If sugar is listed in the first three ingredients (or listed too often in the ingredients list), avoid the product.

CHAPTER TWENTY-ONE

STEP 4—HOW TO HANDLE EATING IN A RESTAURANT

Americans enjoy restaurants. Gourmet, ethnic, family-style, fast-food, deli . . . more people are eating out than ever before. According to the American Restaurant Association, over half of all meals in the United States today are eaten in restaurants. And this figure is predicted to climb steadily into the next century. Restaurant meals (including fast-food meals and deli take-out) represent 40% of the American food budget.

Pleasurable as the experience may be, dining out can pose a serious problem for cardiac health. Restaurant foods generally contain liberal amounts of fat in the form of oil, butter, cream, lard, meat drippings, fatty meat, cheese and cheese sauce. In addition, many items are fried, deep-fried, pan-fried and sautéed. As a result, restaurant meals can be extremely high in total fat and saturated fat as well as in salt, sugar and total calories. Such meals can be in direct opposition to healthful eating.

There are few available options. You could avoid restaurants altogether, but that isn't very realistic. The fact is that eating out frequently is an accepted part of modern American life. Calling for a rollback of the clock to the time of Ward and June Cleaver on TV's *Leave It to Beaver* won't work. In addition, eating out can be a pleasurable experience, so why banish it forever?

Another option is to stick your head in the sand and eat what the restaurant serves. This is just what many people do, but it doesn't make much sense. Why read food labels in a grocery store and change your meals at home, only to break your fat budget in a restaurant? Even seemingly good choices can be "fat traps." Kung Pao chicken, for instance, can contain over 75 grams of fat in a restaurant serving! In order to create low-fat habits, restaurant eating must be taken into consideration.

A third option is to apply fat budgeting to menu selection in order to make smarter, healthier decisions.

Of the three alternatives, only the third makes sense. It's the best way to reconcile dining out with eating right. Dining in a restaurant can be both enjoyable and healthful when a few simple guidelines are employed.

Understand the Basic Principles

Knowing the basic principles and how they apply to food selection in restaurants is fundamental to success. This comes, of course, with the practice of the Positive Diet at home. If you're just beginning to change your dietary habits, my advice is to stay away from restaurants until you feel comfortable with your new way of eating. Research shows that learning to manage meals at home is much easier than handling restaurant meals. So, by delaying, you have more time to concentrate total effort on understanding and practicing healthy eating at home and on making the basic principles a permanent fixture in your life. When this is achieved, usually within four to six weeks, you're in a better position to manage restaurant meals.

Whether or not you take this course, however, total familiarity with the principles of healthful eating (reduce fat, saturated fat, dietary cholesterol, salt and sugar; increase complex carbohydrates and fiber) is necessary before you can apply them to restaurant foods.

KNOW YOUR PERSONAL FAT BUDGET

Your fat budget is the most important criterion for selecting restaurant foods. While there are a number of other important considerations, such as the sodium content of the food or meal, fat budgeting is the most practical way to ensure healthful choices. Research shows that when you track total fat and choose low-fat foods, other important elements such as saturated fat tend to fall in line. Also, there is a practical limit to how much information on food makeup you can process. If you try to set a criterion for each aspect of the basic principles, you'll feel as if you're in a chemistry lab rather than a restaurant.

Your fat budget is a guideline for the day. Make a point of knowing how many grams of fat you have to "spend" before you go to the restaurant. Don't think of restaurant eating as being distinct from your at-home efforts to stay within your budget. Instead, see it as an extension of those efforts. Develop a healthy mind-set. Eating out is not a "special occasion" on which to eat whatever you want until you're stuffed. Understand how restaurant eating fits into your overall dietary plan. If you do "break" your budget ("I just couldn't turn down the chocolate cake for dessert!"), that's okay. You don't have to be perfect. Simply redouble your efforts the following day—take a longer walk when you exercise, for example, and strive for three meals that are low in fat. You can't undo a high-fat yesterday, but you can bring your dietary life into balance today so that your budget evens out.

KNOW HOW MUCH FAT COMES IN RESTAURANT FOODS

Unfortunately, in the past this information has been virtually impossible to get. A few of the fast-food chains put out some information (if you requested it and if they happened to have it on hand), but the fat content of the vast majority of restaurant foods and meals was a mystery. Said one registered dietitian, "We're so worried about packaged food labels that we've overlooked a greater problem—what comes in restaurant foods."

With the publication of my book *The Fat Tooth Fat-Gram Counter & Restaurant Guide*, this information is now available for over 3,500 of the most commonly ordered restaurant foods and meals, including fast foods. It provides you, in effect, with labels for restaurant foods. Without such information, you have no idea what the true fat content of the food really is. For example, let's use McDonald's Big Mac as a standard for comparison purposes. You may be utterly surprised at how other restaurant foods stack up to it.

Food*	Grams of Fat	Food*	Grams of Fat
McDonald's Big Mac	**26**	Baked potato with butter, bacon, sour cream and chives	34
Cheese Nachos	55	Pork sausage patty	33
Chicken-fried steak	82	Turkey and cream cheese sandwich	28
Beef pot pie	62	Reuben sandwich	28
Pasta Alfredo (cream sauce)	61	Fried chicken	28
Ice cream sundae	61	Cheese and crab tart	28
Quiche Lorraine	61	Tuna submarine sandwich	27
Chicken Cordon Bleu	50	Grilled tuna with cheese sandwich	26
Shrimp scampi	49	French onion soup	25
Sole Amandine	49	Double cheese/ pepperoni pizza	25
Chicken Caesar salad	48	Dove bar	22
Fried onion rings	47	Bran muffin	21
Chicken fajitas with guacamole, cheese and sour cream	44	Large mocha specialty coffee	21
BBQ ribs	43		
Mud pie	41		
Biscuit and sausage	38		
Taco salad (without salt)	37		

* "Average serving size" for restaurants, according to the American Restaurant Association.

CHOOSE A RESTAURANT CAREFULLY

Compile a list of restaurants where you know you can get low-fat items and dishes. If you don't, your options may be severely limited. It's more difficult to stick to your budget at a prime rib restaurant that specializes in oversize portions, for instance, or at a fried chicken or fish-and-chips fast-food restaurant. If you think that a Chinese restaurant is a good choice, be aware that an order of Kung Pao chicken can have more fat than three McDonald's Quarter Pounders. Almost all restaurants that prepare food to order, however, will modify their offerings according to your desires. Just be sure to speak up! Another good technique is to think about what you want to order before you get to the restaurant. This will keep you from being caught off guard and ending up with a high-fat meal.

A good suggestion is to check out the restaurants in hotels. Acting on a restaurant industry survey that indicated 40% of Americans were committed to healthful eating when away from home, some hotel chains have begun to offer healthy alternative cuisines. Hyatt Hotels, for example, has developed "Cuisine Naturelle" dishes that have no more than 25% of calories from fat and no more than 800 milligrams of sodium. The Radisson chain's "Inspired Cuisine" offers dishes in which at least half of calories are from carbohydrates and fat makes up no more than 30% of calories. Four Seasons, Ritz-Carlton, Westin, Hilton and Marriott hotels also offer creative, low-fat selections. Their chefs try to avoid butter, cream and salt, and rely on low-fat staples like broth-based salad dressings.

Don't Set Yourself Up to Overeat

If you skip meals all day long to "save calories" for a restaurant meal, chances are that you'll overeat. You'll arrive at the restaurant famished, so your resistance to fatty foods will be low. It's also easy to rationalize breaking your fat budget when you're ravenous. A better plan is to eat a low-fat breakfast and lunch, for example, to compensate for increased fat at dinner.

A good tip is to be a little full when you order. You might want to have a glass of mineral water or fruit juice, a piece of fruit or some raw vegetables an hour or so before dinner to take the edge off your appetite. Watch out for alcohol, as it can increase your hunger.

Be aware of portion sizes. Avoid buffets and "all you can eat" restaurants. Remember, even if your order is low in fat, restaurant portions are generally twice what you should be eating, so develop a mental picture of what a serving should be. A three-ounce portion of meat or fish, for example, is about the same size as the palm of a woman's hand, and three ounces of chicken is about one-half a chicken breast. If you order beef, ask for the "petite," "queen" or "8-ounce" cut rather than the "king" or "16-ounce" portion. If you order sweet-and-sour pork, eat just one cup (the family-style serving plate can contain five cups). Consider sharing. One person can order an entrée while the other chooses the salad bar. (Speaking of salad bars, you should know that salad dressing ladles generally hold from two to six tablespoons of salad dressing!) If the entrée is higher in fat than you would normally eat, order an appetizer portion. Order a rich dessert, then split it—one piece of chocolate cake shared among four people will give everyone a taste without destroying anyone's fat budget. And finally, don't feel compelled to eat everything just because you paid for it. Enjoy what you eat, but resist the urge to join the "Clean Plate Club." Don't hesitate to get a "doggy bag." This way you can reduce your portion at the restaurant and have enough for lunch the next day.

BE INQUISITIVE

Find out what the restaurant offers and how food is prepared. The same key questions that are posed at home must be asked in restaurants: Is the dish made with butter, margarine, cream, oil or animal fat? Is it fried or deep-fat-fried? Is the dressing made with cream? Are large quantities of salt and sugar added to the food in the cooking process? Practicing low-fat eating at home can provide you with these and other logical questions. Often restaurant personnel, particularly at sit-down restaurants, are very knowledgeable about meal content and cooking methods, and can be helpful in the attainment of your dietary goals. But they cannot help if you don't ask questions and tell them what you want—and what you don't want. It does you little good to understand the principles of low-fat eating if you can't put them into effect in a restaurant. And you can't put them into effect unless you ask the right questions.

I remember a visit to a restaurant soon after I began to change my diet. Being more conscious of the fat content of marbled meats, I avoided the prime rib, New York steak and spareribs in favor of a broiled salmon fillet. But when the fish arrived, it was swimming in a butter sauce! And the same fatty sauce covered the rice and vegetables. I hadn't reduced fat consumption by one whit! This discouraging episode took place because I didn't question the preparation of the food before ordering. Had I realized that butter sauce was "automatically" added, I could have avoided the problem by asking that the sauce be "held."

Look for key words on the menu. Avoid foods described as *buttery, butter sauce, sauté, fried, pan-fried, crispy, creamed, cream sauce, aioli, pesto, in its own gravy, au gratin, in cheese sauce, escalloped, au lait, à la mode, au fromage, marinated, basted, prime, Béarnaise, beurre blanc, Hollandaise*. Better choices are: *steamed, in broth, in its own juice, poached, garden-fresh, roasted, broiled, stir-fried* and *lean*.

BE INNOVATIVE

Creative substitution developed at home can be applied to restaurant offerings to strip away much of the unwanted fat yet preserve the taste of the food. Order a club sandwich, for instance, without the bacon and mayonnaise. Ask for nonfat sour cream for your baked potato; order a side dish of rice or pasta instead of French fries. In place of butter on steamed shellfish, ask for fresh lemon wedges. If you're out for a weekend breakfast and want eggs, order them poached, boiled or shirred, but never fried.

There are many enjoyable restaurant foods that conform to healthy basic principles. Do not take a "gloom and doom" approach, but rather open your mind to the endless possibilities available. If your attitude is positive, and if you are mentally and emotionally committed to low-fat eating, then neither the menu choices offered nor the food selection of others will negatively affect your decision to eat healthfully.

TIPS FOR ORDERING IN A RESTAURANT

FAST-FOOD RESTAURANTS

Make smart choices. Many fast-food restaurants now offer more healthful choices. McDonald's, for instance, has shakes with just 1 or 2 grams of fat, and a McLean Deluxe Burger with only 10 grams of fat. Burger King has cut more than half the fat from its BK Broiler Chicken Sandwich. But most fast foods can provide far more fat that you'd like, such as the Taco Salad at Taco Bell with 61 grams of fat or the

Double Western Bacon Cheeseburger at Carl's Jr. with 63 grams of fat. Use your fat budget to make smart choices.

If you choose a hamburger or roast beef sandwich, order small. As size and number of hamburger patties increase, so does the fat. Order those identified as "single" or "junior," and avoid those labeled "jumbo," "super," "double," "triple," "extra-large" and "big." Don't make the mistake of eating too many small burgers. There is no advantage in eating two Wendy's Junior hamburgers with a combined 18 grams of fat over one Wendy's regular hamburger with 15 grams. Stick with "regular" and "junior" roast beef sandwiches.

Watch out for added fat in the form of cheese, bacon, mayonnaise or mayonnaise-based "special sauces." These can add 30 or more grams of fat to hamburgers and sandwiches. Use mustard and ketchup for condiments. Salad bars and prepackaged salads are healthy choices, but added fat can turn them into nutritional disasters. A prepacked green salad with chicken, for instance, has just 3 or 4 grams of fat. But top it with a two-ounce packet of ranch dressing, and you'll add about 34 grams of fat. It's a far better idea to ask for "lite," "diet" and "no-oil" dressings.

Sandwiches can be a good choice or a disaster. Avoid croissant sandwiches. One croissant has the fat equivalent of four pats of butter. Choose low-fat fillers such as roasted turkey breast, lean roast beef, roasted or grilled chicken breast and lean ham. Avoid cold cuts, tuna salad, egg salad and chicken salad made with mayonnaise, cheese sandwiches and cheese melts. Some delis offer extra-lean corned beef and pastrami sandwiches, which are fine on occasion, but watch out for portion size. Many are made with enough filling to feed two people, so order a half-sandwich or share with a friend. A fried fish fillet sandwich, breaded, fried in grease and covered with mayonnaise and fatty sauces, is not a good choice. Wendy's Fish Fillet Sandwich, for instance, contains 29 grams of fat. It's the same with many chicken sandwiches. Watch out for those that contain fried chicken (Burger King's Fried Chicken Sandwich has 40 grams of fat) or fatty add-ons like mayonnaise and cheese in a chicken club sandwich (Carl's Jr. has 29 grams of fat). The best choice is a sandwich made with a skinless, grilled breast. If you like submarine sandwiches, choose turkey, smoked turkey, ham and lean roast beef over salami, pepperoni, mortadella, bologna and cheese.

Avoid all fried foods. A typical medium order of French fries has 17 grams of fat. KFC's "Extra Crispy" chicken has 21 grams of fat. Six chicken McNuggets yield about 15 grams of fat. A better choice is a skinless, grilled breast. If you eat fried chicken, choose the breast and remove the skin and breading. Fried fish and seafood have the same problem. Avoid deep-fried fish, shellfish and shrimp. Long John Silver's Homestyle Fish Dinner has 39 grams of fat; the Baked Fish with Paprika has only 2 grams of fat. A fried fish fillet sandwich is breaded, fried in grease and covered with tartar sauce; it can cost you more fat-grams than a hamburger.

And finally, don't assume anything. Rotisserie chicken, for instance, may sound better than fried chicken or a hamburger, but this is not always the case. One-half chicken at Boston Chicken or Kenny Rogers Roasters comes with skin and has just under 40 grams of fat. One-quarter chicken with skin at KFC ranges from 19 grams (white meat) to 24 grams (dark meat), while the same order at Roy Rogers has 29 grams (dark meat) and 34 grams (dark meat). A better choice is a skinless white breast with just 6 grams of fat.

Sit-Down Restaurants

Most sit-down restaurants offer a variety of foods and preparation methods that can work to your benefit in restricting fat. The key, of course, is to make basic low-fat choices. Seafood, for instance, is usually lower in fat than meat; pasta in a tomato-based sauce has less fat than pasta in a cream-based sauce. Fried foods are richer in fat than those that are broiled. Watch for fatty add-ons such as creamy sauces and dressings, and practice portion control. Learn to distinguish high- from low-fat foods on the menu.

Appetizers. Stay away from those that are fried or deep-fried, drenched in oil, butter or cheese, or served with creamy dips. Nachos with guacamole and cheese, meat and cheese antipasto, deep-fried mozzarella sticks, egg rolls, tempura vegetables, fried calamari and buffalo wings are good examples. More acceptable choices are oysters (raw, baked or steamed); steamed mussels; clam, crab, oyster and lobster cocktails; seviche; steamed pot stickers; sushi and sashimi; steamed or raw vegetables.

Soups. Skip the cream-based soups, such as clam chowder, and the meat soups. Instead, order gazpacho, minestrone, vegetable soup, beef or chicken consommé with pasta or pastina, cioppino and bouillabaisse (fish soups) and black bean soup (hold the sour cream).

Entrées. Avoid fatty meat, deep-fried chicken and fish, and foods with fatty sauces and gravies. Ask for meat to be lean, well-trimmed and cooked in a low-fat manner. Order a small piece of London broil, veal or sirloin done to "medium" or "well done," and ask that no butter or oil be used in its preparation.

Avoid chicken that is fried, batter-dipped and fried, or served smothered with gravy; order it baked, broiled, roasted or barbecued without skin and with any sauces served on the side. If chicken comes with the skin, remove it before eating. In ethnic restaurants, baked or broiled skinless chicken topped with tomato-based or vegetable sauces and minimal cheese are acceptable. Examples include chicken cacciatore (Italian) and arroz con pollo (Mexican). In Oriental restaurants, ask for chicken stir-fried with as little oil as possible. Be aware that roasted turkey dinners with gravy and stuffing can break your fat budget.

Watch out for fish and chips, and any seafood that is fried, deep-fried, breaded or batter-dipped and fried; served with a cream or cheese sauce, en casserole, Newburg or Thermidor; baked, stuffed, or stuffed and rolled. Better choices are seafood that is broiled, poached, blackened, in marinara sauce, in light wine sauce, grilled, marinated, barbecued, stir-fried or steamed. Seafood stews such as cioppino are also excellent choices.

Pasta dishes with low-fat sauces, such as marinara, are excellent entrée choices.

Salads. Avoid salads with strips of meat and cheese. A chef's salad, for instance, can have 800 calories and 65 grams of fat. A simple green salad is virtually fat-free and runs about 10 calories per ounce, but pour on a few tablespoons of dressing and fat/calories skyrocket. Avoid regular dressings, especially creamy dressings such as sour cream, Thousand Island and blue cheese. Ask for "lite" and "fat-free" versions of salad dressings. Order dressing "on the side" and dip your fork in it—you'll get all the flavor but very little of the fat. Watch out for high-fat salad bar items such as bacon bits, cold cuts, eggs, olives and creamy pasta and potato salads. A typical two-cup salad with all the high-fat extras can have 30 grams of fat—as much fat as a cheeseburger.

Vegetables. Avoid pickled vegetables or those prepared or topped with butter, cream, cheese,

cheese sauce or oil. Ask for sodium-reduced soy sauce, flavored vinegars, lemon juice and hot sauce to flavor vegetables without fat. Order fresh vegetables such as asparagus, broccoli or mushrooms, either raw or slightly steamed. Potatoes, rice and noodles are low in fat without butter, sour cream and other fatty condiments.

Desserts. Avoid commercial pastries, pies, cakes, cookies and candy. Fresh fruit, nonfat yogurt, gelatin, sherbet, sorbet, ices and unfrosted angel food cake are smarter choices. If you do opt for a rich dessert, share it with others.

Breakfasts. Avoid fatty meats, whole eggs, fried foods and sugared cereals. Watch out for the breakfast buffet; not only does it have an array of fatty food (sausages, eggs, hash browns), but it also offers as much as you can eat—a dangerous combination. Instead, center your meal on low-fat cereals, muffins or toast, juice and fresh fruit. If you do order eggs, have them poached, boiled or shirred, but not fried. If you feel that you can't do without breakfast meats, Canadian bacon is preferable to sausage, bacon and ham.

Remember, you can eat with more control at home. But when you do dine out, whether it's a fast-food sandwich or a meal in your favorite Italian restaurant, you can eat as healthfully as possible by using the basic principles as your guide.

Smarter Choices in Ethnic Restaurants

Eating out should be an adventure, not a guilt-ridden experience. The following will give you the ins and outs of some of the most popular ethnic restaurant menus.

ITALIAN

Choose vegetable antipasto (roasted peppers and zucchini, grilled mushrooms); minestrone soup, ribollito (thick vegetarian stew) and cioppino (seafood stew); pasta with meatless tomato-based sauces such as marinara, light red, pomodoro, vegetable and red seafood sauce; pasta e fagioli (shells and beans); grilled game, veal and fish; scampi sautéed in wine; baked or broiled chicken; chicken cacciatore; fish dishes topped with meatless tomato sauce and little or no cheese; Italian ice for dessert.

Go easy on or avoid meat and cheese antipasto; fried calamari; bruschetta (bread drenched in olive oil); pasta in butter, cheese, oil, cream or bacon fat (pancetta), such as Alfredo or carbonara sauces, as well as those made with pesto or sausage; cheese and meat-stuffed pasta dishes (tortellini, ravioli, cannelloni, manicotti, lasagna); fritto misto (a "fried mix" of seafood, meat and vegetables); risotto (heavy with butter and cheese); cheesy eggplant or veal parmigiana; veal piccata and marsala; rich desserts such as tiramisu or cannoli. If you order pizza, hold the meat. Vegetable toppings (easy on the cheese) are much lower in fat.

FRENCH

Choose the foods of southern France, which use seafood, vegetables, wine and olive oil. Smart choices are poached, roasted or broiled fish and chicken (such as coq au vin); lean meat; foods steamed in parchment, or steamed or sautéed in wine; dishes labeled coulis, vegetable purée or reduction; salade niçoise; consommé; stews such as bouillabaisse or ratatouille.

Go easy on or avoid the foods of northern France, which center on meat, sausage, goose, lard, goose fat, butter, cream and fatty sauces; cassoulet and gratins (made with cheese or egg); dishes heavy with eggs, such as quenelles, soufflés and quiche; goose or duck pâté; organ meats; rich sauces such as Béarnaise, beurre blanc, béchamel and Hollandaise; items in a pastry shell; croissants; and pastry.

JAPANESE

Choose dishes centered on low-fat rice and vegetables with little or no fat used in cooking; miso soup; sunomono (cucumber salad); yakitori (broiled chicken); Japanese vegetables; chicken and fish teriyaki; hibachi chicken and lean beef, sushi and sashimi; yosenabe (seafood and vegetable stew); shabu-shabu (vegetables and meats boiled in broth); and rice and noodles.

Go easy on or avoid deep-fried foods (tempura, agemono and katsu); sukiyaki; egg dishes such as oyako-donburi.

CHINESE

Choose hot-and-sour wonton soup; steamed dumplings (Chinese raviolis); stir-fried or steamed dishes with vegetables, chicken, seafood and tofu; steamed or braised whole fish or scallops; steamed rice. Ask for meals with no added salt or MSG, and with as little oil as possible. One-cup servings with less than 10 grams of fat include hot-and- sour soup, stir-fried vegetables, Szechuan shrimp, lo mein, chicken chow mein and Hunan tofu.

Go easy on or avoid dishes made with duck, beef and pork; items that have been fried or deep-fried such as egg rolls, dumplings, fried shrimp, fried wontons and fried rice; sweet-and-sour dishes; anything "crispy" or "batter-coated"; dishes heavy on nuts. Some of the fattest choices include Kung Pao chicken, moo shu pork, sweet-and-sour pork, crispy beef and fried rice.

MEXICAN/SOUTHWESTERN

Choose from the basics: mesquite-grilled chicken, seafood and lean cuts of beef or pork; chili con carne; enchiladas, burritos and soft-shell tacos (unfried) with chicken, seafood and vegetable fillings (hold the sour cream and cheese); and black bean soup or gazpacho.

Go easy on or avoid tortilla chips and nachos; deep-fried and fried dishes such as chimichangas, flautas and taquitos; crispy taco or salad shells; quesadillas; cheese dishes such as chili con queso; refried beans (ask for whole ones); fatty "extras" such as cheese, sour cream, guacamole; dishes with poblano aioli (chili mayonnaise) or cilantro pesto. Watch out for fajitas and taco salads, which often contain a surprising amount of fat; combination dinners are usually heavy in fat and calories.

INDIAN

Choose lentil soups like mulligatawny or dal rasam; yogurt-based curries; chicken or fish prepared tandoori, tikka, vindaloo or masala style.

Go easy on or avoid fried appetizers like samosas and pakoras or fried breads such as poori and paratha. Watch out for any dishes called malai, kandhari and korma, which are made with cream or coconut.

CAJUN

Choose red beans and rice (without sausage); mustard greens, okra and kale (hold the bacon); chicken or seafood jambalaya or gumbo; shrimp Creole and other tomato-sauce based dishes; blackened fish; and boiled seafood dinners.

Go easy on or avoid fried corn bread (hush puppies), dirty rice (fried rice with sausage or other fatty meats); sausage dishes including boudin or andouille; cream-based soups or bisque; étouffe; and batter-fried seafoods.

Summing Up

Eating in a restaurant does not mean that you have to sacrifice either nutrition or delectable food. Wherever you dine, there is an opportunity to make smart choices based on your fat budget and your low-fat knowledge. To make smart choices:

- Know your personal fat budget. Make restaurant meals part of your plan rather than an exception to it.

- Choose a restaurant where you know there will be healthier choices, and don't arrive famished.

- Have some idea of what you want to order before you arrive. Use *The Fat Tooth Fat-Gram Counter & Restaurant Guide* to determine how much fat comes in different restaurant meals.

- Ask for what you want . . . and do not want. Work with the waiter and chef to make the smartest choices.

- Use the sensible rules that work at home. Avoid large portions. Avoid fried foods and fatty sauces. If you order a rich dessert, share it.

CHAPTER TWENTY-TWO

STEP 5–HOW TO MODIFY YOUR OWN RECIPES

Healthy eating today is a way of life in our family, but it wasn't always so. After my open-heart surgery in 1977, my wife Bernie and I were faced with a long list of foods to limit or avoid. In those days, the emphasis was on foods you could no longer have, the so-called "bad" foods—bacon, sausage, hot dogs, cheese, ice cream, French fries and hamburgers, to name but a few. Unfortunately, many of these foods were mainstays of our diet. The forbidden list seemed to contain most of the best-tasting foods on the market and all the foods that our family most enjoyed. If we couldn't eat these foods, what was left?

Meal preparation was further complicated because our new way of eating affected not only the adults in our family (who could understand the grave necessity for change) but also our young children, who were likely to go on a hunger strike if poached fish replaced Big Macs and carrot sticks began to show up in place of French fries. We were also concerned that our friends might dread a dinner invitation to our home for fear of being served bland and tasteless fare.

As a result, there were difficult months for the entire family and many of the meals turned out to be real disasters. But it was also during those months that we made a commitment to somehow master a healthy diet. We became determined to create meals that would be not only heart-healthy but appetizing and appealing as well. In short, our decision was to learn how to *eat,* not how to *diet.* We chose to concentrate on what we *could* have and not on what we *could not* have. The challenge was to make the healthy foods so satisfying that we wouldn't miss the unhealthy ones.

We began by cooking meals from low-fat recipe books. There are a number on the market, and many are quite good. However, while someone else's recipes provide a useful introduction to healthy cooking, we found that they're not enough for success. And that's because we like our own food, our own favorite recipes, better than we like the recipes of other people. The fact is that most American families choose to eat from a narrow band of foods. We have our family favorites, and no matter how good the new cookbook, we want our own recipes. Indeed, research shows that most American families prepare 12 recipes 80% of the time! This means that if your're somewhat typical, you don't have to worry about how to create a hundred new low-fat meals. Instead, concentrate on how to change the recipes your family already enjoys (and that you serve 80% of the time) to reduce fat without changing taste. The key phrase is *without changing taste.* Anyone can make low-fat recipes that taste like cardboard. They may be healthy, but you'll have an uphill fight getting your family to eat them. Lasting changes in dietary habits takes place only when you learn to make your own recipes more healthful. Long-term success, then, comes with learning how to modify your own recipes.

HOW TO MODIFY RECIPES

We are advised today by nutritional experts to eat more fresh fruits and vegetables, more seafood and more complex carbohydrates in the form of rice, pasta and grains, and to consume only moderate amounts of meat, poultry and dairy products. Most of this advice is directed at getting us to eat less fat.

While no one argues with the goal, let's face it—fat tastes good. Simply omitting all high-fat foods can make your diet bland and boring. The chances of "sticking with it" are slim indeed. A better perspective is "How can I reduce the fat in this dish without sacrificing taste?" After all, taste is what eating is all about.

Instead of throwing away your old recipes, analyze them for ways to reduce fat (and increase complex carbohydrates) without sacrificing taste. To modify a recipe, you first need to identify the sources of excessive fat and ask a key question: "Why is this in the recipe?" Many of us learned to cook from our mothers or grandmothers, or from a book. Ingredients or cooking methods were never questioned. Today, such inquiry is necessary.

USE LOW-FAT SUBSTITUTES

Switching to low-fat versions of the foods in your own recipes is one of the best strategies for health ful cooking. This is where creative substitution can make a big difference. One form involves simple "one-for-one" exchanges of lower-fat foods for those higher in fat. If your favorite chili recipe calls for hamburger, for instance, substitute lean ground round or shredded chicken breast. There will be very little change in taste from the original recipe, but the fat content will plummet. Choose the leanest cuts of meat, poultry and fish, and dairy products with the lowest fat that will still satisfy your taste buds.

A second method involves more use of low-fat ingredients. For example, prepare a tuna salad with "light" mayonnaise instead of the regular version. You'll get half the fat and more than enough "real" mayonnaise flavor to keep your taste buds happy. Or make French toast with a mixture of nonfat milk, one whole egg and three-fourths cup egg substitute (instead of a mixture of whole milk and four whole eggs), then cook it in a nonstick pan (rather than the traditional skillet with bacon grease). There will be no change in taste, but fat content will be cut substantially. Check the labels for products that are low in fat, then try them. If one brand of fat-free sour cream or low-fat cheese doesn't meet your taste requirements, try others. Keep looking until you find the one that works for you and your family. There is a whole new world of products in the grocery store to help in low-fat cooking.

Cook Without Extra Fat

How you cook is as important as *what* you cook, so low-fat cooking may be an alteration to your traditional cooking methods. Look for ways to cook without added fat. A well-made heavy-gauge nonstick skillet is indispensable for stir-frying or sautéing in a minimum of fat. You can use one tablespoon of olive oil, for example, to "fry" potatoes, rather than an inch of oil. Grilling fish is more flavorful (and healthier) than deep-fat frying. If you're using ground beef, be sure to drain it before adding it to your recipe. Use herbs and spices like fresh ginger, cilantro, curry powder, mustard and flavored vinegar to zip up food without fat. Change your focus to make grains, legumes, fruits and vegetables the center of your meals.

On the pages that follow you'll find a number of recipes that have been modified. Each example provides the original recipe and a modified version. The intent is to show you how simple it is to make low-fat changes that pay off with big dividends. The goal is to eat home-cooked meals that are delicious but won't destroy your fat budget. Modifying your own recipes will help you reach that goal.

TARRAGON VINAIGRETTE

Original Recipe (1 cup)	Modified Recipe (1 cup)
¼ cup tarragon vinegar ¾ cup olive oil 3 shallots, chopped 2 cloves garlic, chopped ¾ teaspoon salt	¼ cup tarragon vinaigrette ¼ cup olive oil ¼ cup reduced-fat chicken broth 2 shallots, chopped 2 cloves garlic, chopped ¼ teaspoon salt
Combine all ingredients in covered jar. Shake well.	Combine all ingredients in covered jar. Shake well. Store in refrigerator.

Nutritional information per 1 tablespoon:

Original		Modified	
Calories:	92	Calories:	32
Total fat:	10 g	Total fat:	3 g
Percentage of calories from fat:	99%	Percentage of calories from fat:	95%
Carbohydrate:	1 g	Carbohydrate:	0 g
Protein:	0 g	Protein:	0 g
Cholesterol:	0 mg	Cholesterol:	0 mg
Sodium:	100 mg	Sodium:	38 mg
Dietary fiber:	0 g	Dietary fiber:	0 g

Modifications:

- Reduce olive oil.
- Use reduced-fat chicken broth.

Calories saved per serving: 60
Fat saved per serving: 7 grams

BEEF STROGANOFF

Original Recipe (8 servings)	Modified Recipe (8 servings)
3 tablespoons butter	¾ pound extra-lean ground round
¾ cup onion, finely chopped	¾ cup onion, finely chopped
1 clove garlic, minced	1 clove garlic, minced
1½ pounds sirloin steak, cut into bite-size pieces	½ pound fresh mushrooms, sliced
½ pound fresh mushrooms, sliced	¼ teaspoon salt
½ teaspoon salt	⅛ teaspoon pepper
⅛ teaspoon black pepper	⅛ teaspoon rosemary
⅛ teaspoon rosemary	1½ cups low-fat (1%) cream of chicken soup
2 tablespoons all-purpose flour	1 cup nonfat sour cream
2 cups cream of chicken soup	1 pound bow tie pasta, cooked al dente
1 cup sour cream	2 teaspoons poppy seeds
1 pound bow tie pasta, cooked al dente	Fresh parsley for garnish
3 tablespoons poppy seeds	
Fresh parsley for garnish	

Original Recipe:

Melt butter in heavy skillet. Add onion and garlic, and sauté 3 to 4 minutes. Add beef and continue to cook 3 to 4 minutes.

Add mushrooms. Cook 2 to 3 minutes. Sprinkle with salt, pepper, rosemary and flour. Stir in soup. Simmer uncovered for 5 minutes. Stir in sour cream. Heat, but do not boil.

Arrange pasta around edges of large platter. Spoon sauce into center. Sprinkle pasta with poppy seeds. Garnish with fresh parsley.

Modified Recipe:

Sauté ground round, onion and garlic in nonstick skillet. Drain off any excess fat.

Add mushrooms. Cook 3 to 5 minutes. Stir in salt, pepper and rosemary. Simmer uncovered for 10 minutes. Add soup, and heat. Stir in sour cream. Heat, but do not boil.

Arrange pasta around edges of large platter. Spoon sauce into center. Sprinkle pasta with poppy seeds. Garnish with fresh parsley.

Nutritional information per serving:

Original		Modified	
Calories:	604	Calories:	331
Total fat:	30 g	Total fat:	6 g
Percentage of calories from fat:	45%	Percentage of calories from fat:	15%
Carbohydrate:	53 g	Carbohydrate:	51 g
Protein:	29 g	Protein:	18 g
Cholesterol:	89 mg	Cholesterol:	30 mg
Sodium:	734 mg	Sodium:	288 mg
Dietary fiber:	2 g	Dietary fiber:	2 g

Modifications:

- Eliminate butter for sautéing by using nonstick skillet.
- Use fat-free cream of chicken soup.
- Use nonfat sour cream.
- Reduce fat in meat by changing cut.

Calories saved per serving: 273
Fat saved per serving: 24 grams

CHICKEN DIVAN

Original Recipe (6 servings)	Modified Recipe (6 servings)
3 chicken breasts, halved and boned	3 whole chicken breasts, halved
⅓ cup butter	¾ pound asparagus spears or 2 cups broccoli flowerets
2 10-ounce packages frozen asparagus spears	2 10¾-ounce cans fat-free (1%) cream of chicken soup
1 10-ounce can cream of chicken soup	⅓ cup nonfat mayonnaise
⅔ cup mayonnaise	⅓ cup skim evaporated milk
⅓ cup evaporated milk	¼ cup grated reduced-fat cheddar cheese
⅔ cup grated cheddar cheese	1 teaspoon lemon juice
1 teaspoon lemon juice	½ teaspoon curry powder
½ teaspoon curry powder	2 tablespoons bread crumbs
½ cup bread crumbs	
1 tablespoon butter	

(continued on next page)

(continued from preceding page)

Brown chicken breasts in butter. Cook asparagus according to package directions. Drain and arrange in casserole dish. Top with chicken. Combine cream of chicken soup, mayonnaise, milk, cheese, lemon juice and curry. Pour over chicken. Top with bread crumbs. Dot with 1 tablespoon butter. Bake at 350° for 25 to 30 minutes.

Remove skin from chicken, and bone. Brown chicken lightly on both sides in non-stick skillet. Steam asparagus in vegetable steamer basket over boiling water for 1 minute. Arrange in 8-inch-square baking dish and top with chicken. Combine soup, mayonnaise, milk, cheese, lemon juice and curry. Pour over chicken. Sprinkle with bread crumbs. Cover lightly with aluminum foil. Bake at 350° for 25 to 30 minutes.

Nutritional information per serving:

Calories:	630	Calories:	264
Total fat:	53 g	Total fat:	6 g
Percentage of calories from fat:	75%	Percentage of calories from fat:	21%
Carbohydrate:	17 g	Carbohydrate:	18 g
Protein:	27 g	Protein:	33 g
Cholesterol:	126 mg	Cholesterol:	86 mg
Sodium:	957 mg	Sodium:	755 mg
Dietary fiber:	Trace	Dietary fiber:	1 g

Modifications:

- Eliminate butter for sautéing by using nonstick skillet.
- Remove skin from chicken.
- Use fat-free chicken broth.
- Use nonfat mayonnaise.
- Use skim evaporated milk.
- Use reduced-fat Cheddar cheese.
- Reduce amount of bread crumbs.
- Eliminate dots of butter.

Calories saved per serving: 366
Fat saved per serving: 47 grams

CHICKEN ENCHILADAS

Original Recipe (8 servings)	Modified Recipe (8 servings)
2 tablespoons butter	4 cups reduced-fat chicken broth
2 whole boneless chicken breasts	2 whole skinless, boneless broth
1 small ripe tomato, chopped	1 small ripe tomato, chopped
1 onion, chopped	1 onion, chopped
1 8-ounce can chopped green chilies	1 8-ounce can chopped green chilies
1½ cups grated Cheddar cheese	¾ cup grated reduced-fat Cheddar cheese
1 cup tomato salsa	1 cup tomato salsa
8 flour tortillas	8 corn tortillas
1 8-ounce can tomato purée	1 8-ounce can tomato purée
3 cloves garlic	3 cloves garlic
3 drops Tabasco sauce	3 drops Tabasco sauce
½ cup sour cream	½ cup nonfat sour cream

Original Recipe

Melt butter in heavy skillet. Add chicken and sauté 10 to 15 minutes, or until chicken is cooked. Let cool, and tear into shreds.

Combine chicken, tomato, ¼ cup chopped onion, 1 tablespoon green chilies, 3 tablespoons cheese and 1 tablespoon salsa. Set aside.

Heat tortillas on nonstick baking sheet in 350° oven for about 3 minutes on each side to soften.

Put 3 tablespoons chicken filling in center of each tortilla and roll. Arrange seam side down in shallow ovenproof baking dish. Set aside.

Place tomato purée, garlic and remaining onion in blender. Purée until smooth.

Modified Recipe

In saucepan, bring chicken broth to boil. Add chicken breasts and bring to second boil. Reduce heat to medium. Cook 20 minutes, or until chicken is done. Remove chicken, and tear into shreds. Reserve broth for later use.

Combine chicken, tomato, ¼ cup chopped onion, 1 tablespoon chopped green chilies, 1 tablespoon cheese and 1 tablespoon salsa. Set aside.

Heat tortillas on nonstick baking sheet in 350° oven for about 3 minutes on each side to soften.

Put 3 tablespoons chicken filling in center of each tortilla and roll. Arrange seam side down in shallow ovenproof baking dish. Set aside.

(continued on next page)

(continued from preceding page)

Stir in remaining green chilies and Tabasco sauce. Pour over enchiladas. Bake at 375° for 15 minutes. Sprinkle with remaining cheese. Bake 10 minutes longer. Remove from oven. Top each enchilada with remaining salsa and dollops of sour cream.

Place tomato purée, garlic and remaining onion in blender. Purée until smooth. Stir in remaining green chilies and Tabasco sauce. Pour over enchiladas. Bake at 375° for 15 minutes. Sprinkle with remaining cheese. Bake 10 minutes longer. Top with salsa.

Nutritional information per serving:

Calories:	349	Calories:	191
Total fat:	17 g	Total fat:	4 g
Percentage of calories from fat:	45%	Percentage of calories from fat:	19%
Carbohydrate:	30 g	Carbohydrate:	22 g
Protein:	19 g	Protein:	17 g
Cholesterol:	60 mg	Cholesterol:	31 mg
Sodium:	653 mg	Sodium:	568 mg
Dietary fiber:	1 g	Dietary fiber:	1 g

Modifications:

- Eliminate butter for sautéing by using nonstick skillet.
- Remove skin from chicken.
- Use reduced-fat Cheddar cheese and reduce amount.
- Use nonfat sour cream.
- Use corn tortillas.

Calories saved per serving: 158
Fat saved per serving: 13 grams

A Last Word

Undertaking the Positive Diet is a life-style change, and no life-style change is easily accomplished. But we've done it, and so can you. Remember, it's a long-range plan. If you blow it on one day, don't be discouraged. Simply vow to start over again the next day. The important thing is to make steady progress.

CHAPTER TWENTY-THREE

STEP 6–EXERCISE TO CHANGE YOUR DIET

Neither cardiovascular health nor permanent weight control comes about through diet exclusively. A low-fat diet pattern needs to be balanced by regular exercise. Studies show that physically active people have health benefits such as increased cardiovascular stamina, lower heart rate, lower blood pressure, increased bone density, enhanced glucose tolerance, reduced body fat, greater maintenance of muscle mass and strength, increased metabolism, better ability to cope with stress, and greater longevity. Says Dr. Robert Butler, former director of the National Institute on Aging, "If exercise could be packaged into a pill, it would be the single most widely prescribed—and beneficial—medicine in the nation."

Unfortunately, not many of us have taken this advice. It is estimated that only 11% of American adults exercise with the intensity, duration and frequency generally recommended for cardiovascular benefit, while 27% of adults are completely sedentary. Although 40% of American adults report that they play sports regularly, more than a third of the sports cited do not efficiently work the heart and lungs. As one physician told me, "As a nation, Americans do not exercise. What we really do is buy exercise stuff!"

Exercise and Cardiac Health

Physical inactivity is linked directly to coronary heart disease. "Since couch potatoes run nearly twice the risk of coronary heart disease as people who are physically active," says Dr. William L. Haskell of Stanford University, "a sedentary life-style just doesn't pay. Sedentary people are at the same risk for heart attacks as the obese and heavy smokers." While a sedentary life-style by itself may not bring on a heart attack, studies show that a fundamental connection exists. Conversely, these same studies suggest a strong correlation between physical activity—even if moderate—and protection from coronary heart disease. One study involving thousands of Harvard alumni found that physically active men had fewer and milder heart attacks and lived longer than their sedentary classmates. Benefits began to appear as soon as the men expended 500 calories a week in exercise, with peak benefits coming between 2,000 and 3,500 calories a week. The study also showed that benefits tapered off after 3,500 calories, thereby making *moderate, regular exercise* the best prescription.

The same findings come from a study conducted by Dr. Steven Blair at the Aerobics Institute in Dallas. Over 10,000 men and 3,000 women, none with any evidence of heart disease or cancer, were followed for eight years. Participants in the study were divided into groups based on level of fitness. The "least fit" group comprised sedentary people; the "medium fit" group, people who exercised moderately; and the "most fit" group, those who exercised vigorously. Deaths were found to be sharply higher in the "least fit" category than in the "medium fit" and "most fit" categories. The study showed that regular exercise is associated with increased longevity, primarily by decreasing the risks of heart disease and cancer. In addition, it showed that even a minimal amount of exercise—a brisk half-hour walk once a day to produce "medium fitness"—provides significant protection.

Calories Burned Per Minute

	Weight in Pounds				
Activity	**Up to 130**	**131 to 152**	**153 to 170**	**171 to 187**	**188+**
Badminton/volleyball	4.4	5.4	6.1	6.8	7.4
Baseball	3.6	4.5	5.0	5.6	6.1
Basketball	5.5	6.7	7.5	8.4	9.2
Bowling (nonstop)	5.2	6.3	7.1	7.9	8.7
Calisthenics	3.9	4.8	5.4	5.9	6.5
Cycling:					
5½ mph	3.9	4.8	5.4	5.9	6.5
13 mph	8.3	10.2	11.5	12.7	14.0
Dancing:					
Moderate	3.3	4.0	4.4	5.0	5.5
Vigorous	4.4	5.4	6.1	6.7	7.4
Golf:					
Twosome	4.2	5.2	5.8	6.4	7.1
Foursome	3.2	3.9	4.4	4.8	5.3
Handball/squash/racquetball	7.6	9.3	10.4	11.6	12.7
Housework	3.2	3.9	4.4	4.8	5.3
Rope skipping:					
70 counts/minute	6.0	7.4	8.3	9.2	10.0
100 counts/minute	9.9	12.0	13.6	15.0	16.5
Rowing:					
Leisurely	3.9	4.8	5.4	5.9	6.5
Vigorous	10.6	13.0	14.6	16.2	17.8
Running:					
5½ mph	8.3	10.2	11.5	12.7	14.0
7 mph	10.8	13.3	14.9	16.6	18.0
9 mph	12.9	14.8	16.6	19.9	20.2

Calories Burned Per Minute

Activity	Weight in Pounds: Up to 130	131 to 152	153 to 170	171 to 187	188+
Skating	4.4	5.4	6.1	6.6	7.4
Soccer	6.9	8.5	9.6	10.6	11.7
Swimming:					
Crawl (moderate)	3.8	4.6	5.1	5.7	6.3
Crawl (vigorous)	8.3	10.1	11.4	12.6	13.9
Sidestroke	6.5	7.9	8.9	9.9	10.9
Tennis:					
Moderate	5.4	6.6	7.4	8.2	9.0
Vigorous	7.6	9.3	10.4	11.6	12.7
Walking:					
2 mph	2.7	3.3	3.8	4.2	4.6
4½ mph	5.0	6.3	7.1	7.9	8.6
Up/down stairs	9.3	11.4	12.8	14.2	15.6
Weight lifting	6.0	7.2	8.2	8.9	9.4

Source: American College of Sports Medicine.

Exercise improves cardiac health in a number of ways. It *strengthens the heart* as a muscle, thereby increasing its efficiency and ability to perform with less effort. A person who lifts weights, for example, soon finds biceps growing and arm strength increasing. It's the same with cardiac muscle: when exercised regularly, it gets stronger and becomes a more efficient pump. The positive effect of exercise on the heart can often be measured in changes in resting pulse. The "average" resting pulse is 72 beats per minute. But if the heart gains efficiency through exercise, the resting pulse might be reduced to 60 beats per minute, a considerable saving in wear and tear on the heart.

Exercise also *strengthens other muscles*, particularly those that are stimulated by the legs in walking or jogging. A well-trained, "strong" muscle requires less oxygen when compared with an untrained muscle. In this way, by strengthening peripheral muscles, exercise reduces the demands on the heart.

One of the most important benefits of regular exercise is that it *increases HDL cholesterol*. With a level under 35 mg/dl cited as an independent cardiac risk factor, raising HDL levels is very desirable. Unfortunately, "protective" HDL cholesterol responds to only a few life-style habits. Along with weight reduction and smoking cessation, regular exercise is the best action a person can take to boost HDL cholesterol. Studies on walkers show that walking two miles a day, three times a week, can raise HDL levels by one to three points. Larger HDL increases can occur with more extensive training (such as running 20 to 30 miles a week).

EXERCISE AND WEIGHT CONTROL

Physical activity is essential for weight loss and weight control. Although much of our concern is focused on being "overweight," the real problem is being "overfat"—carrying an excess of body fat. Unfortunately, body fat cannot be dieted away. But exercise can *burn body fat* as fuel. Again, moderate exercise is the most effective type. This is because the body burns fat for fuel in longer, slower exercise (such as walking for 45 minutes), whereas it burns sugar in short, intense exercise (such as sprinting). Moderate exercise tends to decrease appetite. Most health professionals recommend balancing a low-fat diet (to decrease caloric intake) with a regular program of moderate exercise (to burn stored body fat) as the most effective method of permanent weight loss.

Exercise also *raises metabolism*, the rate at which the body burns calories. In effect, exercise revs up the body's engine and keeps it running (burning calories) at a higher level for hours after the exercise is completed. One study showed that people who exercised had a metabolic rate 7.5% to 28% higher than if they had not exercised, and that the higher rate continued for four to seven hours after they stopped. By causing the metabolic furnace to burn at a higher level, regular exercise makes it harder for the body to conserve energy (calories) and easier for it to lose weight. Says Dr. Jack Wilmore, an exercise expert at the University of Texas, "If exercising regularly changes your metabolism even slightly, so that you burn an extra 100 calories a day, that small change can add up to 10 pounds of weight loss a year."

And finally, exercise *maintains muscle,* a critical factor because muscle is what burns fat. In addition, muscle tissue has a faster metabolism than fat tissue. Body fat is the fuel, but muscle is the engine. The more muscle you have (the bigger the engine), the easier it is to burn fat (fuel). Health professionals recommend moderate exercise, such as walking, in combination with resistance training (such as light weight lifting, rowing, push-ups or aerobic dance) to build and preserve muscle tissue.

Exercise and a Healthy Diet

While most people know about the benefits of regular exercise for cardiac health and weight control, what is not so readily recognized is that exercise can help you to make healthy dietary changes and stick with them. *Indeed, exercise is the first step to a permanent change in dietary habits.*

There is an axiom that states, "When you're under stress, all roads lead to the refrigerator." Most of us know from our own experience that this is true. When we're hurried and harried, anxious about what is to come and depressed over what has already come, we often make poor life-style decisions. It is at such times that we overeat, binge, or live for days on a diet of fast food, frozen meals and snacks.

Trying to change dietary habits can be stressful. Sometimes the pressure created to "eat right" simply drives us to "eat wrong." "I was so worried about eating less meat," one person told me, "that I ate two chocolate bars before I even noticed."

Exercise, however, *dissipates stress*. This is why physically fit people can better cope with stresses such as dietary change. Described as nature's own tranquilizer, exercise may be the most effective method of dissipating pressure, reducing tension and increasing endorphins (natural painkillers produced by the brain). Studies at Duke and Stanford universities have revealed that people who exercise demonstrate more positive moods, self-esteem, self-confidence and a sense of well-being along with less anxiety, stress and depression than those who exercise little or not at all.

One of the results of dissipating stress is better control over eating habits. People who are calm and relaxed are less likely to have dietary habits that include overeating. In addition, studies show that people who exercise regularly choose to eat more healthful foods and fewer "fat tooth" foods than their more sedentary counterparts. Says Dr. Kenneth R. Pelletier, "When people take time out to exercise regularly, they're demonstrating a psychological stance that in itself is going to give them better control over their food choices."

Exercise also *creates an environment for success*. Dietary change is often frustrating because it usually involves the giving up of favorite, comfortable foods. In this respect, attempting such change can be a negative experience. Exercise, however, can help turn a negative situation into a positive experience by emphasizing what we *can do* rather than what we *can't have.* It serves as a positive distraction by giving people something to focus on besides food.

In addition, unlike dietary change, an exercise program is easy to start and progress can be made quickly. This often produces a feeling of success that carries over to other aspects of life—including making more healthful food choices. In this way, success with exercise breeds success with new dietary habits.

Aerobic Exercise Is Best

Anything you can do to increase physical activity is beneficial—even gardening, using stairs and parking at the far end of the lot. Indeed, the most recent government guidelines on healthy exercise say 30 minutes daily of moderate, intermittent exercise, like a brisk walk, does almost as much good as one heart-pounding, nonstop workout in the gym. One big difference from past recommendations is that the exercise does not have to be continuous. It can be 5 minutes here, 10 minutes there, as long as it adds up to at least 30 minutes and as long as it's brisk. Another difference is that exercise can be of moderate intensity and still produce health benefits.

While mild-to-moderate-intensity exercise can increase general health, it takes moderate-to-high-intensity exercise to increase cardiovascular fitness. From the standpoint of cardiovascular fitness, aerobic exercise is still the best. Aerobic exercise is simply physical activity that makes the large muscles work hard—but not so hard that the heart and lungs cannot keep up with the oxygen demand. Some of the best aerobic exercises include:

Brisk walking
Cross-country skiing
(indoor and outdoor)
Cycling (indoor)
Rowing (indoor)
Running in place
Skipping rope
Swimming
Stair machine

Some of the exercises and activities that can be aerobic, if performed at a continual vigorous pace for a period of time, include:

Aerobic dance
Basketball
Cycling (outdoor)
Handball/squash/
racquetball
Hiking
Rowing (outdoor)
Skating (ice or roller)
Soccer
Tennis (singles)

THE F.I.T. CRITERIA

In order to be aerobic, an exercise must conform to the F.I.T. criteria: frequency, intensity and time. How often, how hard, how long—these are the key elements for building cardiac fitness.

FREQUENCY

Many health professionals counsel an aerobic exercise program of four days a week, once every other day. This takes into account the recommendations of the American College of Sports Medicine, which suggest that:

- Fitness is *improved* if you exercise more than three days a week.
- Fitness is *maintained* if you exercise three days a week.

- Fitness is *lost* if you exercise less than three days a week.

Exercising three or four days a week is optimal for cardiovascular conditioning. People who need to lose a great amount of weight may need to exercise daily. However, anyone who exercises more than four days a week should be certain to alternate non-jarring activities, such as brisk walking and swimming, to minimize strain and other injuries.

INTENSITY

How hard you exercise is an important determinant of effectiveness. Golf, casual walking and similar forms of light exercise may improve general health but simply do not stress the heart muscle sufficiently to improve cardiovascular fitness. Unless you're a competitive athlete, sprinting and other intense exercise may result in injury or fatigue rather than fitness. Research shows that the most effective exercise is done at a moderate pace. Exercise intensity is determined by heart rate, or pulse, during the activity or by perceived exertion.

Pulse rate indicates how many heartbeats it takes to meet the circulation needs of the body. There are many places where a pulse can be taken: chest, neck, temple, wrist, groin, inside of the elbow. Pressing in gently, you can feel the "throb" of rushing blood. Each "throb" is one beat. The "normal" resting pulse is between 60 and 90 beats per minute, with an "average" of 72 beats per minute. During a brisk jog, it might be twice that number.

Aerobic exercise calls for the heart rate to be elevated and maintained within certain parameters. A good way for healthy (non-cardiac) individuals to estimate optimal intensity is to exercise within the target heart-rate zone. (Many physicians do not recommend target heart rates for cardiac patients, particularly those on cardiac medications; instead, they use a perceived exertion scale, which will be explained later in the chapter.) The target heart-rate zone is a function of maximal heart rate, a limit on how fast the heart is capable of beating. This is determined by age, not by physical fitness. The maximal heart rate for healthy (non-cardiac) persons can be estimated by this formula: 220 minus age in years. A 50-year-old person with a maximal heart rate of 170, for instance, will generally have a lower maximum heart rate than a 30-year-old with a maximal heart rate of 190—even if the 50-year-old is in better physical condition.

What is your maximal heart rate?

	Sample 30-Year-Old	**You**
Everyone starts here	220	220
Subtract your age	– 30	–___
Estimated maximum heart rate	=190	=

No one should exercise at the maximum heart rate. Instead, you should try to stay within your target heart-rate zone, which is defined by the American Heart Association as being between 60% and 75% of your maximum heart rate. The target heart-rate zone for a 30-year-old, for instance, is between 114 (60%) and 142 (75%) beats per minute.

The chart that follows offers a quick way to determine maximum heart rate and target zone by age group. Individual ranges may differ from 10 to 20 beats per minute. An exercise stress test can determine true maximum heart rate—another good reason to see your doctor before starting to exercise. Beginners should work at the lower end of this zone, and only competitive athletes should work at 75%.

Target Heart-Rate Zones

Age	Maximum Heart Rate*	Target Zone*
20–24	200	120–150
25–29	195	117–146
30–34	190	114–142
35–39	185	111–132
40–44	180	108–135
45–49	175	105–131
50–54	170	102–127
55–59	165	99–123
60–64	160	96–120
65–69	155	93–116
70 and over	150	90–113

* Heartbeats per minute.

There is no magic at being at the upper end of the target zone. Research indicates that less intensive activities such as brisk walking and low-impact aerobics are very effective.

Indeed, some health professionals believe a zone with a lower end of 55% provides cardiovascular training with less risk of injury. Reduced intensity can be compensated for by increasing the frequency and/or duration of training.

To determine whether or not you're in your target zone, wait until you're about 5 or 10 minutes into the exercise, then stop and locate your pulse on the side of your neck or on the thumb side of your wrist. Press hard enough to find your pulse, but avoid pressing too hard on your neck, which can slow your pulse and give an inaccurate count. Practice taking your pulse while you're at rest. If you have a hard time finding your pulse while exercising, try putting your hand over your heart and counting the beats. Once you've found your pulse, count it for 10 seconds. Use your first two fingers (not your thumb). Be sure to count the first beat as zero. Then multiply the count by six to calculate your exercise pulse for one minute. If your pulse rate is below your target zone, you probably need to increase effort; if it's above, you can ease off a bit.

Remember, cardiac patients generally should not use target heart-rate zones. Cardiac patients, particularly those on medications, should check with their doctor regarding exercise heart rate. Many medications can cause changes in heart rate, so in general people on such medications should not use the target zone as a guide.

A better method is to use a system called Perceived Exertion: how you feel during exercise. This system is based on the simple concept that the mind is an excellent judge of how much work the body is doing. The Perceived Exertion Scale grades exercise levels based on the individual's overall feeling of exertion and physical fatigue: rest; very, very light; very light; fairly light; somewhat hard; hard; very hard; and very, very hard. These ratings correspond well with certain metabolic responses to exercise, such as heart rate and oxygen consumption.

Perceived Exertion Scale

	6	Rest
	7	Very, very light
	8	
	9	Very light
	10	
↑	11	Fairly light
	12	
Target Heart-Rate Zone	13	Somewhat hard
	14	
↓	15	Hard
	16	
	17	Very hard
	18	
	19	Very, very hard
	20	

This personal assessment of exercise intensity should focus on the overall, or total, feeling of exertion without overemphasizing any one factor, such as leg pain. Exercise rated as "fairly light" to "hard" is generally appropriate for cardiovascular conditioning, corresponding to 70% to 85% of maximal heart rate. For more general health benefits, it may be enough to exercise at a perceived level of only "very light."

Pay attention to signs of overexertion, such as pounding in your chest, dizziness or faintness, or profuse sweating. If you're very tired during the exercise or if it takes you more than an hour to recover, you may be working too hard regardless of your heart rate. On the other hand, if the exercise doesn't take any effort and there is no hard breathing or sweating, then your pace probably needs to be increased. If you feel that you're performing the exercise at an appropriate level of intensity, stay at that level—even if you're not in your target zone. Listening to your body is of prime importance when exercising. For example, when jogging or walking, be sure your pace lets you carry on a conversation. If you're too out of breath to talk, you're pushing too hard. Perceived Exertion is a guideline to keep you from overdoing it and hurting yourself.

TIME

It is recommended that you exercise (preferably in your target heart-rate zone) for a minimum of 20 continuous minutes in order to promote cardiovascular fitness. Remember, this is a *minimum.* An ideal duration would be 30 minutes to one hour, depending on the activity. Warm-up and cool-down activities such as stretching are not part of the 20-minute minimum. Be sure to give yourself time to build up a tolerance for exercise. Don't expect to walk briskly for an hour your first day out. Take it slow and easy, build up your stamina and endurance, and you'll be able to go for as long as you like without injuring yourself. As with diet, do not be interested in a quick fix. The proper perspective is: How shall I keep physically active for a lifetime?

BEFORE YOU GET STARTED

Make exercise the first step in changing your dietary habits. But before you exercise, remember to get an okay from your doctor. The American Heart Association recommends a stress test before undertaking anything more strenuous than walking, particularly if you're over 40 years old, have abnormal findings such as high blood pressure, have coronary disease, have a family history of coronary disease or more than one coronary risk factor (e.g., obesity, smoking, elevated blood pressure, a sedentary life-style) or have not had a checkup recently.

Select an activity that is enjoyable. If you hate jogging, don't do it. Try brisk walking instead. Keep looking until you find an activity that suits you.

Listen to your body. If it hurts, stop the activity. Never "go for the burn." Remember, the target heart-rate zone is just a guide. Take time to warm up and cool down. Gentle stretching before and after exercise reduces muscle soreness and injury. Always start your exercise routine slowly, gradually move into your target zone, and end with a gentle slowing down. Build your fitness gradually. Don't try to undo years of sedentary habits in the first week of exercise.

And finally, enjoy yourself. I always thought jogging was a drudge until I had bypass surgery and had to consider a life *without* jogging. Every morning run for me now is a joy, a celebration of the fact that I'm still here and still able to jog.

CHAPTER TWENTY-FOUR

STEP 7—DEVELOP A SENSE OF PERSPECTIVE

While it is critical to make dietary recommendations based upon nutritional science, we should not lose sight of the fact that a diet pattern is about real food for real people. Putting together a healthy diet for a lifetime is more than nutritional advice expressed in percentages and grams.

There is no doubt that high-fat foods, particularly those rich in saturated and trans fat, raise cholesterol levels and increase cardiac risk. So cutting fat must be a nutritional priority. But if we concentrate just on that, we may learn the wrong lesson.

Good food and good health are not the result of single-idea messages. We cut sugar, only to find that it is a minor player compared with fat. We threw out the salt shaker, only to learn that just sodium-sensitive people need to be that diligent. And we overreacted to oat bran, first loving it and virtually sprinkling it on ice cream, then feeling like fools. Now, in our zeal to cut fat down to zero, it has become easy to construct a diet that is nutritionally horrendous . . . but low in fat. Start the day with a low-fat shake or skip breakfast, have a few slices of processed turkey roll on white bread and a no-fat dressing on your salad for lunch, grab a fat-free cookie after work, and then, for dinner, pop a low-fat frozen dinner into the microwave. Sure it's a low-fat day, but what have we missed? How about fiber, beta carotene, vitamin A and vitamin C, for starters?

The point is that we must be sure to temper our obsession with fat and remember food. Counting fat down to the last gram in everything you eat is tedious and misses the point. Who wants to spend half of every meal grilling the waiter on the fat content of every dish? Or swear you'll never again eat another olive, avocado, cashew, scone, Swiss chocolate, marinated vegetables, Brie, or drop of olive oil? *Foods that are low in fat and foods that taste delicious are not in diametric opposition*. Eating well is necessary to establishing low-fat dietary habits.

Today's cooks look for menu ideas that are simple and easy to prepare. But "simple" should not be equated with "dull." We only have to look at the cultures of the Mediterranean region, Japan, China and Mexico to find diet patterns that are both low in fat and rich in delicious foods. We need to adapt their concepts to eating in America.

The proper perspective, I believe, comes from a diet based on foods rich in complex carbohydrates and fiber, particularly whole grains and beans. These are the body's most effective fuel. To this core, add fruits and vegetables, particularly those richly endowed with antioxidants. Eat small amounts of lean meat and poultry; use them as condiments for grains and beans. Eat fish twice a week to get a good supply of protective fish oil. Get your calcium from nonfat dairy foods. When you choose fats, make them monounsaturated and polyunsaturated oils. Enjoy alcohol in moderation. Always use low-fat cooking methods. Use meal planning and creative substitution to ensure variety and palatability.

And give yourself enough time to make changes. Despite hype to the contrary, these changes can be very difficult for many people. Remember, the process is evolutionary, not revolutionary.

There are three places where healthy dietary precepts must be put into practice: in the kitchen, in the supermarket and in a restaurant. If you use a proper perspective in each place, your habits will provide you with good food and good health.

DON'T EAT YOUR HEART OUT
COOKBOOK

NUTRITIONAL ANALYSES

A nutritional analysis is provided for each recipe, usually on a per-serving basis and listing total calories, grams of fat, grams of saturated fat, percentage of calories from fat, grams of protein, grams of carbohydrate, grams of dietary fiber, milligrams of cholesterol and milligrams of sodium.

In the interest of consistency and clarity, these decisions were made concerning the analyses:

- When a range is given for an ingredient, the midpoint amount is analyzed.
- When the ingredients listing gives one or more options, the first ingredient is the one analyzed.
- Figures are rounded off to whole numbers, so there may be slight discrepancies between an analysis for a whole meal and the sum of its parts.
- Fat-grams are rounded off to whole numbers, so there might be slight discrepancies in the percentage of calories from fat. A total of less than 0.5 grams of fat is considered a trace amount.
- In many cases, salads and dressings are analyzed separately. The amount of dressing, which is an individual choice, can greatly alter the calories and fat content of a salad.
- We have used "extra-lean" ground beef that is 90% lean/10% fat, which according to the Meat Board has no more than 11 grams of fat per 3.5 ounces, cooked.

- Recipes that call for "light" soy sauce use a soy sauce yielding 600 milligrams of sodium per tablespoon (about half that of regular soy sauce).

- Recipes that call for chicken or beef stock are analyzed based on the figures for homemade stock.

- Recipes that call for "reduced-fat" cheese use a cheese containing 5 grams of fat and 80 calories per ounce.

- A few recipes use "super light" margarine, which yields 2 grams of fat and 20 calories per tablespoon.

- Recipes that call for homemade salsa yield approximately 132 milligrams of sodium less per tablespoon than commercial brands.

- Some recipes are so low in calories that even a trace of fat causes a high fat percentage. Be more concerned about the number of grams of fat in the food than the percentage of calories from fat.

- In recipes calling for oil-based marinades, only a quarter to a half of the marinade was used in the nutritional analysis if the marinade is drained off before cooking.

- Portions are based on average-size servings and have not been shaved to make the numbers appear more favorable.

The menus and recipes are designed to ensure that meals fall well within the American Heart Association's guidelines for fat, cholesterol and sodium. Bear in mind that in a few cases, in order to have proper taste and texture, a particular recipe may exceed the fat guideline (no more than 30% of calories from fat) even in its fat-reduced version. The great majority of recipes in this book keep well below this percentage and all of them are significantly below the fat content of conventional recipes. However, while accommodating as healthy a diet as possible, this must be balanced with foods that give pleasure rather than simply adhere to strict numerical rules.

Remember, whatever health guideline you use, whether it's 30%, 25% or 20% calories from fat, the reference is to *total daily caloric intake,* meaning that not every recipe or single food must be below that fat percentage. How the meal or the foods for the day go together is more to the point. Thus a low-fat meal might be capped off with a dessert that is relatively higher in fat. The more important perspective is how many grams of fat you're eating for the day, and whether or not that figure falls within your fat budget.

Every effort has been made to ensure the accuracy of nutritional data information; however, we cannot guarantee suitability for specific, medically imposed diets. People with special dietary needs should consult with their physician and/or a registered dietitian.

Recipes have been analyzed for nutritional content by Beverly Utt, M.S., M.P.H., R.D., a registered dietitian in private practice, using Nutri-Calc Plus by Camde Corporation. Each analysis is based on the entry of nutritional data for all ingredients in each recipe. The primary sources for values used in the analyses include the *Agriculture Handbook 8 Series* and information from manufacturers. Occasionally, data are incomplete or unavailable. In those cases, substitutions of similar ingredients are made.

TABLE OF SUBSTITUTIONS

Rather than:	Use:		Save Fat-Grams	Save Calories
Whole milk	Nonfat milk	Per cup:	8	70
	1% milk	Per cup:	6	45
2% milk	Nonfat milk	Per cup:	5	45
	1% milk	Per cup:	3	20
Buttermilk	Nonfat buttermilk	Per cup:	3.5	30
	1% buttermilk	Per cup:	2	20
Evaporated milk	Skim evaporated milk	Per ½ cup:	10	55
	Lite evaporated milk	Per ½ cup:	7	60
Sour cream	Nonfat sour cream	Per Tbs.:	3	—
	Low-fat sour cream	Per Tbs.:	2	10
Yogurt	Nonfat yogurt	Per cup:	8	90
	Low-fat yogurt	Per cup:	3	60
Cheese	Fat-free cheese	Per oz.:	9	70
	Low-fat or light cheese	Per oz.:	6	40
	Reduced-fat cheese	Per oz.:	4	30
Cottage cheese	1% low-fat cottage cheese	Per ½ cup:	4	40
Cream cheese	Nonfat cream cheese	Per 1 oz.:	10	135
	Light cream cheese	Per 1 oz.:	5	40
Whipped cream	Frozen toppings (w/o coconut oil)	Per 2 Tbs.:	5	40
	Pressurized light whipped cream	Per 2 Tbs.:	5	34
Cream:				
In coffee	Nondairy lighteners	Per 2 Tbs.:	4	40
In cooking	Nonfat yogurt	Per ½ cup:	30	235

Rather than:	Use:	Save Fat-Grams	Save Calories
Ice cream:			
Super premium ice cream, 16% fat	Nonfat ice cream	Per ½ cup: 18	190
	"Light" ice cream (ice milk)	Per ½ cup: 14	170
	Premium ice cream, 10% fat	Per ½ cup: 8	130
	Frozen fruit bar	Per ½ cup: 18	210
	Sorbet	Per ½ cup: 17	170
Premium ice cream, 10% fat	Nonfat ice cream	Per ½ cup: 10	60
	"Light" ice cream (ice milk)	Per ½ cup: 6	40
	Frozen fruit bar	Per ½ cup: 10	80
	Sorbet	Per ½ cup: 9	40
"Light" ice cream (ice milk)	Nonfat ice cream	Per ½ cup: 4	20
	Frozen fruit bar	Per ½ cup: 3	—
Frozen yogurt	Nonfat frozen yogurt	Per 3 oz.: 3	30
Whole eggs:			
1 large	2 egg whites	5	60
	Egg substitute, nonfat	Per ¼ cup: 5	50
2 large	1 whole egg and 1 egg white	5	60
	Egg substitute, nonfat	Per ½ cup: 10	125
3 large	1 whole egg and 2 egg whites	10	120
	Egg substitute, nonfat	Per ¾ cup: 15	150
Mayonnaise	Fat-free mayonnaise	Per Tbs.: 11	90
	Light mayonnaise	Per Tbs.: 6	50
	Mustard	Per Tbs.: 11	90

Rather than:	Use:		Save Fat-Grams	Save Calories
Butter or stick margarine	Butter substitute	Per Tbs.:	11	90
	Reduced-calorie soft margarine	Per Tbs.:	6	10
	Super light margarine	Per Tbs.:	9	60
	Nonfat cream cheese	Per Tbs.:	11	75
	Jam/jelly	Per Tbs.:	11	60
Salad dressing	Fat-free (no oil) dressing	Per Tbs.:	7	65
	Light dressing	Per Tbs.:	4	40
	Broth-base home-made dressing	Per Tbs.:	7	60
Flour tortilla	Corn tortilla		2	25
Frying in oil	Nonstick skillet	Per Tbs.:	14	120
	w/ cooking spray	Per 2-sec. spray:	14	115
Oil-packed tuna	Water-packed tuna	Per 2 oz.:	12	90
Top sirloin, broiled	T-bone, broiled	Per 3.5 oz.:	20	145
Regular ground beef (73% lean), broiled	"85% lean" ground beef, broiled	Per 3.5 oz.:	7	51
	"95% extra-lean" ground beef, broiled	Per 3.5 oz.:	15	136
	Round steak, full cut, lean only, broiled	Per 3.5 oz.:	14	105
Beef hot dog	Light beef hot dog	Per 1 reg.:	12	60
Turkey hot dog	Light beef hot dog	Per 1 reg.:	8	25
Chopped ham	Boiled ham	2 slices:	4	40

Rather than:	Use:	Save Fat-Grams		Save Calories
Bacon	Canadian bacon	Per 1 oz.:	5	35
Chicken, light meat w/skin	Chicken, light meat, skinless	Per 3.5 oz.:	4	30
Chicken, dark meat, skinless	Chicken, light meat, skinless	Per 3.5 oz.:	7	45
Chicken, dark meat w/skin	Chicken, light meat, skinless	Per 3.5 oz.:	12	80
Turkey, light meat w/skin	Turkey, light meat, skinless	Per 3.5 oz.:	7	65
Turkey, dark meat, skinless	Turkey, light meat, skinless	Per 3.5 oz.:	4	30
Turkey, dark meat w/skin	Turkey, light meat, skinless	Per 3.5 oz.:	8	65
Ground turkey	Ground turkey breast	Per 3.5 oz.:	6	80
Turkey sandwich on a croissant	Turkey sandwich on whole-wheat bread	Per sandwich:	12	140
Chocolate cookie	Fat-free chocolate cookie	Per cookie:	3	20
Potato chips	Light potato chips	Per oz.:	3	30
Tortilla chips	Light tortilla chips	Per oz.:	3	30
	Oil-free, baked (not fried) tortilla chips	Per oz.:	5	30
Fruit Danish pastry	Bagel w/ 1 Tbs. jam	Per 1 med.:	12	45
Bran muffin	English muffin	Per muffin:	12	205

HERBS AND SEASONINGS

The creative use of herbs and seasonings is a key to preparing delicious foods with less fat and less salt. Dried herbs and spices are readily available in food stores. What is different from the past is the great variety of combinations, such as Mrs. Dash's Garlic and Herb Salt-Free Seasoning. Many are found in low- or no-sodium versions. The best advice is to try a number of different brands until you find one that you like the best.

What is more exciting, however, is the vast array of fresh herbs available all year long in the produce section of supermarkets. Basil, tarragon, dill and other fresh herbs are packed in small amounts, perfect for use in family cooking. Unlike dried herbs, fresh herbs give an intense zip to recipes without added salt or fat.

The list that follows suggests herbs and seasonings that are particularly well-suited to various foods.

Artichokes	Bay leaves, lemon, garlic, onion, black pepper
Asparagus	Lemon, vinegar, garlic, onion, marjoram
Baked beans	Cloves, ginger, oregano, savory
Beef	Allspice, bay leaves, mustard, garlic, mace, mushrooms, marjoram, thyme, basil, chervil, onion, green pepper, parsley, caraway seed, chili powder, cumin, ginger, oregano, rosemary, savory, tarragon
Berries	Anise
Broccoli	Lemon, vinegar, black pepper, onion, tomato, sesame seed, mustard, oregano

Carrots	Bay leaves, caraway seed, celery seed, chives, curry powder, dill, dill seed, ginger, mace, marjoram, nutmeg, savory, tarragon, thyme
Cauliflower	Caraway seed, celery seed, curry powder, dill, dill seed, mustard, nutmeg, oregano, savory, tarragon, thyme
Corn	Chervil, garlic powder, onion powder, lime juice, chili powder, chives
Cucumber	Chives, dill, garlic, onion, vinegar
Eggplant	Oregano, garlic, black pepper, onion, parsley, tomato, green pepper, mushrooms, chili powder, marjoram, sage, thyme
Green beans	Basil, lemon, dill, garlic, tarragon, black pepper, marjoram, onion, mushrooms, water chestnuts, tomato, curry powder, mustard, sesame seed
Gravies	Allspice, basil, bay leaves
Lamb	Allspice, garlic, lemon, curry powder, rosemary, mint, tomato, onion, marjoram, mushrooms, green pepper, basil, dill, dill seed, mustard, tarragon
Melons	Anise, cardamom, ginger
Peas	Almonds, basil, chervil, marjoram, mint, mushrooms, onion, dill, dill seed, mustard, oregano, rosemary, sage
Pork	Caraway seed, chili powder, cloves, curry powder, ginger, marjoram, mustard, mustard seed, oregano, rosemary, sage, tarragon, thyme
Poultry	Lemon, paprika, curry, black pepper, oregano, tarragon, thyme, rosemary, cayenne, celery, onion, garlic, tomato, mushrooms, marjoram, green chilies, parsley, dill, ginger, mustard, sage, turmeric

Rice	Chives, saffron, green pepper, onion, mushrooms, savory
Seafood	Allspice, lemon, ginger, celery, onion, tomato, garlic, fennel, chervil, watercress, basil, mushrooms, bay leaves, marjoram, oregano, paprika
Soups and stews	Bay leaves, chili powder, chives, dill, marjoram, oregano, parsley flakes, rosemary
Squash	Cinnamon, ginger, black pepper, basil, mace, onion, cloves, marjoram, mustard, savory
Stewed fruit	Cinnamon
Sweet potato	Nutmeg, cardamom, cinnamon, cloves, ginger
Veal	Allspice, thyme, black pepper, bay leaves, oregano, garlic, chervil, curry, ginger, marjoram, tomato, parsley, apricot, sage, tarragon
White potato	Paprika, parsley, dill, chervil, chives, mace, rosemary, black pepper, garlic powder, basil, bay leaves, mustard, oregano, savory, sesame seed
Zucchini	Lemon, parsley, black pepper, tomato, garlic

APPETIZERS

BRUSCHETTA

16 servings (1 slice bread with ¼ cup tomato mixture)

1 pound fresh, ripe plum tomatoes, chopped
3 garlic cloves, finely chopped
2 tablespoons olive oil
1 loaf Italian, Tuscan, or peasant bread
16 kalamata olives, pitted and chopped
¼ cup chopped fresh basil
2 tablespoons chopped fresh Italian parsley

Combine tomatoes, garlic, and olive oil. Let stand at room temperature for 1 hour.

Meanwhile, slice bread into approximately 16 half-inch slices. Toast under a preheated broiler or in a toaster oven for 2 to 3 minutes, or until brown on both sides.

Just before serving, add olives, basil, and parsley to tomato mixture. Spoon mixture into a medium-size bowl and place in center of a basket or serving tray. Ring with toasted bread.

Variation: Lightly spread bread with Garlic Olive Oil (page 431) before or after toasting. Pour some oil into a spray bottle and spray it on the bread. (Spraying allows a lot of flavor while using a very small amount of oil.)

Serving Suggestion: Bruschetta works well as an appetizer or first course, especially with pasta, and is great on a picnic with roast or grilled chicken.

APPROXIMATE NUTRITIONAL INFORMATION PER SERVING

Calories: 95
Total fat: 3 g
Saturated fat: 0 g
Percentage of calories from fat: 25%
Carbohydrate: 15 g
Protein: 3 g
Cholesterol: 0 mg
Sodium: 239 mg
Dietary fiber: trace

The Easiest Vegetable Antipasto

10 servings

1 15-ounce jar pickled beans
1 15-ounce jar pickled asparagus
1 15-ounce jar pickled snap peas
1 15-ounce can water-packed baby ears of corn
1 14½-ounce can water-packed artichoke hearts
1 15-ounce can pitted black olives

Chill vegetables in their individual jars or cans. When ready to assemble the hors d'oeuvre, thoroughly drain vegetables. Pat dry with paper towles, if necessary. Arrange beans, asparagus, snap peas, baby corn, and artichoke hearts in individual vegetable mounds on a serving platter or tray. Tuck olives among the mounds.

Serving Suggestion: Goes well with a heaping platter of shrimp cocktail.

APPROXIMATE NUTRITIONAL INFORMATION PER SERVING

Calories: 63
Total fat: 2 g
Saturated fat: 0 g
Percentage of calories from fat: 26%
Carbohydrate: 11 g
Protein: 2 g
Cholesterol: 2 mg
Sodium: 306 mg
Dietary fiber: 1 g

Caponata

8 ½-cup servings

1 large eggplant (about 2 pounds)
1 8-ounce can tomato sauce
3 garlic cloves, minced
1 green pepper, seeded and chopped
1 to 2 teaspoons cumin
¼ teaspoon cayenne
¾ teaspoon salt
1 teaspoon sugar
¼ cup red wine vinegar

Dice unpeeled eggplant; place in a 4-quart saucepan. Add remaining ingredients. Cover and cook over medium heat for 20 minutes, stirring frequently. Uncover and cook 30 minutes more, or until thick.

Serving Suggestion: Serve hot or cold as a vegetable dip with oil-free baked, not fried, tortilla chips or crusty French bread; or as a side dish to roast chicken or beef; or over pasta. Especially nice on a picnic with roast chicken.

APPROXIMATE NUTRITIONAL INFORMATION PER SERVING

Calories: 31
Total fat: trace
Saturated fat: 0 g
Percentage of calories from fat: 8%
Carbohydrate: 8 g
Protein: 1 g
Cholesterol: 0 mg
Sodium: 337 mg
Dietary fiber: 3 g

OYSTERS ROCKEFELLER

6 servings

12 cups trimmed fresh spinach (about 2 bunches)
2 tablespoons dry bread crumbs
2 teaspoons olive oil
1 tablespoon grated onion
½ teaspoon chervil (optional)
½ teaspoon salt
1 fresh tarragon sprig or ¼ teaspoon dried (optional)
⅛ teaspoon pepper
2 to 3 drops Tabasco sauce
30 extra-small oysters
¼ cup grated part-skim mozzarella cheese

Steam spinach 2 to 3 minutes; squeeze dry and chop. Combine bread crumbs, olive oil, onion, and seasonings; toss with spinach. Divide well-drained oysters into 6-inch ramekins and broil or grill 5 to 7 minutes, or until very hot; drain excess liquid. Top oysters with spinach mixture; broil 3 to 4 minutes. Sprinkle with cheese; broil 2 to 3 minutes longer, or until cheese is melted and mixture is piping hot.

Note: If using unshucked oysters, thoroughly wash them. Open shells with an oyster knife or other blunt-tipped knife. Remove oysters and dry. Discard flat-top shells; wash deep-bottom shells. Place each oyster in a shell, then spoon 2 to 3 tablespoons of spinach mixture on top and broil or grill as above.

APPROXIMATE NUTRITIONAL INFORMATION PER SERVING

Calories: 151
Total fat: 6 g
Saturated fat: 0 g
Percentage of calories from fat: 33%
Carbohydrate: 10 g
Protein: 15 g
Cholesterol: 73 mg
Sodium: 398 mg
Dietary fiber: 2 g

Crab and Artichokes with Dijon

8 servings

½ pound crabmeat
1 14½-ounce can water-packed artichoke hearts, drained
2 green onions, minced
2 tablespoons Dijon Vinaigrette (page 420)
Fresh parsley for garnish
8 slices crusty French bread, cut into halves

Combine crab, artichoke hearts, and green onion; chill. Just before serving, toss with Dijon Vinaigrette. Garnish with fresh parsley. Serve with crusty French bread.

APPROXIMATE NUTRITIONAL INFORMATION PER SERVING

Calories: 101
Total fat: 1 g
Saturated fat: 0 g
Percentage of calories from fat: 13%
Carbohydrate: 14 g
Protein: 8 g
Cholesterol: 28 mg
Sodium: 336 mg
Dietary fiber: 1 g

SPINACH AND CRAB COCOTTE

6 servings

6 cups trimmed fresh spinach (about 1 bunch)
¾ pound crabmeat
¼ teaspoon Dijon mustard
2 teaspoons light mayonnaise
3 to 4 drops Tabasco sauce
2 tablespoons grated reduced-fat cheddar cheese
6 cherry tomatoes for garnish

Tear spinach into bite-size pieces. Toss crabmeat with mustard and just enough mayonnaise to moisten; dot with Tabasco sauce. Line individual shells or ramekins with spinach; top with crab mixture. Sprinkle with cheese. Bake at 375° for 5 to 10 minutes, or just until cheese melts. Garnish with cherry tomatoes.

APPROXIMATE NUTRITIONAL INFORMATION PER SERVING

Calories: 81
Total fat: 2 g
Saturated fat: 1 g
Percentage of calories from fat: 24%
Carbohydrate: 2 g
Protein: 13 g
Cholesterol: 58 mg
Sodium: 215 mg
Dietary fiber: 0 g

Steamed Mussels with Wine and Garlic

6 servings

4 pounds fresh mussels
¾ cup dry white wine
3 garlic cloves

Scrub mussel shells with a wire brush. Remove and discard beards. Rinse mussels in cold water, discarding broken or open mussels. Place mussels in a steamer; add wine and garlic. Cover tightly; steam 6 to 8 minutes, or just until shells open. Drain. Serve hot or cold.

APPROXIMATE NUTRITIONAL INFORMATION PER SERVING

Calories: 140
Total fat: 4 g
Saturated fat: 1 g
Percentage of calories from fat: 23%
Carbohydrate: 6 g
Protein: 19 g
Cholesterol: 45 mg
Sodium: 295 mg
Dietary fiber: 0 g

STEAMED CLAMS BORDELAISE

4 servings

2 dozen clams
1 tablespoon olive oil
¼ cup dry white wine
1 small onion, chopped
2 garlic cloves, minced
1 celery stalk, chopped
Fresh parsley
Fresh lemon wedges for garnish

Scrub clams and soak in salt water or cornmeal in water to remove sand (page 513). Rinse thoroughly. Place clams in a steamer. Add olive oil, wine, onion, garlic, and celery. Cover and bring to a boil. Reduce heat; simmer 10 minutes, or just until shells open. Drain. Arrange on a bed of fresh parsley. Garnish with lemon wedges.

APPROXIMATE NUTRITIONAL INFORMATION PER SERVING

Calories: 46
Total fat: 1 g
Saturated fat: 0 g
Percentage of calories from fat: 12%
Carbohydrate: 4 g
Protein: 7 g
Cholesterol: 18 mg
Sodium: 32 mg
Dietary fiber: 1 g

Sea Scallops with Tomatoes and Green Chilies

8 servings

1 ½ pounds fresh sea scallops
½ cup fresh lime juice
¼ cup chopped white onion
¼ cup chopped green chilies
1 large ripe tomato, chopped
¼ cup chopped fresh parsley
2 tablespoons olive oil
½ teaspoon salt
¼ teaspoon pepper
6 drops Tabasco sauce
1 bunch fresh parsley
1 lemon, cut into wedges, for garnish

Cut each scallop into thirds. Cover with lime juice and marinate in refrigerator 4 hours. Pour off juice.

Preheat a nonstick skillet. Add scallops and cook, turning frequently, 4 to 6 minutes, or just until scallops are tender. Remove from pan; drain an excess liquid. Chill scallops for several hours. Combine onion, green chilies, and tomato. Chill several hours.

Just before serving, combine scallops with tomato mixture; add chopped parsley. Toss with olive oil, salt, pepper, and Tabasco. Arrange on a bed of parsley in individual shells or ramekins. Garnish with lemon wedges.

Note: To adjust this recipe, plan on 3 scallops per person. This sea scallop dish makes a great appetizer or first course and may also be served as a salad (page 399).

APPROXIMATE NUTRITIONAL INFORMATION PER SERVING

Calories: 109
Total fat: 4 g
Saturated fat: 1 g
Percentage of calories from fat: 34%
Carbohydrate: 7 g
Protein: 12 g
Cholesterol: 23 mg
Sodium: 247 mg
Dietary fiber: 0 g

LAYERED SHRIMP DIP

10 servings

1 8-ounce container tub-style nonfat cream cheese
⅓ cup cocktail sauce
½ pound small cooked shrimp or crabmeat
6 carrots, peeled and cut diagonally into thirds
6 celery stalks, cut diagonally into thirds
1 7-ounce package oil-free baked, not fried, tortilla chips

Spread cream cheese in center of a 10-inch serving tray, keeping the edges neat and uniform. Use the back of a serving spoon to smooth out the surface. Pour the cocktail sauce over the cream cheese and spread it evenly. Sprinkle shrimp or crabmeat over top. Chill until ready to serve. Ring with celery and carrot sticks and/or oil-free baked, not fried, tortilla chips to scoop up the dip.

APPROXIMATE NUTRITIONAL INFORMATION PER SERVING

Calories: 77
Total fat: 1 g
Saturated fat: 0 g
Percentage of calories from fat: 9%
Carbohydrate: 4 g
Protein: 8 g
Cholesterol: 38 mg
Sodium: 218 mg
Dietary fiber: 0 g

SPRING ROLLS

24 servings

2 dozen spring roll (lumpia) wrappers
¾ pound pork loin, ground
2 tablespoons ginger juice*
1 teaspoon sake
1 teaspoon reduced-sodium soy sauce
¼ pound bamboo shoots, washed and cut into 2-inch lengths
3 to 4 green onions, cut into thin 2-inch lengths
5 to 6 shiitake mushrooms, thinly sliced
½ cup fresh bean sprouts
½ teaspoon potato starch
½ cup water
Olive oil
Fresh parsley for garnish
⅓ cup Soy Sauce and Rice Vinegar Sauce (page 432)

Thaw spring roll wrappers. Sprinkle pork with ginger juice,* sake, and soy sauce; let stand 20 minutes. Brown pork in a nonstick skillet over medium heat; set aside.

Sauté bamboo shoots and onions in a small amount of water or chicken broth using a wok or heavy skillet; when barely tender, add mushrooms and bean sprouts; cook 2 to 3 minutes. Cool to room temperature.

In a small saucepan, bring potato starch and water to a boil. Remove from heat; cool to room temperature.

Separate spring roll wrappers and lay them flat. Toss vegetables with pork; place 3 to 4 tablespoons of mixture in the center of each wrapper. Brush outside edges of wrappers with potato-starch mixture and fold edges over, envelope style. Seal outside seam with potato-starch mixture.

Brown spring rolls in a nonstick skillet over medium heat for 10 minutes, or until very hot, or brown in a heavy skillet using a very small amount of olive oil—just enough to coat bottom of pan. Arrange spring rolls on a bed of fresh parsley and serve with Soy Sauce and Rice Vinegar Sauce.

Note: Spring roll (lumpia) wrappers and shiitake mushrooms are available in Oriental markets and in the Oriental section of many supermarkets. If fresh mushrooms are not available, use dried, but first reconstitute by soaking them in water to cover for 30 minutes, or until soft.

*To make ginger juice, purée a 2½-inch piece of peeled fresh ginger in a food processor; squeeze the pulp to obtain the ginger juice.

APPROXIMATE NUTRITIONAL INFORMATION PER SERVING

Calories: 268
Total fat: 2 g
Saturated fat: 0 g
Percentage of calories from fat: 6%

Carbohydrate: 61 g
Protein: 16 g
Cholesterol: 13 mg
Sodium: 197 mg
Dietary fiber: 0 g

Layered Bean Dip

10 servings

1 15-ounce can red kidney beans
1 tablespoon chili powder
½ teaspoon ground cumin
⅓ cup nonfat sour cream
¾ cup chopped iceberg lettuce
⅓ chopped white onion
1 ripe tomato, diced
¼ cup (1 ounce) grated nonfat cheddar cheese
1½ cups Tomato Salsa, preferably homemade (page 433)

Purée kidney beans in food processor. Add chili powder and cumin and whirl 1 minute longer. Chill for at least 1 hour. Spread onto a 10-inch serving tray. Top with sour cream. Sprinkle with lettuce, then onion, tomato, and cheddar cheese. Accompany with salsa.

Serving Suggestion: Ring with oil-free baked, not fried, tortilla chips and carrot and celery sticks to scoop up the dip.

APPROXIMATE NUTRITIONAL INFORMATION PER SERVING

Calories: 57
Total fat: 1 g
Saturated fat: 0 g
Percentage of calories from fat: 10%
Carbohydrate: 11 g
Protein: 4 g
Cholesterol: 1 mg
Sodium: 133 mg
Dietary fiber: 3 g

MINI CHEESE BURRITOS

4 servings

4 6-inch corn tortillas
⅓ cup grated reduced-fat cheddar cheese
2 tablespoons chopped green chilies
2 tablespoons finely chopped tomato
2 tablespoons finely chopped onion
¼ cup Tomato Salsa, preferably homemade (page 433)
¼ cup nonfat sour cream

Lay tortillas flat; sprinkle with cheese, chilies, tomato, and onion. Roll each into a tight roll. Heat at 350° for 5 to 6 minutes. Serve with salsa and sour cream.

APPROXIMATE NUTRITIONAL INFORMATION PER SERVING

Calories: 98
Total fat: 2 g
Saturated fat: 1 g
Percentage of calories from fat: 21%
Carbohydrate: 15 g
Protein: 5 g
Cholesterol: 7 mg
Sodium: 237 mg
Dietary fiber: 1 g

APPETIZER CHEESE TOSTADOS

4 servings

4 6-inch corn tortillas
½ cup (2 ounces) grated reduced-fat cheddar cheese
½ cup Tomato Salsa, preferably homemade (page 433)

Place tortillas on a nonstick baking sheet; sprinkle with cheese. Bake at 350° until cheese is melted and tortilla is crisp. Serve with salsa.

(continued on next page)

(continued from preceding page)

APPROXIMATE NUTRITIONAL INFORMATION PER SERVING

Calories: 97
Total fat: 3 g
Saturated fat: 2 g
Percentage of calories from fat: 29%
Carbohydrate: 12 g
Protein: 6 g
Cholesterol: 10 mg
Sodium: 153 mg
Dietary fiber: 1 g

NACHOS

2 servings

20 to 22 oil-free baked, not fried, tortilla chips
2 tablespoons chopped green chilies
½ cup (2 ounces) grated reduced-fat or extra-light cheddar cheese
¼ cup Tomato Salsa, preferably homemade (page 433)

Arrange chips on a nonstick baking sheet. Sprinkle with green chilies. Top with cheese, then with salsa. Bake at 350° for 6 to 8 minutes, or until cheese is melted. Serve with additional salsa for dipping.

APPROXIMATE NUTRITIONAL INFORMATION PER SERVING USING REDUCED-FAT CHEESE

Calories: 147
Total fat: 6 g
Saturated fat: 3 g
Percentage of calories from fat: 35%
Carbohydrate: 16 g
Protein: 11 g
Cholesterol: 20 mg
Sodium: 326 mg
Dietary fiber: 0 g

APPROXIMATE NUTRITIONAL INFORMATION PER SERVING USING EXTRA-LIGHT CHEESE

Calories: 117
Total fat: 3 g
Saturated fat: 0 g
Percentage of calories from fat: 21%
Carbohydrate: 16 g
Protein: 9 g
Cholesterol: 0 mg
Sodium: 546 mg
Dietary fiber: 0 g

STUFFED MUSHROOMS

28 mushrooms

1 pound large fresh mushrooms (about 28)
½ cup oil-free Italian dressing
1 bunch fresh spinach leaves, about 3 cups
2 teaspoons light mayonnaise
2 tablespoons grated onion
1 tablespoon lemon juice
6 ounces crabmeat
¼ cup (1 ounce) grated reduced-fat cheddar cheese

Clean and stem mushrooms. Marinate in dressing for 1 hour; drain. Wash spinach leaves; shake, but do not dry. Cook covered in a heavy skillet for 2 to 3 minutes, or until spinach is wilted. Drain, squeeze out excess moisture, and chop. Combine mayonnaise, onion, and lemon juice. Toss with crab and spinach. Stuff mushrooms; sprinkle with cheese. Bake at 375° for 15 minutes.

APPROXIMATE NUTRITIONAL INFORMATION PER MUSHROOM

Calories: 15
Total fat: trace
Saturated fat: 0 g
Percentage of calories from fat: 28%
Carbohydrate: 1 g
Protein: 2 g
Cholesterol: 7 mg
Sodium: 35 mg
Dietary fiber: trace

Marinated Mushrooms

28 mushrooms

1 pound fresh mushrooms (about 28)
Juice of 1 lemon
1 cup oil-free dressing
2 garlic cloves
1 bunch fresh parsley for garnish
1 lemon, cut into thin rounds

Clean and stem mushrooms. Place in a large saucepan, and toss with lemon juice. Add dressing and garlic. Cook over medium-high heat for 20 to 30 minutes, stirring frequently. Remove from heat; cool to room temperature. Drain.* Chill.

Cover a serving plate with fresh parsley; top with lemon rounds. Spoon mushrooms over lemons.

Note: Marinated mushrooms will keep several days in the refrigerator.

*Remaining liquid may be used as a marinade for another batch of mushrooms. It also works well as a marinade for artichoke hearts, or as a salad dressing.

APPROXIMATE NUTRITIONAL INFORMATION PER MUSHROOM

Calories: 9
Total fat: trace
Saturated fat: 0 g
Percentage of calories from fat: 9%
Carbohydrate: 2 g
Protein: 0 g
Cholesterol: 0 mg
Sodium: 127 mg
Dietary fiber: 0 g

LITTLE RED POTATO APPETIZERS

10 servings (1 whole potato each)

10 bite-sized red potatoes
¼ cup nonfat cream cheese
¼ cup nonfat sour cream
3 green onions with tops, finely chopped
2 tablespoons grated nonfat cheddar cheese
2 tablespoons Tomato Salsa, preferably homemade (page 433)

Cut potatoes in half; microwave or steam until just tender. Cool. Using a grapefruit spoon, scoop out about one third of flesh from center of each potato half (reserve for another use).

Combine cream cheese with sour cream. Add green onions.

Just before serving, place about 1 teaspoon of cream cheese mixture in center of each potato. Dot half the potatoes with cheese and the other half with salsa. Arrange on a round serving tray. Serve cold or at room temperature.

Variation: Top some of the potatoes with pitted black olive halves and, for a more festive occasion, a few sprinkles of black caviar.

APPROXIMATE NUTRITIONAL INFORMATION PER SERVING

Calories: 50
Total fat: trace
Saturated fat: 0 g
Percentage of calories from fat: 10%
Carbohydrate: 10 g
Protein: 3 g
Cholesterol: 2 mg
Sodium: 60 mg
Dietary fiber: 1 g

Melon and Prosciutto

12 servings

1 3-pound cantaloupe
¼ pound thinly sliced prosciutto (Italian ham)
1 bunch fresh parsley
¼ pound seedless green grapes
¼ pound seedless red grapes

Cut cantaloupe into 12 thin wedges and remove rind. Wrap each wedge with a slice of prosciutto. Arrange on a parsley-lined tray; tuck grapes in center and among cantaloupe wedges.

APPROXIMATE NUTRITIONAL INFORMATION PER SERVING

Calories: 67
Total fat: 2 g
Saturated fat: 0 g
Percentage of calories from fat: 27%
Carbohydrate: 11 g
Protein: 3 g
Cholesterol: 7 mg
Sodium: 252 mg
Dietary fiber: trace

BEVERAGES

Iced Tea

4 servings

Boiling water
6 to 8 tea bags, or 6 to 8 teaspoons loose tea measured into a tea ball
4 cups boiling water
Fresh mint for garnish
Sugar (optional)
Fresh lemon slices (optional)

Fill a teapot with rapidly boiling water; let stand a few minutes, then empty teapot. Add tea bags or tea ball, then 4 cups boiling water. Cover; let steep 3 to 5 minutes, or until tea is desired strength. Remove tea bags. (For best results, judge the strength by the taste not by the color.) Stir. Let cool at room temperature for 2 hours. Serve over ice. Garnish with mint. Pass sugar and lemon slices, if desired.

Note: Tea that has been steeped too long or refrigerated will become cloudy. To make clear again, pour a small amount of boiling water into the tea.

For Sun Tea: Prepare as above using 6 to 8 tea bags and 1½ quarts cold water. Cover and let stand in full sun or at room temperature for 2 to 3 hours, or until tea reaches desired strength. Remove tea bags. Serve over ice.

APPROXIMATE NUTRITIONAL INFORMATION PER SERVING

Calories: 5
Total fat: trace
Saturated fat: 0 g
Percentage of calories from fat: 8%
Carbohydrate: 2 g
Protein: 0 g
Cholesterol: 0 mg
Sodium: 5 mg
Dietary fiber: 0 g

FRESH LEMONADE

4 servings

1 cup fresh lemon juice
4 cups cold water
4 tablespoons sugar, or to taste
1 lemon, sliced into rings
1 thin orange slice, quartered
4 fresh strawberries
4 fresh mint sprigs

Combine lemon juice, water, and sugar in a large pitcher; stir to dissolve sugar. Add lemon slices to mixture. Chill. Pour into 4 ice-filled glasses. Put an orange quarter, a strawberry and a sprig of mint into each glass for garnish.

APPROXIMATE NUTRITIONAL INFORMATION PER SERVING

Calories: 85
Total fat: trace
Saturated fat: 0 g
Percentage of calories from fat: 2%
Carbohydrate: 25 g
Protein: 1 g
Cholesterol: 0 mg
Sodium: 8 mg
Dietary fiber: 0 g

HOT CIDER

4 1-cup sevings

1 quart apple juice
2 cloves
1 cinnamon stick

Heat apple juice, cloves, and cinnamon over medium heat until juice is piping hot; do not boil. Serve at once.

(continued on next page)

(continued from preceding page)

APPROXIMATE NUTRITIONAL INFORMATION PER SERVING

Calories: 116
Total fat: trace
Saturated fat: 0 g
Percentage of calories from fat: 2%
Carbohydrate: 2 g
Protein: 0 g
Cholesterol: 0 mg
Sodium: 7 mg
Dietary fiber: 0 g

FRUIT SHAKE

2 servings

- 2 cups chilled strawberries, raspberries, or blackberries
- 1½ cups nonfat milk

Frost tall glasses in the freezer for 30 to 60 minutes. Purée fruits in a blender. Add milk; whirl until frothy.

Note: Plums, oranges, peaches, melon, papaya, or pineapple may be used in place of berries.

Variation: For additional sweetness, add a piece of banana. For variety, add a jigger of rum. For a creamier taste, omit milk and fold plain nonfat yogurt into puréed fruits.

APPROXIMATE NUTRITIONAL INFORMATION PER SERVING

Calories: 110
Total fat: 1 g
Saturated fat: 0 g
Percentage of calories from fat: 7%
Carbohydrate: 19 g
Protein: 7 g
Cholesterol: 3 mg
Sodium: 97 mg
Dietary fiber: 2 g

GUILTLESS CHOCOLATE MILKSHAKE

Makes 1 cup

1 cup light or nonfat chocolate ice cream
⅓ cup nonfat milk
1½ tablespoons chocolate syrup
⅛ teaspoon vanilla extract

Combine ice cream, milk, chocolate syrup, and vanilla in a blender. Whirl 2 to 3 minutes.

Note: Some brands of light or nonfat ice cream are better than others. Keep tasting them until you find one you like. I have a favorite brand that I use most often, and I look forward to eating it almost as much as having the "real" thing.

Serving Suggestion: A favorite quick-to-fix guiltless dinner is Grilled Chicken Burgers (page 384) or Cube Steak Sandwiches (page 381), Oven French Fried Potatoes (page 474), with a Guiltless Chocolate Milkshake.

APPROXIMATE NUTRITIONAL INFORMATION PER 1-CUP SERVING USING LIGHT ICE CREAM

Calories: 297
Total fat: 8 g
Saturated fat: 5 g
Percentage of calories from fat: 26%
Carbohydrate: 49 g
Protein: 9 g
Cholesterol: 51 mg
Sodium: 155 mg
Dietary fiber: 0 g

APPROXIMATE NUTRITIONAL INFORMATION PER 1-CUP SERVING USING NONFAT ICE CREAM

Calories: 297
Total fat: trace
Saturated fat: 0 g
Percentage of calories from fat: 1%
Carbohydrate: 67 g
Protein: 9 g
Cholesterol: 1 mg
Sodium: 245 mg
Dietary fiber: 0 g

Strawberry Frost

2 servings

2 cups strawberries
Juice of 2 oranges
Juice of ½ lemon
¼ cup apple juice
5 to 8 ice cubes
Whole berries for garnish

Purée strawberries in a blender; add juices. Add ice cubes one at a time; crush. Pour into tall glasses. Garnish with whole berries.

Variation: For a creamier taste, fold in ½ to 1 cup plain nonfat yogurt.

APPROXIMATE NUTRITIONAL INFORMATION PER SERVING

Calories: 80
Total fat: trace
Saturated fat: 0 g
Percentage of calories from fat: 7%
Carbohydrate: 19 g
Protein: 1 g
Cholesterol: 0 mg
Sodium: 3 mg
Dietary fiber: 2 g

BREADS

Pizza

Makes 2 crusts; 1 9-inch pizza (8 slices)

Crust

1 package active dry yeast
¾ cup warm water
4 cups all-purpose flour
½ teaspoon sugar
½ teaspoon salt
2 tablespoons olive oil
1 egg, beaten
Dab of tub safflower margarine

Sauce per Crust

1 14½-ounce can plum tomatoes
1 tablespoon tomato paste
1 tablespoon olive oil
½ teaspoon minced fresh oregano or ¼ teaspoon dried
2 fresh basil sprigs or ¼ teaspoon dried
¼ teaspoon pepper
½ pound grated reduced-fat mozzarella cheese

Toppings

1 cup fresh ripe tomatoes
½ cup sautéed onions
1 cup fresh mushrooms, sliced and steamed 2 to 3 minutes
½ cup sliced green onions
½ cup diced green chili peppers
½ cup fresh pineapple
½ cup alfalfa sprouts
½ pound extra-lean ground round, cooked and drained of fat
½ pound extra lean Italian sausage, cooked and drained of fat
1 cup chopped clams

Dissolve yeast in warm water. Mix flour with sugar and salt; add to yeast along with oil and egg, and stir until mixed. Knead on a heavily floured board until smooth and elastic. (Add additional water if needed for moisture.) Put dough in a bowl greased with tub safflower margarine; cover, and let rise in a warm place for 1 hour. Punch down. Knead slightly. Let rise 1 hour more. Punch down. Knead slightly. Let rise 1 hour more. Divide dough in half. (Dough may be frozen). Roll into two 9-inch crusts.

Drain tomatoes; dice. Reserve ½ cup of the juice and mix with diced tomatoes, tomato paste, and olive oil. Spread over crust; sprinkle with oregano, basil, and pepper. Add choice of toppings. Sprinkle with cheese. Bake at 450° for 20 minutes, or until crust is done and cheese is melted.

APPROXIMATE NUTRITIONAL INFORMATION PER SLICE (WITH CHEESE AND VEGETABLE TOPPINGS*)

Calories: 202
Total fat: 6 g
Saturated fat: 2 g
Percentage of calories from fat: 29%
Carbohydrate: 28 g
Protein: 8 g
Cholesterol: 21 mg
Sodium: 171 mg
Dietary fiber: 2 g

*For sausage topping, add 28 calories and 2 grams of fat per serving. For ground beef topping, add 26 calories and 2 grams of fat per serving. For chopped clam topping, add 15 calories and a trace of fat per serving.

Pizza Bread

Makes 15 slices

1 1-pound can plum tomatoes
2 tablespoons tomato paste
1 loaf French bread
¼ cup (1 ounce) grated reduced-fat cheddar cheese

Drain tomatoes; dice. Reserve half the juice from the tomatoes and mix with diced tomatoes and tomato paste. Slice French bread in half lengthwise; spread both halves with sauce and sprinkle with cheese. Put loaf back together again. Bake at 450° for 10 to 15 minutes, or until bread is hot and cheese has melted. Just before serving, slice crosswise on the diagonal.

APPROXIMATE NUTRITIONAL INFORMATION PER SLICE

Calories: 65
Total fat: 1 g
Saturated fat: 0 g
Percentage of calories from fat: 9%
Carbohydrate: 13 g
Protein: 2 g
Cholesterol: 1 mg
Sodium: 218 mg
Dietary fiber: 1 g

CHEESE BREAD

Makes 2 loaves (15 slices per loaf)

2 packages active dry yeast
2 cups warm water
2 tablespoons sugar
1 tablespoon salt
¼ cup safflower oil
6 cups all-purpose flour
3¼ cups grated reduced-fat cheddar cheese

Dissolve yeast in water; add sugar, salt, oil, and 3 cups of the flour. Mix. Add remaining flour; knead into a soft dough, about 5 minutes. Divide dough into 2 loaves; knead one half of the cheese into each loaf. Shape into round loaves; flatten slightly. Bake on a nonstick baking sheet or in individual loaf pans at 375° for 30 to 35 minutes.

Note: Since this bread is higher in fat than most we recommend, serve it with a low-fat salad such as Layered Salad (page 393) or a low-fat soup such as Manhattan Clam Chowder (page 355) or Chicken Vegetable Soup (page 338).

APPROXIMATE NUTRITIONAL INFORMATION PER SLICE

Calories: 146
Total fat: 4 g
Saturated fat: 2 g
Percentage of calories from fat: 26%
Carbohydrate: 20 g
Protein: 7 g
Cholesterol: 9 mg
Sodium: 310 mg
Dietary fiber: 1 g

Bread Sticks

Makes 5 dozen

2 packages active dry yeast
⅔ cup warm water
2¾ cups water
2 tablespoons safflower oil
1 tablespoon salt
3⅓ cups whole-wheat flour
4½ cups all-purpose flour
Dab of tub safflower margarine
2 egg whites beaten with 1 tablespoon water until frothy
2 tablespoons sesame seeds

Dissolve yeast in ⅔ cup warm water. Heat 2¾ cup water, safflower oil, and salt to lukewarm; pour into a large mixing bowl. Add whole-wheat flour and dissolved yeast. Mix with a wooden spoon until smooth. Gradually add all-purpose flour. Remove to a lightly floured surface. Knead 10 minutes, or until smooth and elastic. Form into a ball.

Place in a medium bowl greased with tub safflower margarine. Cover. Let rise in a warm place for about 2 hours, or until doubled in size. Punch down.

Cut dough into 5 dozen equal pieces. Roll each between palms into a 6- to 8-inch rope. Place 2 to 3 inches apart on a nonstick baking sheet. Cover. Let rise in a warm place for 30 to 60 minutes, or until doubled in size. Brush with beaten egg whites; sprinkle with seeds. Bake at 375° for 10 minutes. Reduce heat to 300° and bake 20 to 35 minutes. Cool on wire racks.

Variation: Instead of bread sticks, form the dough into the shape of cars, trucks, airplanes, animals, angels, flowers, trees, or gingerbread boys. Bake at

375° for 25 to 30 minutes. Slice the bread characters lengthwise between front and back; fill with chicken, peanut butter, or other sandwich filling.

APPROXIMATE NUTRITIONAL INFORMATION PER BREADSTICK

Calories: 64
Total fat: 1 g
Saturated fat: 0 g
Percentage of calories from fat: 12%
Carbohydrate: 12 g
Protein: 2 g
Cholesterol: 0 mg
Sodium: 110 mg
Dietary fiber: 1 g

SOFT PRETZELS

Makes 1 dozen

1 package active dry yeast
1½ cups lukewarm water
1 teaspoon salt
1 tablespoon sugar
4 cups all-purpose flour
1 egg, beaten

Dissolve yeast in water; add salt, sugar, and flour. Knead 5 to 10 minutes, adding more flour as necessary to reduce stickiness. Divide dough into 12 pieces. Twist dough into the shape of pretzels, cars, trucks, airplanes, flowers, trees, gingerbread boys, numerals, or circles. Place on a nonstick baking sheet. Brush with beaten egg. Bake at 425° for 15 minutes, or until lightly browned.

APPROXIMATE NUTRITIONAL INFORMATION PER PRETZEL

Calories: 159
Total fat: trace
Saturated fat: 0 g
Percentage of calories from fat: 2%
Carbohydrate: 33 g
Protein: 5 g
Cholesterol: 0 mg
Sodium: 184 mg
Dietary fiber: 2 g

Bagels

Makes 1 dozen

2 packages active dry yeast
⅔ cup warm water
2 cups whole-wheat flour
¾ cup water
3 tablespoons sugar
1 tablespoon salt
2 cups enriched all-purpose flour
Dab of tub safflower margarine
1 gallon water
1 teaspoon sugar
1 tablespoon poppy seeds

Dissolve yeast in ⅔ cup warm water. Add whole-wheat flour, ¾ cup water, sugar, and salt. Blend on low speed of electric mixer. Then beat on high speed for 2 minutes. Lower speed to low; gradually add all-purpose flour. When dough becomes too stiff for mixer, remove from bowl onto well-floured surface and knead by hand until smooth. Place in a nonstick pan greased with tub safflower margarine. Cover. Let rest 15 minutes.

Divide dough into 12 portions. Shape into balls. With a nut pick, punch a hole in the center of each; pull to enlarge, keeping the shape uniform. Place on a nonstick baking sheet. Cover. Let rise for 30 minutes.

Bring 1 gallon of water and 1 teaspoon of sugar to a boil; reduce heat to simmer. Add 6 bagels; simmer 3 minutes. Turn with tongs; simmer 4 minutes. Remove from water; pat dry with paper towels. Place on nonstick baking sheet; sprinkle with poppy seeds. Repeat with remaining bagels. Bake at 375° for 30 minutes. Serve warm.

APPROXIMATE NUTRITIONAL INFORMATION PER BAGEL

Calories: 164	Carbohydrate: 34 g
Total fat: 1 g	Protein: 5 g
Saturated fat: 0 g	Cholesterol: 0 mg
Percentage of calories from fat: 6%	Sodium: 538 mg
	Dietary fiber: 3 g

BREAD STUFFING

26 ½-cup servings (enough to accompany a 10- to 14-pound turkey)

- 1 large onion, chopped
- 3 celery stalks, chopped
- 1 tablespoon olive oil
- ½ pound fresh mushrooms, sliced
- 10 cups dried bread cubes
- 2½ cups reduced-fat chicken broth, preferably homemade (page 364)
- 1¼ teaspoons sage
- ½ teaspoon or less salt
- ¼ teaspoon pepper

Sauté onion and celery in olive oil until tender. Add mushrooms; cook 2 to 3 minutes. Remove from heat. Add bread cubes. Gradually moisten with broth, adding a little more or less as necessary. Season and toss. Bake covered at 350° for 30 to 40 minutes, or until piping hot.

APPROXIMATE NUTRITIONAL INFORMATION PER ½-CUP SERVING

Calories: 89	Carbohydrate: 16 g
Total fat: 1 g	Protein: 3 g
Saturated fat: 0 g	Cholesterol: 0 mg
Percentage of calories from fat: 15%	Sodium: 237 mg
	Dietary fiber: 1 g

Sour Cream Pancakes

18 pancakes

2 eggs
½ cup egg substitute
½ cup all-purpose flour, sifted
¼ teaspoon salt
1 teaspoon baking soda
2 cups nonfat sour cream

Combine eggs and egg substitute and beat lightly. Combine dry ingredients; blend with eggs and sour cream, using a wire whisk.

Pour enough batter for each pancake onto a preheated nonstick griddle. Cook until top side is bubbly and a few bubbles have broken. Turn and brown other side.

Note: If batter is too thick, add up to 2 tablespoons of water.

APPROXIMATE NUTRITIONAL INFORMATION PER PANCAKE

Calories: 38
Total fat: 1 g
Saturated fat: 0 g
Percentage of calories from fat: 15%
Carbohydrate: 5 g
Protein: 3 g
Cholesterol: 24 mg
Sodium: 135 mg
Dietary fiber: 0 g

FRENCH TOAST

Makes 6 slices

2 eggs*
⅓ cup nonfat milk
¼ teaspoon sugar
½ teaspoon cinnamon
6 slices day-old crusty French bread

Beat eggs; add milk, sugar, and cinnamon. Blend. Heat a nonstick griddle over medium-high heat. Dip bread one slice at a time into egg mixture, coating both sides evenly, and place on the griddle. Brown, about 2 to 3 minutes. Turn and brown other side, 2 to 3 minutes longer.

*Egg substitute cuts the fat and cholesterol significantly.

APPROXIMATE NUTRITIONAL INFORMATION PER SLICE

Calories: 82
Total fat: 2 g
Saturated fat: 1 g
Percentage of calories from fat: 21%
Carbohydrate: 12 g
Protein: 4 g
Cholesterol: 71 mg
Sodium: 177 mg
Dietary fiber: 1 g

APPROXIMATE NUTRITIONAL INFORMATION PER SERVING USING EGG SUBSTITUTE

Calories: 66
Total fat: trace
Saturated fat: 0 g
Percentage of calories from fat: 3%
Carbohydrate: 12 g
Protein: 4 g
Cholesterol: 0 mg
Sodium: 183 mg
Dietary fiber: 0 g

CRÊPES

15 crêpes

- 2 eggs
- ½ cup nonfat milk
- ½ cup cold water
- 1 cup all-purpose flour, sifted
- 2 tablespoons safflower oil
- ½ teaspoon sugar
- ⅛ teaspoon salt

Lightly beat eggs, milk, and water. Add remaining ingredients; blend with a wire whisk. Pour enough batter into a preheated 5-inch nonstick crêpe pan to coat bottom; tilt pan to spread batter. Cook 1 minute, or just until set. Turn. Cook 1 minute longer, or until browned.

Notes: Crêpes may be prepared in advance, layered between wax paper, and wrapped in aluminum foil for freezing. Bring to room temperature for easy separation before using. To reheat, remove wax paper layers; wrap stack of crêpes in aluminum foil. Heat in a 200° oven for about 10 minutes, or until warm.

Some crêpe fillings may be prepared in advance and refrigerated or frozen for later use.

Serving Suggestion: Especially good with fresh strawberries and Whipped Cream Topping (page 587).

APPROXIMATE NUTRITIONAL INFORMATION PER CREPE

Calories: 60	Carbohydrate: 7 g
Total fat: 3 g	Protein: 2 g
Saturated fat: 0 g	Cholesterol: 29 mg
Percentage of calories from fat: 39%	Sodium: 31 mg
	Dietary fiber: 0 g

SOUPS AND BROTHS

Chicken Noodle Soup

Approximately 5 quarts

12 cups reduced-fat chicken broth, preferably homemade (page 364)
1½ cups diced cooked chicken
4 cups cooked egg pastina, alphabet pasta, or orzo

Heat broth to boiling; add chicken and pastina. Heat and serve.

Note: Ronzoni brand ancini pepe pasta is a good alternative to egg pastina or alphabets.

Variations: Add cooked carrots, celery, or other vegetables. For Chicken with Rice Soup, substitute rice for pasta.

APPROXIMATE NUTRITIONAL INFORMATION PER 1-CUP SERVING

Calories: 78
Total fat: 2 g
Saturated fat: 0 g
Percentage of calories from fat: 18%
Carbohydrate: 8 g
Protein: 7 g
Cholesterol: 21 mg
Sodium: 152 mg
Dietary fiber: 0 g

Chicken Soup with Lemon

3 1-cup servings

3 cups reduced-fat chicken broth, preferably homemade (page 364)
2 tablespoons fresh lemon juice

Heat broth to boiling; add lemon juice. Serve.

Note: Nice as a first course with a seafood entrée.

APPROXIMATE NUTRITIONAL INFORMATION PER SERVING

Calories: 30	Carbohydrate: 1 g
Total fat: 1 g	Protein: 4 g
Saturated fat: 0 g	Cholesterol: 2 mg
Percentage of calories from fat: 30%	Sodium: 275 mg
	Dietary fiber: 0 g

CHICKEN SOUP WITH TOMATO AND GREEN ONION

4 1-cup servings

4 cups reduced-fat chicken broth, preferably homemade (page 364)
4 tomato slices
4 green onions with tops, thinly sliced

Heat chicken broth to boiling. Ladle into soup bowls. To each bowl, add 1 tomato slice and green onion. Serve at once.

APPROXIMATE NUTRITIONAL INFORMATION PER SERVING

Calories: 38	Carbohydrate: 2 g
Total fat: 1 g	Protein: 4 g
Saturated fat: 0 g	Cholesterol: 2 mg
Percentage of calories from fat: 27%	Sodium: 280 mg
	Dietary fiber: 0 g

Chicken Vegetable Soup

Approximately 4 quarts

2 cups fresh French green beans
1 28-ounce can tomatoes, diced
5 cups reduced-fat chicken broth, preferably homemade (page 364)
1 onion, chopped
6 carrots, peeled and diced
2 stalks celery, diced
½ teaspoon salt
½ teaspoon pepper
3 cups chopped savoy cabbage (1 head)
1½ cups cubed cooked chicken
2 cups cooked corkscrew or gemelli pasta
2 tablespoons chopped fresh parsley

Steam beans 5 to 6 minutes, or until crisp-tender; set aside. Combine tomatoes, chicken broth, onion, carrots, celery, salt, and pepper in a stockpot; bring to a boil, reduce heat, and simmer 1 to 1½ hours, or until vegetables are tender. Add cabbage, chicken, and pasta; simmer 5 minutes. Add green beans; heat. Sprinkle with parsley.

APPROXIMATE NUTRITIONAL INFORMATION PER 1-CUP SERVING

Calories: 153
Total fat: 2 g
Saturated fat: 0 g
Percentage of calories from fat: 11%
Carbohydrate: 23 g
Protein: 12 g
Cholesterol: 16 mg
Sodium: 315 mg
Dietary fiber: 3 g

CHICKEN SOUP WITH SOBA NOODLES

Approximately 4 quarts

12 cups reduced-fat chicken broth, preferably homemade (page 364)
1 8-ounce package soba (buckwheat) noodles

Heat broth to boiling; add uncooked noodles and bring to a second boil. Cook 2 to 3 minutes, or until noodles are tender. Do not overcook.

Note: Chinese buckwheat (soba) noodles are found in Oriental markets or in the Oriental section of the supermarket; they look like "ramen" noodles.

APPROXIMATE NUTRITIONAL INFORMATION PER 1-CUP SERVING

Calories: 46
Total fat: 1 g
Saturated fat: 0 g
Percentage of calories from fat: 16%
Carbohydrate: 5 g
Protein: 4 g
Cholesterol: 2 mg
Sodium: 235 mg
Dietary fiber: 0 g

Cantonese Chicken Soup

Approximately 4 quarts

6 cups reduced-fat chicken broth, preferably homemade (page 364)
2 whole chicken breasts, skinned and deboned
2 carrots, diced
12 cups chopped fresh spinach, (2 bunches)
1 head Chinese cabbage, chopped
½ pound fresh mushrooms, sliced
1 8-ounce can whole water chestnuts, slivered
3 cups cooked rice
1 cake firm tofu, cubed

In a small stockpot, bring broth to a boil. Add chicken; cook 10 minutes. Reduce heat to a simmer; add carrots. Simmer 10 to 15 minutes, or until carrots are just tender. Add spinach, cabbage, mushrooms, water chestnuts, and rice. Cook 3 to 4 minutes; add tofu. Ladle into soup bowls.

APPROXIMATE NUTRITIONAL INFORMATION PER 1-CUP SERVING

Calories: 130
Total fat: 2 g
Saturated fat: 0 g
Percentage of calories from fat: 15%
Carbohydrate: 16 g
Protein: 12 g
Cholesterol: 19 mg
Sodium: 129 mg
Dietary fiber: 1 g

Chicken Soup with Chinese Vegetables

Approximately 4 quarts

- 12 cups reduced-fat chicken broth, preferably homemade (page 364)
- ½ pound fresh mushrooms, sliced
- 12 cups fresh spinach, washed and torn into bite-size pieces (2 bunches)
- 1 cup fresh bean sprouts
- 2 to 3 drops hot sauce

Heat chicken broth to boiling. Add mushrooms, then spinach; cook 2 minutes. Add bean sprouts and hot sauce. Serve at once.

APPROXIMATE NUTRITIONAL INFORMATION PER 1-CUP SERVING

Calories: 33
Total fat: 1 g
Saturated fat: 0 g
Percentage of calories from fat: 25%
Carbohydrate: 2 g
Protein: 4 g
Cholesterol: 2 mg
Sodium: 230 mg
Dietary fiber: 2 g

Wonton Soup

Approximately 3 quarts

¾ pound extra-lean boneless pork chops
¼ teaspoon pepper
¾ teaspoon salt
6 shiitake mushrooms, chopped
10 green onions, chopped
2 dozen wonton wrappers, thawed
12 cups reduced-fat chicken broth, preferably homemade (page 364)
1 tablespoon reduced-sodium soy sauce

Grind pork in a meat grinder, blender, or food processor; sprinkle with pepper and salt. Toss with mushrooms and green onions. Place mixture by teaspoonful into center of wonton wrappers; squeeze edges of wrapper together to seal.

Drop wontons into 3½ quarts boiling water; bring to a second boil. Boil 2 minutes; add 2 cups cold water. Bring to a third boil; boil 2 to 3 minutes. Drain. Bring chicken broth just to boiling. Stir in soy sauce. Add wontons. Serve.

Note: Wontons may be cooked ahead and refrigerated. To reheat, drop into boiling broth. If fresh shiitake mushrooms are not available, the dried can be purchased in Oriental markets or in the Oriental section of most supermarkets. To reconstitute dried mushrooms, soak them in enough water to cover for 30 minutes, or until soft; remove and squeeze out the excess water. Remove and discard stems. Reserve soaking liquid; add to chicken broth.

APPROXIMATE NUTRITIONAL INFORMATION PER 1-CUP SERVING WITH 2 WONTONS

Calories: 138
Total fat: 7 g
Saturated fat: 2 g
Percentage of calories from fat: 47%
Carbohydrate: 6 g
Protein: 12 g
Cholesterol: 30 mg
Sodium: 384 mg
Dietary fiber: 0 g

EGG DROP SOUP

Approximately 5 1-cup servings

4 cups reduced-fat chicken broth, preferably homemade (page 364)
1 egg, beaten
6 to 8 cherry tomatoes, thinly sliced
4 green onions with tops, thinly sliced

Heat chicken broth to boiling. Pour egg through a wire strainer into hot broth. Ladle broth into soup bowls; add 1 to 2 sliced cherry tomatoes and sliced green onion to each bowl. Serve at once.

APPROXIMATE NUTRITIONAL INFORMATION PER SERVING

Calories: 46
Total fat: 2 g
Saturated fat: 0 g
Percentage of calories from fat: 38%
Carbohydrate: 2 g
Protein: 5 g
Cholesterol: 44 mg
Sodium: 237 mg
Dietary fiber: 0 g

MINESTRONE

Approximately 4 quarts

4 garlic cloves, minced
1 medium onion, chopped
2 celery stalks, diced
6 cups reduced-fat chicken broth, preferably homemade (page 364)
1 14½-ounce can plum tomatoes, diced
1 tablespoon olive oil
½ cup red wine
3 fresh basil sprigs or 1 tablespoon dried
3 fresh oregano sprigs or 1 tablespoon dried
2 teaspoons salt
½ teaspoon pepper
3 medium-size unpared red potatoes, diced
2 carrots, diced
1 9-ounce package frozen green beans, steamed until just crisp-tender
2 15-ounce cans cannellini beans, drained and rinsed
2 cups cooked macaroni

In a stockpot, combine garlic, onion, celery, chicken broth, tomatoes, olive oil, wine, basil, oregano, salt, and pepper; heat just to boiling. Add potatoes and carrots; reduce heat to a simmer; cook 30 to 45 minutes, or until vegetables are tender. Add green beans, cannellini, and macaroni.

Serving Suggestion: Good with Pizza Bread (page 326) or Cheese Bread (page 327).

APPROXIMATE NUTRITIONAL INFORMATION PER 1-CUP SERVING

Calories: 113
Total fat: 2 g
Saturated fat: 0 g
Percentage of calories from fat: 12%
Carbohydrate: 18 g
Protein: 6 g
Cholesterol: 1 mg
Sodium: 310 mg
Dietary fiber: 5 g

TURKEY VEGETABLE SOUP

Approximately 4 quarts

3 quarts reduced-fat turkey broth (page 365)
3 carrots, peeled and diced
2 celery stalks, peeled and diced
4 cups cooked macaroni, rice, or orzo
½ pound fresh mushrooms, sliced

Heat broth to boiling; add carrots and celery. Cover; reduce heat, and simmer until carrots and celery are tender. Add pasta and mushrooms. Heat to serving temperature.

APPROXIMATE NUTRITIONAL INFORMATION PER 1-CUP SERVING

Calories: 80
Total fat: 1 g
Saturated fat: 0 g
Percentage of calories from fat: 12%
Carbohydrate: 12 g
Protein: 5 g
Cholesterol: 2 mg
Sodium: 216 mg
Dietary fiber: 1 g

Italian Vegetable Soup

Makes 6 quarts

1 28-ounce can plum tomatoes, diced
6 cups reduced-fat beef broth, preferably homemade (page 366)
1 tablespoon olive oil
1 onion, chopped
5 garlic cloves, minced
2 to 3 fresh basil sprigs or 1 teaspoon dried
1 teaspoon fresh oregano or ½ teaspoon dried
1 medium green pepper, seeded and chopped
3 medium zucchini, sliced ¼ inch thick
8 cups cooked orzo or other small Italian pasta
1 8¾-ounce can garbanzo beans, drained
½ teaspoon salt
¼ teaspoon pepper
3 tablespoons chopped flat-leaf Italian parsley for garnish

In a heavy stockpot, combine tomatoes, beef broth, olive oil, onion, and garlic. Heat just to boiling, but do not allow to boil. Reduce heat; simmer 30 minutes. Add basil, oregano, green pepper, and zucchini. Simmer covered 5 to 7 minutes, or until zucchini is just tender. Stir in orzo and garbanzo beans. Heat to serving temperature; season with salt and pepper. Garnish with parsley.

APPROXIMATE NUTRITIONAL INFORMATION PER 1-CUP SERVING

Calories: 101
Total fat: 1 g
Saturated fat: 0 g
Percentage of calories from fat: 13%
Carbohydrate: 17 g
Protein: 4 g
Cholesterol: 1 mg
Sodium: 171 mg
Dietary fiber: 1 g

CREAM OF ARTICHOKE SOUP

Approximately 3 quarts

1 medium onion, chopped
3 celery ribs, chopped
2 leeks with green tops, chopped
1 new potato with skin, quartered
6 cups reduced-fat chicken broth, preferably homemade (page 364)
1 14½-ounce can water-packed artichoke hearts, drained and quartered
1½ cups broccoli florets, cooked until just crisp-tender
Freshly ground pepper

Cook onion, celery, leeks, and potato in chicken broth until all vegetables are tender; pour into a blender and purée. Return to stockpot; simmer 30 minutes. Add artichoke hearts; simmer 10 minutes; add broccoli. Heat to serving temperature. Pass ground pepper.

Variation: Use ¾ pound cooked fresh artichoke hearts in place of the canned.

Serving Suggestion: Serve with Clams Italian Style (page 514), crusty French bread, and fresh fruit.

APPROXIMATE NUTRITIONAL INFORMATION PER 1-CUP SERVING

Calories: 65
Total fat: 1 g
Saturated fat: 0 g
Percentage of calories from fat: 11%
Carbohydrate: 11 g
Protein: 4 g
Cholesterol: 1 mg
Sodium: 181 mg
Dietary fiber: 1 g

Beef Broth with Mushrooms

Approximately 3 1-cup servings

1 leek with green tops, finely chopped
3 cups reduced-fat beef broth, preferably homemade (page 366)
½ cup thinly sliced fresh mushrooms
½ teaspoon fresh tarragon or thyme or ¼ teaspoon dried
¼ cup finely chopped fresh parsley

Sauté leek in a small amount of the broth; add mushrooms and stir over high heat for 1 minute. Add remaining broth and tarragon or thyme. Bring to a boil; cover, reduce heat, and simmer 20 minutes. Just before serving, sprinkle with parsley.

APPROXIMATE NUTRITIONAL INFORMATION PER SERVING

Calories: 57
Total fat: 1 g
Saturated fat: 0 g
Percentage of calories from fat: 18%
Carbohydrate: 4 g
Protein: 6 g
Cholesterol: 2 mg
Sodium: 281 mg
Dietary fiber: 0 g

BARLEY-MUSHROOM SOUP

Approximately 4 quarts

1½ cups barley
9 cups reduced-fat beef broth, preferably homemade (page 366)
½ to ¾ pound fresh mushrooms, sliced

Soak barley for several hours or overnight in enough water to cover. Heat broth to boiling; add barley with its soaking liquid. Cover and simmer 2 to 2½ hours, or until barley is tender. Add mushrooms; simmer 10 to 20 minutes.

Variation: Add ¾ pound extra-lean ground round, cooked and drained, to soup. Serve at once.

APPROXIMATE NUTRITIONAL INFORMATION PER 1-CUP SERVING

Calories: 86
Total fat: trace
Saturated fat: 0 g
Percentage of calories from fat: 11%
Carbohydrate: 9 g
Protein: 5 g
Cholesterol: 13 mg
Sodium: 157 mg
Dietary fiber: 2 g

APPROXIMATE NUTRITIONAL INFORMATION PER 1-CUP SERVING USING EXTRA-LEAN GROUND ROUND

Calories: 118
Total fat: 3 g
Saturated fat: 1 g
Percentage of calories from fat: 21%
Carbohydrate: 13 g
Protein: 9 g
Cholesterol: 14 mg
Sodium: 170 mg
Dietary fiber: 3 g

Fresh Mushroom Soup with Mozzarella Cheese

Approximately 2½ quarts

1 onion, chopped
1 carrot, quartered
1 cup chopped celery
6 cups reduced-fat beef broth, preferably homemade (page 366)
¾ pound fresh mushrooms, thinly sliced
Juice of 1 lemon
½ teaspoon salt
¼ teaspoon pepper
¼ cup sherry (optional)
¾ cup grated reduced-fat mozzarella cheese
3 tablespoons chopped fresh parsley

Boil onion, carrot, and celery in beef broth until vegetables are tender; purée in a blender or food processor. Return to stockpot and simmer. Sauté mushrooms in lemon juice until tender. Add mushrooms, salt, pepper, and sherry to simmering broth. Heat to serving temperature. Ladle into soup bowls. Sprinkle with cheese and parsley.

Variation: Place a slice of toasted French bread in each bowl; ladle soup over bread.

APPROXIMATE NUTRITIONAL INFORMATION PER 1-CUP SERVING

Calories: 73
Total fat: 2 g
Saturated fat: 1 g
Percentage of calories from fat: 26%
Carbohydrate: 5 g
Protein: 6 g
Cholesterol: 6 mg
Sodium: 319 mg
Dietary fiber: 1 g

MACARONI, CHICKEN, AND BEAN SOUP

Approximately 4 quarts

- 4 cups reduced-fat chicken broth, preferably homemade (page 364)
- 1 28-ounce can plum tomatoes, chopped
- 1 small onion, diced
- 1 garlic clove, crushed
- 1 4-ounce can diced green chilies
- 1 15-ounce can pinto beans, drained and rinsed
- 1 15-ounce can garbanzo beans, drained and rinsed
- 1½ cups diced cooked chicken
- 2 cups cooked elbow macaroni

Heat chicken broth and tomatoes just to boiling; immediately reduce heat. Add onion, garlic, and green chilies; simmer 1 hour. Add beans, chicken, and macaroni; simmer 20 minutes.

Serving Suggestion: Serve with corn tortillas.

APPROXIMATE NUTRITIONAL INFORMATION PER 1-CUP SERVING

Calories: 123
Total fat: 1 g
Saturated fat: 0 g
Percentage of calories from fat: 9%
Carbohydrate: 18 g
Protein: 10 g
Cholesterol: 12 mg
Sodium: 166 mg
Dietary fiber: 3 g

Macaroni and Bean Soup

Approximately 3 quarts

1 28-ounce can plum tomatoes, diced
½ pound extra-lean ground beef, sautéed and defatted
1 tablespoon chili powder
⅛ teaspoon cayenne
⅛ teaspoon ground cumin
½ teaspoon paprika
½ teaspoon salt
⅛ teaspoon pepper
4 cups cooked elbow macaroni
2 cups fresh or frozen corn kernels
2 15-ounce cans cannellini beans, drained and rinsed
1 15-ounce can garbanzo beans, drained and rinsed

In a 3-quart saucepan, combine tomatoes with their liquid, ground beef, chili powder, cayenne, cumin, paprika, salt, and pepper. Heat just to boiling, but do not allow to boil. Add macaroni, corn, cannellini and garbanzo beans. Heat to serving temperature.

Variation: Delete the ground beef.

APPROXIMATE NUTRITIONAL INFORMATION PER 1-CUP SERVING USING 85% EXTRA-LEAN GROUND BEEF

Calories: 237
Total fat: 4 g
Saturated fat: 1 g
Percentage of calories from fat: 16%
Carbohydrate: 39 g
Protein: 14 g
Cholesterol: 16 mg
Sodium: 343 mg
Dietary fiber: 8 g

APPROXIMATE NUTRITIONAL INFORMATION PER 1-CUP SERVING WITHOUT GROUND BEEF

Calories: 192
Total fat: 2 g
Saturated fat: 0 g
Percentage of calories from fat: 7%
Carbohydrate: 39 g
Protein: 9 g
Cholesterol: 0 mg
Sodium: 329 mg
Dietary fiber: 8 g

THREE-BEAN SOUP

Approximately 3 quarts

1 28-ounce can plum tomatoes, diced
1 tablespoon chili powder
⅛ teaspoon ground cumin
⅛ teaspoon cayenne
½ teaspoon paprika
½ teaspoon salt
⅛ teaspoon pepper
2 15-ounce cans cannellini beans, drained and rinsed
1 15-ounce can garbanzo beans, drained and rinsed
2 15-ounce cans black beans, drained and rinsed

In a 3-quart saucepan, combine tomatoes, chili powder, cumin, cayenne, paprika, salt, and pepper. Heat just to boiling, but do not allow to boil. Reduce heat and simmer 30 minutes. Add cannellini, garbanzos, and black beans. Heat to serving temperature.

APPROXIMATE NUTRITIONAL INFORMATION PER 1-CUP SERVING

Calories: 171
Total fat: 3 g
Saturated fat: 0 g
Percentage of calories from fat: 14%
Carbohydrate: 30 g
Protein: 9 g
Cholesterol: 0 mg
Sodium: 425 mg
Dietary fiber: 9 g

Shrimp and Cannellini Bean Soup

Approximately 3 quarts

1 28-ounce can plum tomatoes, diced
1 tablespoon olive oil
4 garlic cloves, minced
2 15-ounce cans cannellini beans, drained and rinsed
3 cups cooked elbow macaroni
½ teaspoon salt
¼ teaspoon pepper
⅔ pound small cooked shrimp
2 tablespoons finely chopped flat-leaf Italian parsley
2 to 3 fresh basil leaves for garnish (optional)

In a 3-quart saucepan, combine tomatoes, olive oil, and garlic. Heat just to boiling, but do not allow to boil. Reduce heat; simmer 30 minutes. Add cannellini beans, macaroni, salt, pepper, and shrimp. Heat 2 to 3 minutes, just to serving temperature. Garnish with Italian parsley and fresh basil.

Variation: Delete the shrimp.

APPROXIMATE NUTRITIONAL INFORMATION PER 1-CUP SERVING

Calories: 163	Carbohydrate: 25 g
Total fat: 3 g	Protein: 12 g
Saturated fat: 0 g	Cholesterol: 43 mg
Percentage of calories from fat: 14%	Sodium: 295 mg
	Dietary fiber: 5 g

APPROXIMATE NUTRITIONAL INFORMATION PER 1-CUP SERVING WITHOUT SHRIMP

Calories: 133	Carbohydrate: 24 g
Total fat: 2 g	Protein: 6 g
Saturated fat: 0 g	Cholesterol: 0 mg
Percentage of calories from fat: 14%	Sodium: 257 mg
	Dietary fiber: 5 g

MANHATTAN CLAM CHOWDER

Approximately 3 quarts

- 1 28-ounce can plum tomatoes, chopped
- 1 large white onion, chopped
- 3 celery stalks, thinly sliced
- 1 minced fresh thyme sprig or 1 teaspoon dried
- 1 tablespoon chopped fresh parsley
- ½ teaspoon salt
- 2 peppercorns
- ⅛ teaspoon ground pepper
- ⅛ teaspoon Tabasco sauce
- 1 bay leaf
- 3 medium potatoes, pared and diced
- 2 carrots, thinly sliced
- 3 6½-ounce cans chopped clams with their liquid

Combine tomatoes, onion, celery, thyme, parsley, salt, peppercorns, ground pepper, Tabasco sauce, and bay leaf in a stockpot; bring to a boil, reduce heat, and simmer 20 minutes. Bring to a second boil; add potatoes and carrots; reduce heat and simmer 45 minutes, or until vegetables are just tender. Add clams with their liquid; simmer 15 minutes. Remove bay leaf.

Note: Two pounds fresh clams, steamed, plus 1½ cups of their liquid may be used in place of canned clams.

APPROXIMATE NUTRITIONAL INFORMATION PER 1-CUP SERVING

Calories: 115
Total fat: 1 g
Saturated fat: 0 g
Percentage of calories from fat: 8%
Carbohydrate: 15 g
Protein: 12 g
Cholesterol: 27 mg
Sodium: 262 mg
Dietary fiber: 2 g

SEVICHE SOUP

6 servings

½ pound scallops, chopped
½ cup fresh lime juice
1½ cups Mr. & Mrs. T Bloody Mary Mix
2 cups reduced-fat chicken broth, preferably homemade (page 364)
⅓ cup chopped white onion
3 tablespoons chopped green chilies
½ teaspoon olive oil
¼ teaspoon salt
1 tablespoon chopped fresh parsley
1 slice fresh lime, cut into 6 wedges

Cover scallops with lime juice. Marinate in the refrigerator for 4 hours; pour off lime juice.

Preheat a nonstick skillet; add scallops. Cook, turning frequently, for 4 to 6 minutes, or just until scallops are tender. Remove from pan; drain any excess liquid. Chill scallops several hours.

Combine Bloody Mary mix, chicken broth, onion, green chilies, olive oil, and salt. Chill several hours.

Just before serving, add scallops to Bloody Mary mixture. Ladle into soup bowls. Sprinkle with parsley.

Garnish with fresh lime.

Serving Suggestion: Great first course on a hot summer day.

APPROXIMATE NUTRITIONAL INFORMATION PER 1-CUP SERVING

Calories: 70
Total fat: 1 g
Saturated fat: 0 g
Percentage of calories from fat: 14%
Carbohydrate: 6 g
Protein: 9 g
Cholesterol: 14 mg
Sodium: 559 mg
Dietary fiber: 0 g

SEAFOOD CHOWDER

Approximately 6 servings

1 pound clams
1 pound mussels
1 cup dry white wine
1 14½-ounce can plum tomatoes
3 garlic cloves
2 teaspoons olive oil
¼ teaspoon salt
⅛ teaspoon pepper
1 6½-ounce can chopped clams, drained
¼ pound red snapper, cut into 3-inch cubes
¼ pound cod, cut into 3-inch cubes
¼ pound scallops
¼ pound crab legs
2 tablespoons chopped fresh parsley

Scrub clams and soak in salt water or water and cornmeal to remove sand (page 513). Scrub mussel shells with a wire brush under cold running water. Remove beards and discard broken or open mussels.

Heat wine, tomatoes, garlic, and olive oil; simmer 15 to 20 minutes. Add salt, pepper, and chopped clams; simmer 15 to 20 minutes. Heat just to boiling, but do not allow to boil. Add clams and mussels; cover and steam just until shells begin to open. Add remaining seafood; cook 5 minutes, or until clams and mussels have opened and seafood is cooked. Do not over-cook seafood. Ladle into soup bowls. Sprinkle with fresh parsley.

APPROXIMATE NUTRITIONAL INFORMATION PER 1-CUP SERVING

Calories: 261
Total fat: 5 g
Saturated fat: 1 g
Percentage of calories from fat: 18%
Carbohydrate: 10 g
Protein: 35 g
Cholesterol: 80 mg
Sodium: 560 mg
Dietary fiber: 1 g

Cioppino

8 servings

1 pound mussels
1 pound clams
1 cup dry white wine
2 cups reduced-fat chicken broth, preferably homemade (page 364)
1 8-ounce can tomato sauce
3 tablespoons tomato paste
3 tablespoons olive oil
1 onion, chopped
1 leek with green tops, chopped
2 garlic cloves
3 fresh ripe tomatoes, chopped
1 14½-ounce can plum tomatoes, chopped
2 fresh basil sprigs, or ½ teaspoon dried
1 bay leaf
Dash each of fennel, thyme, and cayenne
2 drops Tabasco sauce
¾ teaspoon salt
1 green pepper, chopped
¼ pound red snapper, cut into 3-inch cubes
¼ pound cod, cut into 3-inch cubes
¼ pound scallops
¼ pound cooked crab legs
4 cups cooked seashell-shaped pasta

Scrub mussel shells with a wire brush. Remove and discard beards. Rinse mussels in cold water; discard broken or open mussels.

Scrub clams. Place in a large bowl and cover with cold water. Sprinkle with cornmeal, and let stand 30 minutes. Drain and rinse; discard cornmeal.

Arrange clams and mussels on a rack in a covered steamer filled with 2 cups hot water. Steam 6 to 8 minutes, or just until shells open. Set aside.

Bring wine, chicken broth, tomato sauce, tomato paste, and all but 1 teaspoon olive oil to a boil. Add onion, leek, and garlic; simmer 20 minutes. Add fresh and canned tomatoes and remaining seasonings; heat just to boiling. Add green pepper.

Meanwhile, preheat a nonstick skillet with remaining 1 teaspoon olive oil: add red snapper, cod, and scallops. Cook, turning frequently, 4 to 6 minutes, or just until seafood is tender. Drain any liquid.

Just before serving, add clams, mussels, sautéed seafood, crab legs, and pasta to sauce.

Serving Suggestion: Serve with freshly baked French bread.

APPROXIMATE NUTRITIONAL INFORMATION PER 1-CUP SERVING

Calories: 304
Total fat: 8 g
Saturated fat: 1 g
Percentage of calories from fat: 23%

Carbohydrate: 33 g
Protein: 22 g
Cholesterol: 36 mg
Sodium: 635 mg
Dietary fiber: 2 g

BOUILLABAISSE

10 servings

2 pounds clams
2 pounds mussels
2 cups dry white wine
4 cups reduced-fat chicken broth, preferably homemade (page 364)
¼ cup olive oil
1 onion, chopped
1 leek with green tops, chopped
4 garlic cloves
4 large ripe tomatoes, chopped
1 28-ounce can plum tomatoes, diced
2 fresh basil sprigs
3 drops Tabasco sauce
½ teaspoon salt
1 bay leaf
Dash each of cayenne, thyme, and fennel
2 green peppers, chopped
¾ pound red snapper, cut into 3-inch cubes
¾ pound cod, cut into 3-inch cubes
¼ pound scallops
¾ pound crab legs
6 red potatoes, steamed in their jackets until just tender and sliced

Scrub clams. Place in a large bowl and cover with cold water. Sprinkle with cornmeal and let stand 30 minutes. Drain and rinse; discard cornmeal.

Scrub mussel shells with a wire brush. Remove and discard beards. Rinse mussels in cold water; discard broken or open mussels.

Bring wine, chicken broth, and olive oil to a boil in a large stockpot. Add onion, leek, and garlic; simmer 20 minutes. Add fresh and canned tomatoes, basil, Tabasco sauce, and seasonings; heat just to boiling, but do not allow to boil. Add clams and mussels. Cover. Steam just until shells begin to open; add green peppers and remaining seafood. Cook 5 minutes. Add potatoes; simmer 2 to 3 minutes, or until clams and mussels have opened and seafood is cooked. Do not overcook seafood.

APPROXIMATE NUTRITIONAL INFORMATION PER 1-CUP SERVING

Calories: 359
Total fat: 9 g
Saturated fat: 1 g
Percentage of calories from fat: 22%
Carbohydrate: 30 g
Protein: 33 g
Cholesterol: 70 mg
Sodium: 546 mg
Dietary fiber: 3 g

Gazpacho

Approximately 3 quarts

1 fresh ripe tomato
1 green pepper
3 celery stalks
1 cucumber
1 small onion
3 tablespoons chopped fresh parsley
4 green onions
2 garlic cloves
¼ cup red wine vinegar
2 tablespoons olive oil
¾ teaspoon salt
6 cups canned plum tomatoes, chopped
¼ teaspoon horseradish

In a blender, combine all ingredients except horseradish; purée. Chill at least 3 hours. Just before serving, stir in horseradish.

Variation: Top each cup with 1 tablespoon small cooked shrimp and 1 teaspoon nonfat sour cream.

APPROXIMATE NUTRITIONAL INFORMATION PER 1-CUP SERVING

Calories: 60
Total fat: 3 g
Saturated fat: 0 g
Percentage of calories from fat: 40%
Carbohydrate: 9 g
Protein: 2 g
Cholesterol: 4 mg
Sodium: 258 mg
Dietary fiber: 2 g

If using shrimp and nonfat sour cream, add 9 calories and no grams of fat per serving.

FRESH TOMATO SOUP

Approximately 3½ quarts

3½ pounds ripe tomatoes, chopped
1 large onion, chopped
1 tablespoon minced fresh dill weed or 1½ teaspoons dried
3 tablespoons tomato paste
3 cups reduced-fat beef broth, preferably homemade (page 366)
1½ teaspoons sugar
Ground pepper to taste
2 to 3 drops Tabasco sauce
Dash of salt
2 to 3 sprigs fresh basil

Combine tomatoes, onion, dill, and tomato paste in a stockpot. Bring to a boil, stirring often; reduce heat, cover, and simmer 15 minutes. Cool to room temperature. Pour into a food processor; whirl until smooth. Return to stockpot; add remaining ingredients. Heat to serving temperature.

Variation: Add 1 cup cooked macaroni.

APPROXIMATE NUTRITIONAL INFORMATION PER 1-CUP SERVING

Calories: 37
Total fat: 1 g
Saturated fat: 0 g
Percentage of calories from fat: 15%
Carbohydrate: 7 g
Protein: 2 g
Cholesterol: 0 mg
Sodium: 146 mg
Dietary fiber: 1 g

If including the macaroni, add 14 calories and no grams of fat per serving.

Chicken Broth

Approximately 3 quarts

1 3-pound chicken
3 quarts cold water
2 celery stalks with leaves
2 carrots, peeled
1 large onion, quartered
2 garlic cloves
1 fresh basil sprig or ¼ teaspoon dried
4 peppercorns
1 tablespoon salt
⅛ teaspoon pepper

Put chicken and water in a stockpot. Cover; simmer 2½ hours, or until chicken is tender and pulls away from bone. Strain. Remove meat from bones (freeze for later use). Refrigerate broth overnight; fat will float to the top. Skim and discard fat. Heat broth to boiling; add vegetables and seasonings. Simmer 2 hours; strain. Reserve vegetables for soup or later use; use broth within 1 week or freeze.

Note: For maximum economy, when a recipe calls for cooked chicken breast, buy a whole chicken. Skin and bone breasts. Discard skin. Freeze the bones along with wings and backs in a plastic freezer bag. When 5 to 6 pounds accumulate, (or if you have a chicken carcass after a meal of roast chicken), place in a stockpot; add water to cover by 2 inches. Add vegetables and seasonings as in above recipe. Bring to a boil. Cover. Reduce heat. Simmer 5 to 6 hours. Strain. Discard bones and vegetables as they will be greasy. Refrigerate broth overnight. Skim and discard fat.

Variations: For a richer broth, add another chicken or more chicken parts. For a hearty chicken soup, do not strain broth. Add 2 to 3 cups cooked pasta or rice.

APPROXIMATE NUTRITIONAL INFORMATION PER 1-CUP SERVING

Calories: 27
Total fat: 1 g
Saturated fat: 0 g
Percentage of calories from fat: 33%
Carbohydrate: 0 g
Protein: 4 g
Cholesterol: 2 mg
Sodium: 275 mg
Dietary fiber: 0 g

TURKEY BROTH

Approximately 3 quarts

1 turkey carcass with meaty bones (from a 10-pound turkey)
About 3 quarts water
2 garlic cloves
1 fresh basil sprig or ¼ teaspoon dried
4 peppercorns
1 tablespoon or less salt
⅛ teaspoon pepper
4 celery stalks with leaves
4 carrots, peeled
1 large onion, quartered

Place turkey carcass in a stockpot; add water to cover. Add seasonings; bring to a boil. Add vegetables. Cover, reduce heat, and simmer 6 to 8 hours. Strain; discard bones and vegetables. Remove any meat from bones and reserve for later use. Refrigerate broth overnight. Skim and discard fat that floats to the top. Reheat broth or freeze for later use. Broth will keep for 1 week in the refrigerator.

APPROXIMATE NUTRITIONAL INFORMATION PER 1-CUP SERVING

Calories: 39
Total fat: 1 g
Saturated fat: 0 g
Percentage of calories from fat: 32%
Carbohydrate: 1 g
Protein: 5 g
Cholesterol: 1 mg
Sodium: 660 mg
Dietary fiber: 0 g

Beef Broth

Approximately 2 quarts

- 6 pounds beef bones, or 2 to 3 pounds beef shank or short ribs
- 9 cups water
- 3 celery stalks with leaves, diced
- 2 carrots, diced
- 1 onion, chopped
- 1 tomato, quartered
- 2 bay leaves
- 2 garlic cloves
- 1 minced fresh thyme sprig or ¼ teaspoon dried
- 1 teaspoon minced fresh sweet marjoram or ½ teaspoon dried
- 8 peppercorns
- 2 teaspoons salt

Put bones, meat, and water in a stockpot. Simmer uncovered for 3 hours (do not boil). Strain. Remove any meat or marrow from bones. Add marrow to stock; reserve meat for later use. Chill stock overnight; skim and discard fat that floats to the top. Bring stock to boiling; add remaining ingredients and simmer uncovered for 2 hours. Strain. Reserve vegetables for soup or later use. Use broth within 1 week or freeze for later use.

Note: For a hearty soup, do not strain broth. Add 2 to 3 cups cooked pasta.

APPROXIMATE NUTRITIONAL INFORMATION PER 1-CUP SERVING

Calories: 37
Total fat: 1 g
Saturated fat: 0 g
Percentage of calories from fat: 24%

Carbohydrate: 0 g
Protein: 5 g
Cholesterol: 2 mg
Sodium: 275 mg
Dietary fiber: 0 g

SANDWICHES

TOASTED CHEESE SANDWICH

Makes 1 sandwich

2 slices whole-grain bread
2 teaspoons tub-style light margarine
1½ teaspoons prepared mustard (optional)
2 nonfat cheddar cheese slices

Spread each slice of bread with margarine (one side only). Spread one unbuttered side with mustard; top with cheese and second slice of bread, buttered side up. Heat a nonstick griddle over medium-high heat; brown sandwiches on both sides until cheese melts.

APPROXIMATE NUTRITIONAL INFORMATION PER SANDWICH

Calories: 224	Carbohydrate: 30 g
Total fat: 5 g	Protein: 15 g
Saturated fat: 1 g	Cholesterol: 10 mg
Percentage of calories from fat: 21%	Sodium: 708 mg
	Dietary fiber: 3 g

VEGGIE SANDWICH

Makes 1 sandwich

2 slices whole-grain bread
1½ tablespoons fat-free cream cheese
4 cucumber slices
2 lettuce leaves
2 tomato slices
1 white onion slice
¼ cup alfalfa sprouts

Spread 1 slice of bread with cream cheese. Layer with remaining ingredients. Top with remaining slice of bread. Serve.

APPROXIMATE NUTRITIONAL INFORMATION PER SANDWICH

Calories: 169
Total fat: 3 g
Saturated fat: 1 g
Percentage of calories from fat: 14%
Carbohydrate: 29 g
Protein: 9 g
Cholesterol: 4 mg
Sodium: 428 mg
Dietary fiber: 4 g

LETTUCE AND TOMATO SANDWICH

Makes 1 sandwich

2 slices whole-grain bread
1½ teaspoons fat-free or light mayonnaise
2 tomato slices
Pepper to taste
Salt to taste
2 lettuce leaves

Toast bread; spread with mayonnaise. Sprinkle tomato slices with pepper and salt. Layer lettuce and tomato between toast slices. Serve.

Variation: Top tomatoes with sliced white onion and nonfat or reduced-fat cheddar or mozzarella cheese slices.

APPROXIMATE NUTRITIONAL INFORMATION PER SANDWICH USING FAT-FREE MAYONNAISE

Calories: 155
Total fat: 3 g
Saturated fat: 0 g
Percentage of calories from fat: 15%
Carbohydrate: 29 g
Protein: 6 g
Cholesterol: 0 mg
Sodium: 398 mg
Dietary fiber: 4 g

(continued on next page)

(continued from preceding page)

APPROXIMATE NUTRITIONAL INFORMATION PER SANDWICH USING LIGHT MAYONNAISE

Calories: 174	Carbohydrate: 28 g
Total fat: 5 g	Protein: 6 g
Saturated fat: 1 g	Cholesterol: 0 mg
Percentage of calories from fat: 26%	Sodium: 358 mg
	Dietary fiber: 4 g

Breast of Chicken Sandwich

Makes 1 sandwich

- 2 slices whole-wheat or multi-grain bread
- 2 teaspoons fat-free or light mayonnaise
- 2 ounces poached chicken breast (page 539)
- 2 Bibb lettuce leaves
- 2 tomato slices

Spread 1 slice of bread with mayonnaise; top with remaining ingredients and other bread slice. Cut sandwich in half or diagonally into quarters and serve.

Variation: Substitute turkey for chicken.

APPROXIMATE NUTRITIONAL INFORMATION PER SANDWICH USING FAT-FREE MAYONNAISE

Calories: 243	Carbohydrate: 30 g
Total fat: 4 g	Protein: 22 g
Saturated fat: 1 g	Cholesterol: 44 mg
Percentage of calories from fat: 16%	Sodium: 466 mg
	Dietary fiber: 4 g

APPROXIMATE NUTRITIONAL INFORMATION PER SANDWICH USING LIGHT MAYONNAISE

Calories: 268	Carbohydrate: 29 g
Total fat: 8 g	Protein: 22 g
Saturated fat: 2 g	Cholesterol: 44 mg
Percentage of calories from fat: 26%	Sodium: 412 mg
	Dietary fiber: 4 g

CHICKEN SALAD SANDWICH

Makes 3 sandwiches

1 cup chopped cooked chicken
½ cup finely chopped celery
¼ cup finely chopped water chestnuts
2 tablespoons fat-free or light mayonnaise
6 slices whole-wheat or pumpernickel bread
6 large lettuce leaves
6 ripe tomato slices

Combine chicken, celery, water chestnuts, and mayonnaise. Chill. Just before serving, spread 3 slices of the bread with filling; top with lettuce, tomato and an additional slice of bread. Cut sandwich in half and serve.

APPROXIMATE NUTRITIONAL INFORMATION PER SANDWICH USING FAT-FREE MAYONNAISE

Calories: 210
Total fat: 4 g
Saturated fat: 0 g
Percentage of calories from fat: 16%
Carbohydrate: 32 g
Protein: 15 g
Cholesterol: 23 mg
Sodium: 422 mg
Dietary fiber: 4 g

APPROXIMATE NUTRITIONAL INFORMATION PER SANDWICH USING LIGHT MAYONNAISE

Calories: 226
Total fat: 5 g
Saturated fat: 1 g
Percentage of calories from fat: 22%
Carbohydrate: 32 g
Protein: 15 g
Cholesterol: 23 mg
Sodium: 381 mg
Dietary fiber: 4 g

Chicken and Shrimp Club Sandwich

Makes 1 sandwich

3 slices whole-wheat toast
6 lettuce leaves
1 ounce cooked chicken breast, sliced
1½ teaspoons fat-free or light mayonnaise
3 tomato slices
1 ounce small cooked shrimp

Top first slice of toast with lettuce, chicken, and mayonnaise. Top with second slice of toast; add tomato slices and shrimp; top with third slice of toast. Slice diagonally into quarters.

APPROXIMATE NUTRITIONAL INFORMATION PER SANDWICH USING FAT-FREE MAYONNAISE

Calories: 300	Carbohydrate: 44 g
Total fat: 5 g	Protein: 23 g
Saturated fat: 1 g	Cholesterol: 77 mg
Percentage of calories from fat: 15%	Sodium: 630 mg
	Dietary fiber: 6 g

APPROXIMATE NUTRITIONAL INFORMATION PER SANDWICH USING LIGHT MAYONNAISE

Calories: 319	Carbohydrate: 43 g
Total fat: 8 g	Protein: 23 g
Saturated fat: 2 g	Cholesterol: 77 mg
Percentage of calories from fat: 21%	Sodium: 590 mg
	Dietary fiber: 6 g

TUNA SALAD SANDWICH

Makes 3 sandwiches

½ teaspoon fresh lemon juice
1 6⅛-ounce can water-packed tuna, drained
3 tablespoons minced onion
2 tablespoons minced celery
2 tablespoons finely chopped water chestnuts
⅓ cup fat-free or light mayonnaise
Dash of prepared mustard
6 slices whole-wheat or rye bread
6 ripe tomato slices
6 large lettuce slices

Sprinkle lemon juice over tuna; toss with onion, celery, and water chestnuts. Moisten with mayonnaise and mustard. Spread 3 slices of bread with filling; top each with tomato and lettuce and second slice of bread. Cut sandwich in half and serve.

APPROXIMATE NUTRITIONAL INFORMATION PER SANDWICH USING FAT-FREE MAYONNAISE

Calories: 236
Total fat: 4 g
Saturated fat: 1 g
Percentage of calories from fat: 14%
Carbohydrate: 35 g
Protein: 18 g
Cholesterol: 18 mg
Sodium: 734 mg
Dietary fiber: 4 g

APPROXIMATE NUTRITIONAL INFORMATION PER SANDWICH USING LIGHT MAYONNAISE

Calories: 291
Total fat: 10 g
Saturated fat: 2 g
Percentage of calories from fat: 32%
Carbohydrate: 33 g
Protein: 18 g
Cholesterol: 18 mg
Sodium: 628 mg
Dietary fiber: 4 g

Hot Tuna Sandwich

4 servings

1 6⅛-ounce can water-packed tuna, drained
2 tablespoons finely chopped green pepper
2 tablespoons finely chopped celery
2 tablespoons finely chopped onion
⅓ cup fat-free or light mayonnaise
2 English muffins, halved and toasted
4 nonfat cheddar cheese slices

Combine tuna, green pepper, celery, and onion; moisten with mayonnaise. Spread on muffin halves. Place under a preheated broiler for 2 to 3 minutes. Top with cheese; broil 2 to 3 minutes, or until cheese melts.

APPROXIMATE NUTRITIONAL INFORMATION PER SERVING USING FAT-FREE MAYONNAISE

Calories: 169
Total fat: 2 g
Saturated fat: 0 g
Percentage of calories from fat: 8%
Carbohydrate: 19 g
Protein: 18 g
Cholesterol: 23 mg
Sodium: 725 mg
Dietary fiber: 2 g

APPROXIMATE NUTRITIONAL INFORMATION PER SERVING USING LIGHT MAYONNAISE

Calories: 220
Total fat: 8 g
Saturated fat: 2 g
Percentage of calories from fat: 15%
Carbohydrate: 16 g
Protein: 18 g
Cholesterol: 23 mg
Sodium: 619 mg
Dietary fiber: 2 g

MONTE CRISTO

Makes 3 sandwiches

1 6⅛-ounce can water-packed tuna, drained
¼ cup fat-free or light mayonnaise
6 slices whole-wheat bread
¼ cup egg substitute, beaten

Moisten tuna with mayonnaise. Dip 1 slice of bread into beaten egg; place on a preheated nonstick griddle. Spread with tuna. Dip second slice of bread into beaten egg; place over tuna. Brown sandwiches on both sides, turning only once. Cut sandwich in half and serve.

Variation: Add sliced tomato or white onion.

APPROXIMATE NUTRITIONAL INFORMATION PER SANDWICH USING FAT-FREE MAYONNAISE

Calories: 240
Total fat: 4 g
Saturated fat: 1g
Percentage of calories from fat: 14%
Carbohydrate: 30 g
Protein: 22 g
Cholesterol: 23 mg
Sodium: 769 mg
Dietary fiber: 4 g

APPROXIMATE NUTRITIONAL INFORMATION PER SANDWICH USING LIGHT MAYONNAISE

Calories: 290
Total fat: 10 g
Saturated fat: 2 g
Percentage of calories from fat: 32%
Carbohydrate: 27 g
Protein: 22 g
Cholesterol: 23 mg
Sodium: 693 mg
Dietary fiber: 4 g

TUNA AND CHEESE BURGERS

Makes 4 burgers

1 6⅛-ounce can water-packed tuna, drained
2 tablespoons chopped onion
2 tablespoons sliced water chestnuts
1 teaspoon prepared mustard
⅓ cup fat-free or light mayonnaise
4 hamburger buns
4 nonfat cheese slices
4 lettuce leaves
4 tomato slices
4 white onion slices

Mix together tuna, onion, water chestnuts, and mustard; moisten with mayonnaise. Toast or warm buns; spread bottom half with tuna. Broil 5 inches from heat for about 3 minutes; add cheese. Broil 2 minutes longer, or until cheese melts; add lettuce, tomato, and sliced onion. Top with upper half of bun.

APPROXIMATE NUTRITIONAL INFORMATION PER BURGER USING FAT-FREE MAYONNAISE

Calories: 248
Total fat: 4 g
Saturated fat: 1 g
Percentage of calories from fat: 13%
Carbohydrate: 32 g
Protein: 20 g
Cholesterol: 23 mg
Sodium: 852 mg
Dietary fiber: 1 g

APPROXIMATE NUTRITIONAL INFORMATION PER BURGER USING LIGHT MAYONNAISE

Calories: 299
Total fat: 10 g
Saturated fat: 2 g
Percentage of calories from fat: 31%
Carbohydrate: 30 g
Protein: 20 g
Cholesterol: 23 mg
Sodium: 746 mg
Dietary fiber: 1 g

CRAB SANDWICH

Makes 4 sandwiches

½ pound crabmeat
2 tablespoons minced celery
2 tablespoons minced white onion
3 tablespoons fat-free or light mayonnaise
½ teaspoon lemon juice
8 slices sourdough bread
8 tomato slices
8 lettuce leaves

Combine crabmeat, celery, onion, mayonnaise, and lemon juice in a medium bowl. Toss. Divide filling over 4 slices of bread. Top each with 2 tomato slices, 2 lettuce leaves and 1 bread slice. Cut sandwich in half and serve.

APPROXIMATE NUTRITIONAL INFORMATION PER SANDWICH USING FAT-FREE MAYONNAISE

Calories: 241
Total fat: 3 g
Saturated fat: 1 g
Percentage of calories from fat: 12%
Carbohydrate: 35 g
Protein: 17 g
Cholesterol: 30 mg
Sodium: 660 mg
Dietary fiber: 3 g

APPROXIMATE NUTRITIONAL INFORMATION PER SANDWICH USING LIGHT MAYONNAISE

Calories: 269
Total fat: 7 g
Saturated fat: 1 g
Percentage of calories from fat: 23%
Carbohydrate: 34 g
Protein: 17 g
Cholesterol: 30 mg
Sodium: 600 mg
Dietary fiber: 3 g

Hot Crab and Cheese Sandwich

Makes 4 open-face sandwiches

½ teaspoon fresh lemon juice
½ pound crabmeat
2 tablespoons minced white onion
2 tablespoons fat-free or light mayonnaise
2 English muffins, halved and toasted
4 tomato slices
4 nonfat cheddar cheese slices

Squeeze lemon juice over crab; toss with onion. Moisten with mayonnaise. Spread over toasted muffin halves. Place under a preheated broiler for 2 to 3 minutes, or until hot. Top each muffin with tomato and cheese slices. Broil 3 to 5 minutes longer, or until cheese melts. Serve.

APPROXIMATE NUTRITIONAL INFORMATION PER SANDWICH USING FAT-FREE MAYONNAISE

Calories: 161
Total fat: 1 g
Saturated fat: 0 g
Percentage of calories from fat: 8%
Carbohydrate: 17 g
Protein: 17 g
Cholesterol: 35 mg
Sodium: 556 mg
Dietary fiber: 1 g

APPROXIMATE NUTRITIONAL INFORMATION PER SANDWICH USING LIGHT MAYONNAISE

Calories: 180
Total fat: 4 g
Saturated fat: 1 g
Percentage of calories from fat: 20%
Carbohydrate: 16 g
Protein: 17 g
Cholesterol: 35 mg
Sodium: 516 mg
Dietary fiber: 1 g

LOBSTER SANDWICH

Makes 3 sandwiches

6 ounces cooked lobster meat
1 teaspoon lemon juice
2 celery stalks, minced
2 tablespoons fat-free or light mayonnaise
6 slices rye or sourdough bread
6 tomato slices
6 lettuce leaves

Sprinkle lobster with lemon juice; toss with celery. Moisten with mayonnaise. Top 3 slices of rye or sourdough bread with lobster mixture, tomatoes, lettuce, and another slice of bread. Cut sandwich in half and serve.

APPROXIMATE NUTRITIONAL INFORMATION PER SANDWICH USING FAT-FREE MAYONNAISE

Calories: 246
Total fat: 3 g
Saturated fat: 0 g
Percentage of calories from fat: 10%
Carbohydrate: 37 g
Protein: 18 g
Cholesterol: 41 mg
Sodium: 793 mg
Dietary fiber: 5 g

APPROXIMATE NUTRITIONAL INFORMATION PER SANDWICH USING LIGHT MAYONNAISE

Calories: 272
Total fat: 6 g
Saturated fat: 1 g
Percentage of calories from fat: 20%
Carbohydrate: 36 g
Protein: 18 g
Cholesterol: 41 mg
Sodium: 740 mg
Dietary fiber: 5 g

Lox and Bagels

4 servings

- 2 fresh bagels
- 3 tablespoons nonfat cream cheese
- 4 thin slices of white onion
- ¼ pound thinly sliced lox or smoked salmon
- 1 tomato, thinly sliced (optional)

Cut bagels in half. Spread each half with cream cheese. Top with onion and lox. Garnish with sliced tomatoes, if desired.

APPROXIMATE NUTRITIONAL INFORMATION PER SERVING

Calories: 139	Carbohydrate: 22 g
Total fat: 2 g	Protein: 10 g
Saturated fat: 0 g	Cholesterol: 7 mg
Percentage of calories from fat: 10%	Sodium: 463 mg
	Dietary fiber: 1 g

French Dip Sandwich

Makes 1 sandwich

- 1 teaspoon horseradish
- 1 French roll
- 2 ounces cooked eye-of-round beef roast, thinly sliced
- ⅓ cup reduced-fat beef broth, preferably homemade (page 366)

Spread horseradish lightly over French roll; top with beef. Heat broth to boiling; ladle into a shallow bowl. Serve the sandwich with the dipping sauce.

APPROXIMATE NUTRITIONAL INFORMATION PER SANDWICH

Calories: 277	Carbohydrate: 31 g
Total fat: 6 g	Protein: 24 g
Saturated fat: 1 g	Cholesterol: 40 mg
Percentage of calories from fat: 18%	Sodium: 441 mg
	Dietary fiber: 2 g

CUBE STEAK SANDWICH

Makes 1 sandwich

3 ounces cube steak
2 slices French bread
1½ teaspoons fat-free or light mayonnaise
2 white onion slices
2 tomato slices
2 lettuce leaves

Place cube steaks on a rack in a broiling pan; broil 3 inches from heat for 2 to 3 minutes on each side. Serve on French bread with mayonnaise, onion, tomato, and lettuce.

APPROXIMATE NUTRITIONAL INFORMATION PER SANDWICH USING FAT-FREE MAYONNAISE

Calories: 271	Carbohydrate: 31 g
Total fat: 5 g	Protein: 24 g
Saturated fat: 2 g	Cholesterol: 50 mg
Percentage of calories from fat: 17%	Sodium: 445 mg
	Dietary fiber: 3 g

APPROXIMATE NUTRITIONAL INFORMATION PER SANDWICH USING LIGHT MAYONNAISE

Calories: 290	Carbohydrate: 30 g
Total fat: 8 g	Protein: 24 g
Saturated fat: 2 g	Cholesterol: 50 mg
Percentage of calories from fat: 24%	Sodium: 405 mg
	Dietary fiber: 3 g

BARBECUED BEEF SANDWICH

Makes 1 sandwich

- 2 ounces cooked eye-of-round beef roast, thinly sliced
- 2 tablespoons barbecue sauce
- 1 French roll

Place beef in a saucepan; cover with sauce. Warm over low heat. Serve on French roll.

Note: Read the label before selecting a barbecue sauce.

APPROXIMATE NUTRITIONAL INFORMATION PER SANDWICH

Calories: 308
Total fat: 6 g
Saturated fat: 1 g
Percentage of calories from fat: 18%
Carbohydrate: 40 g
Protein: 22 g
Cholesterol: 40 mg
Sodium: 806 mg
Dietary fiber: 2 g

BARBECUED HAMBURGERS

4 servings

1 pound extra-lean ground round
4 French rolls or hamburger buns, warmed
4 tomato slices
8 lettuce leaves
4 white onions

Press ground round into patties. Grill over hot coals or broil on a rack 3 inches from heat for 4 to 6 minutes on each side. Turn when juices begin to form on top of meat. Place patties on warm French rolls or buns with tomato slices, lettuce, and onion. Serve immediately.

Variation: Top with 1 slice of nonfat cheese.

APPROXIMATE NUTRITIONAL INFORMATION PER SERVING USING 90% LEAN GROUND BEEF

Calories: 308
Total fat: 11 g
Saturated fat: 4 g
Percentage of calories from fat: 34%
Carbohydrate: 25 g
Protein: 26 g
Cholesterol: 70 mg
Sodium: 311 mg
Dietary fiber: 2 g

APPROXIMATE NUTRITIONAL INFORMATION PER SERVING USING 85% LEAN GROUND BEEF

Calories: 343
Total fat: 15 g
Saturated fat: 5 g
Percentage of calories from fat: 38%
Carbohydrate: 25 g
Protein: 26 g
Cholesterol: 71 mg
Sodium: 310 mg
Dietary fiber: 1 g

GRILLED CHICKEN BURGERS

4 servings

2 tablespoons fresh lemon juice
2 teaspoons olive oil
¼ teaspoon pepper
2 whole boneless, skinless chicken breasts
4 very fresh sesame hamburger buns
1 large ripe tomato, sliced
4 thin slices white onion
4 Bibb lettuce leaves
2 tablespoons Dijon mustard and/or lemon mayonnaise (below)

Lemon Mayonnaise

2 tablespoons light mayonnaise
¾ teaspoon fresh lemon juice
½ teaspoon grated lemon peel

In a bowl, combine lemon juice, olive oil, and pepper. Pour over chicken. Marinate 15 to 20 minutes at room temperature, turning occasionally to coat.

Grill chicken over hot coals for 8 to 10 minutes on each side. Just before removing chicken from grill, arrange buns over top of chicken to warm.

To assemble, place chicken, tomato, onion, and lettuce on bottom half of bun. Spread top half with Dijon mustard and/or combined lemon mayonnaise ingredients.

APPROXIMATE NUTRITIONAL INFORMATION PER SERVING USING MUSTARD

Calories: 310	Carbohydrate: 26 g
Total fat: 8 g	Protein: 31 g
Saturated fat: 2 g	Cholesterol: 73 mg
Percentage of calories from fat: 24%	Sodium: 407 mg
	Dietary fiber: 1 g

APPROXIMATE NUTRITIONAL INFORMATION PER SERVING USING LEMON MAYONNAISE

Calories: 328
Total fat: 10 g
Saturated fat: 2 g
Percentage of calories from fat: 28%
Carbohydrate: 26 g
Protein: 31 g
Cholesterol: 73 mg
Sodium: 364 mg
Dietary fiber: 1 g

GRILLED VEAL BURGERS

4 servings

1 pound extra-lean ground veal
4 French rolls
1 sliced white onion
8 red lettuce leaves
1 sliced tomato

Press ground veal into 4 patties. Grill over hot coals or broil on a rack 3 inches from heat for 4 to 6 minutes on each side. Turn when juices begin to form on top of meat. Place patties on French rolls with onion, lettuce, and tomato. Serve.

APPROXIMATE NUTRITIONAL INFORMATION PER SERVING

Calories: 329
Total fat: 9 g
Saturated fat: 3 g
Percentage of calories from fat: 25%
Carbohydrate: 33 g
Protein: 27 g
Cholesterol: 88 mg
Sodium: 386 mg
Dietary fiber: 2 g

Cheese and Egg on a Muffin

1 serving

1 whole English muffin
1 slice tomato
1 slice white onion
1½-ounce slice fat-free cheddar cheese
1 egg

Split and toast muffin. Cover bottom half of muffin with tomato, onion, and then cheese. Soft boil an egg, or fry an egg over easy in a nonstick pan, or scramble an egg in a nonstick pan. When egg is nearly done, place muffin bottom under the broiler or in a microwave oven until cheese melts. Place egg on cheese. Top with remaining half of muffin.

APPROXIMATE NUTRITIONAL INFORMATION PER SERVING

Calories: 229
Total fat: 6 g
Saturated fat: 2 g
Percentage of calories from fat: 24%
Carbohydrate: 29 g
Protein: 13 g
Cholesterol: 216 mg
Sodium: 413 mg
Dietary fiber: 1 g

EGG DISHES

French Omelet

Makes 2 omelets

2 teaspoons chopped onion
¼ cup sliced mushrooms
1 teaspoon minced green pepper
1 teaspoon wine, broth, or tub-style light margarine

Omelet

1 cup egg substitute or 4 whole eggs
2 tablespoons water
Dash of salt and pepper
4 slices tomato for garnish
Fresh parsley for garnish

Fillings

2 tablespoons grated reduced-fat cheddar cheese
1 teaspoon minced fresh chives
2 teaspoons chopped parsley
2 teaspoons diced green chilies
2 tablespoons chopped tomato
2 tablespoons crabmeat

Sauté onion, mushrooms, and green pepper until tender in wine, broth, or light margarine, or steam in a microwave. Set aside.

Beat egg substitute, water, salt, and pepper with a fork until mixture is well blended but not frothy. Heat an 8-inch nonstick skillet over medium heat until a drop of water sizzles when sprinkled on the pan. Pour in egg mixture. Tilt pan to spread evenly throughout and at an even depth.

Using a fork, stir rapidly through top of uncooked eggs. Shake pan frequently to keep eggs moving. When egg is set but still shiny, remove pan from heat. Spoon desired fillings across center. Flip sides of omelet over, envelope style, to hold in filling. Tilt pan and roll omelet over onto plate. Garnish with sliced tomatoes and fresh parsley.

APPROXIMATE NUTRITIONAL INFORMATION PER OMELET WITH EGG SUBSTITUTE, CHEESE, AND VEGETABLES

Calories: 79
Total fat: 1 g
Saturated fat: 1 g
Percentage of calories from fat: 15%
Carbohydrate: 4 g
Protein: 13 g
Cholesterol: 5 mg
Sodium: 484 mg
Dietary fiber: 0 g

APPROXIMATE NUTRITIONAL INFORMATION PER OMELET WITH EGG SUBSTITUTE, CHEESE, CRAB, AND VEGETABLES

Calories: 93
Total fat: 2 g
Saturated fat: 1 g
Percentage of calories from fat: 15%
Carbohydrate: 4 g
Protein: 15 g
Cholesterol: 10 mg
Sodium: 523 mg
Dietary fiber: 0 g

APPROXIMATE NUTRITIONAL INFORMATION PER OMELET WITH TWO WHOLE EGGS

Calories: 179
Total fat: 11 g
Saturated fat: 4 g
Percentage of calories from fat: 57%
Carbohydrate: 3 g
Protein: 15 g
Cholesterol: 431 mg
Sodium: 450 mg
Dietary fiber: 0 g

Note the calories and fat you save when using the egg substitute.

Huevos Rancheros

Makes 4 servings

1 4-ounce can whole green chilies, drained
3 tablespoons grated reduced-fat Monterey Jack cheese
1½ cups egg substitute, beaten
2 tablespoons grated reduced-fat cheddar cheese
4 6-inch corn tortillas
½ cup Tomato Salsa, preferably homemade (page 433)
1 slice tomato for garnish

Gently slit each chili lengthwise and remove seeds. Stuff with Jack cheese. Press slit edges together to hold cheese in. Cut stuffed chilies into bite-size pieces.

Heat a nonstick skillet over medium heat. Arrange chilies in pan. When cheese begins to melt, pour in beaten egg substitute. When eggs start to firm, lift chilies slightly to allow uncooked eggs to run underneath. When almost fully cooked, sprinkle grated cheddar cheese on top. When cheese melts, remove skillet from heat.

Serve with corn tortillas and salsa. Garnish with sliced tomato.

APPROXIMATE NUTRITIONAL INFORMATION PER SERVING

Calories: 136
Total fat: 2 g
Saturated fat: 1 g
Percentage of calories from fat: 16%
Carbohydrate: 17 g
Protein: 12 g
Cholesterol: 6 mg
Sodium: 258 mg
Dietary fiber: 1 g

SALADS

ANTIPASTO SALAD

6 servings

1 cup torn Bibb lettuce
1 cup torn romaine lettuce
1 cup torn red leaf lettuce
⅓ cup Tarragon Vinaigrette (page 423)
12 cherry tomatoes
1 5-ounce can baby corn, drained
12 Marinated Mushrooms (page 314)
1 green pepper, cut into 2-inch strips
12 water-packed artichoke hearts
6 crab legs (optional)

Toss equal amounts of Bibb lettuce, romaine, and red leaf lettuce; moisten with dressing. Serve on chilled salad plates. Arrange tomatoes, baby corn, mushrooms, peppers, artichoke hearts, and crab legs on a chilled tray. Pass as part of salad.

Serving Suggestion: Great salad to serve with pasta.

APPROXIMATE NUTRITIONAL INFORMATION PER SERVING

Calories: 105
Total fat: 3 g
Saturated fat: 1 g
Percentage of calories from fat: 30%
Carbohydrate: 14 g
Protein: 6 g
Cholesterol: 8 mg
Sodium: 432 mg
Dietary fiber: 1 g

LAYERED SALAD

10 side-dish servings

1 small head iceberg lettuce, finely chopped
½ cup green onion, thinly sliced
1 cup celery, thinly sliced
1 8-ounce can sliced water chestnuts, drained
2 cups fresh baby peas
1 cup fat-free or light mayonnaise
¼ teaspoon salt
¼ teaspoon pepper
2 tablespoons grated reduced-fat cheddar cheese
1 tomato, thinly sliced
3 slices crisp-broiled Canadian bacon, finely chopped

Using a shallow glass bowl, layer lettuce, green onion, celery, water chestnuts, and peas. Cover and chill. Just before serving, spread with mayonnaise. Season with salt and pepper. Sprinkle with cheese and spread tomato and Canadian bacon over top. Do not toss; serve layered.

APPROXIMATE NUTRITIONAL INFORMATION PER SERVING USING FAT-FREE MAYONNAISE

Calories: 89
Total fat: 1 g
Saturated fat: 0 g
Percentage of calories from fat: 12%
Carbohydrate: 16 g
Protein: 5 g
Cholesterol: 5 mg
Sodium: 508 mg
Dietary fiber: 2 g

APPROXIMATE NUTRITIONAL INFORMATION PER SERVING USING LIGHT MAYONNAISE

Calories: 150
Total fat: 9 g
Saturated fat: 2 g
Percentage of calories from fat: 55%
Carbohydrate: 12 g
Protein: 5 g
Cholesterol: 5 mg
Sodium: 380 mg
Dietary fiber: 2 g

Mixed Vegetable Salad

4 servings

1 cup broccoli florets
1 cup cauliflower florets
½ medium zucchini, sliced
½ medium yellow squash, sliced
2 large carrots, sliced
1 head lettuce, shredded
2 cups nonfat cottage cheese
2 large ripe tomatoes, quartered
1 cup Salsa Cruda (page 432)

Steam broccoli, cauliflower, zucchini, squash, and carrots for 2 to 3 minutes, or just until crisp-tender. Drain excess moisture. Chill.

Line salad plates with shredded lettuce. Mound ½ cup cottage cheese in the center of each plate. Arrange chilled vegetables and tomatoes around cottage cheese. Accompany with salsa.

Serving Suggestion: Perfect lunch after a weekend of too much eating. Serve without the cottage cheese for a great side-dish dinner salad.

APPROXIMATE NUTRITIONAL INFORMATION PER SERVING

Calories: 132
Total fat: 1 g
Saturated fat: 0 g
Percentage of calories from fat: 5%
Carbohydrate: 17 g
Protein: 17 g
Cholesterol: 6 mg
Sodium: 602 mg
Dietary fiber: 3 g

MARKET VEGETABLE SALAD

Serves 6 as a main course; 15 as a side dish

½ head cabbage, shredded
½ head lettuce, shredded
½ zucchini, sliced
½ white onion, sliced
15 fresh mushrooms, sliced
5 celery stalks, sliced
½ green pepper, chopped
3 slices crisp-broiled Canadian bacon, finely chopped
1 bunch broccoli florets
1 8-ounce can sliced water chestnuts, drained
2 cups fresh baby peas
1⅓ cups fat-free or light mayonnaise
⅔ cup grated reduced-fat cheddar cheese

Using a large salad bowl, layer ingredients, except mayonnaise and cheese, in order given. Cover and chill. Just before serving, spread mayonnaise over top and to edges of bowl. Sprinkle with cheese.

Note: Makes great luncheon fare or a light supper.

APPROXIMATE NUTRITIONAL INFORMATION PER 1-CUP SERVING USING FAT-FREE MAYONNAISE

Calories: 64	Carbohydrate: 10 g
Total fat: 1 g	Protein: 4 g
Saturated fat: 1 g	Cholesterol: 5 mg
Percentage of calories from fat: 18%	Sodium: 324 mg
	Dietary fiber: 2 g

APPROXIMATE NUTRITIONAL INFORMATION PER 1-CUP SERVING USING LIGHT MAYONNAISE

Calories: 110	Carbohydrate: 8 g
Total fat: 7 g	Protein: 4 g
Saturated fat: 2 g	Cholesterol: 5 mg
Percentage of calories from fat: 59%	Sodium: 230 mg
	Dietary fiber: 2 g

Caesar Salad

6 servings

2 large heads romaine, torn into bite-size pieces
Juice of ½ lemon
⅓ cup olive oil (preferably Garlic Olive Oil, page 431)
2½ tablespoons red wine vinegar
1 coddled egg,* chilled
½ teaspoon salt
¼ teaspoon pepper
½ teaspoon Worcestershire sauce
6 anchovy fillets, finely chopped (optional)
¾ cup unseasoned croutons
⅓ cup freshly grated Parmesan cheese

Arrange romaine in a large salad bowl. Drizzle with lemon juice. Add olive oil, vinegar, coddled egg, salt, pepper, and Worcestershire sauce; toss. Add anchovies and croutons; toss again. Sprinkle with Parmesan and toss lightly again.

Note: As with most Caesar salad recipes, this one is not low in fat. I have included it because it is part of one of my favorite "serve to company" menus.

As a first course, I serve Gazpacho (page 362). I accompany the salad with Marinated Grilled Prawns (page 517), fresh cracked crab, and sourdough French bread. For dessert, Lemon Ice (page 603) served with watermelon, honeydew, and cantaloupe slices garnished with fresh mint.

By accompanying the salad with these other low-fat foods, and selecting low-fat foods for breakfast and lunch, it's possible to control your fat budget for the day.

*To make a coddled egg, place a cold egg in a saucepan with enough warm water to completely cover egg. Meanwhile, in a separate saucepan, bring an equal amount of water to a boil. Immerse egg in boiling water; remove from heat and let stand 1 minute. Immediately cool egg in cold water to prevent further cooking. Put egg in refrigerator to chill.

APPROXIMATE NUTRITIONAL INFORMATION PER SERVING

Calories: 174	Carbohydrate: 6 g
Total fat: 15 g	Protein: 6 g
Saturated fat: 3 g	Cholesterol: 39 mg
Percentage of calories from fat: 76%	Sodium: 465 mg
	Dietary fiber: 1 g

SHRIMP CAESAR SALAD

6 servings

Caesar Salad (see preceding recipe)
1½ cups small cooked shrimp

Prepare recipe for Caesar Salad as directed. Divide salad among individual salad plates. Top with shrimp.

Variation: Substitute crabmeat or chicken breast for shrimp.

APPROXIMATE NUTRITIONAL INFORMATION PER SERVING

Calories: 213	Carbohydrate: 6 g
Total fat: 15 g	Protein: 13 g
Saturated fat: 3 g	Cholesterol: 95 mg
Percentage of calories from fat: 65%	Sodium: 514 mg
	Dietary fiber: 1 g

Shrimp and Soba Noodle Salad

8 servings

¼ cup rice wine vinegar
1 tablespoon soy sauce
1 tablespoon olive oil
1 tablespoon sesame oil
2 teaspoons brown sugar
½ teaspoon hot chili oil
2 cups chicken broth, preferably homemade (page 364)
2 cups water
1 5-ounce package soba (buckwheat) noodles
4 cups chopped Chinese cabbage or Napa cabbage
1 recipe Pan-Steamed Broccoli and Cauliflower with Lemon and Hot Chili Sauce (page 465)
½ pound small cooked shrimp

Combine rice wine vinegar, soy sauce, olive oil, sesame oil, brown sugar, and hot chili oil. Set aside.

In 2-quart saucepan, bring chicken broth and water to a boil. Add soba noodles. Stir lightly. Boil 5 to 8 minutes, or until noodles are just tender. Drain and rinse.

Layer chopped cabbage in bottom of a serving bowl. Top with soba noodles and pan-steamed broccoli and cauliflower. Drizzle with dressing. Arrange the shrimp. Serve at once.

APPROXIMATE NUTRITIONAL INFORMATION PER SERVING

Calories: 167
Total fat: 5 g
Saturated fat: 1 g
Percentage of calories from fat: 30%
Carbohydrate: 21 g
Protein: 11 g
Cholesterol: 44 mg
Sodium: 531 mg
Dietary fiber: 2 g

BIBB LETTUCE, TOMATO, AND SCALLOP SALAD WITH TOMATO SALSA

8 servings

3 heads Bibb lettuce
1 recipe Sea Scallops with Tomatoes and Green Chilies (page 306)
1½ cups Tomato Salsa, preferably homemade (page 433)

Divide Bibb lettuce among 8 salad plates. Spread with scallop mixture. Top with salsa.

APPROXIMATE NUTRITIONAL INFORMATION PER SERVING

Calories: 129
Total fat: 4 g
Saturated fat: 1 g
Percentage of calories from fat: 31%
Carbohydrate: 11 g
Protein: 14 g
Cholesterol: 23 mg
Sodium: 274 mg
Dietary fiber: 1 g

Salade Niçoise

6 servings

1 bunch leaf lettuce, torn into bite-size pieces
1 6⅛-ounce can water-packed tuna, drained
3 red potatoes, quartered and steamed
¾ pound fresh green beans, cooked al dente
6 water-packed artichoke hearts, quartered
3 large carrots, sliced on the diagonal and steamed
½ green pepper, cut into thin strips
½ red pepper, cut into thin strips
1 jalepeño or serrano pepper, cut into thin strips (optional)
½ white onion, halved, thinly sliced, and separated
6 ripe plum tomatoes, quartered
12 Greek olives
⅓ cup Low-fat Niçoise (page 430) or Niçoise Dressing (page 429)

Arrange lettuce over a tray or shallow salad bowl. Mound tuna in center. Arrange potatoes, green beans, artichoke hearts, carrots, and peppers around tuna. Add onion slices, tomatoes, and olives. Chill. Just before serving, drizzle with dressing

APPROXIMATE NUTRITIONAL INFORMATION PER SERVING USING LOW-FAT NIÇOISE DRESSING

Calories: 203	Carbohydrate: 31 g
Total fat: 5 g	Protein: 12 g
Saturated fat: 1 g	Cholesterol: 12 mg
Percentage of calories from fat: 21%	Sodium: 518 mg
	Dietary fiber: 7 g

APPROXIMATE NUTRITIONAL INFORMATION PER SERVING USING TRADITIONAL NIÇOISE DRESSING

Calories: 254
Total fat: 11 g
Saturated fat: 2 g
Percentage of calories from fat: 37%
Carbohydrate: 31 g
Protein: 12 g
Cholesterol: 12 mg
Sodium: 459 mg
Dietary fiber: 7 g

MIXED GREENS SALAD WITH CRAB LEGS

4 servings

1 cup torn red leaf lettuce
1 cup torn fresh spinach
1 cup torn romaine lettuce
¼ cup Tarragon Vinaigrette (page 423)
½ cup heart-healthy croutons
4 crab legs for garnish

Toss greens with vinaigrette. Top with croutons. Garnish with crab legs.

Variation: Also good with Tomato Vinaigrette (page 422).

APPROXIMATE NUTRITIONAL INFORMATION PER SERVING

Calories: 89
Total fat: 4 g
Saturated fat: 1 g
Percentage of calories from fat: 42%
Carbohydrate: 8 g
Protein: 5 g
Cholesterol: 14 mg
Sodium: 167 mg
Dietary fiber: 1 g

Crab Louis

4 servings

1 head lettuce
½ pound crabmeat
¼ cup sliced water chestnuts
2 celery stalks, thinly sliced
3 green onions with tops, thinly sliced
½ green pepper, chopped
⅔ cup Tomato Vinaigrette (page 422)
2 tomatoes, cut into wedges
1 bunch asparagus spears, steamed 2 to 4 minutes
Lemon wedges

Line chilled salad bowls with outside leaves of lettuce; shred remaining lettuce. Toss shredded lettuce, crabmeat, water chestnuts, celery, green onion, and green pepper with dressing to moisten; spoon into lettuce-lined bowls. Arrange tomatoes, asparagus, and lemon wedges around the salad. Accompany with Tomato Vinaigrette.

Variation: Substitute shrimp for crabmeat. The fat content will be the same.

APPROXIMATE NUTRITIONAL INFORMATION PER SERVING

Calories: 162
Total fat: 5 g
Saturated fat: 1 g
Percentage of calories from fat: 27%
Carbohydrate: 18 g
Protein: 16 g
Cholesterol: 57 mg
Sodium: 212 mg
Dietary fiber: 3 g

FRESH SPINACH SALAD

4 servings

- 6 cups fresh spinach torn into bite-size pieces (1 bunch)
- ¼ pound fresh mushrooms, sliced
- 3 to 4 green onions, sliced diagonally
- 3 tablespoons fresh Lemon and Olive Oil Dressing (page 427)

Combine spinach, mushrooms, and onions. Add enough dressing to moisten; toss.

APPROXIMATE NUTRITIONAL INFORMATION PER SERVING

Calories: 44
Total fat: 3 g
Saturated fat: 0 g
Percentage of calories from fat: 58%
Carbohydrate: 4 g
Protein: 2 g
Cholesterol: 0 mg
Sodium: 145 mg
Dietary fiber: 2 g

Fresh Spinach Salad with Sesame Seeds

2 servings

6 cups fresh spinach torn into bite-size pieces (1 bunch)
½ teaspoon sesame oil
4 teaspoons lemon juice
4 teaspoons toasted sesame seeds

Toss spinach with sesame oil. Sprinkle with lemon juice and sesame seeds; toss again.

APPROXIMATE NUTRITIONAL INFORMATION PER SERVING

Calories: 71
Total fat: 5 g
Saturated fat: 1 g
Percentage of calories from fat: 57%
Carbohydrate: 6 g
Protein: 4 g
Cholesterol: 0 mg
Sodium: 89 mg
Dietary fiber: 2 g

Corn and Tomatillo Salad

6 servings

2 cups fresh or frozen corn kernels
1 white onion, chopped
1 18-ounce can tomatillos, drained and diced
1 tablespoon rice wine vinegar
2 tablespoons fresh lime juice
2 tablespoons olive oil
½ teaspoon salt
¼ teaspoon pepper
¼ cup chopped fresh cilantro
12 whole fresh cilantro leaves for garnish

In a medium bowl, combine corn, onion, and tomatillos. In a covered jar, combine rice wine vinegar, lime juice, olive oil, salt, and pepper; pour over corn. Add chopped cilantro. Garnish with remaining cilantro, and serve at once.

APPROXIMATE NUTRITIONAL INFORMATION PER SERVING

Calories: 120
Total fat: 5 g
Saturated fat: 1 g
Percentage of calories from fat: 41%
Carbohydrate: 18 g
Protein: 2 g
Cholesterol: 0 mg
Sodium: 276 mg
Dietary fiber: 2 g

TOMATO, MOZZARELLA, AND BASIL SALAD

6 servings

- 2 cups fresh basil leaves
- 3 large ripe tomatoes, sliced
- 2 ounces reduced-fat mozzarella cheese, thinly sliced
- 2 tablespoons olive oil
- ½ teaspoon salt
- ¼ teaspoon freshly ground pepper

Arrange basil leaves on chilled salad plates. Alternate slices of tomato and cheese over basil. Drizzle with olive oil. Season with salt and pepper.

APPROXIMATE NUTRITIONAL INFORMATION PER SERVING

Calories: 87
Total fat: 6 g
Saturated fat: 2 g
Percentage of calories from fat: 66%
Carbohydrate: 5 g
Protein: 4 g
Cholesterol: 5 mg
Sodium: 244 mg
Dietary fiber: 1 g

Tomatoes Vinaigrette

4 servings

1 head Bibb lettuce
3 large ripe tomatoes, sliced
¼ cup Tarragon Vinaigrette (page 423)
2 tablespoons finely chopped onion
1 tablespoon finely chopped fresh parsley for garnish

Arrange lettuce on chilled salad plates. Layer tomato slices over lettuce. Drizzle with dressing. Sprinkle with onion. Garnish with parsley.

APPROXIMATE NUTRITIONAL INFORMATION PER SERVING

Calories: 74	Carbohydrate: 9 g
Total fat: 4 g	Protein: 3 g
Saturated fat: 1 g	Cholesterol: 0 mg
Percentage of calories from fat: 49%	Sodium: 56 mg
	Dietary fiber: 2 g

Zucchini and Tomato Salad with Dijon Vinaigrette

6 servings

2 small zucchini, peeled and sliced lengthwise into julienne strips
¼ cup Dijon Vinaigrette (page 420)
1 head Bibb lettuce
12 cherry tomatoes, halved

Toss zucchini with vinaigrette. Line a salad bowl with lettuce leaves; fill with zucchini. Dot with tomatoes.

APPROXIMATE NUTRITIONAL INFORMATION PER SERVING

Calories: 31
Total fat: 2 g
Saturated fat: 0 g
Percentage of calories from fat: 61%
Carbohydrate: 3 g
Protein: 1 g
Cholesterol: 0 mg
Sodium: 77 mg
Dietary fiber: 1 g

TOMATO AND CUCUMBER SALAD

6 servings

- 1 medium white onion, coarsely chopped
- 2 large ripe tomatoes, coarsely chopped
- 1 English cucumber, peeled and coarsely chopped
- ⅓ cup Tarragon Vinaigrette (page 423)
- 2 cups mixed torn lettuce greens
- ½ teaspoon freshly ground pepper

Combine onion, tomato, and cucumber. Toss with dressing. Serve over lettuce. Sprinkle with freshly ground pepper.

APPROXIMATE NUTRITIONAL INFORMATION PER SERVING

Calories: 65
Total fat: 3 g
Saturated fat: 1 g
Percentage of calories from fat: 48%
Carbohydrate: 8 g
Protein: 2 g
Cholesterol: 0 mg
Sodium: 43 mg
Dietary fiber: 1 g

Cucumber and Red Onion Salad

4 servings

1 English cucumber, peeled and diced
¼ cup red onion, chopped
2 tablespoons fresh lemon juice
1 teaspoon olive oil
2 teaspoons tarragon-flavored white wine vinegar
½ teaspoon salt
¼ teaspoon pepper
Spinach leaves

Combine cucumber with onion. Combine lemon juice, olive oil, vinegar, salt, and pepper. Pour over cucumber and onion mixture. Chill at least 1 hour. Just before serving, line salad plates with spinach leaves. Top with cucumbers and onions.

APPROXIMATE NUTRITIONAL INFORMATION PER SERVING

Calories: 37
Total fat: 1 g
Saturated fat: 0 g
Percentage of calories from fat: 34%
Carbohydrate: 6 g
Protein: 2 g
Cholesterol: 0 mg
Sodium: 291 mg
Dietary fiber: 2 g

GREEN BEANS, TOMATOES, ARTICHOKES, AND MUSHROOMS IN VINAIGRETTE

Makes approximately 10 cups

- 1 pound fresh green beans, cooked
- 1 14½-ounce can water-packed artichoke hearts
- 1 8-ounce can sliced water chestnuts
- ½ pound fresh mushrooms, steamed 2 to 3 minutes, sliced
- ½ cup Tarragon Vinaigrette (page 423)
- 15 cherry tomatoes, chilled

Drain beans, artichokes, water chestnuts, and mushrooms. Chill. Just before serving, moisten with dressing; toss with chilled tomatoes.

APPROXIMATE NUTRITIONAL INFORMATION PER 1-CUP SERVING

Calories: 64
Total fat: 3 g
Saturated fat: 0 g
Percentage of calories from fat: 42%
Carbohydrate: 9 g
Protein: 2 g
Cholesterol: 0 mg
Sodium: 110 mg
Dietary fiber: 2 g

GREEN CHILI AND TOMATO SALAD

Makes approximately 9 ½-cup servings

2 ripe tomatoes, chopped
1 4-ounce can chopped green chilies
4 green onions, chopped
1 bunch leaf lettuce, torn into bite-size pieces
¼ pound sliced fresh mushrooms, steamed 2 to 3 minutes
½ cup commercially prepared oil-free Italian dressing

Combine tomatoes, green chilies, and onions. Chill for 3 hours. Just before serving, toss tomatoes, chilies, onions, and lettuce with mushrooms. Drizzle with dressing. Toss.

Serving Suggestion: Great salad with Chili con Carne (page 450) or Macaroni with Chicken and Beans (page 506). Garnish with heart-healthy oil-free baked, not fried, tortilla chips.

APPROXIMATE NUTRITIONAL INFORMATION PER SERVING USING COMMERCIALLY PREPARED OIL-FREE DRESSING

Calories: 18
Total fat: trace
Saturated fat: 0 g
Percentage of calories from fat: 10%
Carbohydrate: 4 g
Protein: 1 g
Cholesterol: 0 mg
Sodium: 200 mg
Dietary fiber: 1 g

TOMATO, SPINACH, AND CHICKEN SALAD

4 servings

1 large ripe tomato, diced
½ pound fresh spinach, torn into 2-inch pieces
½ pound skinless chicken breast, cooked and cut into 2-inch cubes
2 fresh lemons, quartered
Freshly ground pepper

Chill diced tomato, spinach, and chicken. Layer spinach on 4 individual salad plates. Cover with diced tomato. Top with chicken. Squeeze lemon juice over top. Sprinkle with pepper.

Serving Suggestion: Serve as a first course with Minestrone (page 344) or Three-Bean Soup (page 353).

APPROXIMATE NUTRITIONAL INFORMATION PER SERVING

Calories: 97
Total fat: 2 g
Saturated fat: 0 g
Percentage of calories from fat: 17%
Carbohydrate: 10 g
Protein: 15 g
Cholesterol: 33 mg
Sodium: 77 mg
Dietary fiber: 2 g

Rice, Smoked Turkey, and Sun-Dried Tomato Salad

8 servings

3½ cups chicken broth, preferably homemade (page 364)
1 cup wild rice
10 fresh mushrooms, sliced
1 cup long-grain brown basmati rice
¼ cup olive oil
2 tablespoons red wine vinegar
½ teaspoon salt
¼ teaspoon pepper
4 plum tomatoes, diced
10 sun-dried tomatoes, diced
1 English cucumber, peeled and diced
1 bunch green onions, diced
½ pound smoked turkey breast, diced
Fresh spinach leaves

In a 2-quart saucepan, bring chicken broth and wild rice to a boil. Reduce heat. Cover and simmer 40 minutes, or until rice is tender and broth is nearly absorbed. Add mushrooms. Cover; simmer 4 to 5 minutes longer, or until mushrooms are cooked and moisture is absorbed.

Meanwhile, cook basmati rice according to package directions.

In a small covered jar, combine olive oil, vinegar, salt, and pepper.

In a large salad bowl, combine wild rice, basmati rice, plum tomatoes, sun-dried tomatoes, cucumber, green onion, and turkey. Just before serving, toss with dressing. Serve on spinach-lined salad plates.

Note: This recipe is not low in sodium. By accompanying the salad with other low-sodium foods and selecting low-sodium foods at breakfast and lunch, it's possible to keep the total sodium intake for the day in balance.

Serving Suggestion: Perfect main meal salad. For dessert, serve Lemon Ice (page 603) and skewered fresh seasonal fruit.

APPROXIMATE NUTRITIONAL INFORMATION PER SERVING

Calories: 288
Total fat: 8 g
Saturated fat: 1 g
Percentage of calories from fat: 26%
Carbohydrate: 39 g
Protein: 16 g
Cholesterol: 12 mg
Sodium: 790 mg
Dietary fiber: 3 g

Super Taco Salad

8 servings

1 28-ounce can plum tomatoes
¾ teaspoon salt
¾ teaspoon dry mustard
1¼ teaspoons chili powder
¼ teaspoon ground cumin
¼ teaspoon cayenne
1 small garlic clove, minced
2½ cups cubed cooked, skinless chicken breast
1 19-ounce can red kidney beans, drained
2 15-ounce cans black beans, drained
¾ head lettuce, chopped
1 medium onion, chopped
½ cup grated reduced-fat cheddar or mozzarella cheese
36 heart-healthy oil-free baked, not fried, tortilla chips
1 cup Tomato Salsa, preferably homemade (page 433)
½ cup nonfat sour cream

Purée tomatoes in a blender or food processor; pour into a medium saucepan. Add salt, dry mustard, chili powder, cumin, cayenne, and garlic; heat just to boiling. Reduce heat and simmer 5 minutes; add chicken, kidney beans, and black beans. Heat.

Just before serving, spoon mixture into individual bowls. Top with lettuce, onion, cheese; add tortilla chips, salsa, and sour cream.

Note: Save 288 milligrams of sodium per serving by using dried beans and reconstituting them in place of canned beans, or by rinsing the canned beans.

Variation: Substitute 1 pound extra-lean ground round for chicken.

APPROXIMATE NUTRITIONAL INFORMATION PER SERVING USING CHICKEN

Calories: 315	Carbohydrate: 39 g
Total fat: 6 g	Protein: 30 g
Saturated fat: 1 g	Cholesterol: 52 mg
Percentage of calories from fat: 17%	Sodium: 710 mg
	Dietary fiber: 9 g

APPROXIMATE NUTRITIONAL INFORMATION PER SERVING USING EXTRA-LEAN GROUND ROUND

Calories: 355	Carbohydrate: 39 g
Total fat: 12 g	Protein: 28 g
Saturated fat: 4 g	Cholesterol: 53 mg
Percentage of calories from fat: 29%	Sodium: 710 mg
	Dietary fiber: 9 g

TACO SALAD

6 servings

1 pound extra-lean ground round
1 onion, chopped
2 large tomatoes, chopped
1 head lettuce
½ cup grated reduced-fat cheddar cheese
36 oil-free baked, not fried, tortilla chips
½ cup nonfat sour cream
1 cup Tomato Salsa, preferably homemade (page 433)

In a nonstick skillet, brown ground round with onion; drain. Toss with tomatoes. Line salad bowls with outside leaves of lettuce; shred remaining lettuce and add to bowls. Cover with ground round and tomatoes. Top with cheese. Line rim of bowls with chips. Pass with sour cream and salsa.

Variation: Substitute 1 skinless chicken breast for ground round.

APPROXIMATE NUTRITIONAL INFORMATION PER SERVING USING GROUND ROUND

Calories: 242
Total fat: 11 g
Saturated fat: 4 g
Percentage of calories from fat: 40%
Carbohydrate: 16 g
Protein: 21 g
Cholesterol: 54 mg
Sodium: 222 mg
Dietary fiber: 3 g

APPROXIMATE NUTRITIONAL INFORMATION PER SERVING USING CHICKEN BREAST

Calories: 203
Total fat: 5 g
Saturated fat: 2 g
Percentage of calories from fat: 22%
Carbohydrate: 16 g
Protein: 24 g
Cholesterol: 54 mg
Sodium: 218 mg
Dietary fiber: 3 g

MIXED FRUIT SALAD

4 servings

Lettuce leaves
2 cups nonfat vanilla or fruit-flavored yogurt
½ cup 2-inch-cubed watermelon
½ cup 2-inch-cubed cantaloupe
½ cup 2-inch-cubed honeydew
½ cup 2-inch-cubed fresh pineapple
½ cup 3-inch-cubed fresh papaya
1 cup raspberries, strawberries, or blueberries
Fresh mint for garnish

Arrange lettuce on 4 chilled salad plates. Spoon yogurt into 1-cup-size soufflé dishes, and center each dish in a salad plate. Surround with fruit. Garnish with mint.

Note: Perfect lunch or light supper after a night or two of overeating.

APPROXIMATE NUTRITIONAL INFORMATION PER SERVING

Calories: 116
Total fat: 1 g
Saturated fat: 0 g
Percentage of calories from fat: 4%
Carbohydrate: 25 g
Protein: 5 g
Cholesterol: 1 mg
Sodium: 56 mg
Dietary fiber: 4 g

WATERMELON BASKET SALAD

Approximately 10 quarts

1 10- to 12-pound watermelon
1 2-pound honeydew
1 3-pound cantaloupe
2 pounds grapes
4 cups strawberries
4 cups raspberries
4 cups blueberries
Fresh mint for garnish

Pick a rolly-polly watermelon, which will be carved into a basket. Cut off the top third of the watermelon by cutting lengthwise from each end toward the center. Leave a center portion 2½ inches wide for the handle. Using a serrated knife, make big scallops around the rim of the watermelon.

With a melon baller, form balls from watermelon, honeydew, and cantaloupe. Toss with grapes and berries. Scrape inside of watermelon with a spoon to remove excess melon. Fill with fruit. Tie a bow on the basket handle to coordinate with table setting and napkins. Garnish with fresh mint.

Note: At the end of the meal, rinse watermelon basket; pat dry and freeze for later use.

APPROXIMATE NUTRITIONAL INFORMATION PER 1-CUP SERVING

Calories: 68
Total fat: trace
Saturated fat: 0 g
Percentage of calories from fat: 8%
Carbohydrate: 17 g
Protein: 1 g
Cholesterol: 0 mg
Sodium: 7 mg
Dietary fiber: 4 g

SALAD DRESSINGS, SAUCES, AND CONDIMENTS

DIJON VINAIGRETTE

Makes 1¼ cups

4 tablespoons Dijon mustard
3 tablespoons red wine vinegar
1 tablespoon white wine vinegar
¼ cup chicken broth, preferably homemade (page 364)
¼ teaspoon salt
2 garlic cloves
1 tablespoon chopped fresh basil or ½ teaspoon dried
⅛ teaspoon pepper
2 drops hot sauce
1 tablespoon grated onion
¼ cup olive oil

Combine mustard and vinegars in a blender. Add chicken broth, salt, garlic, basil, pepper, hot sauce, and onion; whirl. With machine running, add olive oil, 1 tablespoon at a time. Chill. Keeps several weeks.

Variation: Omit the chicken broth and increase the olive oil to ¾ cup.

APPROXIMATE NUTRITIONAL INFORMATION PER 1-TABLESPOON SERVING

Calories: 28
Total fat: 3 g
Saturated fat: 0 g
Percentage of calories from fat: 93%
Carbohydrate: 1 g
Protein: 0 g
Cholesterol: 0 mg
Sodium: 69 mg
Dietary fiber: 0 g

APPROXIMATE NUTRITIONAL INFORMATION USING EXTRA OLIVE OIL PER 1-TABLESPOON SERVING

Calories: 75
Total fat: 8 g
Saturated fat: 1 g
Percentage of calories from fat: 99%
Carbohydrate: 1 g
Protein: 0 g
Cholesterol: 0 mg
Sodium: 66 mg
Dietary fiber: 0 g

RASPBERRY VINAIGRETTE

Makes ⅔ cup

- ⅓ cup chicken broth, preferably homemade (page 364)
- 1½ teaspoons arrowroot
- ¼ cup raspberry vinegar
- ¼ cup olive oil
- 1½ teaspoons sesame oil
- ½ teaspoon salt
- ¼ teaspoon pepper
- 1 tablespoon chopped fresh basil (optional)

Heat chicken broth just to boiling, but do not allow to boil. Remove from heat; gradually stir in arrowroot, and stir until broth is slightly thickened. Pour into a food processor; add raspberry vinegar, olive oil, sesame oil, salt, and pepper. Chill. Just before serving, add chopped fresh basil, if desired.

APPROXIMATE NUTRITIONAL INFORMATION PER 1-TABLESPOON SERVING

Calories: 53
Total fat: 6 g
Saturated fat: 1 g
Percentage of calories from fat: 96%
Carbohydrate: 1 g
Protein: 0 g
Cholesterol: 0 mg
Sodium: 108 mg
Dietary fiber: 0 g

Tomato Vinaigrette

Makes ¾ cup

½ pound ripe tomatoes, chopped
3 garlic cloves, chopped
1 shallot, chopped
¼ cup chicken broth, preferably homemade (page 364)
1 tablespoon olive oil
2 tablespoons tomato paste
1 tablespoon chopped fresh basil or 1½ teaspoons dried
¼ teaspoon pepper
3 tablespoons balsamic vinegar
¼ cup chopped fresh basil, (optional)

Combine tomatoes, garlic, shallot, chicken broth, olive oil, and tomato paste in a medium saucepan. Heat just to boiling, but do not allow to boil. Reduce heat and simmer 20 to 30 minutes, stirring frequently. Pour mixture into a food processor and purée. Add basil, pepper, and balsamic vinegar. Chill. Just before serving, add ¼ cup chopped fresh basil, if desired.

Variation: Add 1½ teaspoons fresh dill and/or ½ teaspoon fresh tarragon.

APPROXIMATE NUTRITIONAL INFORMATION PER 1-TABLESPOON SERVING

Calories: 19
Total fat: 1 g
Saturated fat: 0 g
Percentage of calories from fat: 59%
Carbohydrate: 2 g
Protein: 0 g
Cholesterol: 0 mg
Sodium: 10 mg
Dietary fiber: 0 g

TARRAGON VINAIGRETTE

Makes ¾ cup

¼ cup tarragon vinegar
¼ cup olive oil
¼ cup chicken broth, preferably homemade (page 364)
2 shallots, chopped
2 garlic cloves, finely chopped
¼ teaspoon salt

Combine all ingredients in a covered jar; shake well. Chill. Store in refrigerator.

APPROXIMATE NUTRITIONAL INFORMATION PER 1-TABLESPOON SERVING

Calories: 32
Total fat: 3 g
Saturated fat: 0 g
Percentage of calories from fat: 95%
Carbohydrate: 0 g
Protein: 0 g
Cholesterol: 0 mg
Sodium: 38 mg
Dietary fiber: 0 g

Safflower Mayonnaise

Makes 1½ cups

1 egg
1 teaspoon red wine vinegar
2 teaspoons fresh lemon juice
1 teaspoon Dijon mustard
½ teaspoon salt
¼ cup olive oil
1¼ cups safflower oil

Combine egg, vinegar, lemon juice, mustard, salt, and olive oil in a blender; whirl. With machine running, add safflower oil, 1 tablespoon at a time. Refrigerate. Keeps several weeks.

Variation: To make herbed mayonnaise, add 1 teaspoon chopped fresh basil, dill, tarragon, or parsley, or ½ teaspoon dried, just before serving.

Note: If you are going to eat mayonnaise, this is the one to eat, but do so in moderation. The flavor is so good that a little goes a long way. I reserve it for special occasions.

APPROXIMATE NUTRITIONAL INFORMATION PER 1-TABLESPOON SERVING

Calories: 124
Total fat: 14 g
Saturated fat: 1g
Percentage of calories from fat: 100%
Carbohydrate: trace
Protein: trace
Cholesterol: 9 mg
Sodium: 50 mg
Dietary fiber: 0 g

OIL AND VINEGAR DRESSING

Makes 1 cup

¾ cup olive oil
¼ cup cider vinegar
¾ teaspoon salt
¼ teaspoon pepper

Combine ingredients in a covered jar; shake.

APPROXIMATE NUTRITIONAL INFORMATION PER 1-TABLESPOON SERVING

Calories: 90
Total fat: 10 g
Saturated fat: 1 g
Percentage of calories from fat: 100%
Carbohydrate: 0 g
Protein: 0 g
Cholesterol: 0 mg
Sodium: 100 mg
Dietary fiber: 0 g

OIL AND VINEGAR DRESSING WITH LEMON

Makes 1 cup

½ cup olive oil
¼ cup cider vinegar
3 tablespoons fresh lemon juice
½ teaspoon salt
¼ teaspoon pepper
1 garlic clove

Combine ingredients in a covered jar; shake.

APPROXIMATE NUTRITIONAL INFORMATION PER 1-TABLESPOON SERVING

Calories: 61
Total fat: 7 g
Saturated fat: 1 g
Percentage of calories from fat: 99%
Carbohydrate: 1 g
Protein: 0 g
Cholesterol: 0 mg
Sodium: 67 mg
Dietary fiber: 0 g

Fresh Lemon Dressing

Makes 1 serving

Juice of ½ lemon
⅛ teaspoon freshly ground pepper
¼ teaspoon salt

Squeeze lemon over salad greens or vegetables; sprinkle with pepper and salt.

APPROXIMATE NUTRITIONAL INFORMATION PER 1-TABLESPOON SERVING

Calories: 9
Total fat: trace
Saturated fat: 0 g
Percentage of calories from fat: 1%
Carbohydrate: 3 g
Protein: 0 g
Cholesterol: 0 mg
Sodium: 575 mg
Dietary fiber: 0 g

LEMON AND OLIVE OIL DRESSING

Makes ½ cup

6 tablespoons fresh lemon juice
2 tablespoons olive oil
¼ teaspoon freshly ground pepper
½ teaspoon salt

Combine ingredients in a covered jar; shake. Drizzle over salad greens and season to taste.

APPROXIMATE NUTRITIONAL INFORMATION PER 1-TABLESPOON SERVING

Calories: 33
Total fat: 3 g
Saturated fat: 0 g
Percentage of calories from fat: 92%
Carbohydrate: 1 g
Protein: 0 g
Cholesterol: 0 mg
Sodium: 133 mg
Dietary fiber: 0 g

Lemon and Hot Mustard Dressing

Makes ¼ cup

¼ cup fresh lemon juice
¼ teaspoon Oriental hot mustard
¼ teaspoon freshly ground pepper

Combine all ingredients in a covered jar; shake well. Use at once.

Serving suggestions: Great on fresh spinach greens.

APPROXIMATE NUTRITIONAL INFORMATION PER 1-TABLESPOON SERVING

Calories: 5
Total fat: trace
Saturated fat: 0 g
Percentage of calories from fat: 11%
Carbohydrate: 2 g
Protein: 0 g
Cholesterol: 0 mg
Sodium: 0 mg
Dietary fiber: 0 g

NIÇOISE DRESSING

Makes ¾ cup

½ cup olive oil
2 tablespoons tarragon-flavored vinegar
2 tablespoons fresh lemon juice
2 garlic cloves, chopped
1½ teaspoons dry mustard
¾ teaspoon salt
½ teaspoon pepper

Combine all ingredients in a covered jar. Shake well.

APPROXIMATE NUTRITIONAL INFORMATION PER 1-TABLESPOON DRESSING

Calories: 83
Total fat: 9 g
Saturated fat: 1 g
Percentage of calories from fat: 99%
Carbohydrate: 1 g
Protein: 0 g
Cholesterol: 0 mg
Sodium: 134 mg
Dietary fiber: 0 g

Low-Fat Niçoise Dressing

Makes ⅓ cup

¼ cup fresh lemon juice
1 tablespoon Garlic Olive Oil (facing page)
½ teaspoon salt
¼ teaspoon pepper

Combine all ingredients in a covered jar. Shake well.

APPROXIMATE NUTRITIONAL INFORMATION PER 1-TABLESPOON DRESSING

Calories: 26
Total fat: 3 g
Saturated fat: 0 g
Percentage of calories from fat: 89%
Carbohydrate: 6 g
Protein: 0 g
Cholesterol: 0 mg
Sodium: 200 mg
Dietary fiber: 0 g

Hot Mustard and Sesame Seeds

8 servings

½ cup hot Chinese mustard
¼ cup toasted sesame seeds

Mound hot mustard in center of a salad-size plate. Ring with sesame seeds.

Note: Hot Chinese mustard and toasted sesame seeds are available in Oriental markets and in Oriental sections of many supermarkets.

Serving Suggestion: Use with Roast Chicken Oriental Style (page 538) and Spring Rolls (page 308).

APPROXIMATE NUTRITIONAL INFORMATION PER SERVING OF 1-TABLESPOON MUSTARD AND ½ TABLESPOON SESAME SEEDS

Calories: 38	Carbohydrate: 2 g
Total fat: 3 g	Protein: 1 g
Saturated fat: 0 g	Cholesterol: 0 mg
Percentage of calories from fat: 67%	Sodium: 190 mg
	Dietary fiber: trace

GARLIC OLIVE OIL

Makes 1½ cups

1½ cups olive oil
1 head garlic, separated into cloves and peeled

Pour olive oil into a pint-size jar; add garlic. Cover tightly and let mellow 2 to 3 days; remove garlic. Store in a dark place. Keeps 3 to 4 weeks.

Note: Garlic Olive Oil is very flavorful. A little goes a long way, making it possible to use a lot less oil and still have great taste. It works well in salad dressings, in marinades for grilled vegetables, and over toasted bread such as bruschetta, focaccia, and garlic bread.

APPROXIMATE NUTRITIONAL INFORMATION PER 1-TABLESPOON SERVING

Calories: 121	Carbohydrate: 0 g
Total fat: 14 g	Protein: 0 g
Saturated fat: 2 g	Cholesterol: 0 mg
Percentage of calories from fat: 100%	Sodium: 0 mg
	Dietary fiber: 0 g

Soy Sauce and Rice Vinegar Sauce

Makes approximately ⅓ cup

¼ cup reduced-sodium soy sauce
2 tablespoons rice vinegar
½ teaspoon hot chili oil

Combine all ingredients. Mix well.

APPROXIMATE NUTRITIONAL INFORMATION PER 1-TABLESPOON SERVING

Calories: 21
Total fat: trace
Saturated fat: 0 g
Percentage of calories from fat: 18%
Carbohydrate: 3 g
Protein: 1 g
Cholesterol: 0 mg
Sodium: 585 mg
Dietary fiber: 0 g

Salsa Cruda

Makes 2¾ cups

1½ cups chopped ripe tomatoes
3 tablespoons chopped green onion
½ cup chopped red onion
2 finely chopped, fresh jalapeño peppers
2 garlic cloves, minced
1 tablespoon fresh lemon juice
¼ teaspoon salt
½ teaspoon pepper

Combine all ingredients in a glass bowl. Chill.

Serving Suggestion: Great on Mixed Vegetable Salad (page 394) and on grilled chicken.

APPROXIMATE NUTRITIONAL INFORMATION PER 1-TABLESPOON SERVING

Calories: 3
Total fat: trace
Saturated fat: 0 g
Percentage of calories from fat: 11%
Carbohydrate: 1 g
Protein: 0 g
Cholesterol: 0 mg
Sodium: 13 mg
Dietary fiber: trace

TOMATO SALSA

Makes 4 cups

4 whole jalapeño peppers
2 fresh tomatoes
1 14½-ounce can plum tomatoes with liquid
¼ teaspoon cumin (optional)
¼ teaspoon cayenne (optional)
¾ teaspoon salt

Dice peppers, fresh tomatoes, and canned tomatoes into 1-inch pieces. Combine all ingredients in a covered jar. Chill. Season just before serving.

Variation: For a hotter sauce, add Tabasco sauce to taste.

Note: Great as a salad dressing or as a dip.

APPROXIMATE NUTRITIONAL INFORMATION PER 1-TABLESPOON SERVING

Calories: 3
Total fat: trace
Saturated fat: 0 g
Percentage of calories from fat: 13%
Carbohydrate: 1 g
Protein: 0 g
Cholesterol: 0 mg
Sodium: 38 mg
Dietary fiber: 0 g

Low-Fat Pesto

Makes 1 cup

3 cups fresh basil leaves
2 cups torn fresh spinach leaves
6 garlic cloves
2 tablespoons pine nuts
2 tablespoons fresh lemon juice
½ teaspoon salt
¼ cup olive oil
¼ cup freshly grated Parmesan cheese

Combine basil, spinach, garlic, pine nuts, lemon juice, and salt in a blender or food processor. Purée. With machine running, add olive oil 1 tablespoon at a time; process until smooth. Just before serving, stir in Parmesan.

Note: Keeps 2 to 3 weeks in the refrigerator. Pesto can be frozen. (Pour a little olive oil over the top of the pesto to seal it if you are going to freeze it or store it in the refrigerator.)

Serving Suggestion: Pesto is delicious on pasta, chicken, seafood, vegetables, and potatoes.

APPROXIMATE NUTRITIONAL INFORMATION PER 1-TABLESPOON SERVING

Calories: 49
Total fat: 5 g
Saturated fat: 1 g
Percentage of calories from fat: 92%
Carbohydrate: 1 g
Protein: 2 g
Cholesterol: 2 mg
Sodium: 99 mg
Dietary fiber: 1 g

CRANBERRY RELISH

Makes 2 quarts

1 pound (4 cups) fresh cranberries
2 oranges, unpeeled and cut into eighths
2 red delicious apples, unpeeled and cut into eighths
⅓ cup sugar, or to taste

Wash cranberries; discard any that are soft or blemished. Put cranberries, oranges, and apples through the medium blade of a grinder or chop in a food processor. Drain off excess juice; reserve. Add sugar; stir. Pour about half of the reserved juice into the relish (relish should be very moist, but not runny). Chill 24 hours. Keeps 2 to 3 weeks.

APPROXIMATE NUTRITIONAL INFORMATION PER ¼-CUP SERVING

Calories: 45
Total fat: trace
Saturated fat: 0 g
Percentage of calories from fat: 3%
Carbohydrate: 12 g
Protein: 0 g
Cholesterol: 0 mg
Sodium: 0 mg
Dietary fiber: 1 g

Fat-Free Gravy

Makes 2½ cups

- 2 cups chicken or beef broth, preferably homemade (page 364 or 366)
- 3 tablespooons defatted meat juices and drippings (optional)
- ¼ cup all-purpose flour
- ½ cup cold water
- Salt and pepper to taste

Bring broth and defatted meat drippings to a boil. Shake flour and water in a covered jar to form a smooth paste; gradually add to boiling broth. Reduce heat; simmer 5 to 10 minutes, stirring constantly, until thick. Season.

Notes: To defat meat juices and drippings, pour the juices and drippings into a bowl; add a few ice cubes. Chill in the freezer for 10 to 15 minutes, or until the fat congeals at the top and around ice cubes. Discard ice cubes and congealed fat.

It is not necessary to use meat juices and drippings to make a satisfactory gravy with the above recipe.

Variation: For a gravy that is especially good with poultry, instead of 2 cups broth use 1 cup nonfat milk and 1 cup broth, or mix the milk with reduced-fat (1%) cream of chicken soup.

APPROXIMATE NUTRITIONAL INFORMATION PER ¼-CUP SERVING

Calories: 17
Total fat: trace
Saturated fat: 0 g
Percentage of calories from fat: 12%
Carbohydrate: 2 g
Protein: 1 g
Cholesterol: 0 mg
Sodium: 55 mg
Dietary fiber: 0 g

RICE, BEANS, AND OTHER GRAINS

Soak beans using method 1 or method 2.

Soaking Method 1. Wash beans. Stir 1 teaspoon salt into 6 cups of water for each 1 pound of dried beans. Add beans to salted water. Soak overnight. Drain. Rinse. Discard soaking water.

Soaking Method 2. Wash beans. Bring 8 cups of water for each 1 pound of beans to a boil. Add beans to boiling water. Bring to a second boil; boil 2 minutes. Remove from heat; cover and let soak for 1 hour. Drain. Rinse. Discard soaking water.

Cook soaked beans as follows: For 1 pound of soaked beans, bring 6 cups of water, chicken broth (or beef broth), 1 teaspoon salt, and 1 onion to a boil. Add beans; boil gently, uncovered, 25 minutes to 2 hours, or until tender. Cooking times will vary according to type of beans used. Add more water or broth as necessary during cooking to keep beans covered.

One pound beans yields 6 cups cooked beans.

Note: Dry legumes are important sources of B vitamins, iron, calcium, and potassium. They contain no cholesterol, are low in sodium, and are good sources of fiber.

Although home-cooked beans are preferable, canned beans are an invaluable help to shorten meal preparation time. Just be sure to select a brand that uses only heart-healthy ingredients.

Progresso makes a heart-healthy canned black bean, as well as a cannellini bean and kidney bean. Canned beans tend to be higher in sodium than home-cooked beans, so watch the sodium intake in the other foods consumed throughout the day. Rinsing canned beans will reduce the sodium by one half.

SAFFRON RICE

6 servings

2 tablespoons pine nuts
½ teaspoon olive oil
½ cup finely chopped onion
2 garlic cloves, minced
2 cups chicken broth, preferably homemade (page 364)
1 cup uncooked, long-grain white rice
1 teaspoon saffron threads or ¼ teaspoon powdered saffron
1 tablespoon finely chopped fresh parsley

Heat a nonstick skillet over medium-high heat; add pine nuts. Sauté 2 to 3 minutes, or until lightly toasted. Remove from skillet and set aside.

Add olive oil to skillet and heat. Add onion and garlic and sauté 5 minutes, or until tender.

Bring chicken broth to a boil; add onion, garlic, rice, and saffron. Stir lightly. Cover; reduce heat and simmer 15 to 20 minutes, or until rice is tender and moisture is absorbed. Toss with parsley and pine nuts.

APPROXIMATE NUTRITIONAL INFORMATION PER SERVING

Calories: 188
Total fat: 5 g
Saturated fat: 1 g
Percentage of calories from fat: 22%
Carbohydrate: 31 g
Protein: 6 g
Cholesterol: 1 mg
Sodium: 82 mg
Dietary fiber: 1 g

Wild Rice, Brown Rice, and Mushroom Pilaf

7 1-cup servings

1 small onion, chopped
2½ cups chicken broth or beef broth, preferably homemade (page 364 or 366)
2¼ cups water
⅔ cup wild rice
1 cup long-grain brown rice
½ pound fresh mushrooms, sliced
2 tablespoons chopped fresh parsley

In a nonstick skillet, sauté onion in a small amount of the broth until tender. Transfer to a 5- to 6-quart saucepan and combine onion, remaining broth, water, wild rice, and brown rice. Bring to a boil. Reduce heat; stir once. Cover and simmer for 35 to 40 minutes, or until rice is tender and most of the moisture is absorbed. Add mushrooms; simmer 5 minutes longer. Sprinkle with parsley.

APPROXIMATE NUTRITIONAL INFORMATION PER SERVING

Calories: 190
Total fat: 2 g
Saturated fat: 0 g
Percentage of calories from fat: 8%
Carbohydrate: 37 g
Protein: 7 g
Cholesterol: 1 mg
Sodium: 87 mg
Dietary fiber: 2 g

SHRIMP FRIED RICE

6 servings

½ teaspoon olive oil
2 eggs
2 tablespoons water
2 green onions, chopped
3 cups cooked basmati rice, prepared according to instructions on the box and cooled
½ pound cooked baby shrimp
1 tablespoon reduced-sodium soy sauce

Heat olive oil in a nonstick skillet; lightly stir eggs with water; pour egg mixture into skillet. Stir in green onion and scramble eggs with green onion. Just as eggs begin to set, stir in cooked rice. Gently toss eggs and rice until rice is coated and eggs are cooked. Toss with shrimp. Transfer to a serving dish. Sprinkle with soy sauce.

APPROXIMATE NUTRITIONAL INFORMATION PER SERVING

Calories: 181
Total fat: 3 g
Saturated fat: 1 g
Percentage of calories from fat: 13%
Carbohydrate: 24 g
Protein: 13 g
Cholesterol: 128 mg
Sodium: 178 mg
Dietary fiber: 1 g

Rice with Grilled Garden Vegetables

10 servings

Balsamic Marinade

⅔ cup balsamic vinegar
3 tablespoons olive oil
2 garlic cloves, minced
2 tablespoons chopped shallots
3 tablespoons finely chopped fresh basil or 1½ tablespoons dried
1 teaspoon chopped fresh oregano or ¼ teaspoon dried
½ teaspoon chopped fresh rosemary or ¼ teaspoon dried
1½ teaspoons fresh lemon thyme or ¾ teaspoon dried

2 Italian eggplants, halved lengthwise and then quartered
1 tablespoon salt (to be rinsed off)
⅔ cup wild rice
1 cup long-grain brown rice
2½ cups chicken broth, preferably homemade, (page 364)
2½ cups water
2 red onions, peeled and quartered
3 medium zucchini, cut diagionally into ½-inch slices
8 large mushrooms
1 red pepper, seeded and quartered
1 yellow pepper, seeded and quartered
1 green pepper, seeded and quartered
6 plum tomatoes, halved

Combine marinade ingredients in a covered jar. Shake well.

In a colander, toss eggplant with salt and allow to drain for 30 to 60 minutes. Rinse eggplant with water and drain well.

In a 5- to 6-quart saucepan, combine wild rice, brown rice, chicken broth, and water. Bring to a boil. Reduce heat. Stir once. Cover and simmer 40 to 45 minutes, or until rice is tender and moisture is absorbed.

While rice is cooking, prepare coals.

Arrange vegetables in a 13 x 9 x 2-inch casserole. Toss with ½ of the marinade. When coals are hot, place grill 4 to 6 inches above heat. Arrange onions and eggplant on top of grill, cook 5 to 10 minutes, turning often and basting frequently. Add remaining vegetables and continue cooking about 10 minutes longer, turning frequently and basting often until vegetables are tender.

To serve, mound rice in center of a serving platter. Ring with vegetables.

APPROXIMATE NUTRITIONAL INFORMATION PER SERVING

Calories: 185
Total fat: 4 g
Saturated fat: 1 g
Percentage of calories from fat: 20%
Carbohydrate: 34 g
Protein: 6 g
Cholesterol: 1 mg
Sodium: 75 mg
Dietary fiber: 1 g

Rice with Chicken, Prawns, and Clams

8 servings

2 teaspoons olive oil
2 cups chopped onion
3 garlic cloves, chopped
4 whole boneless, skinless chicken breasts, halved
6 cups chicken broth, preferably homemade (page 364)
2 cups uncooked, long-grain white rice
¾ teaspoon saffron
½ teaspoon salt
¼ teaspoon cayenne
1 14½-ounce can water-packed artichoke hearts, drained and quartered
2 cups frozen peas
1 28-ounce can plum tomatoes, drained and coarsely chopped
1½ pounds cooked prawns
24 steamer clams, steamed (page 513)
1 4-ounce jar pimientos, drained

Heat olive oil in a nonstick skillet; add onion and garlic. Sauté 3 to 5 minutes. Add chicken breasts; brown 5 to 7 minutes on each side. Set aside.

Bring chicken broth just to boiling; add rice. Reduce heat; cover and simmer 15 to 20 minutes. Add saffron; simmer 5 to 10 minutes longer, or until rice is tender and moisture is absorbed. Add salt and cayenne.

Transfer rice to a 4-quart casserole; add chicken, artichoke hearts, peas, and tomatoes. Bake uncovered at 350° for 30 minutes. Arrange prawns and clams on top of casserole; cook 3 to 5 minutes longer. Garnish with pimiento.

APPROXIMATE NUTRITIONAL INFORMATION PER SERVING

Calories: 448	Carbohydrate: 53 g
Total fat: 6 g	Protein: 44 g
Saturated fat: 1 g	Cholesterol: 53 mg
Percentage of calories from fat: 11%	Sodium: 624 mg
	Dietary fiber: 4 g

SPICY MEXICAN RICE

6 ½-cup servings

- ½ teaspoon olive oil
- ½ cup finely chopped onion
- 1 cup chicken broth, preferably homemade (page 364)
- 1 cup Mr. and Mrs. T Bloody Mary Mix
- 1 cup uncooked long-grain Texmati or basmati rice

Heat olive oil in a nonstick skillet; add onion and sauté. In a medium saucepan, heat chicken broth and Bloody Mary mix to boiling; add onion and rice. Stir lightly. Cover; reduce heat, and simmer 15 to 20 minutes, or until rice is soft and moisture is absorbed.

Note: Although low in fat, this recipe is high in sodium due to the Bloody Mary mix. Be sure to limit your sodium in other meals to keep the sodium intake for the day in balance.

APPROXIMATE NUTRITIONAL INFORMATION PER SERVING

Calories: 127	Carbohydrate: 25 g
Total fat: 1 g	Protein: 4 g
Saturated fat: 0 g	Cholesterol: 0 mg
Percentage of calories from fat: 4%	Sodium: 479 mg
	Dietary fiber: 1 g

ORIENTAL STICKY RICE

4 ¾-cup servings

1 cup short-grain rice (available in Oriental section of supermarket)
1¼ cups water

Place rice in a fine wire strainer; wash under cold running water until water runs clear. Put rice and water in a medium saucepan; cover and heat to boiling. Reduce heat; simmer 10 to 20 minutes, or until rice is tender and moisture is absorbed. Add additional water, if necessary.

APPROXIMATE NUTRITIONAL INFORMATION PER SERVING

Calories: 149	Carbohydrate: 32 g
Total fat: trace	Protein: 3 g
Saturated fat: 0 g	Cholesterol: 0 mg
Percentage of calories from fat: 2%	Sodium: 7 mg
	Dietary fiber: trace

LONG-GRAIN RICE PILAF

6 ½-cup servings

1 cup chicken broth, preferably homemade (page 364)
1 cup water
1 cup long-grain Texmati or basmati rice
1 tablespoon finely chopped fresh parsley

In a 2-quart saucepan, bring chicken broth and water to a boil. Add rice; stir lightly with a fork. Reduce heat; cover and simmer for 15 to 20 minutes, or until rice is soft and moisture is absorbed. Stir in parsley.

APPROXIMATE NUTRITIONAL INFORMATION PER SERVING

Calories: 115
Total fat: trace
Saturated fat: 0 g
Percentage of calories from fat: 1%
Carbohydrate: 23 g
Protein: 4 g
Cholesterol: 0 mg
Sodium: 41 mg
Dietary fiber: 1 g

BROWN RICE, WILD RICE, AND BARLEY PILAF

4 servings

2 14½-ounce cans chicken broth
½ cup chopped onion
¼ cup pearl barley
¼ cup wild rice
⅓ cup Texmati or basmati long-grain brown rice
2 tablespoons soft wheat berries

In a medium saucepan, combine chicken broth and onion; bring to a boil. Stir in barley, wild rice, long-grain rice, and wheat berries. Cover, reduce heat, and simmer 30 to 35 minutes, or until grains are tender and moisture is absorbed.

APPROXIMATE NUTRITIONAL INFORMATION PER SERVING

Calories: 114
Total fat: 1 g
Saturated fat: 0 g
Percentage of calories from fat: 9%
Carbohydrate: 21 g
Protein: 5 g
Cholesterol: 0 mg
Sodium: 87 mg
Dietary fiber: 2 g

Barley and Mushroom Pilaf

Makes 8 cups

1¾ cups pearl barley
2 teaspoons olive oil
1 onion, chopped
½ pound fresh mushrooms, sliced
4 cups beef broth, preferably homemade (page 366)

Soak barley several hours or overnight in enough cold water to cover. Drain.

Heat olive oil in a nonstick skillet. Sauté onion and barley in oil until onion is tender and barley is toasted. Add mushrooms; cook 2 to 3 minutes longer. Spoon into a large casserole.

Heat broth to boiling; pour over barley. Stir. Bake, covered, at 350° for 1 hour. Uncover; bake 1 to 1½ hours longer, or until liquid is absorbed.

APPROXIMATE NUTRITIONAL INFORMATION PER 1-CUP SERVING

Calories: 184
Total fat: 3 g
Saturated fat: 0 g
Percentage of calories from fat: 13%
Carbohydrate: 32 g
Protein: 8 g
Cholesterol: 1 mg
Sodium: 144 mg
Dietary fiber: 2 g

TABBOULEH

Makes 6 cups

1 tablespoon olive oil
1 medium onion, chopped
½ cup chopped celery
½ pound fresh mushrooms, sliced
1 cup uncooked cracked wheat bulgur
½ teaspoon minced fresh oregano or ¼ teaspoon dried
¼ teaspoon salt
¼ teaspoon pepper
2 cups chicken or beef broth, preferably homemade (page 364 or 366)

Warm olive oil in a nonstick skillet over medium heat; add onion and celery. Cook 5 minutes. Add mushrooms and bulgur; cook, stirring constantly, for 10 minutes, or until bulgur is golden brown and vegetables are tender. Add oregano, salt, pepper, and broth. Cover and bring to a boil; reduce heat and simmer 15 to 20 minutes, or until broth is absorbed.

Variations: Sprinkle with chopped fresh parsley just before serving. Or add ¼ teaspoon fresh dill weed to broth.

APPROXIMATE NUTRITIONAL INFORMATION PER 1-CUP SERVING

Calories: 125
Total fat: 2 g
Saturated fat: 0 g
Percentage of calories from fat: 17%
Carbohydrate: 22 g
Protein: 6 g
Cholesterol: 1 mg
Sodium: 198 mg
Dietary fiber: 2 g

Chili con Carne

8 servings

1 pound extra-lean ground round
1 onion, chopped
2 garlic cloves, minced
1 28-ounce can tomatoes, chopped
½ teaspoon ground cumin
1 teaspoon cayenne
1 tablespoon chili powder
4 cups cooked red kidney beans, or 2 15-ounce cans red kidney beans, drained
2 cups small elbow macaroni, cooked
1 7-ounce can diced green chilies (optional)

Brown ground beef with onion and garlic; drain off any excess fat. Add tomatoes and seasonings; simmer uncovered for 1½ to 2 hours. Add kidney beans; heat just to boiling. Add macaroni; heat to serving temperature. Sprinkle with green chilies.

Note: This recipe is very hot. For a milder flavor, reduce the cumin and the cayenne by half.

Variation: For a meatless chili, delete the ground round. Add the onions and garlic to the tomatoes and seasonings; simmer according to above instructions. The chili still tastes great and you'll save a lot of calories and fat.

APPROXIMATE NUTRITIONAL INFORMATION PER SERVING

Calories: 283
Total fat: 6 g
Saturated fat: 2 g
Percentage of calories from fat: 18%
Carbohydrate: 38 g
Protein: 22 g
Cholesterol: 35 mg
Sodium: 218 mg
Dietary fiber: 9 g

APPROXIMATE NUTRITIONAL INFORMATION PER SERVING OF MEATLESS CHILI

Calories: 199
Total fat: 1 g
Saturated fat: 0 g
Percentage of calories from fat: 6%
Carbohydrate: 38 g
Protein: 11 g
Cholesterol: 0 mg
Sodium: 150 mg
Dietary fiber: 9 g

COUNTRY BAKED BEANS

6 ½-cup servings

3 cups cooked small red beans or pinto beans
1 large onion, chopped
1 8-ounce can tomato sauce
⅓ cup molasses
⅓ teaspoon dry mustard
1 teaspoon chili powder
Salt to taste

Combine beans, onions, tomato sauce, molasses, mustard, and chili powder; pour into a bean pot or casserole dish. Bake uncovered at 350° for 1 hour. Cover and continue baking for 30 minutes.

APPROXIMATE NUTRITIONAL INFORMATION PER SERVING

Calories: 178
Total fat: 1 g
Saturated fat: 0 g
Percentage of calories from fat: 4%
Carbohydrate: 37 g
Protein: 8 g
Cholesterol: 0 mg
Sodium: 13 mg
Dietary fiber: 6 g

RED BEANS AND RICE

Makes 7 cups

½ teaspoon olive oil
1 onion, finely chopped
2 15-ounce cans red kidney beans, drained
½ teaspoon cayenne
¼ teaspoon Tabasco, or to taste
1 teaspoon pepper
½ teaspoon salt
3 cups Spicy Mexican Rice (page 445)
½ cup Tomato Salsa, preferably homemade (page 433)
½ cup nonfat sour cream

Heat olive oil in a nonstick skillet; add onion and sauté until tender. Transfer to a 2-quart saucepan; add kidney beans, cayenne, Tabasco, pepper, and salt. Simmer over low heat for 20 to 30 minutes.

Prepare Spicy Mexican Rice according to recipe instructions.

Just before serving, ladle beans over rice. Top with salsa and a dollop of sour cream.

APPROXIMATE NUTRITIONAL INFORMATION PER 1-CUP SERVING

Calories: 182
Total fat: 1 g
Saturated fat: 0 g
Percentage of calories from fat: 7%
Carbohydrate: 35 g
Protein: 8 g
Cholesterol: 1 mg
Sodium: 653 mg
Dietary fiber: 5 g

VEGETABLES

There is no more heart-healthy fare than vegetables. To preserve the natural sugars and nutrients of vegetables, do not wash them until just prior to cooking. The most important rule about cooking vegetables is not to overcook—cook until just crisp-tender and still very colorful.

To Steam Vegetables: Bring 1 to 2 inches of water to a boil in a medium saucepan. Place vegetables in a steamer basket and place the basket over the boiling water. Cover saucepan with a tight-fitting lid. Steam until vegetables are crisp-tender and still very colorful.

To Boil Vegetables: Bring a small amount of water or broth to a boil—use the smallest amount possible. Add vegetables; bring to a second boil. Cover; reduce heat. Cook at a gentle boil until crisp-tender and rich in color.

To Cook Frozen Vegetables: Follow package directions; omit salt.

To Stir-Fry Vegetables: Slice vegetables to a uniform thickness of about ⅛ inch. Heat a small amount of chicken or beef broth in a wok or heavy skillet over high heat. Add vegetables requiring longest cooking time first; gradually add remaining vegetables. Stir rapidly with long chopsticks or a flat wooden spoon until vegetables show signs of wilting slightly. Lower heat. Cover with lid—cook only briefly, just until vegetables are crisp-tender. Serve at once.

To Oven-Roast Vegetables: Pare and quarter such vegetables as potatoes, celery, carrots, onions, and green peppers. Place on a rack in a baking dish; add ½ cup water, wine, or broth. Cover. Steam 30 to 40 minutes, or until tender. If using mushrooms, tomatoes, or artichoke hearts, they should be added during the last 15 minutes.

To Microwave Vegetables: Vegetables cooked in the microwave retain their bright color and freshness as well as their vitamins and minerals, because they are usually cooked with little or no additional water. For correct cooking procedure and timing for individual vegetables, consult a microwave manual.

To Blanch Vegetables: Bring 1 to 2 inches of water to a boil in a medium saucepan. Place vegetables in a steamer basket and place the basket in the boiling water. Cover saucepan with a tight-fitting lid. Reduce regular cooking time by three quarters. For example, regular cooking time for fresh peas is 3 to 5 minutes, so the blanching time would be 45 to 80 seconds—at this point vegetables will be rich in color and translucent. Immediately plunge vegetables into ice water to stop additional cooking. Consult a vegetable blanching and freezing chart for blanching times for individual vegetables.

Fresh Artichokes

2 to 3 servings

2 to 3 fresh artichokes
Fresh lemon juice
3 tablespoons chopped onion
3 garlic cloves
1½ cups dry white wine
Dash of salt
⅛ teaspoon pepper
1 lemon, sliced

Wash artichokes. Cut 1 inch off the top; cut off stem and tips of leaves. Brush cut edges with lemon juice.

Combine remaining ingredients. Bring to a boil. Place artichokes upright in mixture; cover and simmer until bottom leaves pull off easily. Drain. Serve hot or cold.

Note: Artichokes are delicious cooked in the microwave. See following recipe.

To Microwave: Place artichokes upright in a microwave-proof baking dish. Pour 4 tablespoons lemon juice and 2 tablespoons water over each artichoke. Cover dish with plastic wrap; prick a hole in the top of plastic wrap to allow steam to escape. For 1 medium artichoke, allow 5 to 7 minutes cooking time at full power; for 2 medium artichokes, allow 7 to 9 minutes.

Variation: Add 2 teaspoons olive oil to the poaching mixture.

Serving Suggestion: Accompany with Dijon Vinaigrette (page 420) or fat-free or light mayonnaise mixed with a touch of fresh lemon juice and some grated onion.

APPROXIMATE NUTRITIONAL INFORMATION PER ARTICHOKE

Calories: 156
Total fat: trace
Saturated fat: 0 g
Percentage of calories from fat: 2%
Carbohydrate: 20 g
Protein: 5 g
Cholesterol: 0 mg
Sodium: 309 mg
Dietary fiber: 7 g

ARTICHOKE HEARTS WITH LEMON, GARLIC, AND OLIVE OIL

4 servings

1 14½-ounce can water-packed artichoke hearts, drained
Juice of ½ lemon
2 garlic cloves
2 teaspoons olive oil

Cut artichoke hearts into quarters. Squeeze lemon juice over. Heat garlic with olive oil in a nonstick skillet; add artichokes with lemon and toss gently to coat. Cook 3 to 5 minutes over medium-high heat, or just until warm.

APPROXIMATE NUTRITIONAL INFORMATION PER SERVING

Calories: 46
Total fat: 2 g
Saturated fat: 0 g
Percentage of calories from fat: 44%
Carbohydrate: 6 g
Protein: 2 g
Cholesterol: 0 mg
Sodium: 181 mg
Dietary fiber: 1 g

Fresh Asparagus with Lemon

4 servings

1 pound fresh asparagus
Juice of ½ lemon

Wash asparagus; snap stalks. Place on a vegetable steamer rack over boiling water; cover and steam 5 to 6 minutes, or just until barely tender. Drizzle with lemon juice.

To microwave: Arrange asparagus in a single layer, tender tips toward center, in a microwave-proof baking dish. Cover with plastic wrap; prick a hole in the top of the plastic with a fork to allow steam to escape. Cook at full power 3 to 4 minutes, or just until barely tender. Drizzle with lemon juice.

APPROXIMATE NUTRITIONAL INFORMATION PER SERVING

Calories: 27
Total fat: trace
Saturated fat: 0 g
Percentage of calories from fat: 8%
Carbohydrate: 5 g
Protein: 3 g
Cholesterol: 0 mg
Sodium: 2 mg
Dietary fiber: 2 g

Green Beans with Lemon and Black Pepper

4 servings

¾ pound fresh green beans
1 dill sprig (optional)
Juice of ½ lemon
Black pepper to taste

Place beans on a vegetable steamer rack over boiling water; sprinkle with dill and lemon juice. Cover and steam 4 to 6 minutes; sprinkle with pepper. Cook 10 to 15 minutes, or until beans are tender (do not overcook).

APPROXIMATE NUTRITIONAL INFORMATION PER SERVING

Calories: 28	Carbohydrate: 7 g
Total fat: trace	Protein: 2 g
Saturated fat: 0 g	Cholesterol: 0 mg
Percentage of calories from fat: 3%	Sodium: 5 mg
	Dietary fiber: 3 g

GREEN BEANS WITH FRESH LEMON AND TARRAGON

4 servings

¾ pound fresh green beans
2 teaspoons olive oil
½ cup fresh lemon juice
2 garlic cloves, minced
1 tablespoon fresh tarragon or 1 teaspoon dried
2 teaspoons minced fresh oregano or 1 teaspoon dried
¼ teaspoon salt
⅛ teaspoon pepper

Wash beans; remove ends and strings. Place on a vegetable steamer rack over boiling water; cover and steam 15 to 20 minutes, or until tender (do not overcook). Combine remaining ingredients; pour over cooked beans. Serve hot or cold.

APPROXIMATE NUTRITIONAL INFORMATION PER SERVING

Calories: 57	Carbohydrate: 9 g
Total fat: 2 g	Protein: 2 g
Saturated fat: 0 g	Cholesterol: 0 mg
Percentage of calories from fat: 38%	Sodium: 139 mg
	Dietary fiber: 2 g

Green Beans, Italian Style

6 servings

1 pound fresh green beans
½ cup chicken broth, preferably homemade (page 364)
1 teaspoon olive oil
2 cups canned plum tomatoes
Dash of oregano
½ teaspoon salt
¼ teaspoon pepper

Wash beans. Remove ends and strings; cut on the diagonal into 1-inch pieces. Set aside. Combine remaining ingredients and bring to a boil. Add beans; cook covered for 15 to 20 minutes, or until beans are tender (do not overcook).

APPROXIMATE NUTRITIONAL INFORMATION PER SERVING

Calories: 49
Total fat: 1 g
Saturated fat: 0 g
Percentage of calories from fat: 23%
Carbohydrate: 9 g
Protein: 2 g
Cholesterol: 0 mg
Sodium: 394 mg
Dietary fiber: 3 g

GREEN BEANS WITH MUSHROOMS

6 servings

¾ pound fresh green beans
½ pound fresh mushrooms, sliced
3 green onions with tops, chopped
¼ cup fresh lemon juice
2 teaspoons olive oil
½ teaspoon or less salt
¼ teaspoon pepper

Wash beans. Remove ends and strings; cut on the diagonal into thirds. Place on a vegetable steamer rack over boiling water; cover and steam until just tender, 15 to 20 minutes (do not overcook). Combine beans with mushrooms and green onions; toss with lemon juice, olive oil, salt, and pepper. Serve hot or cold.

APPROXIMATE NUTRITIONAL INFORMATION PER SERVING

Calories: 44
Total fat: 2 g
Saturated fat: 0 g
Percentage of calories from fat: 36%
Carbohydrate: 7 g
Protein: 2 g
Cholesterol: 0 mg
Sodium: 182 mg
Dietary fiber: 4 g

Green Beans with Mushrooms and Water Chestnuts

7 ½-cup servings

¾ pound fresh green beans
½ pound fresh mushrooms, sliced
1 8-ounce can sliced water chestnuts
2 tablespoons lemon juice
½ teaspoon salt
⅛ teaspoon pepper

Place beans on a vegetable steamer rack over boiling water; cook 15 to 20 minutes, or until beans are nearly tender. Add mushrooms the last 5 minutes, add water chestnuts the last 3 minutes. Spoon beans into a serving bowl; toss with lemon juice, salt, and pepper.

APPROXIMATE NUTRITIONAL INFORMATION PER SERVING

Calories: 38
Total fat: trace
Saturated fat: 0 g
Percentage of calories from fat: 5%
Carbohydrate: 9 g
Protein: 2 g
Cholesterol: 0 mg
Sodium: 158 mg
Dietary fiber: 1 g

FRESH BROCCOLI WITH LEMON

4 ½-cup servings

1 bunch fresh broccoli
Juice of ½ lemon

Wash broccoli; remove outer leaves and tough part of stalks. Place on a vegetable steamer rack over boiling water; cover and steam 5 to 10 minutes, or just until tender (do not overcook). Squeeze lemon juice over broccoli.

To microwave: Arrange broccoli in a single layer, florets toward center, in a microwave-proof baking dish. Cover with plastic wrap; prick a hole in the top of plastic wrap to allow steam to escape. Cook at full power 3 to 4 minutes, or just until barely tender.

APPROXIMATE NUTRITIONAL INFORMATION PER SERVING

Calories: 24
Total fat: trace
Saturated fat: 0 g
Percentage of calories from fat: 10%
Carbohydrate: 5 g
Protein: 2 g
Cholesterol: 0 mg
Sodium: 20 mg
Dietary fiber: 4 g

Stir-Fried Broccoli

6 ½-cup servings

1 large bunch broccoli
½ cup chicken broth, preferably homemade (page 364)
1 teaspoon sesame oil
2 teaspoons cornstarch
2 tablespoons water
2 teaspoons sesame seeds

Wash broccoli; cut florets from stems and set aside. Peel stems; cut diagonally into ¼-inch pieces.

Heat chicken broth and sesame oil in a wok or heavy skillet. Stir-fry stems for 2 minutes; add florets and stir-fry 2 more minutes. Add cornstarch dissolved in water and toss quickly to coat and glaze broccoli. Sprinkle with sesame seeds.

APPROXIMATE NUTRITIONAL INFORMATION PER SERVING

Calories: 40
Total fat: 2 g
Saturated fat: 0 g
Percentage of calories from fat: 36%
Carbohydrate: 5 g
Protein: 3 g
Cholesterol: 0 mg
Sodium: 43 mg
Dietary fiber: 2 g

PAN-STEAMED BROCCOLI AND CAULIFLOWER WITH LEMON AND HOT CHILI SAUCE

7 ½-cup servings

½ small head cauliflower
½ pound broccoli
2 tablespoons fresh lemon juice
2 tablespoons water
½ teaspoon hot chili oil

Break cauliflower and broccoli into florets.

In a wok or heavy skillet, heat the lemon juice and water. Add cauliflower; cover and steam 3 to 4 minutes. Add broccoli; cover and steam 2 to 3 minutes longer, or just until cauliflower and broccoli are crisp-tender. Add hot chili oil and toss.

APPROXIMATE NUTRITIONAL INFORMATION PER SERVING

Calories: 17
Total fat: trace
Saturated fat: 0 g
Percentage of calories from fat: 23%
Carbohydrate: 3 g
Protein: 1 g
Cholesterol: 0 mg
Sodium: 11 mg
Dietary fiber: 2 g

Grilled Corn on the Cob

4 servings

4 ears fresh corn, with silks and husks
1 fresh lime or lemon, cut into wedges
Salt to taste (optional)
Ground pepper to taste

Leaving husks and silks on, soak corn for 30 minutes in enough water to cover. Remove corn from water and pull the husks a little way down from the top to drain any excess water.

Arrange corn on a grill over hot coals and close lid of barbecue. Cook 25 to 30 minutes, turning frequently, until corn is tender. Shuck.

Squeeze fresh lime or lemon juice over corn. Sprinkle with salt and pepper.

To microwave: Arrange ears in an oblong microwave-proof dish. Cover with waxed paper; prick a hole in the top of the waxed paper to allow steam to escape. Cook at full power 4 to 6 minutes for 2 ears; 7 to 8 minutes for 4 ears. Turn once during cooking time.

Note: For added butter flavor, sprinkle the corn with Molly McButter before eating. It has 4 calories, 0 g fat, and 90 mg sodium per ½ teaspoon.

Variations: To steam, husk corn; remove silks. Arrange corn on a vegetable steamer rack over boiling water; cover and steam 6 to 8 minutes.

APPROXIMATE NUTRITIONAL INFORMATION PER SERVING

Calories: 59
Total fat: trace
Saturated fat: 0 g
Percentage of calories from fat: 7%
Carbohydrate: 14 g
Protein: 2 g
Cholesterol: 0 mg
Sodium: 3 mg
Dietary fiber: 2 g

BAKED EGGPLANT

8 servings

- 1 medium eggplant, cut crosswise into ¼-inch slices
- 1 tablespoon salt (to be rinsed off)
- 1 medium onion, chopped
- 1 garlic clove, minced
- 2 tablespoons red wine
- 1 14½-ounce can plum tomatoes
- 1 8-ounce can tomato sauce
- ⅓ cup tomato paste
- 4 teaspoons minced fresh oregano or 2 teaspoons dried
- ½ pound fresh mushrooms, sliced
- ⅓ cup all-purpose flour
- 1 cup egg substitute, beaten
- 1 cup bread crumbs
- ½ cup grated reduced-fat mozzarella cheese

In large colander, toss eggplant with salt and allow to drain for 30 to 60 minutes. Rinse eggplant with water and drain well.

Sauté onion and garlic in red wine until tender; add tomatoes, tomato sauce, tomato paste, oregano, and mushrooms. Bring to a boil; reduce heat and simmer uncovered for 30 minutes.

Coat eggplant with flour. Dip into egg substitute, then into bread crumbs. Cook in a nonstick skillet until lightly browned, turning once.

In the bottom of a 13 x 9 x 2-inch baking dish, spread half the tomato mixture, layer half the eggplant slices, top with half the cheese, and spread with sauce. Repeat layers, leaving sauce to pour over the top. Bake uncovered at 350° for 20 to 30 minutes.

(continued on next page)

(continued from preceding page)

APPROXIMATE NUTRITIONAL INFORMATION PER SERVING

Calories: 156	Carbohydrate: 26 g
Total fat: 2 g	Protein: 9 g
Saturated fat: 1 g	Cholesterol: 4 mg
Percentage of calories from fat: 14%	Sodium: 465 mg
	Dietary fiber: 3 g

By using egg substitute instead of a fresh egg, you save 3 grams of fat and 107 milligrams of cholesterol per serving.

Roasted Garlic

4 servings

4 whole garlic heads
2 teaspoons olive oil

Leaving garlic head intact, remove outer layer of skin from the head. Lay each head on the side and cut about ½ inch straight across the top. Arrange garlic in a small, shallow ovenproof casserole. Drizzle ½ teaspoon olive oil on top of each head, letting it run between the individual cloves. Cover pan with foil. Bake at 350° for 30 to 45 minutes, until garlic is tender when pierced with a toothpick. Serve the heads on individual bread or dinner plates.

To eat, peel off individual cloves and squeeze the roasted garlic onto bread, potatoes, or vegetables.

APPROXIMATE NUTRITIONAL INFORMATION PER SERVING

Calories: 60	Carbohydrate: 10 g
Total fat: 2 g	Protein: 2 g
Saturated fat: 0 g	Cholesterol: 0 mg
Percentage of calories from fat: 37%	Sodium: 10 mg
	Dietary fiber: 0 g

SAUTÉED MUSHROOMS

6 ½-cup servings

3 tablespoons white wine or vermouth
1 garlic clove
1 pound fresh mushrooms, caps or pieces

Heat wine or vermouth and garlic in a heavy skillet. Add mushrooms. Cook uncovered over medium heat, stirring frequently, for 3 to 4 minutes

APPROXIMATE NUTRITIONAL INFORMATION PER SERVING

Calories: 25	Carbohydrate: 4 g
Total fat: trace	Protein: 2 g
Saturated fat: 0 g	Cholesterol: 0 mg
Percentage of calories from fat: 12%	Sodium: 3 mg
	Dietary fiber: 1 g

GRILLED PEPPERS AND ONIONS

4 servings

1 large red pepper
1 large yellow pepper
1 large green pepper
1 medium white onion
1 medium red onion

Wash peppers and remove seeds. Cut into 2-inch chunks. Peel onions and cut into 2-inch cubes.

Alternate peppers and onions on skewers. Grill over hot coals about 10 minutes, turning frequently.

(continued on next page)

(continued from preceding page)

APPROXIMATE NUTRITIONAL INFORMATION PER SERVING

Calories: 36	Carbohydrate: 8 g
Total fat: trace	Protein: 1 g
Saturated fat: 0 g	Cholesterol: 0 mg
Percentage of calories from fat: 5%	Sodium: 3 mg
	Dietary fiber: 3 g

Sautéed Mushrooms with Artichokes and Tomatoes

8 ½-cup servings

- 1 14½-ounce can water-packed artichoke hearts, drained
- ¼ cup white wine or vermouth
- 1 garlic clove
- 1 pound fresh mushrooms, caps or pieces
- 10 cherry tomatoes

Cut artichoke hearts into quarters. Heat wine or vermouth and garlic in a heavy skillet; add mushrooms and artichokes. Cook uncovered over medium heat, stirring frequently, for 3 to 4 minutes. Add tomatoes; toss.

APPROXIMATE NUTRITIONAL INFORMATION PER SERVING

Calories: 41	Carbohydrate: 7 g
Total fat: 1 g	Protein: 2 g
Saturated fat: 0 g	Cholesterol: 0 mg
Percentage of calories from fat: 11%	Sodium: 21 mg
	Dietary fiber: 1 g

ROASTED SWEET PEPPERS

8 peppers

8 large red and green sweet peppers
1 tablespoon olive oil
2 garlic cloves
2 teaspoons tarragon wine vinegar
3 chopped fresh basil, or ½ teaspoon dried
½ teaspoon fresh rosemary or ¼ teaspoon dried
½ teaspoon minced fresh oregano or ¼ teaspoon dried

Preheat oven to broil. Arrange peppers on a foil-lined baking sheet. Broil until the skin of the peppers blisters and turns black, turning 2 to 3 times so that all sides are blistered and blackened. Remove from oven. Place in a glass bowl; cover with a kitchen towel. Cool 1 hour. Hold each pepper under cold running water; rub off charred skin. Remove stem and seeds; slice into strips. Combine remaining ingredients; pour over peppers. Chill 24 to 48 hours. Serve with tomato slices or add to sandwiches or pizza.

APPROXIMATE NUTRITIONAL INFORMATION PER 1-PEPPER SERVING

Calories: 42
Total fat: 2 g
Saturated fat: 0 g
Percentage of calories from fat: 4%
Carbohydrate: 7 g
Protein: 1 g
Cholesterol: 0 mg
Sodium: 2 mg
Dietary fiber: 2 g

Potatoes Arrosto

8 servings

1 pound bite-size red potatoes
1½ tablespoons olive oil, preferably Garlic Olive Oil (page 431)
Pinch of salt and pepper to taste

Scrub potatoes and cut each one in half. Toss with olive oil. Arrange cut side up in a shallow roasting pan. Pour ¼ cup water into the bottom of pan. Roast at 375° for 50 to 60 minutes, or until tender and well browned. Just before serving, sprinkle lightly with salt and pepper if desired.

APPROXIMATE NUTRITIONAL INFORMATION PER SERVING

Calories: 48	Carbohydrate: 6 g
Total fat: 3 g	Protein: 1 g
Saturated fat: 0 g	Cholesterol: 0 mg
Percentage of calories from fat: 48%	Sodium: 1 mg
	Dietary fiber: 1 g

Cottage Fries

2 servings

2 medium potatoes
2 teaspoons olive oil

Boil or steam potatoes in their jackets. Slice thin. Toss with oil. Brown in a nonstick skillet over medium heat, turning frequently.

Variation: For Potatoes O'Brien, sauté chopped onion and chopped green pepper in a small amount of water or broth until tender. Toss with potatoes and oil. Brown.

APPROXIMATE NUTRITIONAL INFORMATION PER SERVING

Calories: 260	Carbohydrate: 51 g
Total fat: 5 g	Protein: 5 g
Saturated fat: 1 g	Cholesterol: 0 mg
Percentage of calories from fat: 16%	Sodium: 16 mg
	Dietary fiber: 3 g

FRIED POTATOES WITH GARLIC AND ROSEMARY

4 servings

4 medium potatoes with skins, diced
2 teaspoons olive oil
8 large garlic cloves, unpeeled
2 fresh rosemary sprigs

Microwave or steam potatoes until just crisp-tender.

Heat olive oil in a nonstick skillet; add potatoes and garlic and sauté over medium-high heat for 10 to 12 minutes. Turn; add rosemary. Brown 8 to 10 minutes longer, or until potatoes are tender.

APPROXIMATE NUTRITIONAL INFORMATION PER SERVING

Calories: 156	Carbohydrate: 31 g
Total fat: 3 g	Protein: 4 g
Saturated fat: 0 g	Cholesterol: 0 mg
Percentage of calories from fat: 14%	Sodium: 7 mg
	Dietary fiber: 1 g

Oven French Fried Potatoes

2 servings

2 medium potatoes
2 teaspoons olive oil

Cut potatoes into strips. Toss with olive oil. Arrange on a nonstick baking sheet. Bake at 425° for 15 to 20 minutes, or until brown. Turn; bake 15 to 20 minutes longer, or until tender.

Note: To shorten baking time, parboil potatoes 15 minutes; slice and bake.

APPROXIMATE NUTRITIONAL INFORMATION PER SERVING

Calories: 260
Total fat: 5 g
Saturated fat: 1 g
Percentage of calories from fat: 16%
Carbohydrate: 51 g
Protein: 5 g
Cholesterol: 0 mg
Sodium: 16 mg
Dietary fiber: 3 g

Hash Brown Potatoes

2 servings

2 medium potatoes
1½ teaspoons chopped onion (optional)
2 teaspoons olive oil
Dash of salt and pepper

Boil or steam potatoes in their jackets. Chill. Peel. Shred. Toss with onion, olive oil, salt, and pepper. Pat potatoes into thin patties. Brown in a nonstick skillet over medium heat for 10 to 12 minutes. Turn. Brown 8 to 10 minutes longer, or to desired brownness. For extra crispness, using two spatulas, cut horizontally through center of patty; flip one half over the other.

APPROXIMATE NUTRITIONAL INFORMATION PER SERVING

Calories: 160	Carbohydrate: 28 g
Total fat: 5 g	Protein: 3 g
Saturated fat: 1 g	Cholesterol: 0 mg
Percentage of calories from fat: 26%	Sodium: 273 mg
	Dietary fiber: 2 g

BAKED POTATOES WITH SOUR CREAM AND CHIVES

2 servings

- 2 medium potatoes
- ½ cup nonfat sour cream
- ¼ cup chopped chives or green onions
- ¼ cup Tomato Salsa, preferably homemade (page 433) (optional)

Scrub potatoes in their jackets (do not use new potatoes); prick with a fork. Bake at 425° for 40 to 60 minutes, or at 350° for 60 to 80 minutes. Cut potatoes open and top with sour cream, chives, and salsa.

APPROXIMATE NUTRITIONAL INFORMATION PER SERVING*

Calories: 266	Carbohydrate: 58 g
Total fat: trace	Protein: 8 g
Saturated fat: 0 g	Cholesterol: 1 mg
Percentage of calories from fat: 1%	Sodium: 362 mg
	Dietary fiber: 3 g

*A plain potato has 220 calories and only a trace of fat.

New Potatoes with Sour Cream and Dill

4 servings

1 pound small new potatoes, unpeeled
1 small red onion, thinly sliced
1 green pepper, thinly sliced into rings
1 cup nonfat sour cream
1 tablespoon chopped fresh dill, or ¼ teaspoon dried
½ teaspoon or less salt
¼ teaspoon pepper

Scrub potatoes; boil or steam until just tender. Place whole or sliced into a serving bowl; tuck onion and green pepper slices among potatoes. Combine sour cream, dill, salt and pepper. Pass with potatoes.

APPROXIMATE NUTRITIONAL INFORMATION PER SERVING

Calories: 150	Carbohydrate: 29 g
Total fat: 2 g	Protein: 5 g
Saturated fat: 1 g	Cholesterol: 7 mg
Percentage of calories from fat: 12%	Sodium: 300 mg
	Dietary fiber: 3 g

Parsleyed Potatoes

4 servings

4 new potatoes (approximately 1 pound)
1 tablespoon tub-style light margarine
Juice of ½ lemon
1 tablespoon chopped fresh parsley

Scrub potatoes; steam in their jackets until just tender. Toss with margarine. Drizzle with lemon juice. Sprinkle with parsley.

APPROXIMATE NUTRITIONAL INFORMATION PER SERVING

Calories: 137	Carbohydrate: 29 g
Total fat: 2 g	Protein: 3 g
Saturated fat: 0 g	Cholesterol: 0 mg
Percentage of calories from fat: 11%	Sodium: 37 mg
	Dietary fiber: 2 g

STEAMED RED POTATOES

4 servings

1 pound small red potatoes
2 tablespoons beef or chicken broth, preferably homemade (page 366 or 364)
¼ cup fresh lemon juice
Zest of ½ lemon
¼ teaspoon pepper
Chopped fresh chives
Chopped fresh parsley
Dash of fresh or dried rosemary

Slice potatoes in their jackets into thin rounds; steam until just tender. Heat broth, lemon juice, and lemon zest, but do not boil; pour over potatoes. Season with pepper. Sprinkle with chives, parsley, and rosemary.

APPROXIMATE NUTRITIONAL INFORMATION PER SERVING

Calories: 102	Carbohydrate: 24 g
Total fat: trace	Protein: 2 g
Saturated fat: 0 g	Cholesterol: 0 mg
Percentage of calories from fat: 1%	Sodium: 46 mg
	Dietary fiber: 2 g

Mashed Potatoes

4 servings

3 medium potatoes (1 pound)
2 to 4 tablespoons hot nonfat milk

Peel potatoes; cut into quarters. Boil or steam until tender; drain and mash with potato masher. Beat with electric mixer until light and fluffy, gradually adding hot milk as needed.

APPROXIMATE NUTRITIONAL INFORMATION PER SERVING

Calories: 95	Carbohydrate: 21 g
Total fat: trace	Protein: 2 g
Saturated fat: 0 g	Cholesterol: 0 mg
Percentage of calories from fat: 1%	Sodium: 12 mg
	Dietary fiber: 2 g

Ratatouille

10 servings

1 medium eggplant, cut into 1-inch cubes
1 tablespoon salt (to be rinsed off)
1 large onion, sliced into rings
3 medium zucchini, cut into ½-inch slices
2 green peppers, seeded and cut into ½-inch pieces
3 large tomatoes, chopped
1 cup minced fresh parsley
½ teaspoon salt
1 tablespoon chopped fresh basil, or ½ teaspoon dried
4 garlic cloves, pressed
1 tablespoon olive oil
Ground pepper to taste

In large colander, toss eggplant with salt and allow to drain for 30 to 60 minutes. Rinse eggplant with water and drain well.

Layer vegetables in a deep ovenproof casserole; sprinkle with parsley, salt, basil, and garlic. Drizzle with olive oil. Chill overnight. Bake, covered, in a 350° oven for 3 hours. Sprinkle with ground pepper.

APPROXIMATE NUTRITIONAL INFORMATION PER SERVING

Calories: 43
Total fat: 2 g
Saturated fat: 0 g
Percentage of calories from fat: 35%
Carbohydrate: 7 g
Protein: 1 g
Cholesterol: 0 mg
Sodium: 114 mg
Dietary fiber: 2 g

SESAME SPINACH

2 servings

1 bunch fresh spinach
½ teaspoon sesame oil
4 teaspoons lemon juice
2 teaspoons toasted sesame seeds

Wash spinach in ice water; remove thick stems. Pat dry; tear into bite-size pieces. Toss with sesame oil; sprinkle with lemon juice and sesame seeds. Toss again.

APPROXIMATE NUTRITIONAL INFORMATION PER SERVING

Calories: 48
Total fat: 3 g
Saturated fat: 0 g
Percentage of calories from fat: 55%
Carbohydrate: 5 g
Protein: 3 g
Cholesterol: 0 mg
Sodium: 66 mg
Dietary fiber: 2 g

BAKED SQUASH

4 servings

1 pound Hubbard squash
1 tablespoon tub-style light margarine
½ teaspoon salt
½ teaspoon pepper

Wash squash; cut into halves or squares; remove seeds; brush with light margarine. Place cut side down in a shallow pan. Bake at 350° for 30 minutes; turn. Bake 30 minutes longer, or until tender. Season lightly with salt and pepper.

APPROXIMATE NUTRITIONAL INFORMATION PER SERVING

Calories: 54	Carbohydrate: 11 g
Total fat: 2 g	Protein: 1 g
Saturated fat: 0 g	Cholesterol: 0 mg
Percentage of calories from fat: 27%	Sodium: 302 mg
	Dietary fiber: 3 g

VERA CRUZ TOMATOES

4 servings

¼ cup chopped onion
Wine or broth
6 cups trimmed fresh spinach (1 bunch), chopped
½ cup nonfat sour cream
Dash of Tabasco sauce
4 medium tomatoes
3 tablespoons grated part-skim mozzarella cheese

Sauté onion in a small amount wine or broth until tender; add spinach and cook 3 to 4 minutes. Cool, drain, and squeeze excess water from spinach. Mix spinach and onion with sour cream and Tabasco sauce. Cut tops from tomatoes and remove centers, leaving shells. Fill shells with spinach mixture. Place in a baking dish. Bake at 375° for 20 to 25 minutes. Top with cheese.

APPROXIMATE NUTRITIONAL INFORMATION PER SERVING

Calories: 70
Total fat: 2 g
Saturated fat: 1 g
Percentage of calories from fat: 30%
Carbohydrate: 10 g
Protein: 5 g
Cholesterol: 7 mg
Sodium: 82 mg
Dietary fiber: 2 g

HERBED TOMATOES

2 servings

2 medium tomatoes
2 teaspoons red wine vinegar
Pinch of chopped fresh parsley
Pinch of fresh or dried thyme
Pinch of fresh or dried basil
Pinch of fresh or dried marjoram
Dash of pepper

Slice tomatoes. Sprinkle with vinegar and herbs.

APPROXIMATE NUTRITIONAL INFORMATION PER SERVING

Calories: 28
Total fat: trace
Saturated fat: 0 g
Percentage of calories from fat: 14%
Carbohydrate: 6 g
Protein: 1 g
Cholesterol: 0 mg
Sodium: 12 mg
Dietary fiber: 1 g

Grilled Tomato Halves

4 servings

2 ripe tomatoes, halved
½ teaspoon olive oil
⅛ teaspoon freshly ground pepper
2 tablespoons chopped fresh basil
1 teaspoon bread crumbs

Cut tomatoes into halves; brush lightly with olive oil. Sprinkle with pepper and basil. Top with bread crumbs. Grill 2 to 3 minutes.

APPROXIMATE NUTRITIONAL INFORMATION PER SERVING

Calories: 27
Total fat: 1 g
Saturated fat: 0 g
Percentage of calories from fat: 30%

Carbohydrate: 5 g
Protein: 1 g
Cholesterol: 0 mg
Sodium: 13 mg
Dietary fiber: trace

SKEWERED GRILLED VEGETABLES

6 servings

12 cherry tomatoes
1 14½-ounce can water-packed artichoke hearts, drained
12 fresh mushrooms
1 onion, cut into 2-inch cubes
1 green pepper, cut into 2-inch cubes
1 tablespoon olive oil
1 tablespoon red wine vinegar
¼ teaspoon salt
⅛ teaspoon pepper

Toss vegetables with olive oil, vinegar, salt, and pepper; drain, reserving marinade. Alternate vegetables on skewers. Broil 4 inches from heat, turning often and basting frequently with marinade.

APPROXIMATE NUTRITIONAL INFORMATION PER SERVING

Calories: 85
Total fat: 3 g
Saturated fat: 0 g
Percentage of calories from fat: 30%
Carbohydrate: 15 g
Protein: 3 g
Cholesterol: 0 mg
Sodium: 117 mg
Dietary fiber: 2 g

Stir-Fried Vegetables

10 servings

2 tablespoons olive oil
1 small onion, thinly sliced
2 carrots, cut crosswise into rounds
2 celery stalks, cut diagonally into 1-inch pieces
1 cup broccoli florets
1 green pepper, cut into strips
¼ pound sliced mushrooms
1 cup snow pea pods
1 8-ounce can sliced water chestnuts, drained
½ cup bean sprouts

Heat olive oil in a wok or nonstick skillet; add vegetables, beginning with those requiring the most cooking time. Stir-fry until vegetables are just crisp-tender.

Note: If using a wok, pull vegetables up onto side of pan as they finish cooking.

Variation: Toss stir-fried vegetables with cooked soba (buckwheat) noodles, asparagus, scallops, or chicken. Accompany with reduced-sodium soy sauce.

APPROXIMATE NUTRITIONAL INFORMATION PER SERVING

Calories: 64
Total fat: 3 g
Saturated fat: 0 g
Percentage of calories from fat: 41%
Carbohydrate: 9 g
Protein: 2 g
Cholesterol: 0 mg
Sodium: 18 mg
Dietary fiber: 2 g

VEGETABLES ORIENTALE

8 ½-cup servings

1 pound fresh snow pea pods
1 8-ounce can water chestnuts, drained
¼ pound fresh forest mushrooms, steamed 2 to 3 minutes and sliced
1 cup bean sprouts

Snap ends of snow peas and remove strings. Arrange snow peas on a vegetable steamer rack over boiling water. Cover and steam 2 minutes; add water chestnuts and mushrooms. Steam 45 to 60 seconds longer, or until snow peas are deep green and crisp-tender.

APPROXIMATE NUTRITIONAL INFORMATION PER SERVING

Calories: 55
Total fat: trace
Saturated fat: 0 g
Percentage of calories from fat: 5%
Carbohydrate: 11 g
Protein: 3 g
Cholesterol: 0 mg
Sodium: 6 mg
Dietary fiber: 3 g

HOLIDAY YAMS WITH MARSHMALLOWS

8 servings

2 Red Delicious apples, sliced
⅓ cup chopped pecans
⅓ cup brown sugar
½ teaspoon cinnamon
1 28-ounce can yams, drained
1 cup miniature marshmallows

(continued on next page)

(continued from preceding page)

Toss apples and nuts with combined brown sugar and cinnamon. Alternate layers of apple mixture and yams in a 1½-quart ovenproof casserole. Cover and bake at 350° for 35 to 40 minutes. Sprinkle with marshmallows; broil 6 to 8 minutes or until lightly browned.

APPROXIMATE NUTRITIONAL INFORMATION PER SERVING

Calories: 141	Carbohydrate: 32 g
Total fat: 2 g	Protein: 1 g
Saturated fat: 0 g	Cholesterol: 0 mg
Percentage of calories from fat: 11%	Sodium: 10 mg
	Dietary fiber: 2 g

GRILLED ZUCCHINI

4 servings

2 small zucchini
Juice of ½ lemon
Freshly ground pepper

Cut zucchini lengthwise into quarters. Sprinkle with lemon juice and black pepper. Wrap in foil. Grill 10 to 15 minutes, or until hot and crisp-tender.

APPROXIMATE NUTRITIONAL INFORMATION PER SERVING

Calories: 11	Carbohydrate: 3 g
Total fat: trace	Protein: 1 g
Saturated fat: 0 g	Cholesterol: 0 mg
Percentage of calories from fat: 7%	Sodium: 2 mg
	Dietary fiber: 0 g

PASTA

Spaghetti and Meatballs

16 servings

1 28-ounce can plum tomatoes
1 28-ounce can tomato purée
1 12-ounce can tomato paste
1 8-ounce can tomato sauce
3 cups water
1½ teaspoons salt
1 tablespoon chopped fresh basil or
  1½ teaspoons dried
1½ teaspoons minced fresh oregano or
  ¾ teaspoon dried
3 extra-lean pork loin chops

Meatballs

2 pounds extra-lean ground round
Freshly ground black pepper to taste
1 cup dry bread crumbs
2 eggs
½ cup nonfat milk
½ cup chopped parsley

2 pounds spaghetti, cooked al dente

Purée tomatoes in a blender; pour into a stockpot. Add tomato purée, tomato paste, tomato sauce, water, salt, basil, and oregano. Stir thoroughly to combine ingredients. Heat just to boiling, but do not allow to boil. Reduce to a simmer.

Trim all visible fat from pork chops. In a nonstick skillet, brown chops for 3 to 4 minutes on each side. Drain and discard any excess fat. Add chops to sauce.

In a medium bowl, sprinkle ground round with pepper; add bread crumbs, eggs, milk, and parsley.

Knead until mixture is smooth and ingredients are combined, adding a little milk if needed for moisture. Form into approximately 32 firm golf-ball-size meatballs. Add meatballs to sauce and continue to simmer the sauce over low heat for 2 to 2½ hours.

APPROXIMATE NUTRITIONAL INFORMATION PER SERVING (1 CUP PASTA, ¾ CUP SAUCE, AND 1 MEATBALL)

Calories: 369
Total fat: 8 g
Saturated fat: 2 g
Percentage of calories from fat: 19%
Carbohydrate: 54 g
Protein: 22 g
Cholesterol: 49 mg
Sodium: 265 mg
Dietary fiber: 2 g

APPROXIMATE NUTRITIONAL INFORMATION PER EACH ADDITIONAL MEATBALL

Calories: 62
Total fat: 3 g
Saturated fat: 1 g
Percentage of calories from fat: 40%
Carbohydrate: 3 g
Protein: 6 g
Cholesterol: 31 mg
Sodium: 52 mg
Dietary fiber: 1 g

MEATLESS SPAGHETTI SAUCE

Prepare recipe for Spaghetti and Meatballs above; omitting the pork chops and the meatballs.

APPROXIMATE NUTRITIONAL INFORMATION PER SERVING (1 CUP PASTA AND ¾ CUP SAUCE)

Calories: 263
Total fat: 3 g
Saturated fat: 0 g
Percentage of calories from fat: 9%
Carbohydrate: 52 g
Protein: 11 g
Cholesterol: 0 mg
Sodium: 398 mg
Dietary fiber: 2 g

Spaghetti and Meatballs with Sausage

16 servings

6 extra-lean Italian sausages
1 recipe Spaghetti and Meatballs (page 488)

Select the leanest Italian sausages you can find (ask the butcher in your supermarket if he can special order or make extra-lean sausages in house for you).

In a nonstick skillet over medium-high heat, sauté the sausages for 8 to 10 minutes, turning frequently, or microwave the sausages in a covered, microwave-proof dish at full power for 8 to 10 minutes, turning once.

Cut the partially cooked sausages into thirds; add to spaghetti sauce along with the meatballs. Simmer over low heat for 2 to 2½ hours as directed in the recipe.

APPROXIMATE NUTRITIONAL INFORMATION PER SERVING (1 CUP PASTA, ¾ CUP SAUCE, ⅓ SAUSAGE, 1 MEATBALL)

Calories: 466	Carbohydrate: 54 g
Total fat: 15 g	Protein: 27 g
Saturated fat: 4 g	Cholesterol: 49 mg
Percentage of calories from fat: 29%	Sodium: 460 mg
	Dietary fiber: 2 g

PASTA WITH MARINARA SAUCE

8 servings

1 28-ounce can plum tomatoes
2 tablespoons tomato paste
1 teaspoon minced fresh oregano or ½ teaspoon dried
¼ cup chopped fresh basil or ½ teaspoon dried
½ teaspoon pepper
2 teaspoons olive oil
½ teaspoon salt, or to taste (optional)
1 8-ounce can mushroom stems and pieces, drained
¾ pound penne or corkscrew pasta, cooked al dente

Purée tomatoes in a blender or food processor; pour into a medium saucepan. Add tomato paste, oregano, basil, and pepper. Simmer 20 minutes (do not allow to boil). Stir in olive oil, salt, if needed, and mushrooms. Simmer 5 minutes. Serve over pasta.

Note: This is one of my favorite quick-to-fix dinners.

APPROXIMATE NUTRITIONAL INFORMATION PER SERVING

Calories: 197
Total fat: 3 g
Saturated fat: 0 g
Percentage of calories from fat: 15%
Carbohydrate: 36 g
Protein: 8 g
Cholesterol: 0 mg
Sodium: 284 mg
Dietary fiber: 1 g

LASAGNE

10 servings

1½ pounds extra-lean ground round
1 garlic clove
1 small onion
3 14½-ounce cans plum tomatoes
2 tablespoons olive oil
3 8-ounce cans tomato sauce
1 teaspoon salt
1 teaspoon minced fresh oregano or ½ teaspoon dried
3 fresh basil sprigs or 1 teaspoon dried
¼ teaspoon pepper
2 bunches fresh spinach
2 cups skim ricotta cheese
1 12-ounce package lasagne, cooked and drained
Crushed red pepper
1 pound reduced-fat mozzarella cheese, grated

Brown ground round with garlic and onion in a nonstick skillet; drain excess fat. Set aside. Purée tomatoes in a blender; add olive oil, tomato sauce, and spices. Whirl 2 to 3 minutes. Set aside.

Wash spinach; shake dry and remove any tough stems. Steam in a covered skillet for 2 to 3 minutes, or until wilted. Squeeze dry; chop. Combine spinach, ground round, and ricotta.

Cover bottom of a 13 x 9 x 2-inch pan with tomato sauce. Add a layer of lasagne. Spread with meat mixture. Sprinkle with red pepper. Add a layer of mozzarella. Cover with sauce. Repeat layers two to three more times. Pour remaining sauce over final layer. Top with additional cheese. Bake covered at 350° for 45 to 60 minutes. (For a smaller group, use two 8-inch square pans and freeze one.)

This dish is not low in sodium. By accompanying it with low-sodium foods and selecting low-sodium foods at breakfast and lunch, it's possible to keep the sodium intake for the day in balance.

Variation: Use extra-lean Italian sausage in place of ground round. Remove and discard the casing and brown the sausage in place of ground round.

APPROXIMATE NUTRITIONAL INFORMATION PER SERVING USING EXTRA-LEAN GROUND ROUND

Calories: 423
Total fat: 15 g
Saturated fat: 3 g
Percentage of
calories from fat: 31%
Carbohydrate: 40 g
Protein: 34 g
Cholesterol: 55 mg
Sodium: 938 mg
Dietary fiber: 3 g

APPROXIMATE NUTRITIONAL INFORMATION PER SERVING USING SAUSAGE IN PLACE OF GROUND ROUND

Calories: 430
Total fat: 17 g
Saturated fat: 4 g
Percentage of
calories from fat: 35%
Carbohydrate: 40 g
Protein: 30 g
Cholesterol: 60 mg
Sodium: 1122 mg
Dietary fiber: 3 g

MEATLESS LASAGNE

Prepare recipe for Lasagne omitting the ground round or sausage. It's equally delicious.

APPROXIMATE NUTRITIONAL INFORMATION PER SERVING

Calories: 321
Total fat: 9 g
Saturated fat: 1 g
Percentage of
calories from fat: 24%
Carbohydrate: 40 g
Protein: 23 g
Cholesterol: 20 mg
Sodium: 906 mg
Dietary fiber: 3 g

LINGUINE WITH CLAM SAUCE

8 servings

4 to 5 garlic cloves*
1 tablespoon olive oil*
1 28-ounce can plum tomatoes, diced
1 cup dry white wine
¾ teaspoon salt
¼ teaspoon pepper
2 6½-ounce cans chopped clams with liquid
2 pounds fresh steamer clams, cleaned and steamed (page 513)
1 pound linguine
¼ cup chopped fresh parsley

Combine garlic and olive oil (if time permits let mellow at least 24 hours—several days is even better).

In a small stockpot, combine garlic and oil with tomatoes, wine, salt, pepper, and chopped clams; simmer uncovered for 15 to 20 minutes. Meanwhile, steam clams and cook linguine.

To serve, ladle linguine into soup bowls, cover with sauce. Top with freshly steamed clams in their shells. Sprinkle with parsley.

Note: Orvieto Classico is our favorite wine to use in preparing this dish.

* Or use 1 tablespoon Garlic Olive Oil (page 431).

APPROXIMATE NUTRITIONAL INFORMATION PER SERVING

Calories: 348
Total fat: 4 g
Saturated fat: 0 g
Percentage of calories from fat: 10%
Carbohydrate: 50 g
Protein: 22 g
Cholesterol: 36 mg
Sodium: 439 mg
Dietary fiber: 3 g

LINGUINE WITH CALAMARI

8 servings

1½ pounds squid
1 cup white wine
2 garlic cloves
1 pound linguine, cooked al dente
¼ cup olive oil
Juice of 1 lemon
½ teaspoon salt
¼ teaspoon pepper
3 ripe tomatoes, coarsely chopped
2 tablespoons chopped fresh parsley

Thoroughly wash squid; split and remove cartilage, eyes, and ink sacs.

Heat wine and garlic in a wok or heavy skillet. Sauté squid for 3 to 5 minutes, or just until color changes and squid become tender; do not overcook or squid will become rubbery. Drain off liquid.

Arrange squid over pasta; sprinkle with olive oil, lemon juice, salt, pepper, tomatoes, and parsley. Toss until squid and linguine are well coated.

Note: If you are not familiar with the proper method to clean squid, ask the personnel at your fish market to show you.

Variation: To make a red calamari sauce, decrease the olive oil to 3 tablespoons and add 1 28-ounce can plum tomatoes, diced, and an additional ¼ teaspoon salt.

(continued on next page)

(continued from preceding page)

APPROXIMATE NUTRITIONAL INFORMATION PER SERVING

Calories: 371	Carbohydrate: 43 g
Total fat: 10 g	Protein: 22 g
Saturated fat: 1 g	Cholesterol: 198 mg
Percentage of calories from fat: 25%	Sodium: 176 mg
	Dietary fiber: 2 g

APPROXIMATE NUTRITIONAL INFORMATION PER SERVING FOR RED CALAMARI SAUCE

Calories: 377	Carbohydrate: 47 g
Total fat: 9 g	Protein: 23 g
Saturated fat: 1 g	Cholesterol: 198 mg
Percentage of calories from fat: 21%	Sodium: 413 mg
	Dietary fiber: 3 g

ORZO WITH STEAMED VEGETABLES

8 servings

- 1 bunch fresh asparagus
- ½ bunch fresh broccoli florets
- ⅓ head cauliflower florets
- 1½ cups snow peas
- 1 pound orzo, cooked al dente
- 1 English cucumber, peeled, halved, and sliced
- 2 tablespoons reduced-sodium soy sauce

Separately steam asparagus, broccoli, cauliflower, and snow peas in the microwave or in a vegetable steamer rack over boiling water for 2 to 3 minutes, or until just crisp-tender. Arrange orzo in a casserole dish. Toss with steamed vegetables. Sprinkle cucumber over top. Add soy sauce and toss lightly.

APPROXIMATE NUTRITIONAL INFORMATION PER SERVING

Calories: 247	Carbohydrate: 49 g
Total fat: 1 g	Protein: 11 g
Saturated fat: 0 g	Cholesterol: 0 mg
Percentage of calories from fat: 5%	Sodium: 157 mg
	Dietary fiber: 3 g

MOSTACCIOLI WITH TOMATOES AND BASIL

8 servings

- 6 large ripe tomatoes
- 1½ cups basil leaves
- 6 large garlic cloves, minced
- ⅓ cup olive oil
- ¾ teaspoon salt
- ¼ teaspoon pepper
- 1 pound mostaccioli or other tubular pasta
- 1 cup freshly grated Parmesan cheese

Cut tomatoes into ½-inch chunks. Coarsely chop 1 cup of the basil leaves; reserve the remaining basil leaves for garnish. Combine tomatoes with chopped basil; add garlic, olive oil, salt, and pepper; toss. Let stand for 1 hour at room temperature.

Cook pasta; drain. Toss with tomatoes while pasta is still hot. Sprinkle with Parmesan cheese. Garnish with remaining ½ cup basil leaves.

APPROXIMATE NUTRITIONAL INFORMATION PER SERVING

Calories: 373	Carbohydrate: 49 g
Total fat: 14 g	Protein: 14 g
Saturated fat: 4 g	Cholesterol: 10 mg
Percentage of calories from fat: 34%	Sodium: 442 mg
	Dietary fiber: 3 g

Seafood Fettuccine

6 servings

1 pound mussels
1 pound steamer clams
3 gallons water for soaking solution
1 cup cornmeal for soaking solution
1 medium onion, chopped
3 garlic cloves, minced
1 tablespoon olive oil
1 14½-ounce can plum tomatoes
1 16-ounce can tomato purée
1 6-ounce can tomato paste
1½ cups water
½ teaspoon minced fresh oregano or ¼ teaspoon dried
3 fresh basil sprigs or 1 teaspoon dried
1 teaspoon salt, or to taste
½ green pepper, sliced
½ pound sea scallops, red snapper, bass, or cod
1 pound fettuccine, cooked al dente
¼ pound crab legs for garnish

Scrub mussel shells with a wire brush. Remove and discard beards. Rinse mussels in cold water; discard broken or open mussels.

Scrub clams. Place in a large bowl and cover with cold water. Sprinkle with cornmeal and let stand 30 minutes. Drain and rinse; discard cornmeal.

Arrange clams and mussels on a rack in a steamer; add 2 cups hot water. Cover tightly and steam over medium-high heat 6 to 8 minutes, or just until shells open. Set aside.

Sauté onion and garlic in olive oil; add all remaining ingredients except seafood and pasta. Bring to a boil; reduce heat. Simmer 20 to 30 minutes. Meanwhile, preheat a nonstick skillet; add scallops. Cook, turning frequently, 4 to 6 minutes, or just until scallops are tender. Drain any liquid.

Just before serving, add clams, mussels, and scallops to sauce. Divide pasta among individual bowls. Serve sauce over pasta. Garnish with crab legs.

APPROXIMATE NUTRITIONAL INFORMATION PER SERVING

Calories: 478
Total fat: 8 g
Saturated fat: 1 g
Percentage of calories from fat: 14%
Carbohydrate: 75 g
Protein: 30 g
Cholesterol: 40 mg
Sodium: 661 mg
Dietary fiber: 4 g

PENNE WITH PRAWNS, OLIVES, AND TOMATOES

10 servings

2 teaspoons Garlic Olive Oil (page 431), or 2 teaspoons olive oil plus 2 minced garlic cloves
1 pound large prawns, shelled and deveined
¼ cup olive oil
2 tablespoons balsamic vinegar
3 large garlic cloves
1 teaspoon salt
½ teaspoon pepper
3 cups fresh basil leaves
1 pound penne or other tube-shaped pasta, cooked al dente
1½ pounds ripe tomatoes, cut into 1-inch cubes
1 cup kalamata olives, pitted and halved

In a nonstick skillet over medium-high heat, heat Garlic Olive Oil; add prawns and cook 5 to 6 minutes, or until prawns are cooked. Remove from heat.

(coninued on next page)

(coninued from preceding page)

In a blender or food processor, combine olive oil, vinegar, garlic, salt, pepper, and 2 cups of the basil; whirl 1 minute. Pour over penne while pasta is still warm. Add tomatoes and olives, toss. Add prawns; toss again. Garnish with remaining basil leaves.

Serving Suggestion: Serve with French bread and fresh fruit.

APPROXIMATE NUTRITIONAL INFORMATION PER SERVING

Calories: 311	Carbohydrate: 39 g
Total fat: 12 g	Protein: 13 g
Saturated fat: 1 g	Cholesterol: 52 mg
Percentage of calories from fat: 33%	Sodium: 274 mg
	Dietary fiber: 1 g

PENNE WITH SUN-DRIED TOMATOES

8 servings

- 4 large ripe tomatoes, coarsely chopped
- 10 oil-packed sun-dried tomatoes, drained and coarsely chopped
- 6 large garlic cloves, chopped
- ¼ cup olive oil
- ½ teaspoon salt
- ¼ teaspoon pepper
- 1½ cups fresh basil leaves
- 1 pound penne
- Crushed red pepper (optional)

Combine ripe tomatoes, sun-dried tomatoes, garlic, olive oil, salt, and pepper. Let stand at room temperature for 1 hour. Coarsely chop 1 cup of the basil leaves; reserve the remaining leaves for garnish.

Cook pasta; drain. While pasta is still hot, toss with tomato mixture. Add chopped basil and toss again. Just before serving, garnish with remaining basil leaves. Accompany with crushed red pepper, if desired.

Serving Suggestion: Great as a main course with crusty French bread or as an accompaniment to an entrée of grilled salmon or swordfish.

APPROXIMATE NUTRITIONAL INFORMATION PER SERVING

Calories: 299
Total fat: 10 g
Saturated fat: 1 g
Percentage of calories from fat: 29%
Carbohydrate: 46 g
Protein: 10 g
Cholesterol: 0 mg
Sodium: 197 mg
Dietary fiber: 3 g

FUSILLI WITH CHICKEN AND VEGETABLES

8 servings

1 tablespoon sesame oil
1 whole chicken breast, skinned, boned and diced
1 tablespoon minced fresh ginger
5 garlic cloves, minced
5 cups broccoli florets
1½ cups snow peas
1 bunch green onions, chopped
⅓ cup reduced-sodium soy sauce
⅓ cup dry sherry
1 tablespoon olive oil
2 tablespoons rice wine vinegar
¾ drops hot chili oil
2 8-ounce packages soba noodles

(continued on next page)

(continued from preceding page)

Heat sesame oil in a nonstick skillet or wok. Add chicken and stir-fry 2 to 3 minutes. Add ginger, garlic, broccoli, snow peas, and green onion, and stir-fry 2 to 3 minutes longer. Meanwhile, combine soy sauce, sherry, olive oil, rice vinegar, and hot chili oil. Pour over chicken and vegetables; cook 30 seconds longer. Remove wok from heat. Add pasta. Toss.

APPROXIMATE NUTRITIONAL INFORMATION PER SERVING

Calories: 336	Carbohydrate: 52 g
Total fat: 5 g	Protein: 17 g
Saturated fat: 1 g	Cholesterol: 18 mg
Percentage of calories from fat: 15%	Sodium: 572 mg
	Dietary fiber: 4 g

Pasta and Cannellini Beans

8 servings

- 2 tablespoons olive oil, preferably Garlic Olive Oil (page 431)
- 4 garlic cloves, finely chopped
- 1½ pound ripe plum tomatoes, coarsely chopped
- 15 fresh sage leaves, chopped
- 1 15-ounce can cannellini beans, rinsed and drained
- ¼ teaspoon salt
- ¼ teaspoon pepper
- 1 pound rigatoni, cooked al dente
- 10 whole fresh sage leaves for garnish

Heat olive oil in a medium saucepan; add garlic and sauté 3 to 4 minutes, or until just tender. Add tomatoes and chopped sage leaves; simmer 5 minutes, until tomatoes begin to soften. Add cannellini beans; simmer 5 minutes longer. Season with salt and pepper.

Toss pasta with sauce. Transfer to a serving bowl. Garnish with remaining fresh sage leaves.

APPROXIMATE NUTRITIONAL INFORMATION PER SERVING

Calories: 296
Total fat: 6 g
Saturated fat: 1 g
Percentage of calories from fat: 19%
Carbohydrate: 52 g
Protein: 13 g
Cholesterol: 0 mg
Sodium: 136 mg
Dietary fiber: 5 g

MEDITERRANEAN PASTA

8 servings

3 large ripe tomatoes, chopped
2 tablespoons olive oil
½ cup chopped fresh parsley
1 bunch green onions with tops, chopped
½ teaspoon chopped fresh basil, or ¼ teaspoon dried
1 lemon
1 6⅛-ounce can water-packed tuna, drained
1 teaspoon pepper
1 pound penne, cooked al dente

Combine tomatoes, olive oil, parsley, green onion, and basil; cook 5 to 7 minutes. Squeeze lemon over tuna. Grate rind of lemon; sprinkle over tuna and toss with pepper. Add to tomatoes and onion; cook 5 to 7 minutes. Serve over penne.

APPROXIMATE NUTRITIONAL INFORMATION PER SERVING

Calories: 285
Total fat: 6 g
Saturated fat: 1 g
Percentage of calories from fat: 19%
Carbohydrate: 45 g
Protein: 15 g
Cholesterol: 6 mg
Sodium: 84 mg
Dietary fiber: 2 g

Pasta with Pesto and Tomatoes

8 servings

1 cup loosely packed fresh basil leaves
3 to 4 garlic cloves
¼ cup freshly squeezed lemon juice
⅓ cup pine nuts
½ teaspoon salt
¼ teaspoon pepper
1 pound rotelli, cooked al dente
3 large fresh ripe tomatoes, diced
¼ cup freshly grated Parmesan cheese

In a food processor, combine basil, garlic, lemon juice, pine nuts, salt and pepper; whirl 1 to 2 minutes, or until basil and garlic are coarsely chopped. Pour over pasta. Add tomatoes and toss. Transfer to pasta bowls. Sprinkle with Parmesan cheese.

*Variation**: Rub 1 whole boneless, skinless chicken breast with ½ teaspoon olive oil. Grill over hot coals for 6 to 7 minutes on each side, or until chicken is cooked. Dice. Add to Pasta with Pesto and Tomatoes; toss and sprinkle with Parmesan.

APPROXIMATE NUTRITIONAL INFORMATION PER SERVING

Calories: 267	Carbohydrate: 47 g
Total fat: 5 g	Protein: 10 g
Saturated fat: 1 g	Cholesterol: 2 mg
Percentage of calories from fat: 16%	Sodium: 191 mg
	Dietary fiber: 3 g

*Add 38 calories, 1 g total fat, 1% to percentage of calories from fat, 7 g protein, 18 mg cholesterol, and 16 mg sodium for the addition of the chicken breast.

RIGATONI WITH EGGPLANT, MUSHROOMS, AND TOMATOES

8 servings

- 1 medium eggplant, peeled and diced (about 4 cups)
- 1 tablespoon salt (to be rinsed off)
- ½ teaspoon olive oil
- 2 cups sliced fresh mushrooms (about 20)
- ⅓ cup diced sun-dried tomatoes
- 1 28-ounce can plum tomatoes, diced
- ½ teaspoon salt
- ½ teaspoon pepper
- ½ teaspoon dried oregano
- 3 tablespoons chopped fresh basil or ¾ teaspoon dried
- 1 pound rigatoni, cooked al dente

In a colander, toss eggplant with 1 tablespoon salt and allow to drain for 30 to 60 minutes. Rinse eggplant with water and drain well; pat dry.

In a medium nonstick skillet, heat olive oil. Add eggplant and sauté over medium-high heat 3 to 4 minutes; add mushrooms and sauté 2 to 3 minutes longer. Set aside.

In a medium saucepan, combine sun-dried tomatoes, plum tomatoes, salt, pepper, oregano and basil; simmer 8 to 10 minutes. Add eggplant and mushrooms; simmer 5 minutes. Serve over rigatoni.

APPROXIMATE NUTRITIONAL INFORMATION PER SERVING

Calories: 257
Total fat: 2 g
Saturated fat: 0 g
Percentage of calories from fat: 6%
Carbohydrate: 52 g
Protein: 9 g
Cholesterol: 0 mg
Sodium: 630 mg
Dietary fiber: 4 g

Macaroni with Chicken and Beans

Approximately 12 cups

1 28-ounce can plum tomatoes, diced
½ teaspoon salt
1½ teaspoons dry mustard
1½ teaspoons chili powder
2 small garlic cloves, minced
1 pound chicken breast, skinned, boned, cooked, and diced
2 15-ounce cans kidney beans, drained
2 cups cooked elbow macaroni

Combine tomatoes, salt, dry mustard, chili powder, and garlic; simmer uncovered for 20 to 30 minutes. Add chicken and kidney beans; heat just to boiling. Just before serving, stir in macaroni. Heat to serving temperature.

Variation: Ground round can be used in place of chicken.

APPROXIMATE NUTRITIONAL INFORMATION PER 1-CUP SERVING

Calories: 171
Total fat: 2 g
Saturated fat: 0 g
Percentage of calories from fat: 11%
Carbohydrate: 18 g
Protein: 20 g
Cholesterol: 38 mg
Sodium: 282 mg
Dietary fiber: 5 g

APPROXIMATE NUTRITIONAL INFORMATION PER 1-CUP SERVING USING GROUND ROUND INSTEAD OF CHICKEN

Calories: 221
Total fat: 8 g
Saturated fat: 4 g
Percentage of calories from fat: 32%
Carbohydrate: 18 g
Protein: 19 g
Cholesterol: 49 mg
Sodium: 278 mg
Dietary fiber: 5 g

PASTA SALAD WITH TURKEY, PEPPERS, OLIVES, AND TOMATOES

8 servings

1 pound fusilli or rotini, cooked al dente
1 pound smoked turkey breast, diced
1 pound fresh broccoli florets, cooked al dente
1 6-ounce jar roasted peppers, drained and diced
1 14½ ounce can water-packed artichoke hearts, drained and quartered
1 15-ounce can whole baby corn spears, drained
1 cup pitted black olives
8 plum tomatoes, quartered
6 tablespoons olive oil
2 tablespoons cider vinegar
½ teaspoon salt
¼ teaspoon pepper
½ cup freshly grated Parmesan cheese
6 sprigs fresh basil leaves for garnish

In a large salad bowl, toss pasta, turkey, broccoli, roasted red peppers, artichoke hearts, and baby corn. Chill. In a separate bowl, chill olives and tomatoes.

Just before serving, combine olive oil, vinegar, salt and pepper. Pour over pasta and vegetables. Toss. Add olives and tomatoes. Toss again. Sprinkle with Parmesan cheese. Garnish with fresh basil leaves.

APPROXIMATE NUTRITIONAL INFORMATION PER SERVING

Calories: 498
Total fat: 15 g
Saturated fat: 3 g
Percentage of calories from fat: 27%
Carbohydrate: 61 g
Protein: 31 g
Cholesterol: 51 mg
Sodium: 646 mg
Dietary fiber: 3 g

SPICY CHINESE NOODLES

6 servings

1½ cups Ginger-Flavored Chicken, (page 543)
¼ cup reduced-sodium soy sauce
2 tablespoons sesame oil
1½ tablespoons hot chili oil*
2 tablespoons sugar
2 tablespoons balsamic vinegar
2 cups chicken broth, preferably homemade, (page 364)
2 cups water
1 8-ounce package soba noodles
½ pound snow peas
⅓ pound shiitake mushrooms (about 9)**
1 8-ounce can whole water chestnuts, drained
1 5-ounce can whole baby corn spears, drained
1 bunch green onions, cut diagonally into thin strips

Prepare chicken according to recipe. Cut into strings.

Combine soy sauce, sesame oil, hot chili oil, sugar and balsamic vinegar in a covered jar; set aside.

In a 2-quart saucepan, bring chicken broth and water to a boil; add soba noodles. Stir lightly. Boil 5 to 8 minutes, or until noodles are tender. Drain and rinse.

Microwave or steam snow peas 1 to 2 minutes, or until just crisp-tender; set aside. Microwave or steam mushrooms 2 to 3 minutes, or until tender; transfer to a medium-size bowl. Slice mushrooms into thin strips and toss with ¼ cup of the marinade. Add shredded chicken and toss. Let chicken and mushrooms sit in the marinade 5 minutes.

Arrange soba noodles in a serving bowl. Add snow peas, water chestnuts, corn, mushrooms, and chicken. Toss with remaining marinade. Arrange green onions over top. Serve.

*This recipe is spicy. For a less spicy recipe, substitute olive oil for hot chili oil or reduce the amount of the hot chili oil.

**If using dried shiitake mushrooms, reconstitute them by soaking in enough water to cover for about 30 minutes, or until they become soft.

APPROXIMATE NUTRITIONAL INFORMATION PER SERVING

Calories: 182	Carbohydrate: 44 g
Total fat: 10 g	Protein: 10 g
Saturated fat: 1 g	Cholesterol: 6 mg
Percentage of calories from fat: 31%	Sodium: 493 mg
	Dietary fiber: 3 g

TUNA NOODLE CASSEROLE

4 servings

- 1 10¾-ounce can low-fat (1%) cream of chicken soup
- ½ cup nonfat milk
- 1 8-ounce package elbow macaroni, cooked al dente
- 1 6⅛-ounce can water-packed tuna, drained
- 1 8-ounce can sliced water chestnuts, drained

Warm soup in a saucepan; stir in milk. Combine with remaining ingredients. Pour into a 2-quart ovenproof casserole. Bake at 375° for 25 to 30 minutes.

APPROXIMATE NUTRITIONAL INFORMATION PER SERVING

Calories: 357	Carbohydrate: 60 g
Total fat: 3 g	Protein: 22 g
Saturated fat: 0 g	Cholesterol: 21 mg
Percentage of calories from fat: 7%	Sodium: 521 mg
	Dietary fiber: 2 g

Macaroni and Cheese

4 servings

3 large ripe tomatoes, diced
1 cup loosely packed fresh basil leaves, chopped
1 tablespoon olive oil
½ teaspoon salt
¼ teaspoon pepper
3 cups large elbow macaroni or gemelli pasta, cooked al dente
½ cup freshly grated Parmesan cheese

Combine tomatoes, basil, olive oil, salt, and pepper. Toss with pasta.

Spread mixture in a 13 x 9 x 2-inch baking dish. Sprinkle with Parmesan. Bake uncovered in a preheated 400° oven 10 minutes, or until Parmesan is lightly brown. Serve at once.

APPROXIMATE NUTRITIONAL INFORMATION PER SERVING

Calories: 248
Total fat: 6 g
Saturated fat: 2 g
Percentage of calories from fat: 25%
Carbohydrate: 38 g
Protein: 10 g
Cholesterol: 8 mg
Sodium: 288 mg
Dietary fiber: 2 g

SEAFOOD

Mussels Italian Style

Approximately 4 servings

5 dozen mussels
1 leek including greens, chopped
1 medium onion, thinly sliced
1 large garlic clove, halved
1½ cups dry vermouth
¾ cup water
½ teaspoon salt, or to taste
1 14½-ounce can plum tomatoes, diced
1 tablespoon olive oil
¼ cup chopped fresh parsley

Scrub mussel shells with a wire brush. Remove and discard beards. Rinse mussels in cold water; discard broken or open mussels.

Place mussels on a rack in a steamer or Dutch oven; add leek, onion, garlic, vermouth, water, and salt. Cover tightly and steam over medium-high heat for 6 to 8 minutes, or just until shells open. Remove to a serving dish and cover lightly to keep warm.

Boil cooking liquid for 2 to 3 minutes to reduce. Add tomatoes and olive oil. Heat to serving temperature. Pour sauce over mussels. Sprinkle with parsley.

Variation: Serve over linguine.

Serving Suggestion: Serve with tossed green salad and crusty French bread.

APPROXIMATE NUTRITIONAL INFORMATION PER SERVING

Calories: 276
Total fat: 7 g
Saturated fat: 1 g
Percentage of calories from fat: 22%
Carbohydrate: 16 g
Protein: 23 g
Cholesterol: 51 mg
Sodium: 744 mg
Dietary fiber: 2 g

STEAMED CLAMS WITH FRESH LEMON

Approximately 4 servings

5 dozen steamer clams
3 gallons cold water for soaking solution
1 cup cornmeal for soaking solution
1 bunch fresh parsley for garnish
5 fresh lemons, cut into wedges

Scrub clams. Place in a large bowl and cover with cold water. Sprinkle with cornmeal and let stand 30 minutes. Drain and rinse; discard cornmeal; discard any clams that are not tightly closed or that do not close when pressed.

Arrange clams on a rack in a steamer or Dutch oven; add 2 cups hot water. Cover tightly and steam over medium-high heat 5 to 10 minutes, or just until shells open. Discard any clams that do not open. Reserve nectar for chowder.

Arrange clams on a serving platter. Garnish with fresh parsley and lemon wedges.

Serving Suggestion: Serve with tossed green salad, toasted or grilled garlic bread, and baked potato with nonfat sour cream, chives, and green onion.

APPROXIMATE NUTRITIONAL INFORMATION PER SERVING

Calories: 82
Total fat: 1 g
Saturated fat: 0 g
Percentage of calories from fat: 13%

Carbohydrate: 17 g
Protein: 11 g
Cholesterol: 23 mg
Sodium: 47 mg
Dietary fiber: trace

Clams Italian Style

Approximately 4 servings

5 dozen steamer clams
3 gallons cold water for soaking solution
1 cup cornmeal for soaking solution
1 tablespoon olive oil
1 onion, chopped
1 garlic clove, minced
2 celery stalks, chopped
1 28-ounce can plum tomatoes, diced
¼ cup chopped fresh parsley
Freshly ground pepper

Scrub clams. Place in a large bowl and cover with cold water. Sprinkle with cornmeal and let stand 30 minutes. Drain and rinse; discard cornmeal; discard any clams that are not tightly closed or that do not close when pressed.

Arrange clams on a rack in a steamer or Dutch oven, add 2 cups hot water. Cover tightly and steam over medium-high heat 5 to 10 minutes, or just until shells open. Discard any clams that do not open. Reserve nectar for chowder.

Heat olive oil in a nonstick skillet; add onion, garlic, and celery, and sauté until tender. Add tomatoes. Reduce heat and simmer 30 minutes.

To serve, arrange clams in their shells in soup bowls; cover with tomato mixture. Sprinkle with fresh parsley and ground pepper.

APPROXIMATE NUTRITIONAL INFORMATION PER SERVING

Calories: 129	Carbohydrate: 15 g
Total fat: 4 g	Protein: 11 g
Saturated fat: 0 g	Cholesterol: 23 mg
Percentage of calories from fat: 25%	Sodium: 399 mg
	Dietary fiber: 3 g

GRILLED SCALLOPS DIJON

Approximately 4 servings

2 tablespoons prepared Dijon mustard
2 tablespoons honey
¾ teaspoon curry powder
½ teaspoon lemon juice
1 pound sea scallops
2 fresh lemons, cut into wedges
1 bunch fresh parsley for garnish

Combine mustard, honey, curry, and lemon juice; pour over scallops. Marinate 10 minutes. Remove scallops from marinade and shake off excess.

Grill scallops over hot coals or broil 4 inches from heat for 10 minutes, or until browned; turn. Brush with sauce; grill or broil 8 to 10 minutes longer, or until cooked. Serve with fresh lemon wedges. Garnish with parsley.

Variation: Skewer scallops, mushroom caps, cherry tomatoes and green peppers; brush with sauce. Grill or broil.

APPROXIMATE NUTRITIONAL INFORMATION PER SERVING

Calories: 134
Total fat: 1 g
Saturated fat: 0 g
Percentage of calories from fat: 10%
Carbohydrate: 18 g
Protein: 17 g
Cholesterol: 30 mg
Sodium: 250 mg
Dietary fiber: 0 g

APPROXIMATE NUTRITIONAL INFORMATION PER SERVING OF VARIATION

Calories: 151
Total fat: 1 g
Saturated fat: 0 g
Percentage of calories from fat: 10%
Carbohydrate: 23 g
Cholesterol: 30 mg
Sodium: 256 mg
Dietary fiber: 2 g

Pan-Fried Scallops and Prawns

4 servings

½ pound medium prawns
½ teaspoon olive oil
½ pound sea scallops
2 fresh lemons, cut into wedges
1 bunch fresh parsley for garnish

Peel and devein prawns, leaving tails on. Heat olive oil in a nonstick skillet. Add scallops and sauté over medium-high heat for 2 to 3 minutes on each side; add prawns and cook 2 to 3 minutes longer, or until scallops and shrimp are cooked. Serve with plenty of fresh lemon and garnish with parsley.

Note: I peel and devein the prawns early in the day so that I can complete this recipe and have it on the table in only about 5 minutes. This is a great company meal and goes well with Pasta with Pesto and Tomatoes (page 504) or Penne with Sun-Dried Tomatoes (page 500).

APPROXIMATE NUTRITIONAL INFORMATION PER SERVING

Calories: 125
Total fat: 2 g
Saturated fat: 0 g
Percentage of calories from fat: 15%
Carbohydrate: 8 g
Protein: 21 g
Cholesterol: 105 mg
Sodium: 177 mg
Dietary fiber: 0 g

MARINATED GRILLED PRAWNS

4 servings

16 large prawns
¼ cup olive oil
1½ teaspoons balsamic vinegar
2 tablespoons fresh lemon juice
4 garlic cloves, chopped
2 tablespoons chopped fresh basil or
  1 tablespoon dried
1½ teaspoon minced fresh oregano or
  ¾ teaspoon dried
¾ teaspoon pepper
2 tablespoons chopped fresh Italian parsley

Shell and devein prawns; pat dry.

In a shallow glass bowl, combine olive oil, balsamic vinegar, lemon juice, garlic, basil, oregano, pepper, and Italian parsley. Add prawns. Marinate 20 to 30 minutes, turning each prawn two or three times to coat with sauce. Remove prawns from marinade and shake off excess.

Thread prawns onto metal skewers. Grill over hot coals for 8 to 10 minutes, turning frequently, until prawns turn pink and are cooked.

Serving Suggestion: Grilled Peppers and Onions (page 469) are good with this recipe. Skewer them along with the prawns.

APPROXIMATE NUTRITIONAL INFORMATION PER SERVING

Calories: 103
Total fat: 5 g
Saturated fat: 1 g
Percentage of
  calories from fat: 43%

Carbohydrate: 3 g
Protein: 12 g
Cholesterol: 86 mg
Sodium: 85 mg
Dietary fiber: 0 g

TERIYAKI SHRIMP

4 servings

16 large shrimp (approximately ½ pound)
¼ cup reduced-sodium soy sauce
1 tablespoon brown sugar
2 tablespoons fresh lemon juice
½ teaspoon dry sherry
1 2-inch piece fresh ginger root, peeled and sliced
3 garlic cloves, chopped

Shell and devein shrimp; pat dry.

In a shallow glass bowl, combine soy sauce, brown sugar, lemon juice, sherry, ginger root, and garlic. Add shrimp. Marinate 20 to 30 minutes, turning each shrimp two or three times to coat with sauce. Remove shrimp from marinade and shake off excess.

Thread shrimp onto metal skewers. Grill over hot coals for 8 to 10 minutes, turning frequently, until shrimp turn pink and are cooked.

Serving Suggestion: Grilled Peppers and Onions (page 469) are good with this recipe. Skewer them along with the shrimp. Accompany with Saffron Rice (page 439).

APPROXIMATE NUTRITIONAL INFORMATION PER SERVING

Calories: 87
Total fat: 1 g
Saturated fat: 0 g
Percentage of calories from fat: 11%

Carbohydrate: 7 g
Protein: 12 g
Cholesterol: 86 mg
Sodium: 312 mg
Dietary fiber: 0 g

GRILLED LOBSTER TAILS

4 servings

4 6-ounce lobster tails
2 teaspoons olive oil
1 tablespoon dry white wine
2 fresh lemons, cut into wedges
1 bunch fresh parsley for garnish

Split lobster tail lengthwise halfway through the body; spread tail open. Remove whole meat from tails. Bend shells backward until cracked in several places. Replace meat in shells. Insert skewers lengthwise between shell and meat to prevent curling. Baste with olive oil.

Grill over hot coals for 5 to 10 minutes on shell side; turn and cook 5 minutes longer on flesh side. Baste with wine the last 2 minutes. Serve with lemon wedges. Garnish with parsley.

Variation: To broil, place on broiler rack 3 inches from heat; broil 6 to 8 minutes on shell side. Turn; broil 5 to 10 minutes on flesh side. Baste with wine the last 2 minutes. To bake, bake uncovered at 475° for 16 minutes; baste.

Note: If using frozen lobster tails, thaw before cooking.

APPROXIMATE NUTRITIONAL INFORMATION PER SERVING

Calories: 107
Total fat: 3 g
Saturated fat: 0 g
Percentage of calories from fat: 27%
Carbohydrate: 7 g
Protein: 15 g
Cholesterol: 73 mg
Sodium: 439 mg
Dietary fiber: 0 g

STUFFED SALMON

Approximately 8 4-ounce servings

1 3-pound whole salmon, steelhead, trout, cod, or other whole fish, head and tail removed
2 teaspoons olive oil
Fresh or dried sage to taste
Pepper to taste
1 onion, sliced into rings
2 celery stalks, cut into 3-inch lengths
¼ pound fresh mushrooms, sliced
2 carrots, peeled, quartered, and cut into 2-inch lengths
2 fresh lemons, sliced into rounds

Rub fish inside and out with olive oil; season with sage and pepper. Stuff inside cavity to bulging with onions, celery, mushrooms, and carrots.

Arrange fish on aluminum foil; slide a layer of lemon slices under fish. Place more lemon slices on top of fish (fish should be smothered top and bottom with lemon rounds). Wrap in two thicknesses of foil. Bake at 425° or grill over deep coals until fish flakes.

APPROXIMATE NUTRITIONAL INFORMATION PER SERVING

Calories: 286
Total fat: 14 g
Saturated fat: 2 g
Percentage of calories from fat: 45%
Carbohydrate: 7 g
Protein: 33 g
Cholesterol: 102 mg
Sodium: 94 mg
Dietary fiber: 1 g

Grilled Salmon Fillet

Approximately 4 servings

1 pound fillet of salmon, halibut, swordfish, pike, or other similar fish
2 teaspoons olive oil
Pinch of fresh or dried thyme
Pinch of fresh or dried fennel
2 fresh lemons, cut into wedges

Rub fish with olive oil. Season.

Prepare coals. Generously oil grill. Cook fish 3 to 4 inches above the coal bed, turning only once. Serve with plenty of fresh lemon.

APPROXIMATE NUTRITIONAL INFORMATION PER SERVING

Calories: 275
Total fat: 15 g
Saturated fat: 2 g
Percentage of calories from fat: 49%
Carbohydrate: 6 g
Protein: 32 g
Cholesterol: 99 mg
Sodium: 76 mg
Dietary fiber: 0 g

GRILLED SWORDFISH STEAK

Approximately 4 servings

1 pound fillet of swordfish, halibut, lingcod, red snapper, or other white fish
2 teaspoons olive oil
2 garlic cloves, minced
Dash of paprika

Rub fish with olive oil and garlic. Sprinkle with paprika. Grill over hot coals 5 to 10 minutes, or until fish flakes, turning only once; do not overcook.

Notes: The Canadian Department of Fisheries suggests measuring the fish at the thickest point and allowing 10 minutes cooking time per inch. If a salmon measures 3 inches at its thickest point, the total cooking time would be 30 minutes, 15 minutes per side. A halibut fillet that is 1 inch thick would require 10 minutes total cooking time, 5 minutes per side. Always test fish a few minutes early to avoid overcooking.

Fish is done the second it loses translucency and flakes easily when probed with a fork at its thickest point. When testing a whole fish, probe an inch or two below the base of the head, and again at the thickest point behind the abdominal cavity. When fish is opaque and milky and detaches easily from the bone, it is done.

APPROXIMATE NUTRITIONAL INFORMATION PER SERVING USING SWORDFISH

Calories: 198
Total fat: 8 g
Saturated fat: 2 g
Percentage of calories from fat: 37%
Carbohydrate: 1 g
Protein: 29 g
Cholesterol: 57 mg
Sodium: 131 mg
Dietary fiber: 0 g

APPROXIMATE NUTRITIONAL INFORMATION PER SERVING USING HALIBUT

Calories: 181
Total fat: 6 g
Saturated fat: 0 g
Percentage of calories from fat: 28%
Carbohydrate: 1 g
Protein: 30 g
Cholesterol: 47 mg
Sodium: 79 mg
Dietary fiber: 0 g

MARINATED GRILLED TUNA STEAK

4 servings

½ cup reduced-sodium soy sauce
1 tablespoon sesame oil
1 tablespoon fresh lemon juice
2 tablespoons mirin (sweet cooking wine)
3 garlic cloves
1 2-inch piece fresh gingerroot, peeled
1 tablespoon crushed red pepper
1 pound fresh tuna, swordfish, or mahimahi
2 lemons, cut into wedges

Combine soy sauce, sesame oil, lemon juice, mirin, garlic, gingerroot, and red pepper. Pour over tuna. Marinate 20 to 30 minutes. Remove tuna from marinade and shake off excess. Grill over hot coals for 6 to 8 minutes on each side, or until tuna is done. Serve with plenty of fresh lemon.

APPROXIMATE NUTRITIONAL INFORMATION PER SERVING

Calories: 190
Total fat: 3 g
Saturated fat: 1 g
Percentage of calories from fat: 13%
Carbohydrate: 7 g
Protein: 36 g
Cholesterol: 65 mg
Sodium: 451 mg
Dietary fiber: 0 g

Grilled Halibut with Salsa Fresca

4 servings

1 pound fillet of halibut
1 teaspoon olive oil
¼ cup lime juice
2 tablespoons chopped cilantro
4 plum tomatoes, diced
2 tablespoons diced green chilies
3 garlic cloves, chopped
1 small onion, chopped
1 tablespoon olive oil
½ teaspoon salt
½ teaspoon pepper
1 bunch fresh cilantro for garnish
1 fresh lemon for garnish

Arrange halibut in an 8-inch square dish. Mix 1 teaspoon olive oil with lime juice; pour over fish. Sprinkle cilantro over top. Marinate 15 to 20 minutes.

In a separate bowl, combine tomatoes, green chilies, garlic, onion, 1 tablespoon olive oil, salt, and pepper to make the salsa.

Remove halibut from marinade and shake off excess. Grill over hot coals for 4 to 6 minutes; turn; grill 4 to 6 minutes longer, or until fish flakes easily when pricked with a fork. Arrange fresh cilantro over serving tray. Top with halibut. Garnish with lemon. Accompany with salsa.

APPROXIMATE NUTRITIONAL INFORMATION PER SERVING

Calories: 247
Total fat: 8 g
Saturated fat: 1 g
Percentage of calories from fat: 31%
Carbohydrate: 13 g
Protein: 32 g
Cholesterol: 47 mg
Sodium: 359 mg
Dietary fiber: 1 g

ROAST HALIBUT ON A BED OF FENNEL

Approximately 4 servings

- 1 pound fillet of halibut, red snapper, cod, sole, or other white fish
- 2 teaspoons olive oil
- Juice of 1 lemon
- 2 to 3 green onions, finely chopped
- 1 bunch fresh fennel

Brush fish with olive oil; cover with lemon juice. Sprinkle with green onion. Slice fennel lengthwise and place fish on top. Roast uncovered at 375° for 10 to 20 minutes, or until fish flakes.

APPROXIMATE NUTRITIONAL INFORMATION PER SERVING

Calories: 155
Total fat: 5 g
Saturated fat: 1 g
Percentage of calories from fat: 30%
Carbohydrate: 1 g
Protein: 25 g
Cholesterol: 38 mg
Sodium: 66 mg
Dietary fiber: 0 g

CRAB-STUFFED TROUT

Approximately 2 servings

2 6-ounce trout, heads and tails removed
2 teaspoons olive oil
1 small onion, thinly sliced
¼ pound crabmeat
¼ pound fresh mushrooms, sliced
Juice of ½ lemon
3 tablespoons dry vermouth
2 fresh lemons
1 bunch fresh parsley for garnish

Rub trout inside and out with olive oil. Arrange in a 9 x 13 x 2-inch baking dish; stuff cavity with onion, crab, and mushrooms.

Combine lemon juice and vermouth; pour over fish both inside and outside. Cover baking dish with aluminum foil.

Bake at 400° about 20 minutes, or until skin pulls easily away from fish. Baste frequently during cooking. Serve with plenty of fresh lemon; garnish with parsley.

Variation: Any other type of whole fish may be used in place of trout.

Serving Suggestion: For a refreshing dessert, try Lemon Ice (page 603).

APPROXIMATE NUTRITIONAL INFORMATION PER SERVING

Calories: 157
Total fat: 5 g
Saturated fat: 1 g
Percentage of calories from fat: 27%
Carbohydrate: 10 g
Protein: 19 g
Cholesterol: 45 mg
Sodium: 265 mg
Dietary fiber: 2 g

Crab-Stuffed Sole

Approximately 4 servings

2 green onions with tops, chopped
½ green pepper, chopped
½ cup fresh mushrooms, sliced
2 tablespoons dry white wine
¼ pound crabmeat
1 pound fresh sole fillets
1½ tablespoons fresh lemon juice
½ cup chicken broth, preferably homemade (page 364)
¼ cup all-purpose flour

Sauté green onion, green pepper, and mushrooms in wine; drain. Add crab. Lay sole fillets flat; spread crab filling over each fillet. Roll and secure with toothpicks. Pour lemon juice and a quarter of the chicken broth over fish.

Bake uncovered at 350° for 10 to 12 minutes, or until fish flakes easily when tested with a fork. Transfer to a serving plate to keep warm.

Shake flour and remaining broth in a covered jar to form a smooth paste. Pour liquid that fish was baked in into a saucepan; bring to a boil. Gradually add flour thickening, stirring constantly until sauce has thickened; pour over sole. Serve at once.

Variation: Lobster meat may be used in place of crabmeat. Any type of white fish may be used in place of sole.

APPROXIMATE NUTRITIONAL INFORMATION PER SERVING

Calories: 155
Total fat: 1 g
Saturated fat: 0 g
Percentage of calories from fat: 8%
Carbohydrate: 9 g
Protein: 24 g
Cholesterol: 12 mg
Sodium: 485 mg
Dietary fiber: 1 g

Clam-Stuffed Sole

Approximately 4 servings

¼ cup chopped green onion
1 garlic clove, minced
1 teaspoon olive oil
1½ cups sliced fresh mushrooms
1 6½-ounce can chopped clams, drained
2 tablespoons chopped parsley
1 teaspoon minced fresh oregano or ½ teaspoon dried
2 teaspoons minced fresh basil or ½ teaspoon dried
¼ teaspoon salt
⅛ teaspoon pepper
1 pound sole fillets
1 tablespoon lemon juice
Fresh parsley for garnish
Fresh lemon wedges for garnish

Sauté onion and garlic in olive oil until tender. Add mushrooms; cook 2 to 3 minutes. Stir in clams, parsley, oregano, basil, salt, and pepper.

Layer half the sole fillets in a baking dish and drizzle with lemon juice. Cover each with clam and mushroom filling. Stack remaining fillets over top. Bake covered at 350° for 25 minutes. Garnish with fresh parsley and lemon.

Note: Fresh clams may be used in place of canned. Any type of white fish may be used in place of sole.

APPROXIMATE NUTRITIONAL INFORMATION PER SERVING

Calories: 152
Total fat: 3 g
Saturated fat: 0 g
Percentage of calories from fat: 16%

Carbohydrate: 7 g
Protein: 26 g
Cholesterol: 20 mg
Sodium: 158 mg
Dietary fiber: 1 g

ORIENTAL-STYLE SEAFOOD

4 servings

1 pound fillet of sole, cod, turbot, halibut, or other white fish
6 tablespoons sake
3 tablespoons ginger juice*
3 tablespoons lemon juice
Dash of salt
6 fresh shiitake mushrooms
1 to 2 fresh lemons, cut into wedges

Divide fish into 4 servings. Place each portion on a piece of aluminum foil; fold edges of foil upward to make a bowl. Cover each fillet with a generous amount of sake, ginger juice, lemon juice, and salt; top with 1 to 2 mushrooms. Pinch top edges of foil together to seal, leaving a small amount of space between top of fish and top of foil. Place in a 350° oven and steam for 20 minutes, or until done. Garnish with plenty of fresh lemon.

Note: Shiitake mushrooms can usually be found in Oriental markets. If fresh are unavailable, reconstitute dried shiitake mushrooms by soaking them in water for 30 minutes, or until soft.

*To make ginger juice, purée a 2½-inch piece of peeled fresh ginger in a food processor; squeeze the pulp to obtain ginger juice.

APPROXIMATE NUTRITIONAL INFORMATION PER SERVING

Calories: 124
Total fat: 1 g
Saturated fat: 0 g
Percentage of calories from fat: 7%
Carbohydrate: 10 g
Protein: 18 g
Cholesterol: 0 mg
Sodium: 257 mg
Dietary fiber: 0 g

Szechwan-Style Sole

18 spring rolls

1 tablespoon ginger juice*
1 pound sole fillets, cubed
2 green onions with tops, finely chopped
⅛ teaspoon white pepper
⅛ teaspoon salt
2 tablespoons safflower oil
1 tablespoon sesame oil
1 tablespoon sake
1 tablespoon potato starch
1 egg white, beaten
½ teaspoon potato starch plus ½ cup water
18 spring roll (lumpia) wrappers, thawed, if frozen

Sauce

2 cups chicken broth, preferably homemade (page 364)
1½ tablespoons sesame oil
1½ tablespoons sake
3 tablespoons all-purpose flour plus ½ cup cold water
3 to 4 green onions, sliced
2 to 3 drops hot chili oil

Squeeze ginger juice over fish; let stand 10 minutes. Add green onions, pepper, salt, safflower oil, sesame oil, sake, and 1 tablespoon potato starch. Toss. Fold in beaten egg white.

Heat the ½ teaspoon potato starch and the ½ cup water to boiling to form a glue; cool to room temperature.

Lay spring roll wrappers flat; place 2 tablespoons of fish filling in center of each. Brush outside edges of each wrapper with starch mixture; fold edges over, envelope style, and seal outside seam. Preheat a nonstick skillet; brown spring rolls on one side over medium-high heat for 10 to 15 minutes. Turn; brown on other side.

Meanwhile, prepare sauce. Bring broth, sesame oil, and sake to a boil. Combine the flour and water; gradually add to broth, stirring until thickened. Stir in green onions and chili oil; pour over spring rolls. Serve at once.

*To make ginger juice, purée a 2½-inch piece of peeled fresh ginger in a food processor; squeeze the pulp to obtain the ginger juice.

APPROXIMATE NUTRITIONAL INFORMATION PER SPRING ROLL

Calories: 276
Total fat: 4 g
Saturated fat: 0 g
Percentage of calories from fat: 12%
Carbohydrate: 60 g
Protein: 15 g
Cholesterol: 0 mg
Sodium: 45 mg
Dietary fiber: 0 g

APPROXIMATE NUTRITIONAL INFORMATION PER SPRING ROLL WITH 2⅓ TABLESPOONS SAUCE

Calories: 295
Total fat: 5 g
Saturated fat: 0 g
Percentage of calories from fat: 15%
Carbohydrate: 61 g
Protein: 16 g
Cholesterol: 0 mg
Sodium: 76 mg
Dietary fiber: 0 g

Seafood with Vermouth and Orange Sauce

4 servings

1 pound fillet of halibut, red snapper, cod, sole, or other white fish
2 teaspoons olive oil
½ cup fresh orange juice
½ cup dry vermouth
1 orange, thinly sliced for garnish
Watercress for garnish

Rub fish with olive oil. Heat orange juice and vermouth just to boiling; reduce heat and simmer 2 to 3 minutes. Pour over fish. Bake uncovered at 450° for 15 to 20 minutes, basting frequently. When fish is done, pour juices into a saucepan; boil 3 to 4 minutes to reduce. Spread a serving plate with orange slices; top with fish. Cover with sauce. Garnish with watercress.

APPROXIMATE NUTRITIONAL INFORMATION PER SERVING

Calories: 229
Total fat: 6 g
Saturated fat: 1 g
Percentage of calories from fat: 22%
Carbohydrate: 8 g
Protein: 31 g
Cholesterol: 47 mg
Sodium: 83 mg
Dietary fiber: 0 g

SEAFOOD WITH WINE AND TOMATO SAUCE

4 servings

1 onion, chopped
2 to 3 celery stalks, chopped
2 carrots, diced
1 garlic clove, minced
1 cup white wine
2 teaspoons olive oil
1 8-ounce can tomato sauce
3 tablespoons chopped parsley
1 pound fillet of halibut, red snapper, sole, cod, or other white fish

Sauté vegetables and garlic in a small amount of wine until tender; add olive oil, tomato sauce, parsley, and remaining wine. Simmer 15 minutes. Pour a quarter of the sauce into a baking dish; arrange fish on top. Cover with remaining sauce. Bake, covered, at 350° for 15 to 20 minutes.

APPROXIMATE NUTRITIONAL INFORMATION PER SERVING

Calories: 269
Total fat: 6 g
Saturated fat: 1 g
Percentage of calories from fat: 20%

Carbohydrate: 12 g
Protein: 32 g
Cholesterol: 47 mg
Sodium: 488 mg
Dietary fiber: 2 g

Sea Bass with Sun-Dried Tomato Crust

4 servings

8 marinated sun-dried tomatoes, drained
3 garlic cloves
1 teaspoon olive oil
6 fresh lemon slices
1 pound sea bass fillets
1 tablespoon fresh lemon juice
8 kalamata olives, pitted and halved
Lemon wedges

Process sun-dried tomatoes, garlic, and olive oil in a food processor until tomatoes are finely chopped.

Arrange lemon slices on bottom of an 8-inch ovenproof casserole. Layer sea bass over top. Drizzle fish with lemon juice. Using a spatula, spread the sun-dried tomato mixture heavily over top of fish. Bake uncovered at 375° for 10 to 20 minutes, or until fish flakes easily when pierced with a fork. Sprinkle with kalamata olives the last 3 minutes of cooking time. Serve with fresh lemon wedges.

APPROXIMATE NUTRITIONAL INFORMATION PER SERVING

Calories: 154
Total fat: 5 g
Saturated fat: 1 g
Percentage of calories from fat: 30%

Carbohydrate: 7 g
Protein: 21 g
Cholesterol: 91 mg
Sodium: 314 mg
Dietary fiber: 0 g

POULTRY

Roast Chicken

Approximately 4 3½-ounce servings

1 3- to 4-pound broiler-fryer chicken
Fresh or dried sage to taste
Rosemary to taste
Pepper to taste
Garlic powder to taste
Salt to taste
2 celery stalks with leaves, chopped
1 onion, quartered

Wipe inside of chicken with a damp paper towel; wash outside with cold water. Rub inside cavity with sage, rosemary, pepper, garlic powder, and salt. Place celery and onion inside cavity. Skewer neck skin to back; tuck wing tips behind shoulder joints. Place breast side up in a shallow roasting pan. Roast at 350° for 60 to 75 minutes, or until done. Let stand 10 minutes. Remove skin before slicing.

Serving Suggestion: Serve with oven-roasted vegetables. Be sure to save the carcass for soup (page 364).

APPROXIMATE NUTRITIONAL INFORMATION PER SERVING

Calories: 205
Total fat: 7 g
Saturated fat: 2 g
Percentage of calories from fat: 32%
Carbohydrate: 4 g
Protein: 30 g
Cholesterol: 89 mg
Sodium: 104 mg
Dietary fiber: 1 g

ROAST CHICKEN WITH OLIVE OIL AND FRESH LEMON

Approximately 4 3-ounce servings

2 whole chicken breasts, skinned, boned, and halved
2 teaspoons olive oil
¼ cup fresh lemon juice
1 garlic clove, minced
¼ teaspoon dried oregano
¼ teaspoon dried tarragon

Remove skin from chicken breasts; bone. Combine olive oil, lemon juice, garlic, oregano, and tarragon; pour over chicken. Marinate 20 minutes. Roast at 350° for 35 to 45 minutes, or until done. Baste frequently during baking.

To save chicken bones for soup, keep a plastic bag in the freezer just for bones reserved from boning breasts. When bag is full, add extra backs, necks, and wings and make chicken soup.

APPROXIMATE NUTRITIONAL INFORMATION PER SERVING

Calories: 168
Total fat: 5 g
Saturated fat: 1 g
Percentage of calories from fat: 29%
Carbohydrate: 2 g
Protein: 27 g
Cholesterol: 73 mg
Sodium: 63 mg
Dietary fiber: 0 g

Roast Chicken Oriental Style

12 servings

1 bunch leaf lettuce
1 roast chicken, thinly sliced (page 536)
1 bunch green onions with tops
2 tablespoons rice wine vinegar
¼ cup reduced-sodium soy sauce
2 to 3 drops of hot chili oil
12 spring roll (lumpia) wrappers
¼ cup hot Chinese mustard
¼ cup toasted sesame seeds

Tear lettuce into bite-size pieces; arrange on a platter or tray. Layer chicken over lettuce. Slice green onions lengthwise and into 2-inch strips; arrange around edge of lettuce.

Combine rice wine vinegar, soy sauce, and hot chili oil in a small bowl; set aside.

Place spring roll wrappers in a vegetable steamer rack over boiling water, and steam 3 to 5 minutes or until hot; or wrap spring roll wrappers in a damp paper towel, and steam 1 to 2 minutes in the microwave. Remove to a napkin-lined basket.

Everyone prepares his own: Lay each spring roll wrapper flat. Place a slice of chicken, some lettuce, and green onion lengthwise in center of each wrapper. Fold bottom edge up, left and right sides over, and roll as for crepes.

Dip in hot Chinese mustard and sesame seeds and/or soy sauce and rice vinegar.

APPROXIMATE NUTRITIONAL INFORMATION PER SERVING

Calories: 136	Carbohydrate: 12 g
Total fat: 5 g	Protein: 13 g
Saturated fat: 1 g	Cholesterol: 30 mg
Percentage of calories from fat: 33%	Sodium: 107 mg
	Dietary fiber: 1 g

POACHED CHICKEN IN BROTH

4 servings

4 cups chicken broth, preferably homemade (page 364)
2 whole chicken breasts, skinned, boned, and halved

In a saucepan, bring broth to a boil; add chicken breasts and bring to a second boil. Reduce heat to medium; cook 20 minutes, or until chicken is done. Remove chicken and reserve stock for later use. If chicken is to be used for sandwiches, cool 10 minutes and tear into strings or slice diagonally across top. Poached chicken is excellent for salads and stir-fries, as well as for an entrée.

Variation: Substitute turkey breasts for chicken breasts.

APPROXIMATE NUTRITIONAL INFORMATION PER SERVING

Calories: 113	Carbohydrate: 0 g
Total fat: 3 g	Protein: 21 g
Saturated fat: 1 g	Cholesterol: 46 mg
Percentage of calories from fat: 22%	Sodium: 311 mg
	Dietary fiber: 0 g

Chicken and Dumplings

6 servings

3 whole skinless chicken breasts
1 onion, sliced
2 celery stalks, chopped
½ teaspoon salt
5 peppercorns
1 bay leaf
5 cups water
2 carrots, quartered lengthwise
½ pound fresh mushrooms, sliced
2 tablespoons all-purpose flour plus ¼ cup water
¾ cup snow peas

Dumplings

1 cup all-purpose flour
2 teaspoons baking powder
¼ teaspoon or less salt
½ cup nonfat milk
2 tablespoons safflower oil

Combine chicken, onion, celery, salt, peppercorns, bay leaf, and water in a stockpot; heat to boiling. Cover, reduce heat, and simmer 2 to 3 hours. Strain broth. Slice and wrap chicken. Refrigerate chicken and broth overnight.

Skim fat from broth. Shortly before serving, heat broth to boiling; add carrots and cook 10 to 15 minutes, or until tender.

To prepare dumplings, stir together flour, baking powder, and salt. Combine milk and safflower oil and add to dry ingredients; stir just until moistened.

Add chicken and mushrooms to boiling broth; bring

to a second boil. Drop dumplings by tablespoonfuls on top of bubbling stew. Cover tightly; bring to a boil. Reduce heat; simmer 12 to 15 minutes. Caution: Do not lift cover while dumplings are cooking.

Remove dumplings from pan. Combine the 2 tablespoons flour and ¼ cup water to make a smooth paste; quickly stir into broth to make a gravy. Add snow peas. Heat. Divide chicken, dumplings and vegetables among 6 plates. Ladle sauce over top. Serve at once.

APPROXIMATE NUTRITIONAL INFORMATION PER SERVING

Calories: 322
Total fat: 8 g
Saturated fat: 1 g
Percentage of calories from fat: 23%
Carbohydrate: 30 g
Protein: 32 g
Cholesterol: 73 mg
Sodium: 788 mg
Dietary fiber: 3 g

CHICKEN BAKED WITH LEMON AND WINE

4 3-ounce servings

¼ teaspoon tub-style safflower margarine
2 whole chicken breasts, skinned and boned
½ fresh lemon
Dash of pepper
Dash of salt
¼ cup dry white wine
¼ cup chicken broth, preferably homemade (page 364)

Using a piece of waxed paper, grease a baking dish with margarine. Arrange chicken breasts in baking dish; drizzle with lemon juice. Season. Add wine

(continued on next page)

(continued from preceding page)

and broth. Cover dish tightly. Bake at 400° for 10 to 15 minutes, or until tender and no sign of pink remains.

Serving Suggestion: Serve with tomatoes with fresh basil, Oriental Sticky Rice (page 446), and fresh asparagus.

APPROXIMATE NUTRITIONAL INFORMATION PER SERVING

Calories: 168	Carbohydrate: 1 g
Total fat: 3 g	Protein: 27 g
Saturated fat: 1 g	Cholesterol: 73 mg
Percentage of calories from fat: 18%	Sodium: 139 mg
	Dietary fiber: 0 g

CHICKEN LIMONE

4 3½-ounce servings

2 whole chicken breasts
1 teaspoon fresh lemon juice
1 lemon, cut into wedges
Freshly ground pepper

Remove skin from chicken breasts; bone if desired. Place breasts in a vegetable steamer basket over boiling water; add a dash of lemon juice. Cover. Steam 15 to 20 minutes, or until chicken is tender and no sign of pink remains; do not overcook.

Serve with fresh lemon wedges; sprinkle with ground pepper.

Serving Suggestion: For a real low-fat dinner, serve with fresh raw spinach with a dressing of fresh lemon and ground pepper, sliced tomatoes with fresh basil, and Long-Grain Rice Pilaf (page 446).

APPROXIMATE NUTRITIONAL INFORMATION PER SERVING

Calories: 150	Carbohydrate: 0 g
Total fat: 3 g	Protein: 29 g
Saturated fat: 1 g	Cholesterol: 77 mg
Percentage of calories from fat: 18%	Sodium: 63 mg
	Dietary fiber: 0 g

GINGER-FLAVORED CHICKEN

4 3½-ounce servings

2 whole chicken breasts
1 celery stalk with leaves, chopped
1 small onion, chopped
1 carrot, sliced
Piece of fresh ginger

Remove skin from chicken breasts; bone if desired. Place chicken in a small stockpot; add celery, onion, carrot, and a piece of fresh ginger. Add enough cold water to cover by 2 inches; bring to a boil. Cook 10 to 20 minutes, or until chicken is tender and no sign of pink remains; do not overcook.

Note: A great way to prepare chicken for salads or for dishes with soba noodles.

APPROXIMATE NUTRITIONAL INFORMATION PER SERVING

Calories: 171	Carbohydrate: 5 g
Total fat: 3 g	Protein: 29 g
Saturated fat: 1 g	Cholesterol: 77 mg
Percentage of calories from fat: 16%	Sodium: 78 mg
	Dietary fiber: 1 g

Quick Microwave Chicken

4 3-ounce servings

2 whole chicken breasts, skinned, boned, and halved.

Place chicken in a glass pie plate, placing larger pieces to the outside of dish. Cover with plastic wrap; prick a hole in the plastic for steam to escape. Cook at full power for 8 minutes; turn. Rearrange pieces in dish; cook 6 minutes longer, or until done.

APPROXIMATE NUTRITIONAL INFORMATION PER SERVING

Calories: 142
Total fat: 3 g
Saturated fat: 1 g
Percentage of calories from fat: 19%
Carbohydrate: 0 g
Protein: 27 g
Cholesterol: 73 mg
Sodium: 63 mg
Dietary fiber: 0 g

Quick-to-Fix Chicken

4 servings

2 whole skinless, boneless chicken breasts

Preheat a nonstick skillet over medium-high heat. Add chicken breasts; brown 3 to 5 minutes on each side. Reduce heat; sauté 15 to 20 minutes longer, turning occasionally.

Note: When I am out of time and need dinner in a hurry, this is one of my favorite standbys. Served with Pan-Steamed Broccoli and Cauliflower with Lemon and Hot Chili Sauce (page 465), brown rice, and fresh fruit for dessert, I can have the whole dinner on the table within 30 minutes.

APPROXIMATE NUTRITIONAL INFORMATION PER SERVING

Calories: 142	Carbohydrate: 0 g
Total fat: 3 g	Protein: 27 g
Saturated fat: 1 g	Cholesterol: 73 mg
Percentage of calories from fat: 19%	Sodium: 63 mg
	Dietary fiber: 0 g

OVEN-FRIED CHICKEN

4 3-ounce servings

- 2 whole chicken breasts, skinned, boned, and halved
- 1 teaspoon olive oil
- 2 tablespoons all-purpose flour or bread crumbs
- Dash of pepper
- Dash of paprika

Brush chicken with oil. Dredge lightly in flour or bread crumbs. Season with pepper. Sprinkle with paprika. Bake uncovered at 425° for 35 to 40 minutes. Turn; bake 10 to 25 minutes longer, or until tender.

APPROXIMATE NUTRITIONAL INFORMATION PER SERVING

Calories: 166	Carbohydrate: 3 g
Total fat: 4 g	Protein: 27 g
Saturated fat: 1 g	Cholesterol: 73 mg
Percentage of calories from fat: 24%	Sodium: 92 mg
	Dietary fiber: 0 g

EXTRA CRISPY OVEN-FRIED CHICKEN

4 3-ounce servings

2 whole chicken breasts, halved
½ cup nonfat milk
½ cup Grape-Nuts flakes

Remove skin from chicken, bone if desired. Dip chicken in milk, then in Grape-Nuts flakes. Bake in a nonstick pan at 400° for 30 minutes. Reduce heat to 350°. Cover loosely with foil. Bake 20 to 30 minutes longer. Do not turn chicken during baking.

APPROXIMATE NUTRITIONAL INFORMATION PER SERVING

Calories: 203	Carbohydrate: 13 g
Total fat: 3 g	Protein: 29 g
Saturated fat: 1 g	Cholesterol: 74 mg
Percentage of calories from fat: 14%	Sodium: 177 mg
	Dietary fiber: 0 g

BARBECUED CHICKEN BREASTS

4 3-ounce servings

2 whole chicken breasts, skin removed
½ cup barbecue sauce

Place chicken breasts over hot coals; cook 10 minutes. Turn; cook 10 minutes. Turn; baste with barbecue sauce. Cook 5 minutes. Turn; baste. Cook 5 minutes longer. Chicken is done when it can easily be pulled away from the bone.

Note: Be sure to read labels when selecting a barbecue sauce to ensure it contains only heart-healthy ingredients.

APPROXIMATE NUTRITIONAL INFORMATION PER SERVING

Calories: 166	Carbohydrate: 4 g
Total fat: 4 g	Protein: 27 g
Saturated fat: 1 g	Cholesterol: 73 mg
Percentage of calories from fat: 20%	Sodium: 318 mg
	Dietary fiber: 0 g

GRILLED CHICKEN WITH FRESH LIME

6 servings

3 whole chicken breasts, halved
⅔ cup fresh lime juice
Juice of 2 lemons
2 teaspoons olive oil
2 teaspoons dried rosemary
¼ teaspoon pepper

Remove skin from chicken; bone if desired. Combine all ingredients, except chicken, in a covered jar; shake. Pour over chicken. Marinate several hours or overnight in the refrigerator. Grill chicken over medium-hot coals about 50 minutes. Baste with marinade and turn frequently during cooking.

APPROXIMATE NUTRITIONAL INFORMATION PER SERVING

Calories: 161	Carbohydrate: 2 g
Total fat: 5 g	Protein: 27 g
Saturated fat: 2 g	Cholesterol: 73 mg
Percentage of calories from fat: 26%	Sodium: 63 mg
	Dietary fiber: 0 g

Quick-and-Easy Grilled Chicken

4 servings

⅓ cup fresh lime juice
2 whole chicken breasts, skinned and boned

Pour lime juice over chicken and marinate at room temperature for 10 minutes.

Meanwhile, prepare coals and cover the grill with foil if you wish. Grill chicken over hot coals for 10 to 12 minutes on each side, or until done.

Serving Suggestion: Serve with Grilled Peppers and Onions (page 469), Grilled Corn on the Cob (page 466), and Spicy Mexican Rice (page 445).

APPROXIMATE NUTRITIONAL INFORMATION PER SERVING

Calories: 147
Total fat: 3 g
Saturated fat: 1 g
Percentage of calories from fat: 19%
Carbohydrate: 2 g
Protein: 27 g
Cholesterol: 73 mg
Sodium: 63 mg
Dietary fiber: 0 g

Barbecued Chicken Italian Style

6 servings

1 cup oil-free Italian dressing
2 tablespoons Dijon mustard
¼ cup dry white wine
3 whole skinless chicken breasts
½ pound fresh mushrooms
2 onions, quartered
2 tomatoes, halved

Combine dressing, mustard, and wine. Arrange chicken in a bowl separate from the vegetables. Pour half the dressing over the chicken and the other half over the vegetables. Marinate each 2 hours in the refrigerator. Alternate mushrooms, onions, and tomatoes on 6-inch skewers or toothpicks. When coals are ready, arrange chicken on barbecue; grill 20 minutes. Turn; grill 20 minutes longer. Turn; add vegetables. Grill 10 minutes, or until chicken is tender and vegetables are hot. Baste chicken and vegetables frequently with the marinade during cooking.

APPROXIMATE NUTRITIONAL INFORMATION PER SERVING

Calories: 198	Carbohydrate: 10 g
Total fat: 4 g	Protein: 29 g
Saturated fat: 1 g	Cholesterol: 73 mg
Percentage of calories from fat: 17%	Sodium: 721 mg
	Dietary fiber: 3 g

CHICKEN EN BROCHETTE

6 servings

3 whole chicken breasts, skinned and boned
2 tablespoons olive oil
¼ cup fresh lemon juice
1 teaspoon honey
Dash of tarragon
Dash of oregano
12 cherry tomatoes
12 fresh mushrooms
2 onions, cut into 2-inch cubes
2 green peppers, quartered
½ fresh pineapple, cut into chunks

Cut chicken into 2-inch cubes. Combine olive oil, lemon juice, honey, tarragon, and oregano. Pour

(continued on next page)

(continued from preceding page)

marinade over chicken and vegetables. Marinate 20 to 30 minutes.

Alternate chicken, vegetables, and fruit on skewers. Grill over hot coals 4 to 6 inches from heat, turning frequently and basting often, for 20 to 30 minutes, or until chicken is done.

Variation: Instead of chicken parts, roast a whole chicken. Skewer vegetables separately.

APPROXIMATE NUTRITIONAL INFORMATION PER SERVING

Calories: 213	Carbohydrate: 15 g
Total fat: 5 g	Protein: 28 g
Saturated fat: 1 g	Cholesterol: 73 mg
Percentage of calories from fat: 19%	Sodium: 69 mg
	Dietary fiber: 2 g

Thirty Cloves of Garlic Chicken

4 servings

- 1 pound skinless chicken breasts
- ½ teaspoon olive oil
- 3 heads garlic (about 30 cloves), unpeeled
- 1 cup dry white wine
- ¼ teaspoon powdered thyme
- ¼ teaspoon powdered rosemary
- ¼ teaspoon salt
- 4 ½-inch-thick slices French, Tuscan, or peasant bread, toasted

Preheat a nonstick skillet over medium-high heat. Add chicken breasts and brown about 3 minutes on each side. Reduce heat to medium. Remove skillet from heat just long enough to add olive oil and garlic cloves. Return skillet to heat and sauté chicken and garlic 3 to 4 minutes longer, just until garlic cloves begin to turn golden. Keep a close watch on the garlic and stir the cloves often so that they do not burn. Transfer chicken and garlic to an ovenproof casserole.

Pour the wine into the skillet (the remaining heat in the skillet will warm the wine). Stir in thyme, rosemary, and salt. Pour the sauce over the chicken and garlic. Cover the casserole and bake at 350° for 30 to 40 minutes, or until chicken is cooked and garlic is soft.

Serve chicken and several cloves of garlic on each dinner plate. Top with plenty of sauce. Garnish with toasted bread.

To eat, spread several cloves of softened garlic over bread, dunk break into sauce, and top with chicken.

Serving Suggestion: Great meal for a family-style dinner. Also delicious served cold for a picnic lunch. When chilled, the sauce coats the chicken, making it wonderfully flavorful. The soft garlic can be spread on untoasted peasant bread and then the bread can be topped with the sliced chicken.

APPROXIMATE NUTRITIONAL INFORMATION PER SERVING

Calories: 315
Total fat: 5 g
Saturated fat: 1 g
Percentage of
calories from fat: 14%
Carbohydrate: 21 g
Protein: 37 g
Cholesterol: 88 mg
Sodium: 368 mg
Dietary fiber: trace

Chicken and Barley Stuffed Peppers

4 servings

4 medium green peppers
⅓ cup chopped onion
1 14½-ounce can stewed tomatoes
2 cups cooked barley
¼ teaspoon Tabasco sauce
Dash of pepper
2 cups cubed cooked chicken breast
½ cup grated reduced-fat mozzarella or cheddar cheese

Cut tops off green peppers; remove seeds and membrane. Sauté onion in a small amount of tomato liquid; add tomatoes, barley, Tabasco, pepper, chicken, and half the cheese. Stand peppers upright in an 8-inch square baking dish; stuff with tomato-barley filling. Bake, uncovered, at 350° for 25 to 30 minutes, or until hot; sprinkle with remaining cheese. Return to oven until cheese melts.

Variations: In place of chicken, use ¾ pound extra-lean ground round sautéed and thoroughly drained of fat. In place of barley use cooked rice.

APPROXIMATE NUTRITIONAL INFORMATION PER SERVING

Calories: 311
Total fat: 6 g
Saturated fat: 2 g
Percentage of calories from fat: 16%
Carbohydrate: 43 g
Protein: 22 g
Cholesterol: 45 mg
Sodium: 332 mg
Dietary fiber: 5 g

CHICKEN CURRY

8 servings

½ cup chopped onion
2 cups chicken broth, preferably homemade (page 364)
2 cups nonfat milk
½ cup all-purpose flour
½ teaspoon salt
1 tablespoon curry powder
¼ teaspoon ground ginger
1 tablespoon lemon juice
4 cups cubed cooked chicken breast
1 8-ounce can sliced water chestnuts
6 cups steamed rice
¼ cup raisins for garnish (optional)
⅔ cup pineapple chunks for garnish (optional)

Sauté onion in a small amount of chicken broth until tender; add remaining broth. Bring to a boil. Shake milk and flour in a covered jar to form a smooth paste; gradually add to boiling broth, stirring constantly until thick. Add seasonings. Pour lemon juice over chicken; add to broth. Stir in water chestnuts. Heat. Serve over steamed rice. If desired, garnish with raisins and pineapple chunks.

APPROXIMATE NUTRITIONAL INFORMATION PER SERVING

Calories: 413
Total fat: 4 g
Saturated fat: 1 g
Percentage of calories from fat: 9%
Carbohydrate: 62 g
Protein: 30 g
Cholesterol: 57 mg
Sodium: 287 mg
Dietary fiber: 1 g

Chicken Cacciatore

4 servings

1 28-ounce can plum tomatoes
2 teaspoons olive oil
1 onion, chopped
3 carrots, peeled and thinly sliced
3 celery stalks, thinly sliced
2 tablespoons red wine vinegar
¼ teaspoon pepper
¾ teaspoon dried sage
½ teaspoon salt
¼ teaspoon sugar
2 whole chicken breasts, skinned, boned, and halved
½ pound shell-shaped macaroni, cooked al dente

Combine all ingredients, except chicken and pasta, in a stew pot or Dutch oven; bring to a boil. Reduce heat; cover and simmer 25 to 30 minutes. Add chicken to sauce and cook 25 to 30 minutes, or until tender. Serve over cooked pasta.

Serving Suggestion: Serve with crusty French bread and a tossed green salad.

APPROXIMATE NUTRITIONAL INFORMATION PER SERVING

Calories: 427	Carbohydrate: 58 g
Total fat: 8 g	Protein: 32 g
Saturated fat: 1 g	Cholesterol: 54 mg
Percentage of calories from fat: 17%	Sodium: 633 mg
	Dietary fiber: 7 g

CHICKEN WITH FRESH SPINACH

6 servings

- 3 whole chicken breasts, skinned and boned
- 1 tablespoon ginger juice*
- 1 tablespoon sake
- ½ cup fresh lemon juice
- 2 cups chicken broth, preferably homemade (page 364)
- ¼ cup all-purpose flour
- ½ cup water
- 2 tablespoons potato starch
- 6 cups fresh spinach torn into bite-size pieces (1 bunch)

Cut chicken into cubes. Sprinkle with ginger juice and sake. Let stand 10 minutes.

Combine lemon juice and broth in a medium saucepan; reserve ⅓ cup and set aside. Heat remainder to boiling. Shake flour and water in a covered jar to form a smooth paste; gradually add to boiling broth, stirring constantly until thick. Reduce heat and let simmer 5 to 10 minutes.

Sprinkle chicken with potato starch. Heat reserved broth in a wok or heavy skillet; stir-fry chicken. Toss spinach with chicken. Transfer to serving plates; pour sauce over.

*To make ginger juice, purée a 2½-inch piece of peeled fresh ginger in a food processor; squeeze the pulp to obtain the ginger juice.

APPROXIMATE NUTRITIONAL INFORMATION PER SERVING

Calories: 165
Total fat: 3 g
Saturated fat: 1 g
Percentage of calories from fat: 16%

Carbohydrate: 6 g
Protein: 27 g
Cholesterol: 66 mg
Sodium: 351 mg
Dietary fiber: 1 g

CHICKEN ENCHILADAS

10 servings

1 pound chicken breasts, skinned and boned
6 cups chicken broth, preferably homemade (page 364)
3 tablespoons diced green chilies
2 cups reduced-fat Monterey Jack cheese
1 teaspoon olive oil
½ cup chopped onion
3 garlic cloves
1 14½-ounce can plum tomatoes
1 8-ounce can tomato sauce
4 tablespoons chili powder
1 teaspoon ground cumin
½ teaspoon salt
10 6-inch corn tortillas
¾ cup nonfat sour cream
¾ cup Tomato Salsa, preferably homemade (page 433)

Poach chicken breasts in 4 cups of the chicken broth (see instructions on page 539). Remove from broth. Cool. Reserve broth for later use. Dice chicken and mix with green chilies and 1 cup of the cheese. Set aside.

Heat olive oil in a nonstick skillet; add onion and garlic and sauté until tender. Transfer onions and garlic to a food processor; add tomatoes with liquid and purée. Pour mixture into a medium saucepan. Add tomato sauce, remaining 2 cups chicken broth, chili powder, cumin, and salt. Simmer 30 minutes.

Dip tortillas one at a time into simmering sauce, allowing excess to drip back into saucepan. Spoon ¼ to ⅓ cup of the chicken filling across diameter of tortilla.

Roll up tortilla and arrange seam side down in a 9 x 13 x 2-inch ovenproof casserole. Pour remaining sauce over top. Cover pan with foil. Bake at 350° for 15 minutes. Remove foil cover. Sprinkle with remaining 1 cup of cheese. Bake uncovered 5 minutes longer, or until cheese is melted and sauce is bubbly. Accompany with sour cream and salsa.

Serving Suggestion: Serve with Spicy Mexican Rice (page 445).

APPROXIMATE NUTRITIONAL INFORMATION PER SERVING

Calories: 235	Carbohydrate: 18 g
Total fat: 7 g	Protein: 24 g
Saturated fat: 3 g	Cholesterol: 50 mg
Percentage of calories from fat: 29%	Sodium: 539 mg
	Dietary fiber: 1 g

CHICKEN TOSTADOS

4 servings

- 4 6-inch corn or flour tortillas
- 1½ cups cubed poached chicken (page 539)
- ½ head lettuce, diced
- 2 ripe tomatoes, diced
- 1 white onion, diced
- 1 4-ounce can diced green chilies
- ½ cup grated reduced-fat cheddar or mozzarella cheese
- ¾ cup Tomato Salsa, preferably homemade (page 433)
- ¼ cup nonfat sour cream

Place tortillas on a nonstick baking sheet. Heat in a 350° oven for 3 minutes; turn. Heat 3 more minutes

(continued on next page)

(continued from preceding page)

or until warm. For a softer tortilla shell, warm tortillas in a tortilla warmer, in the microwave, or on the stove top. To microwave, wrap tortillas between two slightly dampened paper towels; microwave for 1 to 2 minutes, or until warm. Keep wrapped until ready to serve. To warm tortillas on the stove top, arrange them in a bamboo basket or vegetable steamer basket; steam covered over boiling water for 3 to 5 minutes, or until warm.

Spread tortillas with chicken; top with lettuce, tomato, onion, green chilies, cheese, salsa, and sour cream. Serve with Spicy Mexican Rice (page 445).

Note: When purchasing flour tortillas, select a brand made with soy bean or other heart-healthy oil, not with lard. Corn tortillas generally do not contain any oil or shortening so are more heart-healthy and are lower in calories and fat.

Variation: Substitute extra-lean ground round for chicken.

APPROXIMATE NUTRITIONAL INFORMATION PER SERVING USING CORN TORTILLAS

Calories: 241
Total fat: 6 g
Saturated fat: 3 g
Percentage of calories from fat: 23%
Carbohydrate: 22 g
Protein: 26 g
Cholesterol: 59 mg
Sodium: 172 mg
Dietary fiber: 1 g

APPROXIMATE NUTRITIONAL INFORMATION PER SERVING USING FLOUR TORTILLAS

Calories: 299
Total fat: 8 g
Saturated fat: 3 g
Percentage of calories from fat: 24%
Carbohydrate: 29 g
Protein: 27 g
Cholesterol: 59 mg
Sodium: 299 mg
Dietary fiber: 3 g

CHICKEN CHALUPAS

8 servings

2 cups chicken broth, preferably homemade (page 364)
2 large ripe tomatoes, chopped
1 large onion, chopped
1 garlic clove
2½ cups cubed cooked chicken breast
⅛ teaspoon cayenne
⅛ teaspoon salt
⅛ teaspoon pepper
8 6-inch corn or flour tortillas

Topping

2 ripe tomatoes, chopped
1 large white onion, chopped
½ cup grated reduced-fat cheddar cheese
1 cup Tomato Salsa, preferably homemade (page 433)
½ cup nonfat sour cream

Bring chicken broth to a boil; add tomatoes, onion, and garlic. Bring to a second boil; cook about 1 hour, or until liquid is nearly absorbed. Stir in chicken, cayenne, salt, and pepper; simmer 45 to 60 minutes, or until all liquid is absorbed.

Place tortillas on a nonstick baking sheet. Heat in a 350° oven for 3 minutes; turn. Heat 3 more minutes, or until warm. For a softer tortilla shell, warm tortillas in a tortilla warmer, in the microwave, or on the stove top. To microwave, wrap tortillas between two slightly dampened paper towels; microwave for 1 to 2 minutes, or until warm. Keep wrapped until ready to serve. To warm tortillas on the stove top, arrange them in a bamboo basket or vegetable steamer

(continued on next page)

(continued from preceding page)

basket; steam covered over boiling water for 3 to 5 minutes, or until warm.

Top each tortilla with chicken filling, then with tomato, onion, and cheese. Sprinkle with salsa; top with nonfat sour cream.

Variation: Just before serving, drain 1 15-ounce can black beans and stir into chicken filling; heat to serving temperature.

APPROXIMATE NUTRITIONAL INFORMATION PER SERVING

Calories: 200	Carbohydrate: 19 g
Total fat: 5 g	Protein: 21 g
Saturated fat: 2 g	Cholesterol: 47 mg
Percentage of calories from fat: 20%	Sodium: 361 mg
	Dietary fiber: 3 g

APPROXIMATE NUTRITIONAL INFORMATION PER SERVING USING BLACK BEANS

Calories: 269	Carbohydrate: 32 g
Total fat: 5 g	Protein: 25 g
Saturated fat: 2 g	Cholesterol: 47 mg
Percentage of calories from fat: 16%	Sodium: 514 mg
	Dietary fiber: 3 g

STIR-FRIED CHICKEN WITH VEGETABLES

4 servings

1 tablespoon ginger juice*
1 teaspoon sake
1 pound chicken breasts, skinned, boned, and cut into bite-size pieces
2 tablespoons potato starch
2 teaspoons olive oil

1 onion, thinly sliced
¼ pound bamboo shoots, cut into 2-inch lengths
3 celery stalks, sliced
1 carrot, sliced crosswise into rounds
2 green peppers, seeded and cut into thin strips
½ pound fresh snow peas
1 8-ounce can sliced water chestnuts
½ pound mushrooms, sliced
1 cup chicken broth (optional), preferably homemade (page 364)

Mix ginger juice with sake; pour over chicken. Let stand 10 minutes; sprinkle with potato starch.

Cook chicken in a preheated nonstick skillet over medium-high heat until chicken turns white throughout. Set aside.

Spray a nonstick wok or heavy skillet with nonstick spray coating; add olive oil and heat. Add onion, bamboo shoots, celery, and carrot, and stir-fry until just crisp-tender. Stir in green peppers and snow peas; stir-fry 2 to 3 minutes. Add water chestnuts and mushrooms; stir-fry 1 to 2 minutes. Add broth as needed for moisture during cooking. Toss chicken with vegetables. Serve at once.

Variation: Warm 3 tablespoons prepared stir-fry sauce and toss with chicken and vegetables before serving.

*To make ginger juice, purée a 2½-inch piece of peeled fresh ginger in a food processor; squeeze the pulp to obtain ginger juice.

APPROXIMATE NUTRITIONAL INFORMATION PER SERVING

Calories: 317
Total fat: 6 g
Saturated fat: 1 g
Percentage of calories from fat: 18%
Carbohydrate: 27 g
Protein: 39 g
Cholesterol: 88 mg
Sodium: 309 mg
Dietary fiber: 4 g

Szechwan Chicken

4 servings

1 tablespoon cornstarch
3 tablespoons reduced-sodium soy sauce
2 whole chicken breasts, skinned, boned, and cut into ½-inch cubes
1 tablespoon dry sherry
2 teaspoons sugar
1 teaspoon cider vinegar
2 teaspoons olive oil
1 teaspoon crushed red pepper
1 shallot, sliced
1 2-inch piece fresh ginger, peeled and sliced

Combine cornstarch and 1 tablespoon of the soy sauce in a shallow bowl. Add chicken and toss to coat.

Combine remaining 2 tablespoons of the soy sauce, sherry, sugar, and vinegar; set aside.

Heat oil in a nonstick skillet. Add chicken and stir-fry 2 to 3 minutes; sprinkle chicken with crushed red pepper. Add shallot and ginger; continue to stir-fry 3 to 4 minutes, or until chicken is cooked. Remove from heat. Add sauce and toss.

APPROXIMATE NUTRITIONAL INFORMATION PER SERVING

Calories: 194
Total fat: 5 g
Saturated fat: 1 g
Percentage of calories from fat: 25%
Carbohydrate: 6 g
Protein: 28 g
Cholesterol: 73 mg
Sodium: 514 mg
Dietary fiber: 0 g

CHICKEN STIR-FRIED WITH GREEN PEPPERS

4 4-ounce servings

1 pound chicken breast, skinned and boned
1 tablespoon sake
2 tablespoons potato starch
½ cup chicken broth, preferably homemade (page 364)
4 green peppers, seeded and cut lengthwise into thin strips

Cut chicken into bite-size pieces; toss with sake. Let stand 10 minutes; sprinkle with potato starch. Cook in a preheated nonstick skillet over medium-high heat until chicken turns white throughout. Set aside. Heat chicken broth in a wok or heavy skillet; stir-fry green peppers for 2 to 3 minutes, or until just crisp-tender. Toss with chicken.

APPROXIMATE NUTRITIONAL INFORMATION PER SERVING

Calories: 227
Total fat: 4 g
Saturated fat: 1 g
Percentage of calories from fat: 13%
Carbohydrate: 27 g
Protein: 39 g
Cholesterol: 88 mg
Sodium: 309 mg
Dietary fiber: 2 g

Roast Turkey

Approximately 15 3-ounce servings

6- to 8-pound turkey
Fresh or dried sage to taste
Pepper to taste
Garlic powder to taste
Salt to taste
2 to 3 celery stalks, cut into 2-inch pieces
1 to 2 onions, quartered

Wipe inside of turkey with a damp paper towel; wash outside with cold water. Rub inside cavity with seasonings. Place celery and onions inside cavity. Skewer neck skin to back; tuck wing tips behind shoulder joints.

Place breast side up on a rack in a shallow roasting pan; roast at 325°. Turkey is done when drumsticks move easily or twist out of joint. A meat thermometer should register 185°. If turkey browns too quickly, cover it with a cap of aluminum foil. Remove skin before slicing.

ROASTING CHART

6-8 pounds: 2¾ to 3½ hours
8-12 pounds: 3¼ to 4 hours
12-16 pounds: 3¾ to 5 hours
16-20 pounds: 4¾ to 6½ hours
20-24 pounds: 6¼ to 8 hours

ROASTING CHART FOR HALVES AND QUARTERS

5-8 pounds: 2½ to 3 hours
8-10 pounds: 3 to 3½ hours
10-12 pounds: 3½ to 4 hours

Notes: To be heart-healthy, the turkey should not be stuffed, as fat from the turkey will drip into the dressing. There is an excellent stuffing recipe (page 331) that is cooked alongside the turkey.

Be sure to save the carcass for soup (page 365).

Variation: To roast a half turkey or quarter turkey, season as for roast turkey. Place skin side up on a rack in a shallow roasting pan. Insert meat thermometer so tip is in thickest part of thigh muscle or breast meat and does not touch bone.

APPROXIMATE NUTRITIONAL INFORMATION PER SERVING

Calories: 140	Carbohydrate: 1 g
Total fat: 3 g	Protein: 25 g
Saturated fat: 1 g	Cholesterol: 77 mg
Percentage of calories from fat: 21%	Sodium: 68 mg
	Dietary fiber: 0 g

POACHED BREAST OF TURKEY

Approximately 8 3-ounce servings

2 pounds fresh turkey breast
1 teaspoon lemon juice

Remove skin from turkey breast. Place breast in a steamer over boiling water and add a dash of lemon juice. Cover. Steam 30 to 35 minutes, or until juices run clear when pricked with a fork.

Serving Suggestion: Great for sandwiches.

APPROXIMATE NUTRITIONAL INFORMATION PER SERVING

Calories: 131	Carbohydrate: 0 g
Total fat: 3 g	Protein: 25 g
Saturated fat: 1 g	Cholesterol: 58 mg
Percentage of calories from fat: 18%	Sodium: 54 mg
	Dietary fiber: 0 g

Barbecued Turkey

Approximately 15 3-ounce servings

8 to 12 pound turkey
Fresh or dried sage to taste
Pepper to taste
Garlic powder to taste
Salt to taste
2 celery stalks, chopped
1 large onion, chopped
2 teaspoons olive oil

Wipe inside of turkey with a damp paper towel; wash outside with cold water. Rub inside cavity with seasonings. Place celery and onion inside cavity. Skewer neck skin to back; tuck wing tips behind shoulder joints. Rub outside of turkey with olive oil.

Place 25 briquets on each side of barbecue kettle. When coals are ready, put in drip pan. Put turkey in roast holder and position on grill. Every hour add 8 briquets per side. For a 12-pound turkey, allow 2½ hours cooking time; for a 20-pound turkey, allow 11 minutes per pound. Remove skin before slicing.

Note: The roast holder and drip pan that are necessary to barbecue a turkey are inexpensive and available in hardware stores, discount stores, and kitchen stores.

APPROXIMATE NUTRITIONAL INFORMATION PER SERVING

Calories: 146
Total fat: 4 g
Saturated fat: 1 g
Percentage of calories from fat: 24%
Carbohydrate: 1 g
Protein: 25 g
Cholesterol: 77 mg
Sodium: 66 mg
Dietary fiber: 0 g

MEAT

Shish Kebab

4 servings

2 teaspoons olive oil
½ cup dry white wine or vermouth
1 teaspoon lemon juice
¼ tablespoon or less salt
1 pound lamb loin, cut into 1-inch cubes
2 green peppers, seeded and quartered lengthwise
12 cherry tomatoes
8 water-packed artichoke hearts
12 fresh mushrooms
1 onion, cut into wedges
2 cups fresh pineapple chunks

Combine oil, wine, lemon juice, and salt; pour over lamb and vegetables. Arrange lamb, vegetables, and pineapple alternately on skewers. Grill over hot coals or broil 4 to 6 inches from heat, basting frequently and turning often, until lamb is done.

Serving Suggestion: Balance your meal with steamed brown rice and fresh fruit.

APPROXIMATE NUTRITIONAL INFORMATION PER SERVING

Calories: 327
Total fat: 11 g
Saturated fat: 3 g
Percentage of calories from fat: 32%

Carbohydrate: 24 g
Protein: 29 g
Cholesterol: 80 mg
Sodium: 196 mg
Dietary fiber: 4 g

BARBECUED LAMB ROAST

8 servings

1 3-pound leg of lamb, boned and butterflied
Dried thyme
Garlic powder
Powdered rosemary
Pepper
16 cherry tomatoes
16 mushroom caps, steamed 2 to 3 minutes
16 asparagus spears, steamed 3 to 5 minutes
Fresh parsley for garnish
Fresh lemon wedges for garnish

Have butcher remove bone from leg of lamb and open roast; season with thyme, garlic powder, rosemary, and pepper. Allow to stand at room temperature for about 1 hour before grilling.

Build a medium-hot fire in a grill. Grill lamb 4 inches from heat, turning every 10 minutes, for 30 to 40 minutes for rare, 40 to 50 minutes for medium, and 50 to 60 minutes for well-done. Place on a carving platter and let set 10 minutes. Carve into diagonal slices. Arrange tomatoes, mushrooms, and asparagus. Garnish with parsley and lemon wedges.

Variation: To oven roast, arrange lamb on rack in roasting pan. Cook 15 minutes at 450°; reduce heat to 350° and roast approximately 1¼ hours, or until lamb reaches desired doneness. Baste frequently.

APPROXIMATE NUTRITIONAL INFORMATION PER SERVING

Calories: 254
Total fat: 10 g
Saturated fat: 4 g
Percentage of calories from fat: 36%
Carbohydrate: 2 g
Protein: 37 g
Cholesterol: 114 mg
Sodium: 90 mg
Dietary fiber: 1 g

ROAST TENDERLOIN OF PORK

6 servings

1 1½-pound extra-lean pork tenderloin roast
Pepper to taste
Fresh or dried sage to taste
Garlic powder to taste

Heat oven to 350°. Season meat. Place fat side up on a roasting pan. Insert a meat thermometer through outside fat into thickest part of meat. Roast 40 minutes per pound; meat thermometer should register 185°.

Serving Suggestion: Serve with warm Applesauce (page 592).

APPROXIMATE NUTRITIONAL INFORMATION PER SERVING

Calories: 142
Total fat: 4 g
Saturated fat: 1 g
Percentage of calories from fat: 26%
Carbohydrate: 0 g
Protein: 24 g
Cholesterol: 78 mg
Sodium: 57 mg
Dietary fiber: 0 g

ROAST LOIN OF VEAL

8 servings

1 2-pound veal loin roast
1 teaspoon olive oil
Juice of ½ lemon
Pinch of fresh or dried thyme
Garlic powder to taste
Pepper to taste

Let meat stand at room temperature for 1 hour; rub with olive oil. Sprinkle with lemon juice; season with thyme, garlic powder, and pepper. Place fat side up on a rack in roasting pan. Insert a meat thermometer through outside fat into thickest part of meat. Roast uncovered at 325° for 15 to 30 minutes per pound; meat thermometer should register 170°.

APPROXIMATE NUTRITIONAL INFORMATION PER SERVING

Calories: 154
Total fat: 6 g
Saturated fat: 2 g
Percentage of calories from fat: 37%
Carbohydrate: 1 g
Protein: 22 g
Cholesterol: 89 mg
Sodium: 81 mg
Dietary fiber: 0 g

Grilled Veal Steaks with Fresh Lemon and Mushrooms

4 servings

1 pound veal round steaks, pounded very thin
1 teaspoon olive oil
½ cup dry white wine
1 tablespoon fresh lemon juice
1 pound fresh mushrooms, thinly sliced
1 14-ounce can water-packed artichoke hearts, quartered
2 lemons, cut into quarters

Grill veal over hot coals or broil on a rack 3 inches from heat. Turn when juices begin to form on top of meat; cook 3 to 4 minutes longer, or to desired doneness.

While meat is cooking, combine olive oil, wine, and lemon juice; pour half of the mixture into a skillet and heat. Add mushrooms and sauté; add artichokes during the last few minutes of cooking. Remove mushrooms and artichokes to a platter; cover to keep warm. Quickly heat remaining sauce. Garnish veal with mushrooms and artichokes, squeeze lemon over; drizzle with wine sauce.

APPROXIMATE NUTRITIONAL INFORMATION PER SERVING

Calories: 223
Total fat: 5 g
Saturated fat: 1 g
Percentage of calories from fat: 20%
Carbohydrate: 16 g
Protein: 29 g
Cholesterol: 88 mg
Sodium: 93 mg
Dietary fiber: 2 g

VEAL ITALIAN STYLE

4 servings

2 small garlic cloves, minced
3 tomatoes, peeled, seeded, and chopped
Dash of fresh or dried oregano
Dash of pepper
1 pound veal round steaks, sliced very thin and pounded extra-thin
4 ounces (1 cup) grated reduced-fat mozzarella cheese

Heat garlic, tomatoes, oregano, and pepper just to boiling. Remove from heat; cover to keep warm. Place veal on a rack in broiler pan; broil 3 inches from heat for 2 to 3 minutes. Turn when juices begin to form on top of meat; broil 1 to 2 minutes longer, or to desired doneness. Cover with cheese. Return to broiler until cheese melts. Serve with sauce.

APPROXIMATE NUTRITIONAL INFORMATION PER SERVING

Calories: 187
Total fat: 5 g
Saturated fat: 3 g
Percentage of calories from fat: 26%
Carbohydrate: 5 g
Protein: 28 g
Cholesterol: 96 mg
Sodium: 133 mg
Dietary fiber: 1 g

DUTCH MEAT LOAF

6 servings

1 15-ounce can tomato sauce
¼ cup water
2 tablespoons prepared mustard
1 tablespoon cider vinegar
1 pound extra-lean ground round
1 cup bread crumbs
1 egg
1 medium onion, chopped
¼ teaspoon pepper

Combine tomato sauce, water, mustard, and vinegar. Mix beef with bread crumbs, egg, onion, pepper, and a quarter of the tomato sauce mixture. Shape into a loaf pan. Pour enough sauce over top of meat loaf to coat. Bake uncovered at 350° for 1 hour, basting often. Warm remaining sauce; serve over sliced meat loaf.

APPROXIMATE NUTRITIONAL INFORMATION PER SERVING

Calories: 218
Total fat: 8 g
Saturated fat: 3 g
Percentage of calories from fat: 33%
Carbohydrate: 19 g
Protein: 18 g
Cholesterol: 47 mg
Sodium: 431 mg
Dietary fiber: 1 g

COUNTRY POT ROAST

6 servings

1 1½-pound chuck roast
1 28-ounce can plum tomatoes, diced
2 teaspoons caraway seeds
½ teaspoon salt
2 to 3 drops Tabasco sauce (optional)
1 bay leaf
¼ teaspoon pepper
4 potatoes, peeled and quartered
6 carrots, peeled and quartered
6 celery stalks, peeled and quartered
4 small onions
12 fresh mushrooms

Brown meat in a small amount of liquid from the plum tomatoes; drain, if necessary, to remove any excess fat. Add tomatoes and seasonings. Cover and simmer 1½ hours; add potatoes, carrots, celery, and onions. Cover and simmer about 1 hour, or until vegetables are crisp-tender. Add mushrooms and simmer 15 minutes.

APPROXIMATE NUTRITIONAL INFORMATION PER SERVING

Calories: 381
Total fat: 12 g
Saturated fat: 4 g
Percentage of calories from fat: 28%

Carbohydrate: 38 g
Protein: 31 g
Cholesterol: 90 mg
Sodium: 532 mg
Dietary fiber: 8 g

Beef Stew

8 servings

2 pounds chuck roast, cubed
1 28-ounce can plum tomatoes
¼ teaspoon pepper
¼ cup red wine (optional)
4 celery stalks, sliced on the diagonal into quarters
1 onion, cut into eighths
5 carrots, peeled and quartered
½ pound fresh mushrooms, sliced
½ pound fresh green beans, cooked
1 14-ounce can water-packed artichoke hearts
½ teaspoon safflower oil
3 to 4 drops of hot chili oil
2 cups cooked macaroni

Brown chuck roast in a small amount of tomato liquid; drain, if necessary, to remove any excess fat. Add tomatoes, pepper, and wine; bring to a boil. Add celery, onion, and carrots; simmer 45 minutes. Add mushrooms, beans, and artichoke hearts; simmer 15 minutes. Add safflower oil, chili oil, and macaroni. Heat.

Note: Hot chili oil is available in Oriental markets or in the Oriental section of the supermarket.

APPROXIMATE NUTRITIONAL INFORMATION PER SERVING

Calories: 382
Total fat: 13 g
Saturated fat: 5 g
Percentage of calories from fat: 29%
Carbohydrate: 32 g
Protein: 33 g
Cholesterol: 90 mg
Sodium: 283 mg
Dietary fiber: 5 g

BEEF STROGANOFF

8 servings

¾ pound extra-lean ground round
¾ cup finely chopped onion
1 garlic clove, minced
½ pound fresh mushrooms, sliced
¼ teaspoon salt
⅛ teaspoon pepper
⅛ teaspoon dried rosemary
1½ cups low-fat (1%) cream of chicken soup
1 cup nonfat sour cream
1 1-pound package bow tie pasta, cooked al dente
2 teaspoons poppy seeds
Fresh parsley for garnish

Sauté ground round, onion, and garlic; drain off any excess fat. Add mushrooms; cook 3 to 5 minutes. Stir in salt, pepper, and rosemary; simmer, uncovered, 10 minutes. Add soup and heat. Stir in sour cream; heat, but do not boil. Arrange pasta around edges of a large platter; spoon stroganoff into center. Sprinkle pasta with poppy seeds. Garnish with fresh parsley.

APPROXIMATE NUTRITIONAL INFORMATION PER SERVING

Calories: 331
Total fat: 6 g
Saturated fat: 2 g
Percentage of calories from fat: 15%
Carbohydrate: 51 g
Protein: 18 g
Cholesterol: 30 mg
Sodium: 288 mg
Dietary fiber: 2 g

Skewered Beef Kebabs

4 servings

1 tablespoon olive oil
¼ cup red wine vinegar
½ cup dry red wine
1 garlic clove, minced
¼ teaspoon pepper
1 pound extra-lean round steak, cut into 1-inch cubes
¾ pound fresh mushrooms
12 cherry tomatoes
12 artichoke hearts
1 white onion, cut into 2-inch cubes
2 green peppers, seeded and quartered lengthwise

Combine oil, vinegar, wine, garlic, and pepper; pour over meat and vegetables. Cover. Chill 1 to 4 hours. Drain. Alternate meat and vegetables on skewers. Grill over medium-hot coals or broil 4 to 6 inches from heat, basting frequently and turning often, until beef is done.

Variation: Marinate a rump roast or a chuck roast; grill or roast. Skewer vegetables separately; grill or broil.

APPROXIMATE NUTRITIONAL INFORMATION PER SERVING

Calories: 264
Total fat: 9 g
Saturated fat: 2 g
Percentage of calories from fat: 30%
Carbohydrate: 19 g
Protein: 30 g
Cholesterol: 67 mg
Sodium: 89 mg
Dietary fiber: 4 g

MARINATED FLANK STEAK

8 servings

½ cup reduced-sodium soy sauce
½ cup vermouth
1 tablespoon brown sugar
1 tablespoon Worcestershire sauce
1½ teaspoons unseasoned meat tenderizer, (optional)
2 garlic cloves, sliced
1 piece of fresh gingerroot, thinly sliced
2 pounds flank steak, all visible fat removed

Combine soy sauce, vermouth, brown sugar, Worcestershire sauce, meat tenderizer, if using, garlic, and gingerroot. Arrange flank steak in a 9 x 13 x 2-inch glass casserole. Pour sauce over top; cover with plastic wrap. Marinate in refrigerator for 2 to 24 hours. Drain marinade. Grill over hot coals for 6 to 8 minutes on each side, or to desired doneness. Remove to a cutting board. Slice on the diagonal.

APPROXIMATE NUTRITIONAL INFORMATION PER SERVING

Calories: 204
Total fat: 10 g
Saturated fat: 4 g
Percentage of calories from fat: 43%
Carbohydrate: 0 g
Protein: 26 g
Cholesterol: 65 mg
Sodium: 155 mg
Dietary fiber: 0 g

BARBECUED ROUND STEAK

8 servings

2 teaspoons olive oil
3 tablespoons lemon juice
1 tablespoon red wine vinegar
2 garlic cloves, sliced
Pinch of fresh or dried thyme
½ teaspoon chili powder
2 pounds extra-lean round steak
1 large onion, sliced
Pepper to taste

Combine olive oil, lemon juice, vinegar, garlic, and seasonings; pour over steak. Top with onion. Cover. Marinate in refrigerator for 2 hours, turning several times to coat. Drain. Grill steak over hot coals 7 to 8 minutes on each side, or to desired doneness. Sprinkle with pepper.

APPROXIMATE NUTRITIONAL INFORMATION PER SERVING

Calories: 162
Total fat: 5 g
Saturated fat: 2 g
Percentage of calories from fat: 28%
Carbohydrate: 2 g
Protein: 25 g
Cholesterol: 67 mg
Sodium: 56 mg
Dietary fiber: 0 g

MEXICAN-STYLE STEAK

8 servings

1 barbecued round steak (facing page)
8 6-inch corn tortillas
½ head of lettuce, chopped
2 ripe tomatoes, chopped
1 white onion, chopped
1 cup Tomato Salsa, preferably homemade (page 433)

Prepare steak according to recipe. Slice steak into very thin strips. Wrap tortillas in aluminum foil and heat in a 325° oven until warm, about 15 minutes. Place several strips of steak on each tortilla. Top with lettuce, tomato, and onion. Roll. Serve with salsa.

APPROXIMATE NUTRITIONAL INFORMATION PER SERVING

Calories: 244
Total fat: 6 g
Saturated fat: 2 g
Percentage of calories from fat: 22%
Carbohydrate: 19 g
Protein: 28 g
Cholesterol: 67 mg
Sodium: 390 mg
Dietary fiber: 2 g

Swiss Steak

4 servings

1 pound extra-lean round steak
¼ cup all-purpose flour
Dash of pepper
1 onion, cut into rings
¼ cup red wine
1 14½-ounce can plum tomatoes

Shake meat in a paper bag with flour and pepper. Brown meat and onion on both sides in wine. Drain, if necessary, to remove any excess fat. Stir in tomatoes. Cook slowly 1½ to 2 hours, or until tender.

APPROXIMATE NUTRITIONAL INFORMATION PER SERVING

Calories: 237
Total fat: 5 g
Saturated fat: 2 g
Percentage of calories from fat: 18%
Carbohydrate: 16 g
Protein: 27 g
Cholesterol: 67 mg
Sodium: 303 mg
Dietary fiber: 2 g

Beef Tostados

6 servings

6 6-inch corn or flour tortillas
1 pound extra-lean ground round, cooked and drained of fat
½ head of lettuce, chopped
2 ripe tomatoes, chopped
1 white onion, chopped
½ cup grated reduced-fat mozzarella or cheddar cheese
1 cup Tomato Salsa, preferably homemade (page 433)

Place tortillas on a nonstick baking sheet. Heat in a 350° oven 3 minutes on each side, or until warm. For a softer shell, warm tortillas in a tortilla warmer, in the microwave, or on the stove top. To microwave, wrap tortillas between two slightly dampened paper towels; microwave 1 to 2 minutes, or until warm. Keep wrapped until ready to serve. To warm tortillas on the stove top, arrange them in a bamboo basket or vegetable steamer basket; steam covered over boiling water for 3 to 5 minutes, or until warm. Spread with ground round. Top with lettuce, tomato, onion, cheese, and salsa.

Note: If purchasing flour tortillas, select a brand made with soy or other heart-healthy oil, not with lard. Corn tortillas generally do not contain any oil or shortening, so are more heart-healthy and are lower in calories and in fat.

APPROXIMATE NUTRITIONAL INFORMATION PER SERVING USING CORN TORTILLAS

Calories: 247
Total fat: 11 g
Saturated fat: 4 g
Percentage of calories from fat: 40%
Carbohydrate: 17 g
Protein: 20 g
Cholesterol: 57 mg
Sodium: 135 mg
Dietary fiber: 3 g

APPROXIMATE NUTRITIONAL INFORMATION PER SERVING USING FLOUR TORTILLAS

Calories: 304
Total fat: 13 g
Saturated fat: 5 g
Percentage of calories from fat: 38%
Carbohydrate: 25 g
Protein: 21 g
Cholesterol: 57 mg
Sodium: 262 mg
Dietary fiber: 3 g

Beef Tacos

4 servings

4 6-inch corn tortillas
¾ pound extra-lean ground round, cooked and drained of fat
¼ cup grated reduced-fat cheddar cheese
1 white onion, chopped
1 green pepper, seeded and chopped
2 tablespoons chopped green chilies (optional)
2 ripe tomatoes, chopped
½ head of lettuce, chopped
½ cup sprouts
1 cup Tomato Salsa, preferably homemade (page 433)
¼ cup nonfat sour cream (optional)

Spread tortillas on a nonstick baking sheet. Place ground round lengthwise in the center of each tortilla. Cover meat with cheese. Top cheese with onion, green pepper, green chilies, if using, and tomatoes. Bake at 400° for 10 to 15 minutes, or until cheese melts. Remove from oven. Top with lettuce, sprouts, and salsa. Fold left and right edges of tortilla over center to cover filling. Top with nonfat sour cream, if desired.

Note: Corn tortillas generally do not contain any oil or shortening so are more heart-healthy and lower in fat and calories than flour tortillas.

APPROXIMATE NUTRITIONAL INFORMATION PER SERVING

Calories: 268
Total fat: 9 g
Saturated fat: 4 g
Percentage of calories from fat: 31%

Carbohydrate: 25 g
Protein: 22 g
Cholesterol: 58 mg
Sodium: 463 mg
Dietary fiber: 3 g

DESSERTS

Fresh Strawberries with Sour Cream and Brown Sugar

4 servings

1 pint strawberries with stems
4 tablespoons nonfat sour cream
Fresh mint leaves for garnish
2 tablespoons brown sugar

Arrange berries in a basket or serving bowl. Place sour cream in a chilled bowl; garnish with mint. Pass with brown sugar. To eat, dip berries first in sour cream, then in brown sugar.

APPROXIMATE NUTRITIONAL INFORMATION PER SERVING

Calories: 55
Total fat: trace
Saturated fat: 0 g
Percentage of calories from fat: 5%
Carbohydrate: 13 g
Protein: 1 g
Cholesterol: 0 mg
Sodium: 15 mg
Dietary fiber: 1 g

Strawberry Shortcake

4 servings

4 slices angel-food cake
1 pint fresh strawberries, crushed or sliced
2 cups Whipped Cream Topping (see following recipe)
4 whole strawberries

Slice cake; top with crushed or sliced berries. Garnish with Whipped Cream Topping and whole berries.

Note: Read the cake-mix label to ensure that the one you select is made with heart-healthy ingredients. However, most angel-food cake mixes are.

Variation: Select a heart-healthy biscuit, scone, or shortcake mix and prepare according to package directions. Bake. Cool 5 to 10 minutes. Slice biscuits, scones, or shortcakes in half.

APPROXIMATE NUTRITIONAL INFORMATION PER SERVING

Calories: 175	Carbohydrate: 39 g
Total fat: trace	Protein: 4 g
Saturated fat: 0 g	Cholesterol: 0 mg
Percentage of calories from fat: 2%	Sodium: 270 mg
	Dietary fiber: 2 g

WHIPPED CREAM TOPPING

8 ⅔-cup servings

- ½ teaspoon unflavored gelatin
- ¼ cup cold water
- ¼ cup granulated sugar
- 3 egg whites
- ¼ teaspoon cream of tartar
- 1 teaspoon vanilla extract

In a small saucepan, soften gelatin in cold water. Stir in sugar. Cook over low heat, stirring constantly for 2 to 3 minutes, or until mixture is hot (do not boil). Set aside.

Fill bottom of a double boiler one-third full with water and bring to a boil. Meanwhile, in top of the double boiler, using an electric mixer, beat egg whites to stiff peaks; place pan over the boiling water. Add cream of tartar; beat 2 minutes. Rewarm

(continued on next page)

(continued from preceding page)

gelatin and pour in a steady stream into egg whites, beating at high speed to stiff peaks, about 1 minute.

Pour hot water out of the double-boiler bottom and fill with ice water. Put top of double boiler over ice water. Add vanilla extract; beat 3 minutes. Serve.

APPROXIMATE NUTRITIONAL INFORMATION PER SERVING

Calories: 32
Total fat: 0 g
Saturated fat: 0 g
Percentage of calories from fat: 0%
Carbohydrate: 6 g
Protein: 1 g
Cholesterol: 0 mg
Sodium: 19 mg
Dietary fiber: 0 g

Poached Pears with Fresh Berries

4 servings

1 cup white wine
1 vanilla bean, split open
4 firm ripe pears
¼ cup lemon juice
2 tablespoons orange juice
1 cup fresh blueberries, strawberries, or raspberries
Fresh mint for garnish

Place wine and vanilla bean in a medium saucepan; bring to a boil. Peel and quarter pears; dip in lemon juice. Place pears in a vegetable steamer basket over boiling wine; cover and steam 8 to 10 minutes, or until tender. Remove from pan. Boil poaching liquid for 2 to 3 minutes to reduce. Remove and discard vanilla bean. Combine 2 tablespoons poaching liquid with 2 tablespoons of the lemon juice and 2 tablespoons orange juice.

Serve pears at room temperature on individual dessert plates with a small amount of sauce. Add berries and garnish with fresh mint.

Variation: In place of berries, substitute other fresh fruits in season such as sliced fresh peaches (dip in lemon juice to preserve color), grapes, kiwi, bananas, cantaloupe, watermelon, plums, peeled orange segments, or mandarin oranges.

APPROXIMATE NUTRITIONAL INFORMATION PER SERVING

Calories: 166
Total fat: 1 g
Saturated fat: 0 g
Percentage of calories from fat: 4%
Carbohydrate: 33 g
Protein: 1 g
Cholesterol: 0 mg
Sodium: 7 mg
Dietary fiber: 6 g

POACHED PEARS WITH RASPBERRY SAUCE

4 servings

4 Bosc or Bartlett pears
2 cups white wine (Soave Bolla works well)
1 10-ounce box frozen raspberries with sugar, thawed
3 to 4 tablespoons cornstarch
½ cup cold water
1 cup whole fresh raspberries
1 cup fresh blueberries
Fresh mint for garnish

Carefully peel pears, leaving stems intact. Slice a small piece off the bottom so pear will stand alone. Pour wine into a deep saucepan; simmer 10 minutes. Stand pears upright in the wine. Cover pan with lid;

(continued on next page)

(continued from preceding page)

simmer 20 to 30 minutes, or until pears are tender when pierced with a fork.

Heat thawed raspberries in a saucepan. In a small bowl, mix cornstarch with cold water to make a smooth paste; gradually add to warm raspberries.

Divide sauce among 4 dessert plates. Stand pears upright in center of sauce. Ring with fresh raspberries and blueberries. Garnish with mint. Or chill until ready to use.

APPROXIMATE NUTRITIONAL INFORMATION PER SERVING

Calories: 337
Total fat: 1 g
Saturated fat: 0 g
Percentage of calories from fat: 3%
Carbohydrate: 66 g
Protein: 2 g
Cholesterol: 0 mg
Sodium: 13 mg
Dietary fiber: 6 g

Baked Apples

6 servings

- 6 medium baking apples
- ¼ cup brown sugar
- 1 teaspoon cinnamon
- 1 tablespoon tub-style light margarine
- ⅓ cup raisins

Remove core from apples. Mix sugar, cinnamon, margarine, and raisins. Fill center of apples. Place upright in a baking dish. Pour 1 cup water around apples. Bake uncovered at 375° for 45 to 60 minutes, basting frequently.

Note: If using a Crock-Pot, reduce water to ½ cup. Cook on low for 8 hours or overnight.

APPROXIMATE NUTRITIONAL INFORMATION PER SERVING

Calories: 147	Carbohydrate: 37 g
Total fat: 1 g	Protein: 1 g
Saturated fat: 0 g	Cholesterol: 0 mg
Percentage of calories from fat: 5%	Sodium: 23 mg
	Dietary fiber: 3 g

APPLE CRISP

8 servings

6 tart cooking apples, peeled and sliced
1 tablespoon lemon juice
⅓ cup granulated sugar
1 teaspoon cinnamon
¾ cup rolled oats
½ cup all-purpose flour
1 cup brown sugar
3 tablespoons tub-style light margarine

Place apples in a pie plate; sprinkle with lemon juice, sugar, and cinnamon. Combine remaining ingredients; pour over apples. Bake uncovered at 375° for 30 minutes, or until apples are tender.

APPROXIMATE NUTRITIONAL INFORMATION PER SERVING

Calories: 240	Carbohydrate: 58 g
Total fat: 1 g	Protein: 2 g
Saturated fat: 0 g	Cholesterol: 0 mg
Percentage of calories from fat: 5%	Sodium: 51 mg
	Dietary fiber: 3 g

APPLESAUCE

8 servings

8 to 10 large cooking apples, peeled, cored, and cut into chunks
½ cup water
½ cup sugar
1 teaspoon cinnamon

Put apples and water in a saucepan; cover and simmer, stirring frequently, until apples are barely tender. Add sugar and continue cooking about 30 minutes, or until sugar dissolves. Stir in cinnamon.

Notes: For a smooth sauce, purée apples in a blender or food processor before adding sugar.

If using a Crock-Pot, combine all ingredients. Cover. Cook on low for 8 hours or overnight.

APPROXIMATE NUTRITIONAL INFORMATION PER ½-CUP SERVING

Calories: 150
Total fat: 1 g
Saturated fat: 0 g
Percentage of calories from fat: 4%
Carbohydrate: 39 g
Protein: 0 g
Cholesterol: 0 mg
Sodium: 2 mg
Dietary fiber: 2 g

RHUBARB SAUCE

5 servings

4 cups sliced rhubarb stalks, all leaves removed
½ cup sugar
¼ cup water

Combine all ingredients in a 2-quart saucepan; cover. Cook slowly about 10 minutes, or until fruit is tender.

Serving Suggestions: Warm, serve over sliced bananas. Serve with 1 cup plain nonfat yogurt combined with the juice and zest of ½ lemon; add a dash of honey.

APPROXIMATE NUTRITIONAL INFORMATION PER SERVING

Calories: 98	Carbohydrate: 24 g
Total fat: trace	Protein: 1 g
Saturated fat: 0 g	Cholesterol: 0 mg
Percentage of calories from fat: 2%	Sodium: 5 mg
	Dietary fiber: 2 g

STRAWBERRY-RHUBARB SAUCE

5 servings

- 3 cups sliced rhubarb stalks, all leaves removed
- ¾ cup sugar
- ½ cup water
- 1 cup fresh strawberries, hulled and sliced

Combine rhubarb, sugar, and water in a 2-quart saucepan; cover. Cook slowly about 10 minutes, or until rhubarb is tender. Stir in strawberries; heat just to boiling.

APPROXIMATE NUTRITIONAL INFORMATION PER SERVING

Calories: 141	Carbohydrate: 35 g
Total fat: trace	Protein: 1 g
Saturated fat: 0 g	Cholesterol: 0 mg
Percentage of calories from fat: 2%	Sodium: 5 mg
	Dietary fiber: 2 g

The single and the double pie-crust recipes that follow are made with oil rather than butter or solid shortening. Although the oil produces a non-cholesterol crust, it lacks the flakiness and flavor of those made with butter or solid shortening.

I have tried many times to reduce the amount of oil and still produce a tasty crust, but so far have been disappointed in the results.

There are some pie-crust mixes on the market that have 5 grams of fat per eighth of a 9-inch pie shell and the flavor is very acceptable. Krusteaz is the brand I'm most familiar with. The nutritional analysis of the pie recipes has been calculated with Krusteaz mix as well as with a homemade crust.

Due to the amount of fat in the crust, limit yourself to fruit pies with no added fat in the filling. And budget for them. I try to serve them when the main meal is a low-fat soup, or only for a company meal or special occasion.

SINGLE PASTRY CRUST

1 9-inch crust

1½ cups all-purpose flour
1½ teaspoons sugar
¾ teaspoon salt
½ cup canola oil
2 tablespoons nonfat milk

Combine flour, sugar, and salt. Mix together oil and milk; add to flour. Using a pastry blender or fork, work mixture into a soft dough. Add additional milk if needed. Form into a ball. Roll out on a well-floured pastry cloth. Place in a 9-inch pie plate. Adjust crust. Flute edges.

Note: If a baked shell is needed, prick bottom and sides of crust with a fork. Bake at 450° for 10 to 12 minutes, or until golden. If filling and crust are to be baked together, do not prick crust.

APPROXIMATE NUTRITIONAL INFORMATION PER SERVING

Calories: 214	Carbohydrate: 19 g
Total fat: 14 g	Protein: 3 g
Saturated fat: 1 g	Cholesterol: 0 mg
Percentage of calories from fat: 60%	Sodium: 202 mg
	Dietary fiber: 1 g

DOUBLE PASTRY CRUST

2 9-inch pie crusts

2 cups all-purpose flour
½ teaspoon salt
4 tablespoons ice water
⅔ cup safflower mayonnaise
1½ tablespoons nonfat milk

Combine flour and salt. Mix ice water with mayonnaise; add to flour. Using a pastry blender or fork, work mixture together; add milk. Form into a ball. Divide dough in half. Roll out each half on a well-floured pastry cloth. Place one half in a 9-inch pie plate; adjust crust. Fill. Add top crust; flute edges. Prick.

Note: It is important that the ice water be ice cold.

APPROXIMATE NUTRITIONAL INFORMATION PER SERVING

Calories: 247	Carbohydrate: 25 g
Total fat: 15 g	Protein: 4 g
Saturated fat: 2 g	Cholesterol: 0 mg
Percentage of calories from fat: 55%	Sodium: 240 mg
	Dietary fiber: 1 g

Strawberry-Rhubarb Pie

8 slices

½ cup sugar
¼ cup all-purpose flour
¼ teaspoon salt
¼ teaspoon nutmeg
3 cups sliced rhubarb stalks, all leaves removed
1 cup sliced strawberries
1 9-inch double pastry crust (page 595)

Combine sugar, flour, salt, and nutmeg. Add fruit. Toss to coat. Let stand 20 minutes. Spoon into pastry-lined pie plate. Add top crust. Flute edges. Prick. Bake at 400° for 40 to 45 minutes.

APPROXIMATE NUTRITIONAL INFORMATION PER SERVING

Calories: 325
Total fat: 15 g
Saturated fat: 2 g
Percentage of calories from fat: 42%
Carbohydrate: 43 g
Protein: 5 g
Cholesterol: 0 mg
Sodium: 309 mg
Dietary fiber: trace

APPROXIMATE NUTRITIONAL INFORMATION PER SERVING USING KRUSTEAZ PIE-CRUST MIX

Calories: 258
Total fat: 10 g
Saturated fat: 1 g
Percentage of calories from fat: 36%
Carbohydrate: 39 g
Protein: 3 g
Cholesterol: 0 mg
Sodium: 269 mg
Dietary fiber: trace

FRESH BERRY PIE

8 slices

1 9-inch double pastry crust (page 595)
2 tablespoons all-purpose flour
½ cup sugar
⅛ teaspoon salt
4 cups fresh raspberries, strawberries, or blackberries
1 teaspoon lemon juice

Line a 9-inch pie plate with pastry. Mix together flour, sugar, and salt; sprinkle a quarter of the mixture on uncooked bottom crust. Coat berries with lemon juice and toss with remaining sugar mixture. Spoon into pie plate. Add top crust; flute edges. Prick. Bake at 450° for 15 minutes. Reduce heat to 350° and continue baking 25 to 30 minutes.

APPROXIMATE NUTRITIONAL INFORMATION PER SERVING

Calories: 333
Total fat: 15 g
Saturated fat: 2 g
Percentage of calories from fat: 41%
Carbohydrate: 46 g
Protein: 4 g
Cholesterol: 0 mg
Sodium: 274 mg
Dietary fiber: trace

APPROXIMATE NUTRITIONAL INFORMATION PER SERVING USING KRUSTEAZ PIE-CRUST MIX

Calories: 266
Total fat: 10 g
Saturated fat: 1 g
Percentage of calories from fat: 35%
Carbohydrate: 41 g
Protein: 3 g
Cholesterol: 0 mg
Sodium: 234 mg
Dietary fiber: trace

Apple Pie

8 slices

6 cups pared and sliced apples
1¼ tablespoons lemon juice
¼ cup sugar
½ teaspoon cinnamon
⅛ teaspoon salt
2 tablespoons all-purpose flour
1 9-inch double pastry crust (page 595)

Toss apples with lemon juice. Combine sugar, cinnamon, salt, and flour; mix with apples. Spoon into a pastry-lined pie plate. Add top crust. Flute edges. Prick. Bake at 450° for 10 minutes. Reduce heat to 375° and continue baking 40 to 50 minutes.

APPROXIMATE NUTRITIONAL INFORMATION PER SERVING

Calories: 340
Total fat: 15 g
Saturated fat: 2 g
Percentage of calories from fat: 41%
Carbohydrate: 48 g
Protein: 4 g
Cholesterol: 0 mg
Sodium: 274 mg
Dietary fiber: trace

APPROXIMATE NUTRITIONAL INFORMATION PER SERVING USING KRUSTEAZ PIE-CRUST MIX

Calories: 273
Total fat: 10 g
Saturated fat: 1 g
Percentage of calories from fat: 34%
Carbohydrate: 44 g
Protein: 2 g
Cholesterol: 0 mg
Sodium: 234 mg
Dietary fiber: trace

PUMPKIN PIE

8 slices

1 1-pound can pumpkin
¾ cup firmly packed brown sugar
¾ cup egg substitute
¼ teaspoon salt
1 teaspoon cinnamon
½ teaspoon ginger
½ teaspoon nutmeg
¼ teaspoon cloves
1 12-ounce can evaporated skim milk
1 9-inch single pastry crust (page 594)

Combine pumpkin, brown sugar, egg substitute, salt, and spices; add milk and blend. Pour into pie shell. Bake at 400° for 50 minutes, or until done.

Note: To test for doneness, insert a knife into center of pie. When pie is done, the knife will come out clean.

APPROXIMATE NUTRITIONAL INFORMATION PER SERVING

Calories: 362
Total fat: 15 g
Saturated fat: 1 g
Percentage of calories from fat: 36%
Carbohydrate: 50 g
Protein: 9 g
Cholesterol: 2 mg
Sodium: 370 mg
Dietary fiber: trace

APPROXIMATE NUTRITIONAL INFORMATION PER SERVING USING KRUSTEAZ PIE-CRUST MIX

Calories: 239
Total fat: 5 g
Saturated fat: 0 g
Percentage of calories from fat: 20%
Carbohydrate: 41 g
Protein: 7 g
Cholesterol: 2 mg
Sodium: 268 mg
Dietary fiber: trace

Cobbler Batter

- 1 cup all-purpose flour, sifted
- ½ teaspoon salt
- 1½ teaspoons baking powder
- ⅓ cup nonfat milk
- 3 tablespoons safflower oil

Combine flour, salt, and baking powder. Mix milk with oil; add to flour. Using a fork or pastry blender, work dough into a ball. Drop by spoonfuls onto fruit cobbler (recipes follow).

APPROXIMATE NUTRITIONAL INFORMATION PER ⅛ OF RECIPE

Calories: 106	Carbohydrate: 13 g
Total fat: 5 g	Protein: 2 g
Saturated fat: 0 g	Cholesterol: 0 mg
Percentage of calories from fat: 45%	Sodium: 139 mg
	Dietary fiber: 1 g

Cherry Cobbler

8 servings

- 1 16-ounce can pitted tart pie cherries with liquid
- ½ cup sugar
- 1 tablespoon minute tapioca
- 1 recipe cobbler batter (above)

Combine cherries, sugar, and tapioca in a medium saucepan; cook, stirring constantly, until sugar is dissolved and syrup is clear. Pour into a 9-inch pie plate. Dot with cobbler batter. Bake at 425° for 25 to 30 minutes, or until topping is lightly browned.

APPROXIMATE NUTRITIONAL INFORMATION PER SERVING

Calories: 191
Total fat: 5 g
Saturated fat: 1 g
Percentage of calories from fat: 25%
Carbohydrate: 34 g
Protein: 4 g
Cholesterol: 0 mg
Sodium: 141 mg
Dietary fiber: 1 g

BERRY COBBLER

8 servings

- ¾ cup water
- 2 tablespoons cornstarch
- ½ cup sugar
- 3 cups strawberries, raspberries, blueberries, or blackberries
- 1 recipe cobbler batter (see facing page)

In a medium saucepan, combine water, cornstarch, and sugar; bring to a boil. Cook for 1 minute, stirring constantly. Add berries and remove from heat. Pour into a 9-inch pie plate. Top with cobbler batter. Bake at 425° for 25 to 30 minutes, or until topping is lightly browned.

APPROXIMATE NUTRITIONAL INFORMATION PER SERVING

Calories: 179
Total fat: 5 g
Saturated fat: 0 g
Percentage of calories from fat: 28%
Carbohydrate: 31 g
Protein: 2 g
Cholesterol: 0 mg
Sodium: 141 mg
Dietary fiber: 2 g

RHUBARB COBBLER

8 servings

4 cups sliced rhubarb stalks, all leaves removed
½ cup sugar
1 to 2 tablespoons water
2 tablespoons cornstarch
1 recipe cobbler batter (page 600)

In a medium saucepan, combine rhubarb, sugar, water, and cornstarch. Bring to a boil; cook for 1 minute, stirring constantly. Pour into a 9-inch pie plate. Dot with cobbler batter. Bake at 425° for 25 to 30 minutes, or until topping is lightly browned.

APPROXIMATE NUTRITIONAL INFORMATION PER SERVING

Calories: 175
Total fat: 5 g
Saturated fat: 0 g
Percentage of calories from fat: 28%
Carbohydrate: 30 g
Protein: 3 g
Cholesterol: 0 mg
Sodium: 143 mg
Dietary fiber: 2 g

LEMON ICE

4 servings

2 cups water
4 tablespoons sugar
½ cup fresh lemon juice
Grated zest of 2 lemons

Combine water and sugar in a saucepan; boil without stirring for 5 minutes. Cool. Add lemon juice and zest; stir. Pour into an ice-cream freezer and process according to manufacturer's instructions, or pour into large bowl suitable for freezing and follow instructions for freezing and beating ices in the following recipe.

APPROXIMATE NUTRITIONAL INFORMATION PER SERVING

Calories: 53
Total fat: 0 g
Saturated fat: 0 g
Percentage of calories from fat: 0%

Carbohydrate: 15 g
Protein: 0 g
Cholesterol: 0 mg
Sodium: 4 mg
Dietary fiber: 0 g

Fresh Strawberry Ice

4 servings

4 cups hulled strawberries
1½ teaspoons lemon juice
1½ tablespoons sugar

Purée berries in a blender; add lemon juice and sugar and whirl 2 to 3 minutes. Process in an ice-cream freezer according to manufacturer's instructions, or pour into a large bowl and follow the instructions that follow for freezing and beating ices.

Pour mixture into a large mixing bowl suitable for freezing. Cover. Freeze 1 to 2 hours, or until solid around edges but still slightly slushy in center. Remove from freezer. Beat with an electric mixer on medium speed until mixture is smooth and no large crystals remain. Cover. Refreeze for 1 hour. Serve at once or refreeze. If frozen, allow mixure to soften for 5 to 10 minutes at room temperature, or for 30 minutes at refrigerator temperature, before serving.

Notes: It is important that the bowl used for freezing be large because the mixture must not be too deep if it is to freeze properly. When doubling a recipe, use two bowls rather than one.

Ices can fit into your meal plans in a number of ways because you can serve ices as a first course, with or between courses of a meal, or for dessert. They are also fun to make with children or grandchildren.

Serving Suggestion: Serve ices in chilled, stemmed glasses, in fresh lemon or orange shells, or in cantaloupe or other melon boats. Garnish with whole fresh fruits and a sprig of mint.

APPROXIMATE NUTRITIONAL INFORMATION PER SERVING

Calories: 62	Carbohydrate: 15 g
Total fat: trace	Protein: 1 g
Saturated fat: 0 g	Cholesterol: 0 mg
Percentage of calories from fat: 8%	Sodium: 2 mg
	Dietary fiber: 2 g

WATERMELON ICE

4 servings

3 cups watermelon flesh
⅓ cup sugar
Juice of 1 large orange

Purée watermelon in a blender; add remaining ingredients and whirl 3 to 4 minutes. Process in an ice-cream freezer according to manufacturer's instructions, or pour into a large bowl suitable for freezing and follow instructions for freezing and beating ices (see preceding recipe).

Serving Suggestion: Spoon into cantaloupe or honeydew boats. Garnish with fresh mint.

APPROXIMATE NUTRITIONAL INFORMATION PER SERVING

Calories: 108	Carbohydrate: 27 g
Total fat: 1 g	Protein: 3 g
Saturated fat: 0 g	Cholesterol: 0 mg
Percentage of calories from fat: 5%	Sodium: 3 mg
	Dietary fiber: trace

Granita de Caffè con Panna

4 servings

2 cups brewed espresso coffee
¼ cup sugar
½ cup Whipped Cream Topping (page 587)

Combine brewed coffee and sugar. Pour into a large mixing bowl suitable for freezing. Follow instructions for freezing and beating ices (page 604). Spoon into stemmed glasses. Garnish with topping.

Variation: To save time, use pressurized prepared light whipped cream topping.

APPROXIMATE NUTRITIONAL INFORMATION PER SERVING

Calories: 96
Total fat: 1 g
Saturated fat: 1 g
Percentage of calories from fat: 13%
Carbohydrate: 21 g
Protein: 0 g
Cholesterol: 21 mg
Sodium: 73 mg
Dietary fiber: 0 g

APPROXIMATE NUTRITIONAL INFORMATION PER SERVING USING PRESSURIZED LIGHT WHIPPED CREAM TOPPING

Calories: 106
Total fat: 3 g
Saturated fat: 1 g
Percentage of calories from fat: 23%
Carbohydrate: 20g
Protein: 0 g
Cholesterol: 4 mg
Sodium: 77 mg
Dietary fiber: 0 g

Peanut Butter Cookies

40 cookies

4 egg whites
2 cups nonhydrogenated peanut butter
1⅔ cups granulated sugar

Beat egg whites until stiff. Combine peanut butter and sugar; fold in egg whites. Drop by teaspoonfuls onto nonstick baking sheets. Flatten slightly with prongs of a fork. Bake at 325° for 20 minutes. Remove to wire racks to cool.

APPROXIMATE NUTRITIONAL INFORMATION PER COOKIE

Calories: 109
Total fat: 6 g
Saturated fat: 1 g
Percentage of calories from fat: 53%
Carbohydrate: 11 g
Protein: 4 g
Cholesterol: 0 mg
Sodium: 67 mg
Dietary fiber: 1 g

RICE KRISPIES COOKIES

24 cookies

- 3 tablespoons tub-style light margarine
- 40 regular marshmallows
- ½ teaspoon vanilla
- 4 cups Rice Krispies cereal

Warm margarine. Add marshmallows and cook over medium heat until marshmallows are melted, stirring constantly. Add vanilla. Pour in cereal. Mix well. Using a small piece of waxed paper, press mixture evenly into a waxed paper-lined 13 x 9 x 2-inch pan. Cut into 24 2 x 2-inch squares when cool.

APPROXIMATE NUTRITIONAL INFORMATION PER COOKIE

Calories: 50
Total fat: trace
Saturated fat: 0 g
Percentage of calories from fat: 5%
Carbohydrate: 12 g
Protein: 0 g
Cholesterol: 0 mg
Sodium: 18 mg
Dietary fiber: 0 g

MOLASSES COOKIES

4 dozen cookies

2 cups all-purpose flour
¼ teaspoon salt
1 teaspoon baking powder
1 teaspoon baking soda
½ teaspoon ground cloves
1¼ teaspoons ground ginger
1¼ teaspoons cinnamon
⅔ cup safflower oil
¼ cup molasses
1 egg
1 cup firmly packed brown sugar
¼ cup granulated sugar

Sift together flour, salt, baking powder, baking soda, cloves, ginger, and cinnamon. Set aside. Using lowest speed of an electric mixer, blend oil, molasses, and egg; add brown sugar. Blend. Gradually add flour mixture; mix well.

Chill dough for 2 hours. Form into 1-inch balls. Roll each ball in granulated sugar. Place on nonstick baking sheets. Sprinkle each cookie with 2 to 3 drops of water. Bake at 375° for 8 to 10 minutes, or until set and tops are crackled. Cool cookies on a wire rack.

APPROXIMATE NUTRITIONAL INFORMATION PER COOKIE

Calories: 74
Total fat: 3 g
Saturated fat: 0 g
Percentage of calories from fat: 39%

Carbohydrate: 11 g
Protein: 1 g
Cholesterol: 4 mg
Sodium: 41 mg
Dietary fiber: 0 g

TAPIOCA PUDDING

6 servings

1 egg, well beaten
2½ cups nonfat milk
3 tablespoons quick-cooking tapioca
¼ cup sugar
1 teaspoon vanilla extract

In a medium saucepan, combine egg, milk, tapioca, and sugar; let stand 5 minutes. Cook tapioca over medium heat, stirring constantly, until mixture comes to a full boil, 6 to 8 minutes. Add vanilla. Stir only enough to mix. Pour into bowl or individual serving cups. Let cool for 20 minutes. Chill.

Variation: For chocolate tapioca, add 3 tablespoons semisweet cocoa powder along with the vanilla to completed recipe.

APPROXIMATE NUTRITIONAL INFORMATION PER SERVING

Calories: 130
Total fat: 1 g
Saturated fat: 1 g
Percentage of calories from fat: 7%
Carbohydrate: 22 g
Protein: 9 g
Cholesterol: 37 mg
Sodium: 63 mg
Dietary fiber: 0 g

APPROXIMATE NUTRITIONAL INFORMATION PER SERVING OF CHOCOLATE TAPIOCA

Calories: 136
Total fat: 1 g
Saturated fat: 1 g
Percentage of calories from fat: 9%
Carbohydrate: 23 g
Protein: 9 g
Cholesterol: 37 mg
Sodium: 64 mg
Dietary fiber: 0 g

Chocolate Cake

12 slices

2 eggs, separated
1¼ cups sugar
1¾ cups all-purpose flour
¾ teaspoon baking soda
¾ teaspoon salt
½ cup safflower oil
1 cup nonfat milk plus 1 tablespoon vinegar
¼ cup unsweetened cocoa powder
½ teaspoon vanilla extract

Beat egg whites until frothy. Gradually beat in ½ cup of the sugar; beat until egg whites are stiff. Set aside.

In a large mixing bowl, sift together remaining sugar, flour, baking soda, and salt; add oil and half the milk and vinegar. Beat 1 minute on medium speed; add remaining milk, egg yolks, cocoa powder, and vanilla. Beat 1 minute longer. Fold in egg whites.

Pour into 2 nonstick 9-inch round cake pans or 24 paper-lined muffin cups. Bake at 350° for 30 to 35 minutes, or until a toothpick inserted near the centers comes out clean. Cool on wire racks for 10 minutes. Remove from pans. Cool thoroughly on racks.

Serving Suggestion: Frost with Seven-Minute Icing (see following recipe), if desired.

APPROXIMATE NUTRITIONAL INFORMATION PER SLICE

Calories: 251
Total fat: 10 g
Saturated fat: 1 g
Percentage of calories from fat: 37%
Carbohydrate: 37 g
Protein: 4 g
Cholesterol: 36 mg
Sodium: 234 mg
Dietary fiber: 1 g

APPROXIMATE NUTRITIONAL INFORMATION PER SLICE OF CAKE WITH ICING

Calories: 334
Total fat: 10 g
Saturated fat: 1 g
Percentage of calories from fat: 28%
Carbohydrate: 58 g
Protein: 5 g
Cholesterol: 36 mg
Sodium: 288 mg
Dietary fiber: 1 g

SEVEN-MINUTE ICING

- 2 egg whites
- 1¼ cups sugar
- Dash of salt
- ½ cup water
- ¼ teaspoon cream of tartar
- 1 teaspoon vanilla extract

Bring 2 cups water to a boil in bottom of a double boiler. In top of double boiler, combine egg whites, sugar, salt, water, and cream of tartar; beat 1 minute. Place over boiling water. Using highest speed of electric mixer, beat constantly for 5 to 7 minutes, or until frosting stands in stiff peaks. Remove from heat. Stir in vanilla.

Frost tops and sides of two 8- or 9-inch layers or top and sides of one 10-inch tube cake.

APPROXIMATE NUTRITIONAL INFORMATION FOR 1/12 OF RECIPE

Calories: 84
Total fat: 0 g
Saturated fat: 0 g
Percentage of calories from fat: 0%
Carbohydrate: 21 g
Protein: 1 g
Cholesterol: 0 mg
Sodium: 54 mg
Dietary fiber: 0 g

BIBLIOGRAPHY

Anderson, J.W., et al. "Effects of Oat Bran or Bean Intake for Hypercholesterolemic Men." *American Journal of Clinical Nutrition* 40, 1984.

Armstrong, M.L., et al. "Regression of Coronary Atherosclerosis in Rhesus Monkeys." *Circulatory Research*, 1959.

Assembly of Life Sciences, National Research Council. "Diet, Nutrition, and Cancer Committee Report on Diet, Nutrition and Cancer." Washington, D.C.: GPO, 1984.

Austin, M.A., et al. "Atherogenic Lipoprotein Phenotype: A Proposed Genetic Marker for Coronary Heart Disease Risk." *Circulation* 82, 1990.

Banks, T., N. Ali and K. Dais. "Dietary Management of the Patient with Atherosclerosis: Are the New National Cholesterol Education Panel Recommendations Enough?" *Journal of the National Medical Association* 81, 1989.

Barnett, Robert. "Why Fat Makes You Fatter." *American Health*, May 1986.

Bennett, W., and J. Gurin. *The Dieter's Dilemma: Eating Less and Weighing More.* New York: Basic Books, 1982.

Bernard, N.D., L.W. Scherwitz, et al. "Adherence and Acceptability of a Low-Fat Vegetarian Diet Among Patients with Cardiac Disease." *Journal of Cardiopulmonary Rehabilitation* 12, 1992.

Blankenhorn, D.H., et al. "The Influence of Diet on the Appearance of New Lesions in Human Coronary Arteries." *Journal of the American Medical Association* 263, 1990.

Blankenhorn, D.H., and D.M. Kramsc. "Reversal of Atherosis and Sclerosis. The Two Components of Atherosclerosis." *Circulation* 79, 1989.

Block, G., et al. "Nutrient Sources in the American Diet: Quantitative Data from the NHANES II Survey. *American Journal of Epidemiology* 122, 1985.

Bray, G.A. "Obesity—A Disease of Nutrient or Energy Balance?" *Nutrition Reviews* 45, 1987.

Brody, J.E. *Jane Brody's Good Food Book.* New York: W.W. Norton & Co., 1985.

Brown, A.G., J.J. Albers, L.D. Fisher, et al. "Regression of Coronary Artery Disease as a Result of Intensive Lipid-Lowering Therapy in Men with High Levels of Apolipoprotein B." *New England Journal of Medicine,* Vol. 323, 1990.

Brown, M.S., and J.L. Goldstein. "How LDL Receptors Influence Cholesterol and Atherosclerosis." *Scientific American* 251, 1984.

———. "Lowering Plasma Cholesterol by Raising LDL Receptors." *New England Journal of Medicine* 305, 1981.

Bulliyya, G., et al. "Lipid Profiles Among Fish-Consuming Coastal and Non-Fish Consuming Inland Populations." *European Journal of Clinical Nutrition* 44, 1990.

Burkitt, D. *Don't Forget Fiber in Your Diet.* New York: Arco Publishing, 1984.

Caggiula, A.W., et al. "The Multiple Risk Intervention Trial (MRFIT). IV. Intervention on Blood Lipids." *Preventive Medicine* 10, 1981.

Castelli, William P., et al. "Incidence of Coronary Heart Disease and Lipoprotein Cholesterol Levels—The Framingham Study." *Journal of the American Medical Association,* Vol. 256, 1986.

Connor, S.L., and W.E. Connor. *The New American Diet.* New York: Simon & Schuster, 1986.

Connor, W.E., and S.L. Connor. "Diet, Atherosclerosis and Fish Oil." In *Advances in Internal*

Medicine, H. Stollerman and M.D. Siperstein, eds. Chicago: Year Book Publishers, 1989.

———. "The Dietary Prevention and Treatment of Coronary Heart Disease." In *Coronary Heart Disease: Prevention, Complications and Treatment,* W.E. Connor and D. Bristow, eds. Philadelphia: Lippincott, 1985.

Cooper, Kenneth H. *Controlling Cholesterol.* New York: Bantam Books, 1988.

Corbin, C. *Nutrition.* New York: Holt, Rinehart & Winston, 1980.

DeBusk, R.F., N. Houston-Miller, F.R. Superko, et al. "A Case Management System for Coronary Risk Factor Modification Following Acute Myocardial Infarction." *Annals of Internal Medicine,* 1994.

Drewnowski, Adam, and M. Greenwood. "Cream and Sugar: Human Preferences for High-Fat Foods." *Physiological Behavior* 30, 1983.

Drewnowski, Adam, et al. "Sweet Tooth Reconsidered: Taste Responsiveness in Human Obesity." *Psychology & Behavior,* Vol. 35, 1985.

———. "Taste and Eating Disorders." *American Journal of Clinical Nutrition,* 1987.

Edington, J.D., et al. "Serum Lipid Response to Dietary Cholesterol in Subjects Fed a Low-Fat, High-Fiber Diet." *American Journal of Clinical Nutrition* 50, 1989.

Engblom, E., T. Ronnemaa, et al. "Coronary Heart Disease Risk Factors Before and After Bypass Surgery: Results of a Controlled Trial on Multifactorial Rehabilitation." *European Heart Journal,* 1992.

"Fish, Fatty Acids, and Human Health." Editorials, *New England Journal of Medicine* 7, 1985.

Fisher, M., et al. "The Effect of Vegetarian Diets on Plasma Lipid and Platelet Level." *Archives of Internal Medicine* 146, 1986.

Flatt, J.P. "Dietary Fat, Carbohydrate Balance, and Weight Maintenance: Effects of Exercise." *American Journal of Clinical Nutrition* 45, 1987.

Frick, M.H., O. Elo and K. Haapa. "Helsinki Heart Study: Primary Trial with Gemfibrozil in Middle-Aged Men with Dyslipidemia." *New England Journal of Medicine*, Vol. 317, 1987.

Ginsberg, H.N. "Lipoprotein Physiology and Its Relationship to Atherogenesis." *Endocrinology and Metabolism Clinics of North America* 19, 1990.

Goodnight, S.H. "The Vascular Effects of Omega-3 Fatty Acids." *Journal of Investigative Dermatology* 93, 1989.

Gordon, T., et al. "High Density Lipoprotein as a Protective Factor Against Coronary Heart Disease: The Framingham Study." *American Journal of Medicine* 62, 1977.

Grundy, Scott M. "Comparison of Monounsaturated Fatty Acids and Carbohydrates for Lowering Plasma Cholesterol." *New England Journal of Medicine* 314, 1986.

Guthrie, H.A. *Introductory Nutrition.* St. Louis, Mo.: Times Mirror/Mosby College Publishing, 1989.

Heart Facts. American Heart Association, 1993.

Hegele, R.A. "Lipoprotein (a): An Emerging Risk Factor for Atherosclerosis." *Canadian Journal of Cardiology* 5, 1989.

Hetzel, B.S., et al. "Fall in Coronary Heart Disease Mortality in the U.S.A. and Australia Due to Sudden Health: Evidence for the Role of Polyunsaturated Fat." *Journal of Clinical Epidemiology* 42, 1989.

Kane, J.P., et al. "Regression of Coronary Atherosclerosis During Treatment of Familial Hypercholesterolemia with Combined Drug Regimens." *Journal of the American Medical Association* 264, 1990.

Kannel, W.B., et al. "Serum Cholesterol, Lipoproteins, and the Risk of Coronary Heart Disease:

The Framingham Study." *Annals of Internal Medicine* 74, 1971.

Karvetti, R.L., H. Hamaldinen, et al. "Long-Term Effect of Nutrition Education on Myocardial Infarction Patients: A 10-Year Follow-Up Study." *Nutrition Metabolism of Cardiovascular Diseases,* 1993.

Katch, F., and W.D. McArdle. *Nutrition, Weight Control, and Exercise.* Philadelphia: Lea & Febiger, 1988.

Keys, A. (ed.) "Coronary Heart Disease in Seven Countries." *Circulation* 41, 1970.

LaRosa, J.C., et al. "The Cholesterol Facts: A Summary of the Evidence Relating Dietary Fats, Serum Cholesterol, and Coronary Heart Disease. A Joint Statement by the American Heart Association and the National Heart, Lung, and Blood Institute." The Task Force on Cholesterol Issues, American Heart Association. *Circulation* 81, 1990.

Lipid Research Clinics Program. "The Lipid Research Clinics Coronary Primary Prevention Trial Results. I: Reduction in Incidence of Coronary Heart Disease. II: The Relationship of Reduction in Incidence of Coronary Heart Disease to Cholesterol Lowering." *Journal of the American Medical Association* 25, 1984.

Manson, J.E., et al. "A Prospective Study of Obesity and Risk of Coronary Heart Disease in Women." *New England Journal of Medicine* 322, 1990.

Mattson, F.H. "A Changing Role for Dietary Monounsaturated Fatty Acids." *Journal of the American Dietetic Association* 89, 1989.

Mensink, R.P., and M.B. Katan. "Effect of Dietary Trans Fatty Acids on High-Density and Low-Density Lipoprotein Cholesterol Levels in Healthy Subjects." *New England Journal of Medicine* 323, 1990.

National Cholesterol Education Program (NCEP) Expert Panel on Detection, Evaluation and

Treatment of High Blood Cholesterol in Adults. "Summary of Second Report." National Heart, Lung and Blood Institute, National Institutes of Health, Bethesda, Md. *Journal of the American Medical Association*, Vol. 269, 1993.

National Research Council. *Diet and Health: Implications for Reducing Chronic Disease Risk.* Committee on Diet and Health, Food Nutrition Board, Commission on Life Sciences. Washington, D.C.: National Academy Press, 1989.

———. *Recommended Dietary Allowances,* 10th ed. Washington, D.C.: National Academy Press, 1989.

Nestel, P.J. "Current Strategies for Atherosclerosis and Lowering Cholesterol." *Clinical and Experimental Hypertension* 11, 1989.

Nikolaus, T., G. Schlierf, et al. "Treatment of Coronary Heart Disease with Diet and Exercise—Problems of Compliance." *Annals of Nutritional Metabolism,* 1991.

Nordoy, A., and S.H. Goodnight. "Dietary Lipids and Thrombosis: Relationships to Atherosclerosis. *Arteriorsclerosis* 10, 1990.

Ornish, Dean. *Dr. Dean Ornish's Program for Reversing Heart Disease.* New York: Random House, 1990.

———, et al. "Can Lifestyle Changes Reverse Coronary Heart Disease?" *Lancet* 336, 1990.

Ornish, D., L.W. Scherwitz, et al. "Effects of Stress Management Training and Dietary Changes in Treating Eschemic Heart Disease. *Journal of the American Medical Association,* 1983.

Phillipson, B.E., et al. "The Reduction of Plasma Lipids, Lipoproteins and Apoproteins in Hypertriglyceridemic Patients by Dietary Fish Oils." *New England Journal of Medicine,* Vol. 312, 1985.

Pollock, M., J. Wilmore, and S. Fox. *Health and Fitness Through Physical Activity.* New York: Wiley Publishing, 1978.

"Provisional Dietary Fiber Table." *Journal of the American Dietetic Association* 86, 1986.

Ribiero, J.P., L.H. Hartley, et al. "The Effectiveness of a Low Lipid Diet and Exercise in the Management of Coronary Artery Disease." *American Heart Journal*, 1984.

Sandkamp, M., et al. "Lipoprotein (a) Is an Independent Risk Factor for Myocardial Infarction at a Young Age." *Clinical Chemistry* 36, 1990.

Schuler, Gerhard, et al. "Myocardial Perfusion and Regression of Coronary Artery Disease in Patients on a Regimen of Intensive Physical Exercise and Low-Fat Diet." *Journal of the American College of Cardiology* 19, 1992.

———. "Regular Physical Exercise and Low-Fat Diet: Effects on Progression of Coronary Artery Disease." *Circulation* 86, 1992.

Schuler, G., R. Hambrecht, et al. "Myocardial Profusion and Regression of Coronary Artery Disease in Patients on a Regimen of Intensive Physical Exercise and Low Fat Diet. *Journal of the American College of Cardiology*, 1992.

Shekelle, R.B., and J. Stamler. "Dietary Cholesterol and Ischaemic Heart Disease." *Lancet*, 1989.

Shepherd, R., and L. Stockley. "Fat Consumption and Attitudes Toward Food with a High Fat Content." *Human Nutrition: Applied Nutrition* 39, 1985.

Stone, N.J. "Diet, Lipids and Coronary Heart Disease." *Endocrinology and Metabolism Clinics of North America* 19, 1990.

Stunkard, A.J., et al. "An Adoption Study of Human Obesity." *New England Journal of Medicine* 314, 1986.

Trevisan, M., et al. "Consumption of Olive Oil, Butter and Vegetable Oils and Coronary Heart Disease Risk Factors." *Journal of the American Medical Association* 263, 1990.

U.S. Department of Agriculture. *Composition of Foods.* Agriculture Handbook No. 8. Washington, D.C.: GPO, 1989.

———. *Nutritive Value of American Foods in Common Units.* Agriculture Handbook No. 456. Washington, D.C.: GPO, 1975.

———. *The Surgeon General's Report on Nutrition and Health.* DHHS (PHS) Publication No. 88-50210. Washington, D.C.: GPO, 1988.

Wood, P.D. "The Cholesterol Controversy Is Over!" *Runner's World,* March 1984.

GENERAL INDEX

(Page numbers in *italics* refer to illustrations.)

A

B

C

D

E

F

G

H

I

M

N

P

T

U

V

W

Y

INDEX TO RECIPES

A

C

D

E

F

G

N

R

S

T

V

W

Y

Z

ABOUT THE AUTHORS

Joseph C. Piscatella is the author of four widely acclaimed books—*Don't Eat Your Heart Out Cookbook, Choices for a Healthy Heart, Controlling Your Fat Tooth* and *The Fat Tooth Fat-Gram Counter & Restaurant Guide*—all of which have been enthusiastically endorsed by health professionals. His books are used by more than 5,500 hospitals in cardiac rehabilitation, weight loss and prevention programs. Mr. Piscatella's recovery from open-heart surgery at age 32 and his successful approach to healthy life-style changes, which resulted in coronary regression at age 47, are welcome news to those interested in improving cardiac health.

President of the Institute for Fitness and Health, Inc., in Tacoma, Washington, Mr. Piscatella lectures on life-style management skills to a variety of clients, including Fortune 500 companies, professional associations, hospitals and health professionals. His seminar has been cited in *Time* magazine for its effectiveness.

As a spokesperson on behalf of a healthy life-style, Mr. Piscatella is a frequent guest on television and radio programs, contributes to national publications and has hosted a television series on making healthy life-style changes. He is the only nonmedical member of a National Institutes of Health Cardiac Rehabilitation Expert Panel charged with developing clinical practice guidelines for physicians. He is also a member of the American Association for Cardiovascular and Pulmonary Rehabilitation.

Bernie Piscatella is vice president of the Institute for Fitness and Health and is responsible for all the recipes and nutritional analyses in this book as well as in those named above.

For more information on Mr. Piscatella's seminars, please contact:

Institute for Fitness and Health, Inc.
P.O. Box 98882
Tacoma, WA 98499
Tel. (206) 584-4481
FAX 206-584-6204